TEST MATCH
SPECIAL DIARY

Test Match Special Diary

The Full Story of England's
World Cup-Winning and Ashes Summer –
From the Best Seat in the House

THE *TMS* TEAM
with Jon Surtees

INTRODUCTION BY JONATHAN AGNEW

SIMON &
SCHUSTER

London · New York · Sydney · Toronto · New Delhi

A CBS COMPANY

First published in Great Britain by Simon & Schuster UK Ltd, 2019
A CBS COMPANY

Copyright © Test Match Special, 2019
By arrangement with the BBC
The BBC logo is trademark of the British Broadcasting Corporation
and is used under licence
BBC logo © BBC 1996

1 3 5 7 9 10 8 6 4 2

Simon & Schuster UK Ltd
1st Floor
222 Gray's Inn Road
London WC1X 8HB

www.simonandschuster.co.uk
www.simonandschuster.com.au
www.simonandschuster.co.in

Simon & Schuster Australia, Sydney
Simon & Schuster India, New Delhi

A CIP catalogue record for this book
is available from the British Library

Hardback ISBN: 978-1-4711-8831-2
eBook ISBN: 978-1-4711-8832-9

Typeset in Bembo by M Rules
Printed and bound by CPI Group (UK) Ltd, Croydon, CR0 4YY

CONTENTS

INTRODUCTION BY JONATHAN AGNEW

There is nothing worse in sport than an anti-climax. How often are tournament finals built up to the max, only to disappoint on the day? Don Bradman's second-ball duck in his last Test innings would rank as one of cricket's greatest letdowns, but there are plenty more to choose from throughout the sport's proud history.

One would definitely be the 1999 Cricket World Cup. Staged in England, it was a shocker right from the very start. The hosts were knocked out before the official World Cup song was released and, apart from the memorable tie between Australia and South Africa in the semi-final, overall the event was the dampest of damp squibs.

Fast-forward 20 years, and the pressure was on. Not merely was the World Cup returning to these shores for the first time since then, but it was immediately followed by the Ashes. (Whatever happened to the deal that was supposed to prevent the two events occurring in the same year, let alone virtually within a fortnight?) The steady and alarming slump in participation numbers can be blamed on a number of things, not least the absence of cricket on free-to-view television since 2006 and a lack of school facilities, making this summer an opportunity that simply could not be missed. England had to win the World Cup in order to breathe new life into a sport that was in serious danger of passing most people by. Follow that with a cracking Ashes series, and cricket's decline might just be halted.

Everyone had a part to play, not merely the cricketers. The administrators had to get the format right, broadcasters had to project cricket in the most appealing way possible, the grounds needed to be full of people having fun and, of course, the weather had to behave itself.

My first encounter with CWC 2019 was distinctly unpromising. An opening event had been set up on the Mall, no less, featuring a celebrity-packed cricket match on the famous stretch of tarmac with Buckingham Palace as a backdrop. But it was a cold, wet, bleak afternoon. The 'celebrities' had to be persuaded into a tent to speak gushingly about the forthcoming tournament, while the majority of the public that turned up were, in fact, guests on their way to a garden party at the palace. It was a miserable launch that filled one with dread for what lay ahead. It was, therefore, a massive relief when England overcame the threat of South Africa the following day. Ben Stokes took a wonderful catch in the deep, which the photographers captured brilliantly for the back pages, and we were off and running.

There is no question that the World Cup was a monumental success. And we thought that before the final that blew everyone away. The standard of cricket was top-class throughout and helped by the lack of tedious one-sided matches featuring the weaker teams that have blighted previous tournaments. While there is undoubtedly an argument for World Cups to expand the game by involving more teams, there is a counter view that television showing full grounds is a much better look than the cavernous, deserted stadia that played host to the wannabe giant-killers of the past. All-play-all is a much better format, too.

The crowds were fantastic. One of my favourite games was the Pakistan–Bangladesh clash at Lord's, where a full house of more than 25,000 cricket fanatics had the day of their lives. Their noise, colour and sheer exuberance transformed the traditional home of cricket into something we might likely see in the

IPL, but the realisation finally dawned that the majority were British: British cricket lovers who we see so rarely at mainstream cricket matches other than those involving the country of their family origin, however distant that tie might be. Never has the disconnect been so obvious, but then, with the ECB's Hundred tournament in mind, the challenge that must be addressed could not have been clearer, either.

England's brash, no-holds-barred approach was demonstrated by Jason Roy, Jonny Bairstow and, at Old Trafford, by Eoin Morgan, whose destruction of Afghanistan's attack was as brutal as it was brilliant. As I left that evening, I remember saying to Adam Mountford, the *Test Match Special* producer, that I had not enjoyed a one-day match so much in a very long time and, although England had already slipped up against Pakistan, the dream of lifting the trophy was still very much alive.

But in five days, that all changed. An awful performance against Sri Lanka at Headingley was followed immediately by defeat to Australia at Lord's. England were not only faltering, but it seemed that they were on an irreversible slide that would dump them out of the World Cup before the semi-finals. Every remaining game was now a 'must win': India, the one-day powerhouse, and top-of-the-table New Zealand who had taught England how to transform their game four years ago.

The victory over India was set up by an honest and open team talk and a rip-roaring, audacious opening stand of 160 in just 22 overs by Roy and Bairstow. Stokes thrashed 79 and, although Rohit Sharma added another century to his burgeoning collection, England won comfortably and seemed to have turned the corner. Another hundred by Bairstow demolished New Zealand and not only were England in the semi-finals, they were definitely the better for the tough, pressurised games they had to play to get there.

The destruction of Australia at Edgbaston was not only

spectacular but seemed to strike a blow for the Ashes, which was to follow. The Hollies Stand was at its raucous, bullying best and erupted when David Warner was dismissed by Chris Woakes for 9. Roy and Bairstow tore the bowling apart, with England booking their place in the final with 18 overs to spare. It was a thrashing that ensured that there was, by now, no escape from World Cup fever. Sky TV agreed to show the final on free-to-view, a welcome decision that also played its part in projecting cricket into new territory.

It is incredible how little I remember of the final. What I do know is that a number of us, unconnected other than having written and commentated on the tournament throughout, were all sick and confined to bed two days afterwards. I did an interview for BBC Radio London with Vanessa Feltz the morning after the game and realised how confusing the whole day had been. Did Stokes's ricochet happen in the game, or the Super Over? And that dropped catch on the boundary? It was a blur.

My wife, Emma, was in the Mound Stand, and I popped down to see her. I rarely leave the commentary box, so was blown away by the atmosphere outside. India supporters in their blue shirts were waving England flags. 'Sweet Caroline' boomed round the famous old ground. It was magical. Back upstairs, we received a cake from the Duchess of Cornwall, which featured a beautifully sculptured World Cup trophy. Twice during the course of the Super Over, New Zealand's commentator, Bryan Waddle, was confident enough to lift it in mock celebration. That is how it felt to me, too.

Jofra Archer, in his first international summer, calmly laced his boots before the Super Over. 'I presume I'm bowling it,' he said. No one argued. The noise blared through our open window. My voice kept cracking – not, as someone kindly wrote, through emotion, but because of a persistent throat infection that I could not shake off. It's not possible to prepare to commentate on a finish like that because, for a start, we do not know what is going to happen.

My technique? Short sentences. It stops you gabbling in excitement, keeping you calm and orderly, and lets the crowd noise tell the story for you. That is the advantage radio has over television, because the listeners really have to concentrate hard, and it draws them in to where you are. Martin Guptill was running to the end furthest from us, so it was impossible to see if he had failed to make it. But England's spontaneous reaction and the roars from the crowd sitting with the perfect side-on view in the Grand Stand were good enough for me to go for it, with just enough uncertainty to keep listeners hanging on for a further agonising 30 seconds or so until the replay was finally shown around the ground.

I felt sorry for Bryan. So near but so far; separated by the margin of boundaries in the match. Rules are rules and I do not think that a shared World Cup is really the way to go. But I have also experienced the blow of following your team throughout, before falling at the final hurdle. You feel the disappointment of your listeners. I remember telling our audience that there will never be another day of cricket like it, and enjoyed a couple of drinks with Emma, utterly elated.

If we were all flying with excitement, how would the players cope? I interviewed Joe Root before the Test against Ireland and his face looked vacant. I sent a message to his dad after the match hoping that the captain would get a proper rest before the Ashes, but there simply was not time. At Edgbaston, James Anderson broke down after only four overs with a recurrence of his calf injury. Truth is, whatever the temptation, he should not have returned until he had played a full match, which is the true test of fitness. It was a heavy price, as Anderson took no further part in the Ashes.

But for Steve Smith and with Anderson, England would

probably have won the first Test. Booed to the crease, Smith's two centuries were eccentric, exhausting and quite brilliant. When it was all over, he was booed back to the pavilion. While I did not mind the hostile reminder of what he had done when he walked to the middle, I did not understand the reaction to such a wonderful display of batting. Surely you buy your ticket in the hope of watching the best playing to their very best?

England had the better of the rain-affected Lord's Test and morale was high as Headingley dawned. England's hopeless decline to 67 all out in the first innings seemed certain to end this Ashes contest, and when Australia set England 359 to win, it would require their highest ever run chase in Test cricket.

I can admit it now, but halfway through the final afternoon I dictated my column for the BBC website. England had lost, and here I was delivering my withering verdict on where it had all gone wrong. One hour later, I was describing the most remarkable and exciting finish to a Test match there has ever been. I interviewed Stokes a few minutes after he thrashed Pat Cummins to the boundary, and he was clearly in a different place. 'We won!' was all he could say breathlessly, while videos of the winning moment, shot on listeners' mobile phones from beaches, cricket clubs, pubs and living rooms all over the country, began to pour into *Test Match Special*.

The overall theme of the 2019 Ashes was of two fragile batting line-ups struggling against top-class bowling attacks, with the increasingly colourful Smith standing head-and-shoulders above everyone else. This continued at Old Trafford and The Oval, where England's victory denied Australia their outright series win, and the crowd gave Smith the ovation he deserved when he was dismissed for the last time for a mere 23. The result seemed to be a fitting finale to a series which will be remembered forever for one match, containing one staggering individual performance.

So, did the summer fulfil our ambitions and rekindle interest in cricket? As I walked to my car from The Oval for the last time one September afternoon, I passed what I would consider to be a typical south London playground – except within the high wire fence were maybe 30 children, aged 10 or 11, all playing cricket under the watchful eye of their teacher. I paused to watch for a while and nodded. It had been a brilliant, unforgettable summer.

CHAPTER 1

England's Biggest Ever Summer of Cricket Starts Here

Friday 3 May
England v Ireland – One-day International
Malahide, County Dublin, Ireland

Team *TMS*: Jonathan Agnew, Charles Dagnall, Michael McNamee, Niall O'Brien, Alan Lewis, Ian Bell, Andy Zaltzman

So, here we are. It's the start of this country's greatest summer of cricket for a generation. Over the coming 136 days our sceptered isle will play host to all the world's finest cricketers, the game's most historic rivalry and everything in between.

And Jonathan Agnew is grumpy.

It's not the thought of the long summer ahead, far from it. Aggers is shivering under a large golf umbrella, being buffeted by a coastal westerly coming straight off the Irish Sea and into England's opening match of the summer, a one-off one-day international against Ireland in Malahide.

TMS arrived yesterday, in the middle of a dense rain-storm that has thoroughly irrigated the venue – sadly to the extent that the start of the summer has been delayed due to a wet outfield.

'When does the merchandise place open? I need to go and buy one of those Cricket Ireland rugby shirts,' says the BBC's cricket correspondent as he realises he has come woefully underclubbed for a breezy day in a temporary Portakabin on the east coast of Ireland.

The delayed start sees the game reduced to 45 overs and means a number of the England-based *TMS* team are nervously looking over their shoulders towards the already-booked, early-evening flight from Dublin. It also furthers the wait for England's three ODI debutants: Dawid Malan, Ben Foakes and – of course – Jofra Archer, whose potential participation in the World Cup has been the topic of some substantial conversation over the preceding month.

The match starts at 12.45 p.m. and David Willey delivers its first ball, which shapes away nicely and is left well alone outside the off stump by Ireland captain William Porterfield. The second ball sees more activity as he is rapped on both pads and narrowly survives a DRS review from England. We are under way!

The big story arrives almost immediately as Archer takes the new ball from the other end, bowling the second over of the game. His first ball is drilled through cover by Paul Stirling, and after singles off the fourth and fifth balls, Archer's first over in an England shirt has gone for 6.

Aggers eventually decided against visiting the merchandise store, instead borrowing a warmer top from his *TMS* and Leicestershire colleague Charles Dagnall.

'It comes to something when you have to rely on Charles Dagnall for fashion assistance. I've had to borrow his jumper, it's freezing,' comments Agnew, ungratefully, after earlier also calling out statistician Andy Zaltzman for wearing a beanie at a cricket match.

Later in the day, back in possession of his jumper, Dagnall ruefully declares that it is now stretched.

Tom Curran is brought into the attack and takes England's first wicket of the summer, Archer demonstrating another side to his game by taking a fine diving catch at mid-on. England make early progress, with Ireland four down before summariser Niall O'Brien comes up with the biggest revelation of the day when he states that Boyzone star Ronan Keating is a huge cricket fan and can often be seen having a coffee in Malahide village.

This is particularly pleasing for Aggers, who reveals he once saw the Irishman in concert at Nottingham Ice Arena.

Mark Adair and George Dockrell seem to be dragging Ireland back into the game but Archer returns to the attack and earns his headlines by demolishing Adair's off stump with a 90mph yorker for his first England wicket. When Liam Plunkett accounts for the 'Lambeth Lara' – Tim Murtagh – and Dockrell in the same over the game is virtually up and Ireland set England 199 to win.

'It's really important for Ireland that they make a good start. It's not a big target and one you feel that England will easily overhaul,' opines Aggers as James Vince and Dawid Malan stride out to open the reply.

This is looking to be the case as the two ease to 34 without strife but when Dockrell pulls off a blinding catch at midwicket Vince departs and everything changes. Joe Root, Eoin Morgan, Malan and Joe Denly are all back in the pavilion with England 66 for five.

David Willey and Ben Foakes are slowly rebuilding the chase but the late start has caused time to get on and Agnew and Dagnall are starting to panic about making their flights. Ireland's ebullient wicketkeeper Gary Wilson is giving the stump mic an excellent early-season workout and when Willey picks out Adair on the leg-side boundary, everyone is beginning to wonder whether this might be a repeat of England's infamous early-season slip-up against Scotland at The Grange last summer.

Tom Curran joins his Surrey team-mate Ben Foakes at the crease and, despite some scares, the two keep their heads and save England's blushes, a 98-run partnership securing the win by four wickets.

However well Foakes has played on debut, in the commentary box the man of the match award is given to BBC Radio Ulster's Michael McNamee, who has called the last 45 minutes by himself after Agnew and Dagnall had to make a mad dash to the airport to catch their flights and ensure safe passage back to England for prior commitments the next day!

During that time, McNamee was largely joined on the microphone by Ian Bell. It was a classic Bell performance. He only came into the team at the last minute after Jimmy Anderson was called up by Lancashire, but put in a superb showing, outlasting his fellow Englishmen on the microphone and carefully seeing his side home.

All in all, an excellent start to the season. Embarrassment averted for England, a thrilling spectacle for the Malahide masses and a triumphant return to the airwaves for *TMS*, which closes as it began, shivering under leaden Irish skies, as producer Adam Mountford and 5 Live reporter Kevin Howells pack up all the equipment. Onwards to Cardiff.

Ireland 198 (43.1 overs; Stirling 33; Plunkett 4-35) lost to England 199-6 (42 overs; Foakes 61*; Little 4-45) by four wickets.

Sunday 5 May
England v Pakistan – Royal London Twenty20
International
Sophia Gardens, Cardiff, Wales

Team *TMS*: Isa Guha, Charles Dagnall, Jimmy Anderson, Ramiz Raja,
Andy Zaltzman

Three England T20 debutants today: Ben Foakes, Jofra Archer and Ben Duckett. And three who are making their first on-air start of the summer for *TMS*: Isa Guha, Ramiz Raja and a man who may well play a pretty key role in the latter part of the campaign, Jimmy Anderson.

It is also lovely to see the regular crew of *TMS* engineers for the summer's first game on the mainland of England and Wales.

All the team, including the 'King of the Swingers', always thoroughly enjoy coming to Cardiff. Today particularly, there are two reasons for this. Firstly, the walk to the ground is definitely the most spectacular in Britain, taking you through central Cardiff, past the castle, along the banks of the River Taff and through some extremely picturesque parks.

Secondly, the Welsh hospitality is always excellent and within minutes of arriving in the box the first cakes of the summer are produced – on this occasion they are Welsh cakes and have been provided by the staff at the ground. All five members of the T20 truncated team happily tuck in. Start as you mean to go on.

It is a chilly day but after the Portakabin of Malahide it's nice to be back inside a permanent structure. Pakistan pace bowler Mohammad Amir is spotted asking the television commentators – based on the boundary edge in a commentary 'pod' that looks a little like a burger van – for a cup of the hot chocolate they are gratefully clutching.

5

Early drama as Eoin Morgan takes a stunner to get rid of Fakhar Zaman but the game is almost over before it even began when a piece of the pitch disintegrates beneath David Willey as he runs in to bowl. The England all-rounder is lucky not to suffer a serious injury. Once it becomes clear that the bowler is okay, Zaltzman remarks that he thinks it's probably the first use of a trapdoor in international cricket.

Amid all the drama, Babar Azam and Haris Sohail are putting on a fine partnership, Babar smashing Joe Denly's first two deliveries for huge sixes. However, that man Archer puts an end to both their innings, claiming Sohail with a slower ball before brilliantly running out Babar off his own bowling.

Pakistan end on 173 and, after the early loss of Ben Duckett, James Vince and Joe Root climb into the chase with a partnership of 45 that has Dagnall and Guha purring into their mics.

Dagnall notes that the tourists are 'playing a dangerous game' by offering Vince width to unfurl his 'glorious' cover drives, while Isa confidently states that a dismissal of a Mohammad Hasnain cutter to the boundary is 'Vince at his best'.

England bring up their hundred with two wickets down from 12.1 overs, causing more purring in the box. This time it's Zaltzman who has discovered a rare statistical confluence as Pakistan brought up their century from the same delivery, with the same number of wickets down.

A well-managed chase comes down to England requiring seven from the final over and victory is assured in style when skipper Eoin Morgan pumps Faheem Ashraf straight back down the ground for six.

Oddly enough, that was the sole T20 match that England will play this summer, so no matter what happens, they will have a 100 per cent record in something. Well batted. To The Oval!

Pakistan 173-6 (20 overs; Azam 65) lost to England 175-3 (19.2 overs; Morgan 57*) by seven wickets.

Wednesday 8 May
England v Pakistan – Royal London One-day
International Series – Match 1
The Kia Oval, Kennington, London

Team *TMS*: Isa Guha, Simon Mann, Charles Dagnall, Daniel Norcross, Michael Vaughan, Phil Tufnell, Ebony Rainford-Brent, Ramiz Raja, Alec Stewart, Andy Zaltzman

We start where we will end up, as England's first home one-day international of the summer is played at the same ground that will host the final Ashes Test match come September.

However, the weather is not on our side. An early arrival was greeted with lashing rain and, while conditions have calmed down a bit, there is definitely precipitation in the area all day and just how much cricket gets played will largely depend on how lucky we get with where the clouds that contain the rain are blown. To a chorus of raised eyebrows, assistant producer Henry Moeran – frequently *TMS*'s shining light of optimism – declares that there will be 100 overs bowled.

As the chances of play are discussed, the *TMS* social media feeds light up with news of a BBC scandal. It is always a shame when this sort of thing comes too close to home. News of Greg James's confirmed cheating in a quiz against Jimmy Anderson on the *Tailenders* podcast sees another, metaphorical, cloud fall over the commentary box.

The poor weather at least gives the opportunity for a good chat about the potential make-up of the England World Cup squad and the team are united in their belief that Jofra Archer must be selected, meaning that Tom Curran, Mark Wood, Liam Plunkett and David Willey are competing for the remaining three spots.

Ebony Rainford-Brent selects Mark Wood for the chop, Michael Vaughan cuts Liam Plunkett and Alec Stewart gets rid of David Willey. Former *TMS* commentator Ed Smith, now England's chief selector, has a massive call to make.

The cricket eventually gets going and Jofra Archer immediately backs up what everyone has been talking about by producing a world-class spell of very fast bowling. Former seamer Charles Dagnall is luxuriating in Archer's class as he repeatedly beats the edge and sends well-placed bouncers flying past the noses of Fakhar and Imam-ul-Haq before making the breakthrough in the fourth over as Fakhar edges to Joe Root at slip.

In the summariser's chair, Vaughan says that we will be watching Archer in both the World Cup and the Ashes, while Norcross eyes Plunkett as the bowler with the most similarities to Archer in the squad. Plunkett then proceeds to make his case as he picks up Babar with a cross-seam delivery that highlights his value to the squad.

With all the talk of The Hundred arriving in English cricket next year, many a sly chuckle is had when a rainstorm of biblical proportions arrives and the players sprint from the field after 16.4 overs; precisely 100 balls. A restart comes but only another 2.2 overs are bowled before The Oval is hit by more of the wet stuff and the players return to the dressing rooms, this time for good.

While it is always frustrating to be producing a ball-by-ball cricket commentary when there is no cricket happening, it is always wonderful to see the volume of emails received during bad weather. On this occasion it is even more so, as listeners tell us how much they're anticipating future rain delays because they want to hear the stories and interviews they generate!

Almost to prove their point, the afternoon in the commentary box is enlivened by a visit from Pakistan Cricket Board managing director Wasim Khan, a conversation between Ramiz Raja and Alec Stewart – and an extraordinary incident with a spider.

With Ramiz on the air with Simon Mann, a huge arachnid is suddenly spotted coming down from the roof of the commentary box, causing significant consternation among onlookers as to its immediate future plans. That consternation quickly changes to mild panic, broadcast worldwide on the BBC airwaves, when it rapidly descends and lands on Simon's face while he is on air.

A consummate professional and multitasker, Simon is able to swat it away but not before any slumbering listeners have been woken by his startled reaction!

Given the stress this has caused, Simon is allowed off air and is replaced by Alec Stewart, who is engaged in conversation by Ramiz about a particular match during the 1992 World Cup. While many will remember the final as the primary meeting between the two sides, England had the chance to eliminate the eventual victors had they beaten them in Adelaide earlier in the competition.

When Pakistan were dismissed for 74, bags were being packed. However, some unseasonal rain arrived and sawed off England's chase at 24 for one, allowing Ramiz and his Pakistan side to fight another day. Listening to Alec discuss this, the world 'rueful' comes to mind – and his mood is not improved when Ramiz reminds him that he is currently discussing it with the man who went on to catch Richard Illingworth to win the final, 24 days later!

At 7.11 p.m., after many hours of amateur meteorology, calls to professional meteorologists, World Cup chat and spider battles, the game is officially abandoned, which turns out to be the right decision as the heavens quickly open afterwards.

The series has got off to an inauspicious start, next stop Southampton – where the medium-range forecast looks promising.

Pakistan 80-2 (19 overs). No result.

Saturday 11 May
England v Pakistan – Royal London One-day
International Series – Match 2
The Ageas Bowl, Southampton

Team *TMS*: Isa Guha, Simon Mann, Charles Dagnall, Daniel Norcross, Michael Vaughan, Phil Tufnell, Ramiz Raja, Jimmy Anderson, Andy Zaltzman

There is controversy from the off in Southampton. Not only have England rested Jofra Archer, leading Michael Vaughan to deduce that he will definitely be selected in the World Cup squad, there has been a major change to the commentary facilities.

With Hampshire having constructed a hotel at the Ageas Bowl, when England come to town a number of rooms are converted into commentary facilities. For a certain member of the team, a former England off-spinner who goes by the nick-name 'The Cat', this makes it his favourite box on the circuit, largely because of the impressive double bed covered in expensive Egyptian cotton linen that sits at the back – and the large sofa on one side. However, for today's game, both have been removed, causing a significant drop in Tuffers' morale.

Fortunately for the wider team, they have also removed the bathrobe that previously hung on the door of the en-suite lavatory provided in each commentary room, which gives Tuffers no opportunity to offer a repeat performance of previous years when he occasionally emerged for a stint on the mic garbed in nothing but the official Hampshire CCC dressing gown and slippers!

Compared to Wednesday the weather is superb and, with England's first-choice opening pair of Jason Roy and Jonny Bairstow back together at the top of the order, expectations are high for the series to quickly get back on track.

Before play gets under way there is one further oddity to contend with. Charles Dagnall, committed to his art as he is, has brought along his bass guitar so he can practise ahead of an impending third-grade exam he is due to sit. With Daggers not required on air at the start of the game, he is sat next door watching the action and practising his licks. So far, relatively normal.

The situation changes when the normally ultra-reliable Ramiz Raja fails to show ahead of his opening session of expert analysis and assistant producer Henry Moeran is dispatched to locate the great Pakistani. Guesses abound as to where he might be, but none are correct. The simple truth is discovered almost immediately by Moeran, who begins his search in the neighbouring box. He discovers Ramiz in his own world, wearing some large headphones, as he enjoys a private concert by Daggers, who is keen to get feedback and ensure a good pass in his exam.

England start watchfully but quickly pick up the pace and it's clear that Roy and Bairstow are relishing being back together at the top of the order, with Tufnell declaring that 'they're looking greedy' and Vaughan sensing that a total of 350-plus is well on the way.

At one stage, Roy hits what can only be described as a baseball shot, hard and high over extra cover. Daniel Norcross and Tufnell are in possession of the microphones at the time and are aurally staggered on air, wondering out loud about the England opener's incredible talent, nerve and inventiveness. Later on, Norcross is heard saying that 'it was a shot so extraordinary, I couldn't quite believe what I was seeing as I described it'.

As the two continue to accumulate runs quickly, Daggers takes a position at the back of the main box, bass guitar still in hand. Similarly to former Maccabees guitarist Felix White on the *Tailenders* podcast, occasional flurries of music soundtrack the commentary – and Dagnall takes great delight in handing out a lesson of his own when James Anderson starts to show an interest. The BBC Online text commentary asks its readers to send in names for a potential band featuring the seamers, with favourites including Chas and James, and Iron Maidens.

Despite having only opened together 25 times, Roy and Bairstow set a new England record as they reach their sixth century partnership and it takes a superb catch from Fakhar Zaman at deep square leg to eventually dismiss Bairstow.

Roy, enjoying the chance to spend time at the crease after an injury-hit start to the year, moves on to 87 before he goes shortly after a brief rain break that saw the *TMS* box become the focus of much crowd excitement as displaced fans worked out where the commentators were and started trying to get their attention in a variety of different ways. Fortunately, *TMS* fans are wonderful people and decorum was maintained at all times!

Eoin Morgan and his 'lovely wrists' (according to Isa Guha) maintain momentum and Jos Buttler lifts the second ball he faces well over the boundary to sound the starting gun on an extraordinary innings.

While England have a lot of one-day cricket to play over the next two months, something amazing will have to happen to outshine this innings from Buttler.

The England wicketkeeper is in stunningly brutal form, dispatching the ball over boundaries all around the ground and repeatedly bringing the crowd to their feet. After 40 overs, England are on 261 for three and Simon Mann declares that 'Pakistan are in for a very tough last ten overs'.

Although the tourists start the final ten well, there is only so much they can do when Buttler is playing like this and the commentary soon becomes a series of gasps, superlatives and studied appreciation. 'Timed' says Anderson as the ball is flicked over the leg side; 'remarkable' says Vaughan as Buttler uses his wrists to power one over point for four; 'incredible' says Ramiz as he toe-ends one over deep midwicket; 'that has gone miles and miles and miles and miles' observes Norcross as the delivery from Hasan Ali disappears six rows back.

Buttler stokes his seventh six of the innings over long-off and signals for a drink. 'The way he's playing, he deserves a nice gin and tonic,' reckons Michael Vaughan to amused agreement from an astonished commentary box.

The former England captain is still on the microphone with Dan Norcross as Buttler homes in on the century.

'If it's in the slot, it's going,' he says.

'Oh, it's gone! It has absolutely gone!' adds Norcross, perfectly getting across the feeling of wonderment at the incredible innings.

The onslaught leaves Pakistan requiring 374 to win and Buttler's unique talent is emphasised one last time by off-duty *TMS* statistician Andrew Samson, who tweets that, on average, Buttler takes 69.5 balls to reach a one-day-international century. The next closest in history is A.B.de Villiers, with 81.9.

After an innings break enlivened with the first of four *TMS* documentaries about previous World Cups to be staged in England, Pakistan begin their chase, with Tufnell noting their intent, adding: 'If it's there to be hit, they're hitting it.' It is one of the beautiful bon mots of cricket commentary that looks silly when written down but actually offers excellent insight when read out loud.

It says something about the way one-day cricket has evolved that an opening partnership of nearly 100 from under 15 overs can be considered humdrum but the Buttler innings was so spellbinding that's how it feels.

Imam-ul-Haq falls and the innings is almost remembered for the wrong reasons when Roy hurtles around the rope unsuccessfully attempting to prevent a boundary and only succeeds in violently colliding with a Sky cameraman stationed just behind the rope. Fortunately, all parties walk away unharmed, but it could have been nasty.

Without Jofra Archer and Tom Curran, the England attack looks a little samey and the bowlers are toiling through the middle overs, with Fakhar Zaman bringing up his century from 84 balls and Babar Azam proving an excellent foil at the other end. While England have a monster total on the board, Pakistan are making it very interesting and Simon Mann goes so far as to call them favourites.

This is until Fakhar receives a very wide ball from Chris Woakes and manages to get the thinnest of under edges on it. The umpire is not initially convinced but a 'desperation' review from Morgan sees the back of the opener and returns England to the driving seat – a position further strengthened when Babar gets in a terrible muddle trying to dispatch a half-tracker from Adil Rashid and only bunts an easy catch back to the bowler.

Asif Ali is the latest batsman to produce fireworks, rifling Rashid for some monster sixes, while James Anderson on commentary is ruing his Royal London One-day Cup semi-final, which is to be played on the same pitch tomorrow.

'I cannot stop thinking about my game tomorrow on this pitch. My hamstring has been tightening up and my back has started to spasm as the game has gone on,' he claims. Kindly, Norcross offers to write him a note to present to Lancashire head coach Glen Chapple.

With Asif Ali still at the crease, Pakistan are very much staying in the chase, especially when David Willey presents one that is right in the slot and it disappears back over his head. However, when the same delivery comes out again in the next over, the contact is not so clean and Ben Stokes is able to hang on to an excellent catch at long-on.

The next over goes for 17, swinging the game back in Pakistan's favour once more and the tension is palpable in the box. Producer Adam Mountford is on the edge of his seat and utterly immersed in events until Ramiz Raja, perhaps trying to alleviate a bit of nervous tension, attempts to show him a YouTube video of a traditional Punjabi band playing the *Game of Thrones* theme tune.

In the end, cool heads from Willey, Liam Plunkett and Chris Woakes prevail to see England home by 12 runs.

After the wet disappointment of The Oval, England's – and *TMS*'s – summer of cricket has got off to a classic start in Southampton, with 734 runs scored. Ramiz Raja thinks Pakistan will be 'ruing' the missed chances they had to win the match, while Greg James has taken to Twitter to proclaim that he is 'fully in love' with Jos Buttler, adding that he can't wait for the World Cup when the rest of the country will fall for him too.

Once the main broadcast goes off air, there is the requirement to do a review of the day for BBC Radio 5 Live. Today, this is done somewhat more successfully than the last time *TMS* were in Southampton.

During the 2018 Test series against India, Eleanor Oldroyd and Simon Hughes were sat in the next door 'commentary box' (hotel room) recording the 5 Live review. With speculation rife over the potential retirement of the great Alastair Cook, they had just started a conversation about his Test career and whether they thought that rumours of an impending announcement were true.

As they talked, they became aware of someone coming into the back of their box but, ever the professionals, carried on regardless. It turns out Cook himself was staying in the hotel room on the other side of the corridor and had accidentally walked into the wrong room at the end of a long day's cricket. Desperate for a shower and a sit-down, the cricketing icon had only succeeded in finding two BBC broadcasters discussing the potential end of his career!

Following a game like today, the excitement for the rest of the summer is palpable – and England still have three more one–day internationals to play before they even confirm their squad for the World Cup. Onwards, to Bristol!

England 373-3 (50 overs; Buttler 110*, Roy 87, Morgan 71*)
beat Pakistan 361-7 (50 overs; Fakhar 138) by 12 runs.

Tuesday 14 May
England v Pakistan – Royal London One-day
International Series – Match 3
County Ground, Bristol

Team *TMS*: Alison Mitchell, Simon Mann, Charles Dagnall, Michael
Vaughan, Ramiz Raja, Vic Marks, Andy Zaltzman

It's sun, sun, sun in the West Country and *TMS* are joined by the inestimable Vic Marks for the first time this summer. There is a summer's ODI debut on the outfield too, with Joe Denly included in the XI as England continue to search for spin bowling cover in their final World Cup squad.

Given the relatively tiny dimensions of Bristol, Michael Vaughan thinks that Denly has been 'thrown the shortest straw' by being asked to bowl leg spin today. But at this level you need to take your chances where you can, as Denly is well aware, having waited a decade since his last chance to play one-day cricket for his country.

After his feats of genius in Southampton at the weekend, England are relieved to see the back of Fakhar Zaman, as well as Babar Azam, early on, but Haris Sohail and Imam-ul-Haq are rebuilding when Tom Curran, who is always a particularly enthusiastic participant in England's prematch football sessions, sprints down the wicket after his follow-through, passes Sohail like Usain Bolt racing against Phil Tufnell and shows superb technique to side-foot the ball on to the stumps.

'That's why they play football on a morning,' bellows a jubilant Vaughan!

As Curran is still celebrating beneath us, Adam Mountford receives a message from England media man Danny Reuben. More often than not, these are important breaking news stories. On this occasion he was keen for his opinion that Curran is the worst footballer in the England side to be mentioned on air in the context of this dismissal. The comment is immediately used on air and the politics of the England dressing room left for others to deal with.

At the halfway point of the innings, Pakistan are 142 for three, with Vic Marks describing the bespectacled Imam as 'the glue Pakistan are batting around'. His eyewear is certainly characteristic and generates conversation in the box about great glasses-wearing cricketers over the years, with names like M.J.K.Smith and Zaheer Abbas quickly thrown into the mix.

Denly is introduced into the attack and begins, nervously, with a couple of full tosses. His over goes for nine and that is it as he is whipped out of the attack and immediately replaced by Moeen Ali.

Imam moves to his hundred and starts to up his ambitions, planting David Willey for a huge six over long-on and then blowing a kiss in the direction of the aggrieved England bowler, much to the amusement of all and sundry.

A fierce debate then breaks out in the box as to whether there is a slope or not at Bristol. Charles Dagnall is convinced there is one, others less so. Fortunately, Henry Moeran is on hand to take an extraordinary picture with his mobile phone proving, beyond all doubt, that Dagnall is correct.

Another happy result of this debate is the influx of emails from listeners all over the country, some of whom seem to have played cricket on truly extraordinary outfields. Tales of balls rolling in a horseshoe, Augusta style, and long chases – often with a hangover or after a heavy tea – up steep and unkempt inclines keep the team and the listeners entertained for some time.

With Jofra Archer and Adil Rashid both being rested in the interests of testing squad depth, England are starting to struggle to keep a hold on Imam and the big-hitting Asif Ali, with the ball regularly finding the boundary. Imam is capitalising on his watchful start with some expansive stroke play until Curran squeezes the perfect yorker under his bat and rocks back the off stump, generating a loud roar from a good Bristol crowd.

As he leaves the field, Vaughan and Dagnall are waxing lyrical about the innings and Dagnall asks: 'I wonder how many centuries we're going to see in this World Cup?'

Proving he can now time his broadcasting with the same

quality he used to time a cover drive, Vaughan leaves a perfect beat and simply replies: 'Oh, plenty.'

Chris Woakes grabs his fourth wicket as Pakistan end aggressively, totalling 358 for nine. It will be some excellent chasing practice for England, especially without Buttler.

Jason Roy and Jonny Bairstow, as has become traditional, get off to a stonking start and when Roy deposits Shaheen Afridi into the top tier of the media stand, there is a mad dash as half of the *TMS* team immediately race out of the door in an attempt to retrieve it. There are some things that you do as a child that never become any less thrilling – and returning any kind of ball to a professional sportsperson is certainly one of them.

As the ball was flying towards the box, memories were evoked of a famous incident that happened in a county match down the road at Taunton in 2011. The two doyens of Welsh cricket, Eddie Bevan and Steve James, were commentating on a domestic one-day match between Somerset and Glamorgan when Robert Croft bowled to Peter Trego.

Trego hit a ferocious six, so ferocious in fact that it went sailing straight through the window of the commentary box, splintering glass all over Ed and Steve. The noise the ball made when passing through the window was so loud and clear, listeners genuinely thought it was a sound effect. The reaction and story struck the national chord to such an extent that the clip was even played on *Have I Got News for You* later that week. Both men survived to recount the tale for many years.

Shortly after the ball-retrieving excitement there is further fun to be had as Michael Vaughan discovers that Simon Mann is wearing no shoes. The mood is giddy – as Vaughan gets stuck into his colleague in the box, Roy and Bairstow get stuck into Pakistan on the field and Afridi drops an absolute dolly to give Roy another life.

An excited Andy Zaltzman points out that Roy and Bairstow are now England's highest-scoring opening partnership ever (overtaking *TMS* pair Alastair Cook and Ian Bell) and the two celebrate by Roy smacking Imad Wasim's first delivery on to the third floor of the nearby modern block of flats that looms over Bristol. A group of mates who had previously been enjoying a relaxed evening on their balcony rapidly dive for cover.

Bairstow then wants in on the action, lofting the ball clean over the stands and into the car park. This time it's the turn of a queue of fans blithely waiting for a burger to throw themselves out of harm's way.

When Roy smashes Faheem Ashraf's first ball for six, Zaltzman points out that it's the fourth time today that the Surrey batsman has hit the opening ball of an over for a maximum. A great stat for a great achievement and the box signals its approval to their resident statistician.

Roy goes for 76 but the fact of the matter is the England openers have put on 159 from 105 balls at 9 an over and made what seemed like a testing total look easily gettable.

Bairstow goes to three figures but celebrates in a perfunctory manner and seems to have his sights set on something far bigger. He underlines this by slamming Hasan Ali back down the ground for a sensational boundary and then clears the pavilion, requiring a new ball to be called for. He then smacks the new ball into the stands. Fortunately for Gloucestershire CCC's new-ball budget, this one comes back in a usable condition.

It seems like Bairstow could be on to break Jason Roy's record individual one-day score for England, but just when he is seeming utterly impregnable, he gets an under edge and deflects the ball on to his wicket. The Yorkshireman's fury is such that he immediately swings his bat into the stumps, which could be an expensive reaction.

The boundary breaching is catching on, though, and Joe

Root gets in on the action, thwacking a six, significant in that he had not hit one in his previous 13 ODI innings. Zaltzman is in a rich run of statistical form, pointing out he had gone over 500 balls without hitting one.

With captain Morgan dropping himself down the order to give team-mates time at the crease, the match-winning partnership develops between England's two true all-rounders – Ben Stokes and Moeen Ali.

As the ball continues to fly over the boundary, Vaughan describes England's chase as 'disdainful'. The Ashes-winning captain also comes off his long run at Sarfaraz Ahmed, accusing the Pakistani skipper of being too reactionary. To be fair, he hasn't been helped by some very poor fielding from the tourists, who have dropped three catches they would feel they should have taken.

When looking back at the scorecard, it might seem that running out Ben Stokes was an uplift in the tourists' fielding, but it was actually rank bad luck for Stokes, who departs after Moeen middles a drive down the ground and the ball deflects off Afridi's boot and on to the stumps. His 37 is the first time Pakistan have dismissed an England batsman for less than 40 in this series.

Despite chasing 359 to win, Ramiz Raja hits the nail on the head when he says that 'the way England have played, even a thousand would have looked scarce'.

The game is up when the total is reached with 5.1 overs to spare. It's the fifth-highest ODI chase of all time and England have done it with 31 balls to spare and while resting Jos Buttler, Jofra Archer and Adil Rashid and batting their No 4 batsman deliberately down the order. Extraordinary.

Let's leave the last word to Michael Vaughan, who almost appears starstruck, such is his love of the performance.

'How do you set a target against this England team? What is safe? I don't think anything will be. It's a testament to the team that they go out and make this chase look so easy. They're a tremendous team to watch.'

On the way to the hotel, a debate breaks out as to whether people are happy to call it a night and go straight to their rooms or whether something more adventurous could be afoot. After Adam Mountford points out what happened last time people ventured into the Bristol nightlife after an England cricket match, the team decide to take the early night and leave any curiosity about Mbargo nightclub for another time.

There are only two games to go before the World Cup and *TMS* will now up sticks and make for Trent Bridge.

Pakistan 358-9 (50 overs; Imam 151; Woakes 4-67) lost to England 359-4 (44.5 overs; Bairstow 128, Roy 76) by six wickets.

Friday 17 May
England v Pakistan – Royal London One-day
International Series – Match 4
Trent Bridge, Nottingham

Team *TMS*: Simon Mann, Charles Dagnall, Daniel Norcross, Michael Vaughan, Graeme Swann, Ramiz Raja, Andy Zaltzman

Despite the fact the game doesn't start until lunchtime, it's a hell of a morning for *TMS*.

The southern-based members of the team, Daniel Norcross and Simon Mann, are leaving home early and heading up to Nottingham on the train. This is absolutely fine until the points about a mile outside of Nottingham station decide to pack up and the pair are utterly stranded, with time ticking down towards 12.45 p.m. when the show is due on air.

While the phrase 'don't panic' is used on a text, when word gets around that there could be a vacancy, both Henry Moeran and BBC Asian Network's Nikesh Rughani are seen publicly performing what can only be described as 'commentary stretches' to subtly let Adam Mountford know they're ready for *TMS* action if required.

Mountford sends out a 'Hail Mary' to regular *TMS* commentator Alison Mitchell, not down for this game but potentially due to be commentating for TV today. An excellent plan is foiled when word is received that she is on the same train as Norcross and Mann. Moeran and Rughani renew their warm-ups.

The temperature cools slightly when a message is received from Mann – who is fondly nicknamed 'Grumpy' by colleagues – saying the train is moving and all should be well. It rises again five minutes later when a second missive comes in saying, 'Scrub that, we've stopped moving again.'

Normally, one of the commentators will venture down to the middle to do the toss, before seamlessly handing back to the studio. Today, though, Charles Dagnall – who only needed to make a short hop from the Midlands and has therefore arrived in plenty of time – is required to do both duties, necessitating a hasty dash from the middle to the box before handing over to himself and commencing what will potentially be one of the longest commentary stints of his life.

Dagnall's bacon is saved, though, as, just as the first ball is being delivered, the door to the box flies open and Norcross and Mann exhaustedly fling themselves through and almost straight on air. It's not been the start to the day they dreamed of, but they have made it on time! 'Never in doubt,' mutters Mountford, ruefully, from his producer's desk at the rear of the box.

What the tardy pair don't realise is that they missed one of the great nights of all time the evening before. Those from the team who decided to arrive in Nottingham with time to spare had gathered for a quiet drink in the hotel bar. With 'World Cup fever' running through the veins of all warm-blooded cricket lovers, it was decided to attempt to name every member of every England World Cup squad from 1975 to 2015.

The roar of rejoicing that went up when Andy Zaltzman remembered that the back-up wicketkeeper in 1975 was Warwickshire's John Jameson could be heard for some distance around the city. Who says *TMS* don't know how to have fun?

England ring the changes once again, resting Chris Woakes, Liam Plunkett and David Willey, bringing back Jofra Archer and giving Mark Wood his first start of the summer, creating one of the quickest England attacks many can recall. Jos Buttler returns, captaining the side – Eoin Morgan is suspended after he presided over a very poor over rate on Tuesday – and, after his heroics in Bristol, Jonny Bairstow is given the day off, with James Vince replacing him. Finally, Adil Rashid comes back in, but Joe Denly still retains his spot.

Archer and Wood open up for England, regularly hitting speeds in excess of 90mph. An excellent hour's broadcasting is also enlivened by Graeme Swann's first appearance of the season, which gives him the chance to reminisce about his *Strictly* experience last year, which he describes as 'ten times more fun than I expected'.

Apparently, the prematch nerves were the same as cricket, but it was considerably harder because his faith in his dancing ability was somewhat less than his faith in his cricketing ability! Back on air for the first time this summer, Swann says how happy he is to be returning to his comfort zone and his broadcasting family.

On the field, Imam-ul-Haq takes a wicked blow to the elbow

from Wood and is quickly carted off to hospital for a scan. Joe Denly comes on first change, bowling for just the 41st time in 149 List A matches. His World Cup spot is up in the air and he doesn't bowl badly but the feeling is still that the Kent batsman could be a square peg for a round hole in the World Cup squad.

Pakistan continue well and after 30 overs are 178 for one. It shows how much the game has changed that Simon Mann, now fully recovered from his transport excitements, asks whether Pakistan are going to 'have a real dart' in the final 20 overs.

Babar Azam brings up his ton but is dismissed for 115 off 112 balls and the problem with Pakistan's innings is nailed by Andy Zaltzman, who points out that Babar's ton is the slowest of the six ODI centuries that have been made at Trent Bridge since the last World Cup in 2015.

The pace is picked up towards the end of the innings, and Imam receives a large cheer when, returned from hospital, he emerges at the fall of the seventh wicket to continue his innings. He is still there at the end of the innings, leading to a very odd-looking scorecard as it appears that he has batted through the 50 overs for a score of 6 not out.

TMS commentators are too generous to a colleague to make any Geoffrey Boycott jokes but the email inbox lights up with listeners making some very funny observations indeed.

With Bairstow rested, Jason Roy opens up alongside James Vince and, while the two add 94 for the first wicket, Norcross doesn't see the fluency that characterises Roy and Bairstow's partnership. Vince, who had made a start and reached 43, is undone by Mohammad Hasnain. 'Not a great-looking dismissal,' he adds.

Roy continues unchecked, capitalising on another Pakistani fielding error to progress and bring up his century. The ease of England's chase is exemplified by the fact Roy took

29 fewer balls than Babar to reach three figures. Michael Vaughan is a particular fan of the shot used to bring up the hundred, tweeting: 'To bring up a century with a 6 over extra cover off the back foot to an off spinner is nothing short of ridiculous!!!!!!!!' The exclamation marks are a trademark of social media but hammer home the point about the opener's stunning form.

He is out for 114, strangled down the leg side, and when both Buttler and Moeen Ali go for ducks after Root is dismissed, England are five down and Pakistan are quickly back in the game.

The new partnership is Denly – finally getting a chance to make his case with the bat – and Ben Stokes, who has been searching for form for a little while now.

They steady the ship but Denly, proving the old maxim that it's better to have no luck than bad luck, is dismissed by a stunning catch from Junaid Khan. Given the parlous state of Pakistan's fielding in this series, he can count himself unfortunate.

Tom Curran joins Ben Stokes and England need 83 from 60 balls. Their job is made easier by another fielding howler from Pakistan, this time from Hasan Ali.

Ali is then called back into the attack and is taken for back-to-back fours by Curran, who is once again showing his cool head under pressure. After saving England with Ben Foakes in Malahide, he has really impressed with both the bat and ball in this series and a lot of those who thought he might struggle to make the World Cup squad have changed their minds.

With two overs to go, England are at the same score as Pakistan were at this stage – 322 for seven. However, the difference is that Pakistan had Imam-ul-Haq batting with one good elbow and England have Ben Stokes, who flat-bats a huge six over deep midwicket on the second ball of the 49th over. When Adil Rashid hits the last ball of the over for four, the job is virtually done. Stokes seals the deal with three balls of the final over remaining. England have secured the series.

Potentially even more valuable was the form and confidence Stokes's 71 not out will breed. Other than who to leave out of the squad, England didn't have many concerns before this game but Stokes hadn't produced his vintage form for a little while and this innings will settle a few restless minds.

Speaking after the game, Jason Roy reveals his century was made after he was up all night in the hospital with his young daughter and he only managed to grab two hours' sleep between 8.30 and 10.30 a.m. He describes it as 'not my most fluent of innings'. Vaughan is to the point as ever in response: 'I dread to see him when he is fluent.'

Zaltzman ends the day with aplomb, stating that England have now won 17 home matches in a row when they're chasing a total.

There's now just one full ODI before the World Cup and it's in Leeds on Sunday.

Pakistan 340-7 (50 overs; Azam 115; Curran 4-75) lost to England 341-7 (49.3 overs; Roy 114, Stokes 71) by three wickets.*

Sunday 19 May
England v Pakistan – Royal London One-day
International Series – Match 5
Emerald Headingley, Leeds

Team *TMS*: Simon Mann, Charles Dagnall, Alison Mitchell,
Michael Vaughan, Ebony Rainford-Brent, Ramiz Raja,
Mark Ramprakash, Andy Zaltzman

We have an all-time debutant in our ranks today. Everyone is hugely excited to welcome the last man to hit 100 first-class centuries, one of the finest English batsmen of the last few decades – and a coach who is still regularly working with the England team – Mark Ramprakash.

There is no formal *TMS* policy regarding employing former England cricketers who have been on *Strictly* but there is certainly no shortage of cha-cha-cha skills in the box, with Vaughan, Tufnell, Swann and now particularly Ramprakash all boasting impressive ballroom credentials.

On the field, Jofra Archer and Mark Wood are now the ones to be rested, with David Willey, Tom Curran and Chris Woakes forming the bulk of the seam attack. With the bat, Jason Roy drops out and Jonny Bairstow comes back in, while Eoin Morgan returns following his ban.

Another *TMS* debutant today is the grand new stand at Headingley, revolutionising the Football Ground End. Ex-Yorkshire captain Michael Vaughan admits a slight bias but thinks it looks 'magnificent'. However, all is not quite right in terms of the ground, as a noisy air-conditioning system cannot be silenced using traditional means. Always a resourceful and innovative bunch, Team *TMS* come up with an effective solution as a large number of NatWest '4' and '6' cards are collected from the sponsor's representatives outside and taped across the vents, thus preventing listeners from having to endure the airy drone of the system all day.

A welcome addition to the box is a stunning cake, which has been kindly sent in by Welcome to Yorkshire, the Yorkshire tourist board. They have created a bat and ball, set on a green base. Sadly, though, the ball has become slightly less than perfectly round in transit and, when a picture is posted on the *TMS* social media accounts, the tourist board accuse *TMS* of ball tampering.

While a picture supplied of what the cake looked like

beforehand clearly shows the ball has changed shape somewhat, it is impossible to prove the case and suggestions of an internal investigation are overruled in favour of simply tucking in. Tampering or not, the cake is delicious and the team feels thoroughly welcomed to Yorkshire.

Excitement is really building for the World Cup and, with Eleanor Oldroyd and *5 Live Sport* deciding to broadcast their whole programme from the neighbouring box, it is clear anticipation is growing. There are strong rumours around that today is a 'bowl off' between Tom Curran and David Willey for the final World Cup spot – but that will have to wait as England bat first.

As expected, Vince and Bairstow set off at an excellent clip, Dagnall admiring that 'lots of players can play an extra cover drive but few can make the crowd coo in doing so, like James Vince can', as he languidly strokes another one to the boundary.

The cooing turns to annoyance, though, as Vince is caught on the leg side.

'That's the feeling with Vince, really,' says Simon Mann. 'He was playing splendidly.' The frustration is clearly mutual, with Vince swiping the air with his bat as he walks off the field. Ramprakash, a man who has spent significant time working with Vince over the last few years, speaks of a 'palpable disappointment' that he has not converted another fine start.

'James Vince has scored some very big scores for Hampshire, so he's capable, but it's understanding at the higher level when you need to take on shots and when you don't,' he concludes.

Bairstow perishes trying to slot the ball into the new stand and Root and Morgan 'slow down' the rate. Saying that, England are still 147 for two after 20 overs, which would have been a semi-decent T20 total until relatively recently.

Excitement is growing about potential records. England's

highest ever total at Headingley, 339, looks certain to go but some are arguing that last year's 481 at Trent Bridge is in danger. Alison Mitchell contributes to the debate with an excellent story. Apparently, World Cup scorecards have been reprinted because tallies for fans to keep score initially only went up to 400. It has now been decided they need to be able to reach 500.

Record-breaking excitement dissipates slightly when first Morgan, then Root, Buttler and Moeen Ali are dismissed and England slide from 222 for two to 272 for six.

In the end, a very lively late cameo from Tom Curran gets England to 351 for nine. Amazingly, that seems about par in this series and Pakistan will be hopeful of picking up a consolation victory.

During the interval we're treated to the final episode in Kevin Howells and Andy Zaltzman's excellent history of home World Cups, with Alec Stewart, Angus Fraser and veteran cricket correspondent of the *Sun* newspaper John Etheridge reminiscing about England's efforts in 1999. Stewart – who was skipper for that fateful tournament – mentions the word 'shambles' on more than one occasion but it seems like he can now see the funny side of some of the events that went on 20 years ago.

Chris Woakes gets the England bowlers off to a flyer by getting Fakhar Zaman caught at slip off the third ball of the innings and then following up by trapping both Abid Ali and Mohammad Hafeez LBW in his second over. The tourists are 6 for three – Woakes has followed up a wicket maiden with a double wicket maiden and 352 looks some way away.

Sarfaraz Ahmed, 'nuggety' according to Alison Mitchell, and Babar Azam have dragged Pakistan back to respectability when Adil Rashid produces a sublimely brilliant run-out, taking a dreadful off-balance throw from Jos Buttler, spinning in a circle and back-handing the ball on to the stumps without looking, to get rid of Babar for 80.

Rashid then does it again, this time taking an astonishing diving catch off his own bowling to remove Shoaib Malik, and when Buttler stumps Sarfaraz for 97 it becomes a case of when not if England secure the win.

Chris Woakes returns to the attack and completes his five-fer when Hasan Ali is caught at fine leg and the series is over when Mohammad Hasnain runs past one from Rashid and is also stumped.

Hasnain had scored 28, which by itself is an unremarkable occurrence. However, this is certainly one of the more incredible 28s in international cricketing history, because before this game Hasnain had not made a single run in professional cricket. Zaltzman is boiling over with excitement at this, particularly when the No 11 clobbered David Willey for a giant six over extra cover, exposing all three of his stumps in the process.

England won the match by 54 runs, securing the series 4-0. While not technically a whitewash, England win all four matches that were played to a finish, with only the first game at The Oval falling victim to the weather.

Despite being rested today, Jason Roy is named England's man of the series for his 277 runs in three innings, averaging 92.33.

Speaking after the game, Morgan is clearly still not relishing having to cut his squad down to 15 for the World Cup but the opinions in the box have evolved over the course of the series with most of the team now agreeing that it should be David Willey and Joe Denly who miss out – with Jofra Archer and James Vince being brought in and Tom Curran winning the race for the final seam-bowling spot.

The only place where there is still contention is for the back-up spinner and, while he hasn't played at all in this series, Hampshire left-arm Liam Dawson is seen as the man most likely to step in.

All will be revealed on Tuesday 21 May – and *TMS* have an announcement of their own to come the day before.

England 351-9 (50 overs; Root 84, Morgan 76; Afridi 4-82) beat Pakistan 297 (46.5 overs; Ahmed 97, Azam 80; Woakes 5-54) by 54 runs.

CHAPTER 2

The Phony War

Monday 20 May

TMS confirm their squad for the Cricket World Cup

While former *TMS* mainstay Ed Smith is dealing with one of the more thorny decisions of his professional life, current *TMS* producer Adam Mountford has had a similar job to do in terms of selecting the commentators and pundits who will take fans through the next six weeks of the Cricket World Cup.

With the world's finest cricketing nations all coming to these shores, there are some staggeringly good commentators in the country, on hand to add expertise to their nation's games – and the wider competition.

In the end, Team *TMS* looks like this. Unless stated, the commentators are representing England: Jonathan Agnew; Michael Vaughan; Simon Mann; Sir Alastair Cook; Alison Mitchell; Sir Curtly Ambrose (West Indies); Natalie Germanos (South Africa); Phil Tufnell; Charles Dagnall; Ebony Rainford-Brent; Fazeer Mohammed (West Indies); Graeme Swann; Jimmy Anderson; Jim Maxwell (Australia); Prakash Wakankar (India); Jeremy Coney

(New Zealand); Isa Guha; Alec Stewart; Dan Norcross; Pommie Mbangwa (Zimbabwe); Paul Farbrace; Graeme Smith (South Africa); Bryan Waddle (New Zealand); Ramiz Raja (Pakistan); Vic Marks; Tymal Mills; Mel Jones (Australia); Kevin Howells; Jason Gillespie (Australia); Stuart Law (Australia); Scott Read; Athar Ali Khan (Bangladesh); Geoff Lemon (Australia); Niall O'Brien (Ireland).

It's pleasing to discover that Sir Curtly Ambrose has recently featured on the Australian version of *Strictly – Dancing with the Stars*. You can never have too much dancing expertise in the commentary box at any one time.

There are 34 commentators and summarisers in total – and, similar to the World Cup cricket squads, *TMS* are reserving the right to call up replacements should injuries or train delays occur.

There are 48 games across 45 days and *TMS* will be providing ball-by-ball commentary on every single delivery. That's over 400 hours of live broadcasting in a month and a half. It's an amazing feat of logistics and a balancing act up and down the country. Not only that, English domestic cricket will continue throughout the tournament, with every ball of every match in the County Championship covered online and on BBC Local Radio, *and* England women play West Indies in June before their Ashes series gets under way on 2 July in Leicester, a full 12 days before the World Cup final takes place. It's going to be one of the busiest times in *TMS* history, but we wouldn't have it any other way.

Tuesday 21 May

England confirm their squad for the Cricket World Cup

The big day is here, after months and months of speculation (it could even be years to be honest!). England name their final 15 at 9.30 a.m.

As predicted in Headingley, it's David Willey and Joe Denly who have missed out, with Jofra Archer, James Vince and Liam Dawson coming into the final squad. Alex Hales also misses out after his disciplinary issues earlier in the year.

Other nations are naming their squads every day and there is a feeling that the World Cup is upon us. Time is taken by various members of the wider *TMS* team to recce the ten grounds and ensure everything is as it should be prior to our arrival and it's very exciting to see all the World Cup banners that have gone up around the country.

Just the small matter of a couple of warm-up matches and a Lord's final and the World Cup will be under way.

Saturday 25 May
England v Australia – ICC Cricket World Cup – Warm-up
The Ageas Bowl, Southampton

Team *TMS*: Charles Dagnall, Simon Mann, Geoff Lemon, Mel Farrell, Graeme Swann

While this game is classified as a World Cup warm-up, some rivalries are never just warm-ups and the first meeting between England and Australia of the 2019 summer is unlikely to be anything other than fiercely competitive.

Disappointingly, while *TMS* have been moved to a different

hotel room to the one we were in earlier in the month, there is still no bed or sofa to accessorise the commentary box with. Fortunately, despite such hardships we are able to just about continue and with Phil Tufnell not on duty today there are fewer vociferous protests.

Today's *TMS* debutant is award-winning Australian author Geoff Lemon and one of his first duties is to commentate on a desperate parade of English injuries. First Mark Wood pulls up in his delivery stride and leaves the field, next Jofra Archer goes over in the field and finally Jason Roy gets a whack on the hand while backing up. Eoin Morgan is already sitting this one out after sustaining a fractured finger in practice yesterday.

There are palpable nerves in the commentary box every time a potential injury occurs, but it seems like all three will be okay for Thursday's World Cup opener with a little rest and some light nursing. However, their withdrawal from the field of play does give rise to a very amusing period as England fielding coach Paul Collingwood dons Wood's shirt and jogs out to do some fielding.

With fears of further injuries mounting, the sight of the 42-year-old Collingwood out there immediately prompts the 40-year-old Graeme Swann out on to the balcony to do some light stretching so as to be ready should the call come up into the box for more bodies.

Were the phone to ring, Swann wouldn't be the first member of the *TMS* team to abandon the commentary box for the playing field. When Henry Blofeld was covering the England tour of India in 1963–64 and a virulent bug struck the England team, he was close to replacing Micky Stewart and playing in the second Test of the series.

The great Blowers recalled the incident, saying his response at the time was that 'I would certainly play if needed, but if I scored 50 or upwards in either innings I was damned if I would stand down for the Calcutta Test!' In the end, Stewart checked himself out of hospital and played. But, as ever, Blofeld had an excellent story.

A similar bug befell the England side in Bangladesh a number of years ago and, when a conversation broke out in a distant hotel bar about how many players would have to be sidelined for Charles Dagnall to make his Test match debut, there were cross words spoken when it was suggested that then England coach Mark Ramprakash might still be picked ahead of him as a bowler. After that Dagnall insisted that should the debut materialise he would certainly not be doing any interviews with the BBC.

Away from the injuries, the biggest news on the field is that David Warner and Steve Smith are wielding willow on English turf for the first time since 'Sandpapergate' blew up in South Africa in March last year. As many people expected, both of them are given a rough ride by the English crowd.

Warner is booed to the crease and when he is dismissed by Liam Plunkett, 43 runs later, the crowd roars, pauses for a moment and then boos him back to the dressing room. He is replaced at the crease by Smith, who receives the same treatment on his way to the middle, when he celebrates his fifty and again when he celebrates making a hundred.

It seems like the treatment may follow them around the country all year and become a feature of Australian games, especially when England are the opposition. Jimmy Anderson, not involved in the World Cup but certain to be playing a huge role in the Ashes, had his say on the *Tailenders* podcast yesterday where he said the crowd were certainly within their rights to boo the pair, adding: 'If the shoe was on the other foot and two English guys were in the same situation [in Australia] they'd be getting absolutely everything, both barrels!'

Others in the box think it's slightly unseemly but it certainly doesn't sound like it's going to change any time soon.

Whether it's because of England's splendid retro kit, or a certain lack of firepower in the Australian batting, the innings itself feels quite old-fashioned and they eventually accumulate 297 for nine, somewhere shy of the 373 England totalled on this ground a few weeks ago.

Pleasingly for the crowd, England's innings kicks off with Steve Smith dropping Jason Roy at slip, a chance so easy Graeme Swann adds: 'There is no such thing as an easy slip catch, apart from this.'

The chase is rather emblematic of the game, with England taking few risks and prioritising preparation over delivering scintillating cricket. Jos Buttler, as he did the last time England played in Southampton, provided the highlights with a typically charismatic fifty – including 24 off one over from Nathan Coulter-Nile.

Oddly, England's sedate chase gives rise to an exciting finish, with 15 required from the final over. England do not get them, with Jofra Archer run out trying to take a second from his first ball.

Swann sums up everyone's feeling on the events of the day when he describes it as a 'glorified practice game but it was an important one for both teams'. England have one more of these, at The Oval on Monday, before the World Cup starts at the same ground three days later.

England 285 (49.3 overs; Vince 64) lost to Australia 297-9 (50 overs; Smith 116; Plunkett 4-69) by 12 runs.

Monday 27 May
England v Afghanistan – ICC Cricket World Cup Warm-up
The Oval, Kennington, London

Team *TMS*: Simon Mann, Daniel Norcross, Charles Dagnall, Jonathan Agnew, Ebony Rainford-Brent, Tymal Mills

The final hurdle for England to clear before the World Cup has been placed at The Oval and has the word 'Afghanistan' written on it.

While Afghanistan are nobody's favourites for the World Cup, some have been talking them up as dark horses, notably the Asian cricket experts on the BBC's *Doosra* podcast who have said that 'there's something about this Afghanistan team that reminds me of Sri Lanka in 1996. They could go all the way.' We will see.

Vastly experienced fast bowler Tymal Mills, who has played T20 cricket all around the world, is making his *TMS* debut today and adds, 'This Afghanistan team don't die wondering with the bat. Their opening pair are probably the biggest boom or bust partnership in the World Cup.'

He is proved spectacularly right when, after some early pyrotechnics, Hazratullah Zazai goes for another big one off Jofra Archer and perishes to a simple catch at mid-on.

Jonathan Agnew, who started the summer in Ireland but wasn't heard on air during the Pakistan series, returns to the box today and quickly gets back into the swing of things when he describes Rahmat Shah as not being 'just caught in two minds – he was in four minds!' as he is the second to go.

At 87 for four, the Afghans seem potentially on their way to setting a total but a collapse of four wickets in eight balls for five runs quickly finds them 92 for eight and it's only some pedigree batting from Mohammad Nabi that allows them to post 160.

The feeling among the team is one of disappointment in the Afghan batting, with Norcross summing it up when he glumly says, 'Afghanistan didn't cover themselves in much glory.'

Setting off to chase, unlike in Southampton at the weekend, England are utterly incendiary. Ebony Rainford-Brent thinks 'it's important England make a statement' and that is certainly what they do.

Jason Roy, having been dropped off a ferocious drive, peppers the boundary with an array of dominant shots. At one stage Rainford-Brent, a former colleague of Roy's on the Surrey Academy, says the opener is 'just toying' with the Afghan bowling.

Agnew adds that Roy is 'imperious' as he continues to move through the gears, ending unbeaten 11 short of his century as England chase the runs down off just 17.3 overs, giving everyone a very early night.

England have played some thrilling cricket so far this summer. While there have been four full one-day internationals, none of it feels like it has really mattered in the wider context.

As the team leave The Oval in the mid-afternoon sun, discussing what to do with their unexpected bonus four hours thanks to Jason Roy, there is a frisson in the air.

Next time *TMS* are in their box at The Oval, the World Cup will be up for grabs.

Afghanistan 160 (38.4 overs) lost to England 161-1 (17.3 overs; Roy 89*) by nine wickets.

TMS WORLD CUP COMMENTATORS LISTED BY BATTING AND BOWLING AVERAGES

Batsmen

Surname	Initials	Nationality	First Class Runs	First Class Average	First Class Wickets	First Class Bowling Average	Catches
Smith	G.C.	South Africa	12916	48.73	11	102.90	241
Cook*	A.N.	England	23455	47.67	7	30.14	322
Stewart	A.J.	England	26165	40.06	3	148.66	721
Vaughan	M.P.	England	16295	36.95	78	33.38	118
Raja	R.H.	Pakistan	10392	36.59	6	57.16	103
O'Brien	N.J.	Ireland	9057	35.51	2	9.50	492
Coney	J.V.	New Zealand	7872	35.14	111	31.17	192
Law	S.G.	Australia	11812	34.43	90	35.17	407
Marks	V.J.	England	12419	30.29	859	33.28	144
Jones	M.	Australia	4835	28.44	3	67.33	67
Rainford-Brent	E.J.C.L.C.R	England	2425	24.74	11	43.54	28
Farbrace	P.	England	711	18.23	1	64.00	89

Still playing

Bowlers

Surname	Initials	Nationality	First Class Wickets	First Class Bowling Average	Catches	First Class Runs	First Class Average
Ambrose	C.E.L.	West Indies	941	20.24	88	3448	13.95
Guha	I.T.	England	244	22.45	71	1546	14.86
Anderson*	J.M.	England	950	24.97	144	1815	9.65
Gillespie	J.N.	Australia	613	26.98	68	3742	19.59
Mbangwa	M.M.	Zimbabwe	126	28.41	21	324	6.89
Agnew	J.P.	England	666	29.25	39	2118	11.57
Tufnell	P.C.R.	England	1057	29.35	106	2066	9.69
Dagnall	C.E.	England	87	31.56	5	223	10.13
Swann	G.P.	England	739	32.12	195	7811	25.52
Marks	V.J.	England	859	33.28	144	12419	30.29
Mills	T.S.	England	55	36.50	3	260	11.30
Ali-Khan	A.	Bangladesh	1	109.00	5	48	8.00

Still playing

CHAPTER 3

Stokes Fires Up England

Monday 30 May
England v South Africa – ICC Cricket World
Cup – Match 1
The Oval, Kennington, London

Team *TMS*: Jonathan Agnew, Natalie Germanos, Charles Dagnall,
Isa Guha, Michael Vaughan, Graeme Smith, Phil Tufnell, Sam Curran,
Andy Zaltzman

It's here, it's arrived. Ever since Steve Smith smote Matt Henry to the legside boundary of the Melbourne Cricket Ground on 29 March 2015 we've been patiently waiting for this moment. We've watched the World Cup toured around the globe. We've observed the final warm-up matches and even attended the opening ceremony on The Mall outside Buckingham Palace last night – where the official World Cup song was performed and Kevin Pietersen and Chris from *Love Island* won a game of street cricket for England. Could it be a sign?

The day dawns brightly and the Secret Seven that will

bring today's match to the cosmos arrive, bright-eyed and bushy-tailed, in plenty of time for work. Phil Tufnell is particularly excited, literally telling everyone 'I'm just so excited' on repeated occasions to hammer home the point.

Over the years, *TMS* has broadcast from every corner of the world with some of the finest commentators and summarisers in the game. For the World Cup, all these people are coming to England and Wales, and it feels a lot like friends reunited as Graeme Smith and Natalie Germanos arrive, buzzing with excitement about what lies ahead.

A particularly good moment is when Smith greets Alec Stewart, who is covering the game for BBC Radio 5 Live. As well as being recent colleagues at Surrey, both men were participants in the specific WhatsApp group that was set up for this game by producer Adam Mountford. Smith's first work in the group was to change its icon to a Protea flower – Stewart's was to then immediately change it to a St George's Cross!

As if the first match in the Cricket World Cup was not excitement enough, there is more fervour created when Henry Moeran appears in the box clutching a cup of Costa coffee. 'Where did you get that from?' is uttered simultaneously by many people. When Henry reveals that a brand-new coffee machine has been installed in the press lounge, the box quickly empties as the new arrival goes under the *TMS* microscope and is declared 'a fine addition' by all and sundry.

The World Cup arrives on The Oval outfield under the watchful eye of a very talented aerial gymnast and, after a short address from the Duke of Sussex and two immaculate national anthems, we are under way.

South Africa spring an immediate surprise by opening the bowling with leg-spinner Imran Tahir and his first ball is watchfully knocked for a single by Jason Roy. Disaster has been averted from the first ball and the nation breathes a palpable sigh of relief. However, that sigh of relief is immediately inhaled back again as Jonny Bairstow gets a feathered nick on Tahir's second ball and departs for a golden duck.

Aggers and Tuffers are the men honoured with the mics for the first session and Tuffers has only just said that 'You need to be a brave man to go down the wicket and whack a leg-spinner over mid-off in the first over of the World Cup' when the dismissal happens, as Bairstow attempts to cut and is caught behind.

Joe Root comes to the crease to face the third ball of the innings, which can't have been in the plan. Amazingly, he is serenaded to the crease by a man standing under the scoreboard who is actually playing a guitar made out of a cricket bat. At the back of the box, Dagnall spots another career opportunity and makes a note in his diary.

Often during an international match, the box is full of people coming and going. There are cups of coffee to fetch, old friends to see and occasional other duties to attend to. Today feels different. The size of the game and the anticipation is such that people are hanging on every ball. Despite the immense amount of travel required over the next six weeks, there are no logistics being worked out, no trains being booked and no future days being anticipatorily planned. This is the big one; today is the day everyone's been waiting for.

Roy and Root rebuild, and Smith is 'harping on' about the need for South Africa to get back-to-back wickets when Andile Phehlukwayo and Kagiso Rabada get rid of both Roy and Root. For a second time, England start to rebuild with Eoin Morgan and Ben Stokes gradually finding their form at the crease. Charles Dagnall is enraptured to spot Stephen Fry in the crowd, who is utterly delighted as Stokes carts a six into the stands.

In a sign of England's immense strength in depth, there is a *TMS* debut today for one of the programme's youngest-ever summarisers, 20-year-old Sam Curran – who, despite earning nearly £1 million in this year's IPL, is not even close to joining his elder brother in the current England World Cup squad.

Sam is enjoying an early stint in the summariser's chair and makes the fine point that while people might be excited to watch Jos Buttler in a World Cup, when Morgan and Stokes are playing like this, 'It's no bad thing.' Murmured approval is tempered by a professional jealousy at how someone who was a teenager less than a year ago can be this good at batting, bowling and summarising.

Morgan perishes as England attempt to step on the gas and when Buttler under edges a slower ball from the exciting Lungi Ngidi, Smith tenses, visibly straightens in his chair and then hunches over the microphone and declares it a 'massive, massive moment for South Africa'. In case anybody doubts his thoughts, he adds another 'huge', before taking a deep breath and handing over to Michael Vaughan.

Moeen Ali is the next to fall and any dreams England had of kicking off the World Cup with a total the size they had been regularly posting against Pakistan are firmly out of the window as the boundaries dry up towards the end of the innings. However, Ben Stokes is still there and swinging. The rate picks up slightly towards the end and, when Stokes goes for 89, Aggers is delighted with a beautiful drive for four from Jofra Archer in the final over as England post 311.

So, the World Cup has got under way not with a monstrous batting effort but a well-played innings, especially from 1 for one. Vaughan thinks South Africa captain Faf du Plessis got his tactics spot-on, but when an Oval punter shouts 'Is that enough?' through the open window of the commentary box, Aggers responds that even the vaunted cricketing minds of *TMS* have no idea!

England emerge with the ball and Archer is front and centre.

As he charges in and flies one down at 91mph in the first over, it's amazing to think that, less than a month ago, we were discussing whether or not he should be selected. It's in the second over that he really hits the headlines though, cracking Hashim Amla square on the forehead with a brutal bouncer. The South African isn't felled, but the helmet comes off and he's clearly in a spot of bother. Both resident South Africans in the box, Natalie Germanos and Graeme Smith, are surprised and concerned when Amla is led from the field and thoughts quickly turn to sympathy as the veteran walks off with his hand on his temple.

Archer, very much the man of the moment, continues to be at the heart of the action as he dismisses Aiden Markram, causing Curran to exclaim, almost involuntarily, 'I wish I could do that!' He then bowls a 93mph brute to du Plessis, who top-edges his attempted pull and skies into the deep.

There is then a bizarre incident when an Adil Rashid googly gives the off stump what Aggers describes as 'a good whack' but fails to remove the bails. It also generates an incredible admission from Phil Tufnell, who asks, 'Isn't that out? The bails just have to come up, not fall off.'

'No, Tuffers, the bails have to come off,' responds Aggers on behalf of everyone listening around the world and shouting loudly at their radio.

Another great South African voice appears in the commentary box in the form of former all-rounder Jacques Kallis, who sums up the match situation when he looks at Quinton de Kock, who is playing an uncharacteristically measured innings, and comments, 'He has recognised the importance of him being there for a long time to try and get South Africa close to this total.'

Shortly after another odd incident, where Root almost gets stuck under the covers trying to recover the ball, England are grateful he found his way back onto the field as his occasional off-spin makes the key breakthrough, inducing de Kock to find Liam Plunkett at deep square leg. While Aggers thinks that new man J.P.Duminy 'has a record of not fancying it much' against quick bowling, it is Ali who claims his man, this time Stokes taking another good catch in the deep. The Durham all-rounder is then back in the game once more when his cannon-like arm from the boundary delivers the perfect throw for Morgan to run out Dwaine Pretorius.

South Africa are five down when England bring back Rashid into the attack and the baby-faced Curran comes off like a long-in-the-tooth club player keen to get to the bar when he says the leg-spinner 'will hopefully finish this game nice and early'. However, it's Archer who does the damage – another brutal bouncer seeing Rassie van der Dussen spooning an easy catch. The next man is a re-emerging Amla and he is immediately greeted with another rapid-fire short-pitched delivery from Archer. The new England star has a firm fan in Smith, who is perplexed that South Africa seem unprepared for his pace but adds, 'Jofra Archer will become a hero in England very quickly if he keeps bowling this way.'

Then, just when it seems as if Archer is going to be Man of the Match, Stokes fires the World Cup onto the front page by taking one of the most extraordinary catches you will ever see. Phehlukwayo gets down on one knee and hammers Rashid for a certain six towards the famous Oval gasholders, but Stokes, who seemingly just has to stand there and watch the ball fly over his head, launches himself into the air like Superman and plucks the ball out of the sky with his right hand while almost perfectly horizontal to the turf.

It is the sort of moment a commentator dreams of and Natalie Germanos is more than up to the task of getting the scale of the catch over to the listeners, playing the perfect neutral as she raises her voice to the level of a cricket lover who has just seen something extraordinary, passionately calling out, 'Unbelievable, jumping in the air and – somehow – plucking it out of nowhere.'

Graeme Smith, also slack-jawed, admits, 'Well, you have to smile – what a catch! He never looked like he was going to get anywhere near it. He came in, he went back, it was going to sail over his head and he stuck out the right hand and the big celebrations follow because that is a wonderful catch. It's going to take a lot to beat that in this World Cup!'

While less visually spectacular, Andy Zaltzman then raises excitement levels even further by revealing that it is the first wicket an English leg-spinner has ever taken in the World Cup. There has been a lot of talk about the importance of preparation for this tournament, largely about the actual players, but Zaltzman proves in a stroke that elite statisticians also need to make sure they're able to operate at the top of their game at just the right moment.

Stokes has had a spectacular game. Firstly, his 89 was the lynchpin of England's effort and a very intelligent innings in the circumstances. Next, he took a crucial catch and made a superb run-out, and then he made one of the great World Cup catches of all time. What's he going to do for an encore? The question is answered quickly as he is thrown the ball and immediately takes the final two wickets to finish the match for England with ten overs remaining.

Charles Dagnall is in the chair for the victorious moment, proclaiming proudly that 'South Africa have been outclassed in all departments. A very good victory for England. Ben Stokes can walk off a proud Englishman, knowing he has helped towards a convincing win and the perfect start in this World Cup campaign.'

Tufnell, on the mic at the beginning and the end, adds that it was 'a very, very, very impressive start for England. They were outstanding with the ball.'

The job has been done, the World Cup has started and England have their first two points. However, in a sign of even greater things to come, Jonathan Agnew wistfully adds that he is already 'looking forward to seeing Jofra Archer with a brand-new red ball in his hand, running in at some Australians . . .'

That's as may be, but there's a long road to travel beforehand and it first leads us to Trent Bridge tomorrow, where Pakistan will play the West Indies.

England 311-8 (50 overs; Stokes 89, Morgan 57, Roy 54, Root 51) beat South Africa 207 (39.5 overs; de Kock 68, van der Dussen 50) by 104 runs.

Friday 31 May
West Indies v Pakistan – ICC Cricket World
Cup – Match 2
Trent Bridge, Nottingham

Team *TMS*: Jonathan Agnew, Fazeer Mohammad, Simon Mann, Ramiz Raja, Ebony Rainford-Brent, Graeme Swann, Sir Curtly Ambrose, Phil Long

There is more excitement upon arrival in Trent Bridge and it is all absolutely well founded because it's still just the second day of the World Cup and today we are joined by the great Sir Curtly Ambrose for the first time this summer. Before his arrival it is pointed out that, as a player, Curtly was not exactly known for

49

his huge amounts of 'chat' on the field and therefore the great man may not be the most natural choice as a special summariser.

His mesmeric effect on fellow cricketers clearly carried on long past his retirement though, as when Curtly has occasionally worked for *TMS* before, Charles Dagnall concluded that he had never worked with such an intimidating summariser. 'If Curtly says it's Christmas, I'm singing carols!' he added instructively. Such opinions are not expressed when Sir Curtly arrives at the back of the relatively small commentary box at Trent Bridge – looking every bit of his much-vaunted 6ft 7 – and warmly greets the team.

TMS have the perfect man at the mic as the West Indies start their World Cup by producing an incendiary bout of fast bowling that is impressive even when compared to the halcyon days of Curtly himself in the 1990s. Pakistan are quickly 81 for eight as Andre Russell, Jason Holder and Oshane Thomas bowl fast, hard and aggressively and see it pay off.

Two contrasting reactions to the rapid-fire dismissals some-what sum up the differing feelings on either side of the box. After Russell bowls a 90mph bouncer at Haris Sohail (his fourth in a row), causing the batsman to flick an outside edge through to Shai Hope, Ambrose responds with an almost nostalgic delight that it's 'a brilliant piece of bowling! Andre Russell got it in the perfect area, it bounced and left the batsman. That is high-quality fast bowling.'

Not long has passed before Pakistan lose their seventh wicket, Shadab Khan, causing Ramiz Raja – who has already declared the innings as a disaster – to almost hold his head while declar-ing, 'This is shaping up to be embarrassing for Pakistan. Pace is working for West Indies.'

The game started at 10.30 a.m. and shortly after midday Pakistan are all out for 105. Sadly though, for Graeme Swann, the short game has compounded an avoidable error. The

Nottingham-based pundit thought the game was a day/night affair and apologetically rocks through the door with Pakistan eight down at 11.50 a.m. With Swanny living a short distance from the ground, he cannot fall back on the train-based excuses of Norcross and Mann when a similar incident occurred at this ground earlier in the month.

The innings break is partially taken up with a discussion about Curtly's experience on *Dancing with the Stars*, the Australian *Strictly*. From his point of view, it's nice that he's now known Down Under for something other than magnificent sporting violence against Australian batsmen, but from the point of view of assembled masses – both in the box and in the *TMS* email inbox – it's the fact that his dance partner was 5ft 4 that draws the most reaction.

It also draws the attention of the Trent Bridge IT department as the entire *TMS* crew and wider press box simultaneously look up clips from the show and cause their Wi-Fi signal to spike alarmingly. Nonetheless, it's better than the time a number of years ago when the late, great Tony Cozier, unaware of what he was doing, gave out the private media Wi-Fi password at The Oval and the network blew up as half of the 23,000-strong crowd immediately tried to avail themselves of a free connection.

With Curtly's Australian background, it is decided that we need to organise a *TMS* dance-off later in the summer: Vaughan v Tufnell v Swann v Ramprakash v Ambrose. Other commentators are welcome to enter but they may not have much chance. Agents are contacted and organisational responsibilities are handed out.

Back on the field, the game is over after a brief West Indies chase enlivened by Chris Gayle becoming the World Cup's leading six-hitter and Nicholas Pooran hitting 'a mighty six' to secure the victory by 1.55 p.m. Wrapping the game up, Agnew says that the win 'is about as comprehensive and one-sided as it could be'. No one disagrees, least of all Ramiz Raja, who shakes his head slowly and slinks away contemplatively. By contrast, one man who is delighted with the early finish is Graeme Swann, who completed his two-hour working day in style and was even able to get off in time to take his son to nets. Perfect.

Pakistan 105 (21.4 overs; Thomas 4-27) lost to West Indies 108-3 (13.4 overs; Gayle 50) by seven wickets.

Saturday 1 June
New Zealand v Sri Lanka – ICC Cricket World Cup – Match 3
Cardiff Wales Stadium, Cardiff

Team *TMS*: Scott Read, Alison Mitchell, Bryan Waddle, Kevin Howells, Jeremy Coney, Jimmy Anderson, Paul Farbrace, Phil Long

It's the first World Cup double-header and today *TMS* are in two different cities, situated 55 minutes apart. Both games pit Antipodean favourites against Asian challengers, and everyone is still excited. Walking from the hotel to the ground, James Anderson – experiencing his first World Cup from a fan's perspective – is entranced by the anticipation in people's eyes and delighted to hear there is still a buzz around Ben Stokes's catch from Thursday.

The game gets going and fortune is favouring the brave, with the Sri Lankans going for their shots against a highly fancied New Zealand attack. That cliché becomes more literal in the sixth over when Dimuth Karunaratne attempts to run one down to third man but only succeeds in chopping it onto his own stumps. An open-and-shut case, surely? Actually not, as despite the ball hitting the timbers with a fair crunch, the bails are not dislodged and Karunaratne remains.

After South African wicketkeeper Quinton de Kock got away with one on Thursday, this is now the second time it has happened in the World Cup and serious questions are asked about the weight and behaviour of the LED 'zing' bails that are being used. Sadly, for the Sri Lankans, that's as good as it gets as they fold for just 136 ('A real horror show,' suggests Kevin Howells), and New Zealand, perhaps conscious of the need to drive a good run rate early in the competition, comprehensively knock off the chase in just 16.1 overs. It's just as well that Karunaratne got away with his zing bails incident, as he carries his bat for 52*, 38 per cent of his team's total.

Former Sri Lanka coach Paul Farbrace sums up a brutal day for his old side when he says, 'Sometimes when you have a bad day you've got to move on quickly – and today is one of them for the Sri Lanka team. The best thing today for Sri Lanka will have been the journey from the hotel to the ground.'

Despite the poor game, Cardiff has at least borne witness to a feat of broadcasting today, as, during the Sri Lanka innings, the *Tailenders* podcast goes live on 5 Live for the first time this season. Greg James and Felix White are in London, and Jimmy Anderson joins them from the commentary box, seamlessly juggling his two simultaneous responsibilities with the poise of a seasoned pro.

Sri Lanka 136 (29.2 overs; Karunaratne 52) lost to New Zealand 137-0 (16.1 overs; Guptill 73*, Munro 58*) by ten wickets.*

Saturday 1 June
Afghanistan v Australia – ICC Cricket World Cup – Match 4
The County Ground, Bristol

Team *TMS*: Simon Mann, Charles Dagnall, Geoff Lemon, Vic Marks, Graeme Swann, Mel Jones, Andy Zaltzman

The day/night game sees Australia and Afghanistan get their campaigns under way, but the pre-match chat in the box is at least partially around the Champions League final that is taking place tonight in Madrid. With a 1.30 p.m. start in Bristol, the back end of the game is due to clash directly with the big match and a number of the team are pretty cheesed off at this confluence of events – and therefore delighted when Afghanistan win the toss, choose to bat first and are 0 for one after the third ball when Mitchell Starc utterly castles Mohammad Shahzad with an extremely quick yorker.

Charles Dagnall is the keenest to try to catch some of the football and decides to adopt the most potent and deadly weapon in the commentator's arsenal to ensure watching at least some of the action. Yes, Daggers reaches for the commentator's curse. Every time he approaches the microphone, Dagnall is vociferous in his praise of the Afghan partnership at the crease, knowing full well that fate dictates any fulsome praise will immediately see the victim dismissed, often in a way that humiliates commentator and batsman in equal measure.

However, not truly understanding the official rules of fate,

Dagnall doesn't realise that he is unable to intentionally bring on the curse and is getting increasingly frustrated as Gulbadin Naib and Najibullah Zadran help their side recover from 77 for five to 160 for six before they eventually post a creditable 207.

As the incendiary Aaron Finch and David Warner walk to the crease, the football-fixated Daggers is hopeful of a similar result to the previous two matches, where the chasing side have polished off the requirement in short order to boost their run rate. Sadly for him, though, the Afghans bowl what Graeme Swann describes as an 'immaculate length' and the Australians show no haste to get to the total, treating their opposition with total respect.

As with the ODI earlier in the season, the Bristolian residents of the flats that overlook the ground are having some fun and the innings is enlivened when a couple appear on their balcony dressed as full blocks of sandpaper. It's clearly childish and immature, but equally clearly, it's terrifically amusing to all and sundry. Australia's careful approach is rewarded by a solid seven-wicket victory, the win assured with 15.1 overs remaining.

Dagnall, his dreams of watching the Champions League destroyed, stomps off to his car and sits down in the driver's seat at 7.45 p.m. exactly. He later reports that the game was rubbish anyway and listening to the world-class BBC 5 Live commentary was infinitely preferable to actually watching it.

Simon Mann and Henry Moeran decide to stick it out in the commentary box and, as the floodlights are turned off to leave Gloucestershire County Cricket Club in darkness, the glow of Moeran's iPad can be spotted from around the ground and its many overlooking flats, emanating brightly from the box as the *TMS* pair tune in for the first half.

Afghanistan 207 (38.2 overs; Najibullah 51) lost to Australia 209-3 (34.5 overs; Warner 89*, Finch 66) by seven wickets.

Sunday 2 June
South Africa v Bangladesh –
ICC Cricket World Cup – Match 5
The Oval, Kennington, London

Team *TMS*: Natalie Germanos, Isa Guha, Daniel Norcross, Graeme Smith, Alec Stewart, Phil Tufnell, Athar Ali Khan, Andy Zaltzman

Walking to the ground this morning, it feels like the World Cup has really come alive. The Bangladeshi fans outside The Oval are supporting their team with a contagiously intense fervour – with many thousands of tiger mascots descending on south London. This fervour is also being transmitted throughout the *TMS* box by BBC Radio 5 Live's Roushan Alam, a familiar voice to all fans of the excellent *Doosra* podcast but a man making his 5 Live debut today.

Roushan, whose day job is a producer on Radio 1, is having one of the most nervous days of his life twice over. Firstly, he's a lifelong cricket fan getting his first opportunity to broadcast live on the sport; secondly, if he wasn't working on the game, he'd undoubtedly be in the stands as he's a huge Bangladesh fan, so he's intensely nervous for the start of a World Cup campaign where many have tipped the Tigers as an excellent outside chance.

Indeed, there is a spirited pre-match debate as to whether a Bangladesh win today would count as a shock or not. There's no need to guess where Roushan sits on it – and he points to his side's recent comprehensive victory in a tri-series against Ireland and the West Indies as strong evidence for the defence.

South Africa bowl first, with Daniel Norcross describing the colour of their kit as a 'horrid yellow'. Every Bangladesh run is roared on by the partisan crowd and, as they get off to a good start, Phil Tufnell thinks the atmosphere is 'starting to get to' the South Africans. In the box, there is something that is 'starting to get to' Team *TMS*, too. Not the wonderful racket generated by the Bangladeshis, but the true identity of South Africa's first change bowler, Andile Phehlukwayo. As part of the World Cup preparation, the pronunciation of his name was long discussed.

It was agreed by most that it should be said, phonetically, as 'FELL-U-QUAYE-OH'. However, this was thrown entirely into disarray at his first press conference, when it became apparent that he says 'PELL-OOH-SHWIE-OH'. There was further mud thrown into the process when *TMS*'s South African specialist Natalie Germanos arrived on air and immediately said 'PEH-KLUH-SHWAI-OH'. Overwhelming confusion reigns and it is decided, as there is clearly no correct answer, to respectfully adopt a bastardisation of all three approaches and hope not too many people notice.

Later in the day, Isa Guha is waxing lyrical with Graeme Smith when the former SA skipper's shift comes to an end and he has to hot-foot it down the corridor to start a spell for TV. Normally, there will be another summariser ready and waiting to step seamlessly into the breach. However, on this occasion, the cupboard is bare and Isa is forced to, brilliantly, speak to herself in front of a large worldwide listenership for a good three-minute spell until producer Adam Mountford flies back through the door in possession of our Bangladeshi friend Athar Ali Khan, who had been delayed working for the same TV network that Smith had to join up with!

Mushfiqur Rahim and Shakib Al Hasan are dominating the game and, with Lungi Ngidi injured and out of the attack, South Africa are looking toothless. The 200 comes up from 32 overs and Andy Zaltzman points out that, at 142, it is the highest Bangladesh partnership in the history of the World Cup.

After a brief South African fightback, Bangladesh wallop 70 from the last six overs to end up with 330. Whether it's a shock or not remains debatable, but it would be an impressive job for South Africa to chase it down. They start well, but a calamitous run-out, described as 'chaos in the middle' by Isa Guha and, more bluntly, 'dumb cricket' by Alec Stewart, sets the tone for a quiet period of the game where nobody can quite work out if they're setting a good platform or getting well behind the rate. It turns out to be the latter, as Shakib makes his point with the ball as well as the bat, bowling Aiden Markram and collecting his 250th ODI wicket as he does so.

After a brief visit to the commentary box by England women's captain Heather Knight, the game further swings towards Bangladesh when Faf du Plessis is bowled by Mehedi Hasan, causing Smith to eloquently worry that 'I feel like the game might walk off the field with Faf du Plessis'.

South Africa again threaten to get back into the game, but when Rassie van der Dussen is bowled, they need 103 from the final ten overs and, despite a massive six from Kagiso Rabada that Stewart describes as 'not far off the shot of the day', Bangladesh complete a famous 21-run victory, to the delight of the massed ranks of tiger-waving fans in the stands.

It is similarly pleasing to Roushan, who had virtually abandoned his post and had been furiously pacing around the corridors for the last hour, summoning a deep breath and what he thought was his finest BBC neutrality training whenever he was called on air. Whether the listeners at home considered him a neutral may be a different matter – however, his passion generated some superb broadcasting, really getting across the special atmosphere at The Oval today.

The 'shock or not' debate is returned to in the post-match reckoning, with Stewart nailing his colours firmly to the 'shock' mast, saying, 'This is a massive, massive upset. For South Africa to be turned over by Bangladesh in game two is a shock that'll go around the world.'

It has been noticed that Graeme Smith's voice, a basso profundo at the best of times, has been getting progressively deeper as his anger with the South African performance increases. By the end, as he mournfully admits that 'South Africa will have looked at this as a must-win game,' his pitch is somewhere near the Mariana Trench.

Norcross doesn't then help matters as he espouses the genuine concern being felt by South Africans when he concludes, 'If they lose to India on Wednesday then they are on the brink of going out.' It's hard to argue with him – but it's been a classic World Cup occasion and a small army of cuddly tigers are still being waved as Team *TMS* makes its way into the London night, with minds on England's encounter with Pakistan.

Later that night, the 'shock or not' debate is ended by Roushan, who simply tweets 'not an upset' six times, one under the other. He's had a good day and getting the final word over the legendary Alec Stewart seems like an excellent way to end it.

Bangladesh 330-6 (50 overs; Mushfiqur 78, Shakib 75) beat South Africa 309-8 (50 overs; du Plessis 62) by 21 runs.

CHAPTER 4

Pakistan Hit Back

Monday 3 June
England v Pakistan – ICC Cricket World Cup – Match 6
Trent Bridge, Nottingham

Team *TMS*: Jonathan Agnew, Isa Guha, Charles Dagnall, Fazeer
Mohammad, Michael Vaughan, Ramiz Raja, Graeme Swann,
Andy Zaltzman

The sun is shining, the drums are pounding, and it very much feels like a World Cup as *TMS* approach Trent Bridge this morning. These two sides have played a lot recently and there is a sense of expectation in the air that England will continue the positive start they made to the summer.

After witnessing the brutalisation the West Indies quicks gave to Pakistan on Friday, they bring in Mark Wood for Liam Plunkett to give them two 'nasty fasties' to pepper the unfortunate opposition with.

Eoin Morgan wins the toss, chooses to field first and, to the surprise of many – not least a smiling Ramiz Raja – Pakistan get off to a strong start, shooting to 111 for one after the first 20 overs. As Aggers says, 'We weren't expecting Pakistan to be 100 for one first thing this morning, but that's the beauty of this game.'

The first in a number of crucial moments comes in the 21st over when Mohammad Hafeez plunders Adil Rashid down the ground and hits it straight to Jason Roy. It is representative of the standards England set themselves in the field that when he puts down the straightforward chance, the shockwaves that circulate Trent Bridge are seismic. 'I have never seen Jason Roy drop one like that!' says Michael Vaughan, slightly slack-jawed.

Pakistan continue unchecked and loose lips in the box are mentioning the cherished '400' number before Babar Azam is taken well by Chris Woakes in the deep. However, Roy's dropped catch is compounded with errors breeding errors from what Swanny refers to as some 'very laissez-faire fielding'.

They end up setting England 349 to win, which is the sort of total they chased with impunity during the recent ODI series, but would be the biggest ever achieved in a World Cup, and they'll have to play well to get there. 'England haven't played like the world number one side in the first half of this game,' says Aggers – he's absolutely spot on.

As often in the past, Pakistan have displayed the mercurial side to their game, and when Vaughan says, 'The other Pakistan have arrived today,' it's hard not think back to their sides of the past who have sometimes walked a fine line between brilliance and disaster.

World Cup responsibilities rest heavily on players – and they clearly impact on security guards too, because there is a bit of a *TMS* 'incident' today. Normally when the programme is at Trent Bridge, we are garlanded with some of the most delicious brownies you could imagine by a very friendly listener,

Sue Dewey. During a normal match, the brownies will reach their intended destination in the commentary box very easily, frequently accompanied by Sue. However, today there is an utter disaster as they are intercepted by security and disappear into the Nottingham ether. Whether they are treated as a suspicious package and carefully blown up at the bottom of the River Trent or whether they are simply eaten by others seems unimportant – they haven't arrived with *TMS* and there is a significant drop in morale because of it.

When the normally mild-mannered Aggers contrasts the previous few hours of cricket with 'the absolute shambles' Pakistan produced against the West Indies just three days ago, his uncharacteristically cutting turn of phrase is put down to a lack of sugar in the blood and someone is dispatched to the pick 'n' mix facility in the press box to help him at least partially make up for 'Browniegate'. The sweets are not required though, as Aggers' mood is lifted organically when the great Sir Vivian Richards unexpectedly appears in the commentary box.

Viv is one of the most iconic cricketers in the history of the game and even though he is now 67 years of age, he looks none of them and is still built like a bull – a point proven when he 'jovially' punches assistant producer Henry Moeran high on the arm and the young man woundedly removes himself from the situation to immediately consider shoulder surgery.

However, Aggers' mood is particularly stoked when he and Viv withdraw to the neighbouring box to discuss their days playing against each other, off the air. While Jonathan's Test career has been mentioned on *TMS* many times before – usually quite harshly by Geoffrey Boycott when he has just lost a discussion point – one thing that is not often pointed out is the identity of his first two Test victims, both taken in the second innings of his debut at The Oval in 1984. They were very high-class dismissals: the first was opener Gordon Greenidge; and the second, and no points if you're playing along at home, was a certain I.V.A.Richards.

Richards was trapped LBW for 15 (off 11 balls, superbly) and while the West Indies side he was a part of might have gone on to win by 172 runs, it becomes apparent he has not forgotten the moment at all. Not only has he not forgotten the moment, he vividly remembers the ins and outs of the dismissal and is convinced that, were it to take place in today's game, it would be overturned by DRS!

Aggers is less convinced but, with Moeran still away in the medical room, ensures he avoids any more jocular contact from Sir Viv and heads back to the main box for another commentary stint, clearing the way for Michael Vaughan to slide in for a selfie. There are certainly not many cricketers that Michael Vaughan would bother for a selfie. Viv is one and his presence in the box has energised an already memorable day.

England set off on their chase and Roy's day is compounded when he is dismissed LBW in the second over, burning England's only umpire review in the process. He's not had his finest day, but he will certainly come again. Hopefully he doesn't tune into *TMS* when back in the dressing room and hear Zaltzman pointing out that the stands of 1 and 12 he has put on with Jonny Bairstow in the World Cup thus far compare very unfavourably with the average of 99.6 per partnership they were collectively pooling prior to the tournament.

New man Joe Root is dropped at slip and the game maintains a frenetic pace, with Vaughan maintaining that 'There's a bit of chirp out there,' shortly before Bairstow falls to Wahab Riaz.

Whether Ramiz Raja is aware of Daggers' experiment with the commentator's curse on Saturday in Bristol or not, he collects a belter for himself by stating that 'England need a good solid partnership between Root and Morgan. If they can get to 150, Pakistan will be sweating for sure,' mere moments before Morgan is cleaned up by Mohammad Hafeez to leave England 86 for three.

The 'chirp' Vaughan detected in the middle makes its way into the heart of the commentary box when Hafeez pauses in his delivery stride and warns Ben Stokes, freshly arrived at the crease, that he could easily have 'Mankaded' him. Fortunately, he issued the warning rather than going through with it and likely causing a major international incident. However, even the sniff of a Mankad has Swanny's back right up. 'Oh stop it!' he exclaims down the airwaves to Hafeez. 'I detest a Mankad! It's antagonistic, it's just not cricket. Stokes's feet were not even outside the crease. It leaves a horrible taste.' His viewpoint, however, is not shared by his commentary partner Fazeer Mohammad, who thinks there is nothing wrong with a Mankad because 'batsmen take an unfair advantage'.

While it would be a very unwelcome development for all *TMS* commentators and summarisers to take the same view on everything, it is rare to hear such a passionate debate break out on the air where the two protagonists have viewpoints that are so wide apart and – although the email inbox does prickle with concern about the relationship between the two men when they come off air – a hard-fought debate can only be ended when they simply agree to differ. If a Mankad does actually occur, all bets are off and Viv Richards might have to be brought back to keep the peace.

Stokes goes, replaced by Jos Buttler, and the ground echoes to chants of 'Pakistan! Zindabad!' as the real possibility of Pakistan putting the disastrous ODI series behind them and winning the big one unfolds in front of their massed ranks of support. Root and Buttler are motoring along and Vaughan speaks for many when he says, 'Moeen Ali has not been in tremendous form, so these two have got to take it deep for England.' As Buttler continues to gather pace, avoiding a referred LBW shout and very nearly being caught at slip, Dagnall points out that 'If Buttler stays in for another half-hour, anything is possible.'

Ramiz Raja is backing England, but that's possibly because someone has now quietly explained commentator's curse to him and he's decided to have a crack deliberately. Speaking of commentator's curse, despite the high-octane action, there is still time for the new series of *Love Island* to get its first on-air mention of the year, causing the expected deluge of correspondence – positive and negative – to flood into the inbox.

Root brings up his hundred and the excitement is so all-consuming that *TMS* receive a text from Rolling Stones keyboard player Matt Clifford, who is apparently updating the score for Sir Mick Jagger and Charlie Watts, as the Stones rehearse for their upcoming US tour. Frankly, even in the world of *TMS*, there are extraordinary texts to receive – and then there's that one. Presumably, the nation's greatest rock 'n' roll band are devastated to learn that Root, on 107, doesn't pick the pace on a Shadab Khan delivery and fizzes a catch straight to point.

'We've got a game on our hands here!' shouts Swanny over the noise of the Pakistan fans, who have come back to life and are delighting themselves in making even more noise than before. With ten overs to go, England are 258 for five and require 91.

Buttler and Moeen Ali are running busily in the middle, but Pakistan's fielding – their key weakness for the entirety of the ODI series last month – is transformed and the England pair can't find the boundaries required to stay with the run rate. A four is found to bring up Buttler's century, a shot hit so powerfully that it's probably just as well mid-off wasn't able to get anything on it. But the very next ball, Mohammad Amir produces the moment of the match, disguising his slower ball perfectly so Buttler can't pick the pace and goes the same way as Root, also fizzing a catch straight to point.

While Moeen and Chris Woakes are trying their best, England have only managed six boundaries in the last 15 overs and the ever-climbing rate is getting the better of them. Nonetheless, there is a feeling that anything is possible with this England team and Daggers and Vaughan are both involuntarily standing up while commentating, conveying the excitement and the incredible Trent Bridge atmosphere to the listening public in superb style.

A Moeen boundary causes Vaughan to declare, 'It's still on, this game!' But a Wahab slower ball does for him in the next over and when Woakes edges the very next ball behind, it's clear that – despite losing their last 11 one-day internationals in a row – Pakistan are indeed going to take the big one. Attempting to paper over the impending England defeat, Vaughan is still waxing lyrical about the incredible atmosphere, both at The Oval yesterday and at Trent Bridge today. World Cups in all sports need huge games to really 'catch fire' and the past two days have done that in spades.

Pakistan win by 14 runs and, as Aggers says, 'It's absolutely against the run of form, and there'll be some very surprised people by that result.' But everyone is fulsome in their praise for the victors, who have turned it around at just the right moment to give themselves a big chance in the World Cup. England faces look pretty glum, so the decision is taken to dispatch 5 Live's Eleanor Oldroyd – commonly referred to as the friendliest woman in broadcasting – to the Trent Bridge squash courts to conduct the post-match interviews.

While the rest of the *TMS* team are able to begin their

journeys to wherever it is in the World Cup they are required next, Michael Vaughan and the production staff enjoy a very late night in the commentary box as *The Tuffers and Vaughan Cricket Show* needs to be broadcast on 5 Live almost immediately after *TMS* goes off air.

With Tuffers missing in action today, his place on the show is taken by injured England player Sam Billings, who it's fair to say is a little more 'establishment' than the much-loved 'Cat' – and Vaughan brings an incredibly memorable day to a close by suggesting that although England have lost today, they've done nothing to convince him that they're not still favourites for the World Cup.

Pakistan 348-8 (50 overs; Hafeez 84, Azam 63, Ahmed 55) beat England 334-9 (50 overs; Root 107, Buttler 103) by 14 runs.

JONATHAN AGNEW'S FOUR TEST WICKETS

C.G.Greenidge c Botham b Agnew 34
(England v West Indies, The Oval, August 1984)

I.V.A.Richards LBW b Agnew 15
(England v West Indies, The Oval, August 1984)

A.Ranatunga b Agnew 84
(England v Sri Lanka, Lord's, August 1984)

P.A.de Silva c Downton b Agnew 16
(England v Sri Lanka, Lord's, August 1984)

Tuesday 4 June
Afghanistan v Sri Lanka –
ICC Cricket World Cup – Match 7
Cardiff Wales Stadium, Cardiff

Team *TMS*: Simon Mann, Alison Mitchell, Daniel Norcross, Jeremy Coney,
Mel Jones, Niall O'Brien, Phil Long

There might be rain around the UK, but the Cardiff morning is officially 'okay but murky' and Team *TMS* are buoyed by an early-morning tweet asking Daniel Norcross to inform listeners that there is thick snow in Queensland, so it could be worse.

Sri Lanka go off like an absolute train, with Angelo Mathews – who is wearing a coat, jumper, beanie hat and huge headphones while sitting on the balcony – clearly desperate for the batsmen above him to play all the way through and minimise the amount of time he needs to spend outside today.

There are serious complaints muttered off air about the Afghans, who are now fielding two players with headbands, making the job of identifying fielders – in some commentators' eyes – unnecessarily difficult. Sri Lanka are cracking along at 144 for one in the 21st, but sadly, shortly after the 30th they wind up 178 for seven and eventually limp to just 201.

As the collapse is in full effect, Norcross suggests that 'Afghanistan's fans look like they've just won the World Cup' – Mel Jones adding: 'After a brilliant start for Sri Lanka, things are falling apart completely.' Not only that but, with eight wickets down, the murk gets wetter and the players leave the field for nearly three hours. During the break, commentators are dispatched on a rota to the top of the fire escape outside the box to check on the quality and nature of the rain. For simplicity's sake, they are required to report back one of four categories: mizzle, drizzle, steady rain and stair-rods.

Afghanistan need only 4.56 an over to win – and when statistician Phil Long points out that their second-wicket partnership has increased an Afghan World Cup record of eight runs, hopes are raised. However, an extraordinary catch by Thisara Perera sees the Afghans slip to 44 for three, which becomes 57 for five. When Niall O'Brien reveals that Perera is known as The Big Panda by his team-mates, a stunned silence briefly falls across the box before it's decided to simply take it in stride and carry on with the commentary.

'This is an extraordinary, error-strewn game,' says Simon Mann as Afghanistan try to get back into it. 'It's not been high-level, top cricket but it's been fascinating.'

The hordes of passionate Afghans in Cardiff are willing their underdog heroes to a victory, but when Gulbadin Naib falls LBW to Pradeep, they start slipping behind the tell-tale DRS calculator and – despite some calamitous Sri Lankan fielding – a vintage Lasith Malinga delivery puts them further back and another one secures the DRS win. As Mel Jones says with a rueful tone, 'Afghanistan will be thinking of this as an opportunity missed.'

A cold, soggy day ends with the box warmed up by passionate rage as it is discovered that some Jaffa Cakes that had been sent to *TMS* by a kindly listener were delivered to the wrong radio studio. To make matters worse, they were then consumed by the broadcasters working in that studio. The final insult was how this information was discovered – a picture of the empty Jaffa Cake tube is sent to the mobile phone of a commentator, with a sarcastic comment appended, thanking *TMS* for the snacks. Utterly appalling.

Sri Lanka 201 (36.5 overs; Perera 78; Nabi 4-30) beat Afghanistan 152 (32.4 overs; Pradeep 4-31).

Wednesday 5 June
South Africa v India – ICC Cricket World Cup – Match 8
The Hampshire Bowl, Southampton

Team *TMS*: Prakash Wakankar, Natalie Germanos, Isa Guha, Graeme Smith, Michael Vaughan, Alec Stewart, Andy Zaltzman

On the day before World Cup matches, teams are required to make at least one player available to the media for the purposes of previewing the game they are about to play. Relatively straight-forward, you would think. Not where India are concerned. They make their World Cup debut today, and yesterday, for a reason that will remain known only to themselves, they asked two net bowlers to speak to the media. These bowlers don't play for India and have no association with the team whatsoever, other than the brief privilege of bowling to them in the nets.

So, it's a perplexed *TMS* crew that arrive back in the commentary suite for today's match at the gloriously renamed Hampshire Bowl. The temporary renaming is to protect ICC sponsors, but a brief early-morning discussion is unable to decipher why Hampshire Bowl was chosen over a simple return to the ground's original name, the Rose Bowl.

As ever with Southampton assignments, *TMS* are billeted in a converted hotel room within the ground's on-site Hilton and the morning gets off to a confusing start when Henry Moeran, producing today's game, can't access the box and has to go down to the reception to ask for the key. It takes a while to explain that he's not staying in the room and needs the key to get to work. An understanding is reached in the end, but the 'Do Not Disturb' sign is erected outside just in case.

An early delight is the arrival of Prakash Wakankar on the air for the first time in 2019. A superb Indian commentator and one of *TMS*'s very finest friends, it is wonderful to have his specialist knowledge guiding listeners through an Indian team that are rightly considered one of the favourites for this tournament.

South Africa choose to bat first, and it doesn't go brilliantly. Graeme Smith and Natalie Germanos are obviously concerned about the struggles their countrymen are facing. While they are fulsome in their praise for the Indian bowling, Smith is clearly frustrated, adding, 'This is below the level you expect of South Africa, certainly. Preparation was the key. They knew they would have three tough games first up and I just don't think they prepared enough.'

Another frustration for the team is proliferation of empty seats in Southampton. Official ICC communiques have constantly trumpeted a sold-out tournament, but it has become an ongoing theme that *TMS* will arrive at a ground and see a couple of thousand empty seats. With vast numbers of Indian fans desperate to see their heroes up close, Michael Vaughan sums it up when he says, 'It's such a shame there are so many empty seats. They keep saying it's sold out, but where are the tickets?'

An unexpected highlight of the innings and certainly something to file in the 'didn't think you'd see that at the Cricket World Cup' box is when a loud helicopter is heard approaching the ground. It's a relatively regular sight at certain grounds and not normally something commented on too much, until it becomes apparent that it's no normal helicopter and American President Donald Trump is being transported to today's D-Day commemoration ceremony in nearby Portsmouth via his official helicopter 'Marine One'.

South Africa wind up 227 for nine and a lot of the mid-innings chat is about *TMS* listeners sending in their tales of unexpected cricket fans, a conversation triggered by a recent tweet from star German footballer Thomas Müller, where he is wearing a replica Indian shirt and wishes Virat Kohli, apparently a big fan of the German national football team, a good World Cup. *Game of Thrones* actress Carice van Houten is mentioned as once watching a game in Utrecht, while Premier League club Wolves send in a tweet of their players engaging in some cricket, which is a lovely change from cricketers playing football – although the less said about Portuguese midfielder Rúben Neves's bowling action the better.

With a small total to chase, the massed ranks of blue-and-orange-clad Indian fans expect their side to quickly make mincemeat of it. However, having seen the value some of their bowlers were able to extract from the pitch, it is a cautious but safe chase from India. There are grumbles about the lack of thrilling cricket produced at times – aside from when South African wicketkeeper Quinton de Kock takes a very special catch to remove Indian skipper Virat Kohli – but a masterpiece from Rohit Sharma, who is unbeaten on 122, sees them home with 15 balls to spare.

Ebony Rainford-Brent has enjoyed a memorable day in the box alongside her close friend and former England team-mate Isa Guha. The two won a World Cup/Ashes double together ten years ago and have both flourished on *TMS* in recent years. They have also become the latest *TMS* commentators to get over-excited by the prospect of commentating in a hotel room, keeping themselves entertained during the drier moments of the Indian chase by climbing fully clothed into box's en-suite bath and shower for some very amusing selfies.

Ebony is on air in the end and sums up another poor day for South Africa by saying that they 'have not looked at the races at all since they arrived, but India have shown they mean business [putting in] an all-round solid team performance. This is the way you want to start a tournament. For South Africa there is a lot of pain.' As Smith and Germanos shuffle away, gamely posing with celebrating Indian fans, today has certainly been a tale of two sides.

South Africa 227-9 (50 overs; Chahal 4-51) lost to India 230-4 (47.3 overs; Sharma 122*) by six wickets.

Wednesday 5 June
Bangladesh v New Zealand – ICC Cricket World
Cup – Match 9
The Oval, Kennington, London

Team *TMS*: Daniel Norcross, Alison Mitchell, Bryan Waddle, Jeremy
Coney, Ebony Rainford-Brent, Athar Ali Khan, Phil Long

In London, The Oval has once again been taken over by a horde of passionate Bangladeshi fans. As on Sunday, it's utterly wonderful and the cuddly tiger count is again very high. Bangladesh bat first and get off brilliantly but are dragged back to 60 for two in a competition of two teams who started with a win and would certainly harbour semi-final ambitions.

When one of *TMS*'s two resident Kiwis, Jeremy Coney, suggests that the catch taken by Trent Boult to dismiss Tamim Iqbal could be taken by Boult's mother, there is some furious Googling to work out what her profession is – and whether Trent is a chip off the old block – but it turns out that, sadly, he is just speaking metaphorically.

Tamim is replaced by the diminutive Mushfiqur Rahim, causing Daniel Norcross to suggest that you could fit two of him into one Mohammad Shahzad. It's an amusing line, but potentially lost on all but the most fervent World Cup followers. While the tournament is generating substantial interest in cricket, the two could probably walk down most high streets outside of Dhaka and Kabul unbothered by selfie hunters.

Shakib Al Hasan is looking excellent again but is caught behind by Colin de Grandhomme, and Bangladesh eventually post 244 all out. New Zealand are chasing efficiently, with Ross Taylor joining Kane Williamson, who has been making life look pretty straightforward in the middle. There is a calamity, though, and one of the New Zealanders' key men is seemingly run out, casting the outcome into doubt. However, when the decision is thrown to the third umpire, it becomes clear that Mushfiqur Rahim has broken the stumps with his gloves first and Taylor is reprieved.

'If you're a Bangladesh fan, you're tearing your hair out,' says Alison Mitchell. Despite having played over 400 ODIs between them, Williamson and Taylor continue to provide run-out opportunities to such an extent that Jeremy Coney suggests that 'Ross Taylor and Kane Williamson should go for counselling,' adding that he is 'losing weight watching this'. Such is the normally unperturbable Coney's stress, Mitchell calls for a hot tea and someone is immediately dispatched to the excellent Oval coffee machine.

The two batsmen work out their differences and start to win the game for New Zealand. Coney's fellow Kiwi Brian Waddle – who has been respectfully mocked on air for his recent receiving of the New Zealand equivalent of an OBE – thinks that 'Taylor is looking the class player that he is,' with Coney adding: 'They don't panic, these two. They know how to get runs.'

The commentator's curse is firmly applied as, overs later, Williamson chips the ball to deep mid-off and gives away his wicket, and when Tom Latham goes fourth ball, such is the change in momentum and the uplift in The Oval atmosphere, Alison Mitchell reaches back to her school days to proclaim, 'Wowee!'

Jimmy Neesham becomes the latest to survive the tightest of run-outs and is seemingly taking the game home when Taylor is strangled down the leg side and tigers are once more raised skywards as the game swings again. Colin de Grandhomme is another who looks like he might finish it, but Mushfiqur partially atones for his earlier error by leaping high to take a great catch, and when Neesham picks out long-on and New Zealand still need 27 with three wickets left, Waddle lets out a strained 'Oh nooooooo . . .' before completing his commentary stint and deciding the only thing for it is to pace up and down the same corridor Roushan Alam used earlier in the week for the first Bangladesh game.

Matt Henry and Mitchell Santner show excellent composure to almost take their side over the line, giving the massed ranks of Bangladeshis producing an atmosphere for the ages one last chance to explode when Henry is clean-bowled by a full toss from 'The Fizz' (Mustafizur Rahman). However, Lockie Ferguson squirts one through third man and Santner drives one for four to complete a victory that was far more stressful than required but produced a wonderful spectacle for all at The Oval and the *TMS* listeners around the world.

Daniel Norcross – who has had an eventful day, including being upbraided for smoking in the wrong area but then using the subsequent conversation to persuade the German steward that cricket was actually a wonderful sport – sums the whole thing up afterwards by saying, 'It's been a day full of errors, some magnificent moments, some terrific bowling, some terrific batting, and an absolutely terrific finish.'

Bangladesh 244 (49.2 overs; Shakib 64; Henry 4-47) lost to New Zealand 248-8 (47.1 overs; Taylor 82) by two wickets.

Thursday 6 June
Australia v West Indies –
ICC Cricket World Cup – Match 10
Trent Bridge, Nottingham

Team *TMS*: Jonathan Agnew, Fazeer Mohammad, Charles Dagnall, Geoff Lemon, Sir Curtly Ambrose, Tymal Mills, Stuart Law, Phil Long

A weary statistician and producer, Phil Long and Adam Mountford, are among the first to arrive at Trent Bridge, despite catching the last train from London last night. They are joined by former Australian player and West Indies coach Stuart Law, who is linking up with *TMS* today for a clash of his two former sides. An excellent politician, when asked who he is supporting he flashes a broad smile (as if he'd thought this might crop up) and answers 'Middlesex', where he is currently first-team coach.

As well as Stuart, *TMS* are enjoying one of its most bowler-centric line-ups in recent times with Jonathan Agnew, Charles Dagnall, Curtly Ambrose and Tymal Mills all taking to the airwaves today – and all capable of giving batsmen a good old-fashioned 'hurry up' in their time. In Mills's case, he's very much still capable of it and, similarly to when Sam Curran was with *TMS* at The Oval recently, it offers a great change of pace to hear a player who is still playing commentating on his contemporaries. Although England aren't playing today, Tymal is particularly interesting when discussing his friend and Sussex team-mate Jofra Archer in the pre-match discussion – suggesting that the new England star has the tools to go a very long way indeed in the game.

As the broadcast gets going, it is mentioned that *TMS* has all bases covered: Mills for raw pace; Ambrose for bounce; Agnew for swing and movement – and Dagnall, if required, for declaration bowling.

West Indies bowl first and get rid of Australia captain Aaron Finch and then David Warner early on – and as fast bowler Sheldon Cottrell celebrates with his traditional salute, Law earns his summariser spurs very early by revealing the reason behind that specific celebration is that Cottrell is still a serving member of the Jamaican Army, and the salute is to honour his commanding officer, who has to give him specific permission to play every time he dons the West Indies shirt.

Two more quick ones and Australia are deep in trouble at 38 for four and then, following a brief recovery, 79 for five – with Aggers warming up for later in the summer as he gets stuck into Marcus Stoinis for 'a soft dismissal'. There is talk of a recovery, but when Alex Carey falls, that turns to whether

West Indies can close it out. Geoff Lemon asks whether the first two deliveries faced by new man Nathan Coulter-Nile 'are the least two convincing deliveries you have ever seen anyone face?'

Tucking Lemon's abuse into his back pocket, Coulter-Nile survives his early issues and plays the crucial role of the innings, smacking 92. At one stage, he leathers the ball at Shimron Hetmyer, fielding at square leg, only to see the young West Indian drop the chance, much to the chagrin of *TMS*'s superb West Indian commentator, Fazeer Mohammad.

'Give Hetmyer some slack there – it was absolutely smashed at him,' replies Law, defending the player.

'You sound like his dad,' retorts Fazeer immediately.

'I was his dad for two years!' says the quick-witted Law, drawing the crowd to their feet and winning the point against Fazeer.

As the innings concludes, 'Salutin' Sheldon' brings down the house with a spectacular boundary catch to remove Smith, taking the ball one-handed before throwing it back up, crossing the boundary and taking it again when he's back inside the field of play. 'Quite brilliant!' gasps Dagnall. Coulter-Nile, tantalisingly close to the World Cup record for a No 8 batsman, goes for 92 and Australia post 288 all out – very defendable and much higher than they could possibly have hoped for earlier in their innings.

West Indies get chasing and, after Chris Gayle has survived yet another delivery that hits the stumps but doesn't remove the bails, he plays a characteristically eventful knock. However, there is drama in the commentary box as Curtly Ambrose is not appreciating the English conditions.

'It's chilly. I'm not used to this weather. I've got my big fleece on,' complains the Big Man.

'We've still got to go to Chester-le-Street, Curtly,' quickly replies Daggers.

'Oh gawd,' comes the soulful reply.

Halfway through, the West Indies are 133 for three – and while Australia were 119 for five at the same point, Jason Holder's side really do not feel like the favourites, a position compounded when Shai Hope – beginning to play a totemic innings – gives his wicket away on 68. Andre Russell – who Phil Long points out hit 510 from 249 balls in this year's IPL – whacks his second ball 103m, deep into the Radcliffe Road Stand and Charles Dagnall, quite rightly, says, 'Half an hour of this and the game is done.'

However, the massed crowds get only ten minutes as he mis-cues an outside edge off Starc and has to depart, heightening the tension – which is given a statistical boost after 42 overs as Phil Long once again chips in, this time to reveal that both teams went into the 43rd on 233 for six.

Pat Cummins bowls his final over – with Stuart Law offering up some high praise for the three maidens he achieved – but Starc getting Carlos Brathwaite could be even more key, especially when he gets Jason Holder in the same over for 51. He returns in his next over to complete the five-fer, bowling Cottrell middle stump and effectively securing a topsy-turvy contest for Australia. They go on to win by 15 runs, despite Ashley Nurse smacking four consecutive fours in the final over.

Australia are looming, and when Aggers says that they 'will feel winning the game from where they were that they can beat anybody', there is an ominous look around the box as everyone realises that the Aussies are now firmly stamped with the tag of potential winners.

Australia 288 (49 overs; Coulter-Nile 92, Smith 73) beat West Indies 273-9 (50 overs; Hope 68, Holder 51, Starc 5-46) by 15 runs.

Thursday 6 June
England Women v West Indies Women – Royal London
One-Day Series – Match 1
Grace Road, Leicester

Team *TMS*: Natalie Germanos, Ebony Rainford-Brent, Charlotte Edwards,
Lydia Greenway, Henry Moeran

West Indies are also in action on the other side of the East Midlands as England women kick off a summer campaign that, just like their male colleagues', will end in a hugely anticipated Ashes series. Henry Moeran, *TMS*'s regular assistant producer behind the scenes, takes to the airwaves today alongside an otherwise all-female team that features Charlotte Edwards and Lydia Greenway making their seasonal debuts.

TMS are not often present in Leicester – which is a shame, because for the commentators working here there is one more excuse than usual to enjoy some cake, which is always a wonderful thing. At most international grounds, the *TMS* commentary box is usually located in a 'Broadcast Centre', close to our television colleagues. However, at Grace Road the TV facility is at the other end of the stadium, meaning those who are commentating for both TV and radio need to get around the circumference of the ground in between shifts. This makes for quite a lot of frantic running about, but – with the requirement to only speak rather than potentially be filmed – the team seem to be taking the opportunity of their *TMS* shifts to refuel!

The tone is rather set from the very first ball, a waist-high full toss delivered by Shakera Selman that is hooked for six by Amy Jones. Moeran describes it as 'a horrible loosener' to which Jones 'just said, "Thank you very much!"' England dominate the game with the bat, ending 318 for nine, with Jones scoring 91 and captain Heather Knight 94. As West Indies trudge off following their shellacking, Edwards says, 'They'll be wondering how they can chase this down.'

The frantic nature of switching between TV and radio is catching up with Ebony Rainford-Brent, who declares she 'probably needs less butter in my life', after quickly wolfing down a salmon and king prawn bake for dinner.

Katherine Brunt gets the first breakthrough for England and then bowls Shemaine Campbelle the very next ball to set up a hat-trick opportunity. This isn't taken, but with Amy Jones's first-ball six and then this from Brunt, England are setting out their stall very early in the summer. Only Chedean Nation is able to provide any serious resistance, battling hard for her unbeaten 45, while the remainder of the West Indian batting looks rather like a telephone number as batters are dismissed for 1, 3, 0, 10, 2, 0 and 0.

England win by 208 runs, their biggest-ever victory over the West Indies, and will be very pleased with their start to the summer. The West Indies, meanwhile, looked shell-shocked and Charlotte Edwards 'can't believe it's the same team we saw six months ago'.

England 318-9 (50 overs; Knight 94, Jones 91, Matthews 4-57) beat West Indies 110 (36 overs) by 208 runs.

Friday 7 June
Pakistan v Sri Lanka – ICC Cricket World Cup – Match 11
The County Ground, Bristol

Team *TMS*: Simon Mann, Daniel Norcross, Scott Read, Vic Marks, Ramiz Raja, Paul Farbrace, Andy Zaltzman

As *TMS* arrive in Bristol, the weather is grim, the outlook for the rest of the day is grim and the faces of everyone concerned are grim. However, despite the fact that not a single ball is bowled, *TMS* once again proves that – even with no cricket to actually commentate on – it is still a thoroughly enjoyable listen. A particular highlight is Daniel Norcross and Ramiz Raja spending a superb hour going through the 1992 World Cup game by game.

At 4 p.m., the umpires put everyone out of their misery by calling the game off. *TMS* has been on air for six hours at that stage. It's a shame for everyone, not least the Pakistan and Sri Lanka players, but the wider issue could be the fact that this rain looks like it might stick around for a few days.

Match abandoned.

CHAPTER 5

Roy and the Mallard Protection Society

Saturday 8 June
England v Bangladesh –
ICC Cricket World Cup – Match 12
Cardiff Wales Stadium, Cardiff

Team *TMS*: Jonathan Agnew, Charles Dagnall, Isa Guha, Alison Mitchell,
Michael Vaughan, James Anderson, Graeme Swann, Paul Farbrace,
Andy Zaltzman

Arrival in Cardiff sees the weather better than in Bristol on Friday, but its primary characteristic would be described as 'very windy'. At most grounds, this wouldn't affect *TMS* very much at all. However, due to the size of the media interest in the World Cup, Cardiff have been forced to invest in some temporary media facilities to house everyone. *TMS* are allocated our normal box, but Eleanor Oldroyd, who is presenting *5 Live*

Sport from the ground, has been given one of the temporary spaces on the other side of the stadium.

The strength of the wind is such that from the *TMS* end, the 5 Live box can clearly be seen swaying gently from side to side. Shortly before the start of the game, Jimmy Anderson heads over there nervously, ready for his 11 a.m. call to do *Tailenders* with Greg James and Felix White, both of whom are tucked safely into a studio at the BBC in London. Anderson has certainly had more enjoyable hours and gratefully returns to the *TMS* box green around the gills shortly after the show has finished. However, poor Ellie has to stay over there all afternoon and her safety is not helped by an incendiary performance from England.

After a start that Andy Zaltzman delightedly calls 'an innings of two tenths so far' (England hit just 15 from the first five overs but then 52 from the second five), Jason Roy and Jonny Bairstow once again find their rhythm and turn the 5 Live box into the centre of what Charles Dagnall describes as 'tin pan alley', with huge sixes repeatedly appearing like they are simply going to fly into the box where Ellie is broadcasting.

The dismissal of Bairstow brings some small respite as the more conservative Joe Root hits 21 from 29, but Roy is playing the innings of his life at the other end. Many is the time a *TMS* pundit has wondered what Roy might be capable of on the biggest stage, and here he proves beyond all reasonable doubt that he is one of the most special batsmen in the world.

His hundred comes up in a bizarre way as he knocks what looks like a single into the deep and jogs through. However, a serious misfield sees the ball fly through and unexpectedly reach the boundary, bringing up the landmark. This takes Roy completely unaware, and his first action after scoring a debut World Cup century is to run, full tilt, into umpire Joel Wilson. It looks nasty for a second, but Wilson gamely drags himself to his feet and the match continues, with Roy moving through the gears rapidly.

Anderson, who has returned after being granted a short break to settle his stomach, thinks 'England are in a brilliant position – especially when you talk about doubling the score at 30 overs. That would give them 400.' That looks more than on the cards as Roy marmalises the first three balls of a Mehedi Hasan over for huge sixes. He is looking in so much control that genuine thoughts about six sixes in an over are passing through people's minds before he slices the fourth ball into the air to go for a superb 153.

Former England coach Paul Farbrace is another summariser on today's game and declares that Jason could open in the Ashes, saying, 'Roy took his time at the beginning and that's what he has developed as a player. His options he takes now are so much smarter. If he continues to play as he is, the Ashes are very much in reach for him. Roy could easily open for England in the Ashes; he has shown his temperament has changed. At the beginning he was looking to be playing big shots all the time, but he has matured as a person and a player and I think he has got the capabilities to play Test cricket.' That's certainly an exciting prospect.

With Roy gone, Jos Buttler takes on the role of chief aggressor, sending one into the River Taff and causing Zaltzman to reach deep into his stats book to come up with the gem that, since the last World Cup, he has scored 1,020 runs from 564 balls in the last ten overs of innings. This is a strike rate of 10.8 per over and he is averaging 78.3 in the last ten overs of innings. Disappointed as she is to see the back of some of England's finest batsmen, Ellie breathes a slight sigh of relief when Buttler goes for 64. Given the hitting on show today, it's almost a shock that she hasn't had to take evasive action at one stage or another.

England end on 386 for six, with Zaltzman pointing out that they've now become the first team ever to make 300 in seven consecutive one-day internationals. Agnew, referring to the Trent Bridge defeat against Pakistan earlier in the week, adds: 'If anyone was feeling jittery in and around the England camp, it was a much calmer, authoritative, thoughtful, controlled approach today and that should prove too much for Bangladesh.'

There has been a lot of talk about the extra pace Jofra Archer gives England and there is no clearer demonstration of this than in his second over of the Bangladesh innings, when he clean bowls Sarkar for 2 and then sees the ball ricochet off the stumps and fly, firstly over the wicketkeeper's head and then over the boundary without bouncing. *TMS* usually bring an experienced team, but no one has ever seen that before.

Bangladesh make a comeback of sorts, highlighted by Shakib flicking Archer over fine leg and out of the ground, imperilling a paddling of ducks on the River Taff. On commentary, Graeme Swann wonders whether a Mallard Protection Society exists. If it does, it would be in business today.

The key partnership in the Bangladesh innings is between Shakib and Mushfiqur Rahim. Michael Vaughan is advocating a conservative approach, saying, 'Bangladesh just have to keep going the way they are. If they can't get to 380 then get to 330 and make sure your net run rate isn't damaged too badly.'

As summed up by Vaughan, there is little hope of Bangladesh getting close and when Rahim and Mohammad Mithun go in quick succession, Jimmy Anderson has the kind understatement of a current player when he says, 'It's looking a steep task now for Bangladesh, those couple of quick wickets were just what England needed to put the pressure back on.'

The win is sealed when Archer takes two wickets in the

penultimate over, ending the game with a brutal bouncer to his fellow fast bowler Mustafizur Rahman. 'It was important they put in a real strong performance and they have done exactly what was required,' concludes Vaughan, to widespread agreement, adding: 'If England can clear out the peripheral nonsense – against Pakistan they were agitated – it's about the mentality going forward.'

England 386-6 (50 overs; Roy 153, Buttler 64, Bairstow 51) beat Bangladesh 280 (48.5 overs; Shakib 121) by 106 runs.

Saturday 8 June
New Zealand v Afghanistan – ICC Cricket World Cup – Match 13
County Ground, Taunton

Team *TMS*: Daniel Norcross, Simon Mann, Bryan Waddle, Jeremy Coney, Ramiz Raja, Pommie Mbangwa, Mel Jones, Phil Long

Despite what happened earlier in the summer, Daniel Norcross and Simon Mann are allowed to travel together again. On this occasion they are driving from Bristol to Taunton. In principle, this is fine. However, tradition dictates that a disaster befalls them, and, on this occasion, it is the fault of Norcross's Uber driver, who is supposed to deliver him to Simon's mother's house, where he will be picked up. However, the driver flies straight past the agreed address, with Norcross only aware of what has happened when he sees a hapless Mann frantically attempting to flag them down from the pavement.

Order is eventually restored and the two arrive in plenty of time to see Afghanistan inserted by New Zealand. Afghanistan make three changes, one of which is particularly noteworthy as Noor Ali Zadran is brought in instead of Mujeeb Ur Rahman. Noor Ali is Mujeeb's uncle and there is plenty of speculation as to what the brother/father thinks about the whole situation.

Despite some horrendous conditions the day before, Taunton is a picture for its entry into the World Cup, and with no more rain expected for today, cider country is ablaze with excitement at taking its place on the international stage. A good start is made by the Afghan openers, with Jeremy Coney pointing out that Somerset is generally a batsman-friendly venue and statistician Phil Long giving him credence by pointing out that the last time a World Cup match took place here, Sourav Ganguly and Rahul Dravid put together a 318-run partnership for India!

'This is a wonderful start from Afghanistan,' says Zimbabwean summariser Pommie Mbangwa. 'The batting is the key and they are bang on track now – any side would take 61 for none after ten when being asked to bat first.' That is true, but that becomes 66 for one and then 66 for two, 66 for three and 70 for four. The days of 6.1 an over are long gone as Hashmatullah Shahidi takes 20 balls to get off the mark and any lingering momentum Afghanistan may have had is destroyed by two rain breaks.

Back on the field, Afghanistan slip to 105 for five and end up 172 all out, with Hashmatullah gaining the last laugh as his 59 is the only score of note.

Although Martin Guptill goes from the very first ball of the innings, a characteristically controlled innings of 79 not out from Kane Williamson sees New Zealand home with little drama – other than yet more oddly calamitous running with Ross Taylor – and lots of reserved efficiency. The win is secured with a single, and Mel Jones thinks that Williamson's lengthy innings might have been the New Zealander playing for form, saying, 'Kane Williamson was a bit scratchy at the start but by the end he was timing it well and that's a good sign for New Zealand.'

She's also critical of Afghanistan, adding: 'We've got to start shifting the language about it being a fairy-tale story for Afghanistan now. They're an established side, but they're being caught short in a few different areas. Their footwork to pace and building on starts is wanting.'

From New Zealand's perspective, it's job done. The schedule gave them three easy starts and as Jeremy Coney concludes, 'It is about to get tougher for them and we'll find out in the next four matches whether they're going to reach the semi-finals.'

For Norcross and Mann, the day ends as it began, with a potential transport mishap as it becomes clear that Mann's car only has 37 miles of petrol in the tank and there is not a station in that range. Norcross distracts the driver with old 'Derek and Clive' sketches and Andy Zaltzman's podcast, *The Bugle*, as they limp along the A303, eventually finding salvation near Stonehenge with the car running on fumes.

Afghanistan 172 (41.1 overs; Hashmatullah 59; Neesham 5-31, Ferguson 4-37) lost to New Zealand 173-3 (32.1 overs; Williamson 79*) by seven wickets.

Sunday 9 June
India v Australia – ICC Cricket World Cup – Match 14
The Oval, Kennington, London

Team *TMS*: Prakash Wakankar, Charles Dagnall, Isa Guha, Geoff Lemon,
Michael Vaughan, Phil Tufnell, Mel Jones, Andy Zaltzman

Arrival in central London reveals another amazing Oval occasion, with a sea of Indian blue greeting fans coming off the tube in Kennington. Palpable tension in the air makes it feel like a big one, possibly the biggest of the World Cup so far.

India win the toss and bat first, roared on by their passionate support, but Phil Tufnell reckons that 'Australia seem to have got that strut back and feel that they can beat anyone.' This is demonstrated by an incredible effort from Nathan Coulter-Nile, who almost takes Rohit Sharma with an unlikely catch in the second over. He just got his fingertips to it, with Isa Guha and Phil Tufnell both agreeing that he actually managed to dive too far!

Aside from that dropped 'chance' and a blow to the hand of Shikhar Dhawan, India start superbly and bring up their hundred from 19 overs, with Andy Zaltzman pointing out that they have won on 13 of the previous 15 occasions Rohit and Dhawan have put on a century-opening partnership. In the stands, the Bharat Army, the Indian version of the Barmy Army, have come up with a version of the Yaya/Kolo Toure song, but substituting the Manchester City players' names for Rohit and Dhawan. It's an Indian party all right, a fact underlined when Australian Mel Jones comes on air with her compatriot Geoff Lemon.

'I think we've doubled the Australian support in the crowd today, Geoff,' says Mel dispiritedly. 'I thought I saw a few yellow shirts and went over to talk to them, but it turned out they were Chennai Super Kings fans!'

The arrival of the Aussie pair on the mic does herald a breakthrough, with Rohit caught behind off Coulter-Nile, the deathly silence of surprise only broken when Virat Kohli emerges from the dressing room to hitherto unseen levels of adulation. Kohli, after a few early wobbles, begins to play himself into the game and, after Jason Roy yesterday, Dhawan is the latest World Cup centurion to reach the milestone in an odd way, nearly running out Kohli from a direct hit, but then taking an overthrow from the ricochet. After the third umpire has done the necessary, the runs are given and the roar goes up, Dhawan raising both hands in celebration. Zaltzman is quick on the draw, pointing out it's the opener's third hundred in five ODI innings at The Oval.

India have built the perfect platform and Michael Vaughan says, with Australia's batting line-up, they'll need at least 300 to feel confident. Dhawan is caught on the boundary with 13 overs to go, but all that does is clear the decks for Hardik Pandya to come in and play a superbly brutal knock.

Pandya is described by Dagnall as a 'bar emptier', and that's exactly what happens. The Australian secondary bowlers have been taking the brunt of the Indian bombardment, but when Pandya takes ten from the first two balls of Pat Cummins' first 'death' over, it becomes apparent that no one is safe.

The silence-to-roar equation returns with Indian shock at Pandya's dismissal followed by loud hero worship when M.S.Dhoni joins Kohli at the crease. Kohli hasn't looked at his best in this innings, but perhaps the sight of Dhoni at the other end relieves the pressure somewhat and he unfurls a stunning cover-driven six off Mitchell Starc that causes Mel Jones to embrace her inner teacher and proclaim, 'The report card is in on that shot . . . and it's an A+!'

This is almost bested by Dhoni picking up the same bowler off his legs and depositing him to the back of the stand, with

Geoff Lemon adding: 'A metre higher and it would have been smashing a car window out in the street.'

Dhoni falls to yet another contender for Catch of the Tournament, this time Marcus Stoinis taking an astonishing caught and bowled as he sticks out his hand and somehow holds onto a full-throated drive. He then wonders why he bothered as K.L.Rahul comes in and hits his first ball for six and the final ball of the over for four. He does claim the wicket of Kohli in the meantime though – so it's slings and arrows for the all-rounder as India post 352 for five. As Lemon says, 'This will be a very steep mountain for Australia to climb.'

An oppositional viewpoint is provided by Prakash Wakankar, who says, 'It's probably been as close to a perfect script as you would expect: win the toss, bat first, a wicket with no demons, great weather, a solid start, then people coming in and playing cameos.' However, the veteran adds, 'People here are saying it's game over. I don't think so. I'm expecting a close game.'

Australia almost get off to a disastrous start, as David Warner chops a Jasprit Bumrah delivery on his boot and then onto the stumps. The ball is travelling as it hits the wickets, but once again the bails are not dislodged and Warner isn't out. Dagnall and Vaughan are on air and are astonished by what they are seeing. 'The sound was a real clunk – and I expected the next thing to see the zing bails light up,' says a wide-eyed Dagnall.

'This is ridiculous – it's 80-odd miles per hour and it's hit leg stump. Hard,' adds an astonished Vaughan. 'That ball to Warner thudded into leg stump. If you're not getting out when you're getting bowled, it's a concern. Something needs to be done. It's madness,' he concludes, speaking for many gobsmacked faces in the *TMS* box, the wider Oval and, looking at the *TMS* inbox, many cricket fans around the world.

Warner, known for his frequently aggressive stroke play, is

not playing his normal game and at one stage has played out 14 straight dot balls, something Zaltzman says is the third longest sequence of dot balls in his ODI career. Nobody knows which particular well he drew the stat from, but it's impressive and insightful about an Australian innings that isn't quite getting going.

While Warner is struggling, Aaron Finch is looming dangerously at the other end but is cut off in his prime, run out by Kuldeep Yadav. Steve Smith is the new man to the crease – receiving his now almost-traditional welcome of a round chorus of boos – and he knows he has a lot to do.

Dagnall is in the middle of describing the rebuilding effort when he is suddenly – unexpectedly – handed a glass of champagne by Zaltzman, who seemingly has been passed it through the open window next to him. While *TMS* always like to have an open window to allow the commentary box to properly feel the atmosphere of the crowd, it is not normally utilised for this purpose!

It turns out that one of Andy's friends – fellow comedian Tim Key, who is probably best known for playing Alan Partridge's 'Sidekick Simon' – is watching from the next-door terrace and decided that he shouldn't be having all the fun, so passed a couple through the window. It's already been a long day and Dagnall and Zaltzman are grateful for their unlikely celebrity benefactor.

While Smith and Warner are building a partnership, Dagnall calls out a lack of intensity from the pair as the Australians make only 104 for one after 20 overs. Warner reaches his fifty off 77 balls – his slowest ever in an ODI – and Vaughan isn't sure Australia know what's going on, joking that 'Warner might have forgotten that they're chasing 353 – he thinks they're chasing 252!'

It doesn't seem like Warner is wearing a *TMS* earpiece

in the middle, but he decides to abandon the caution he has been showing thus far and go for a big heave off Yuzvendra Chahal. Sadly for him, it only reaches Bhuvneshwar Kumar on the boundary and his slightly odd innings comes to an end. The new man, Usman Khawaja, is not scoring much quicker than his predecessors, and Geoff Lemon sums up the situation saying, 'Steve Smith is the glue and Usman Khawaja is the glue, too.'

'It's all very sticky out there,' notes Tuffers.

Glenn Maxwell, the batsman with the second highest strike rate in ODI cricket according to Zaltzman, is sitting watching with his pads on, but by the time he reaches the middle when Khawaja is bowled by Bumrah, Australia need more than 11 an over. Tuffers, who has stated confidently that he should have come in a spot higher, nods knowingly as Maxwell immediately sets about the Indian attack, but it's too little too late. Smith and Marcus Stoinis both fall to Kumar in the same over and when Maxwell goes, slicing a big shot into the leg side, it's all over for the Aussies.

Although Australia limit the damage to a 36-run defeat, the result feels much more conclusive than that in the final reckoning. 'A very, very impressive performance from India,' concludes Michael Vaughan. 'They haven't let this huge support down and they're the best team I've seen so far at the tournament. They look like the team to beat.'

India 352-5 (50 overs; Dhawan 117, Kohli 82, Sharma 57) beat Australia 316 (50 overs; Smith 69, Warner 56, Carey 55*) by 36 runs.

Sunday 9 June
England Women v West Indies Women – Royal London
One-Day Series – Match 2
County Ground, Worcester

Team *TMS*: Natalie Germanos, Ebony Rainford-Brent, Charlotte Edwards,
Lydia Greenway, Henry Moeran, Isabelle Westbury

England win the toss and bat in Worcester, hoping for a repeat performance from their dominant win in Leicester earlier in the week. However, they encounter a more spirited West Indian opposition, with Lydia Greenway adding: 'It's a stark contrast to the other day.'

Despite their renewed focus, England are on top when the rain starts to fall in Worcester. The sides are back out by early afternoon, with the game reduced to 41 overs a side. West Indies are right back in it when Afy Fletcher takes both Sarah Taylor and Tammy Beaumont in two balls, but Nat Sciver survives the vital hat-trick delivery and then marshals a rear-guard effort from England as they total 233 for seven, kindly uplifted to 243 by the Duckworth–Lewis–Stern method.

Any confidence felt after the first game in the series is boosted by four wickets in the first 12 overs – the last being the dangerous Stafanie Taylor – leaving West Indies 32 for four shortly before the rains return and the players are again ushered from the field. Twenty overs are needed to constitute a game so England put on spin pair Sophie Ecclestone and Laura Marsh – playing her 100th ODI – who delights Isabelle Westbury with an off-spinner 'that is as good as it gets' to bowl Chedean Nation. The West Indies end up playing a confusing game as they fall irretrievably behind the run rate and eventually lose by 121 runs via the DLS method.

It's a guaranteed ODI series victory for England, but as Natalie Germanos says, 'England haven't had to use Plan B once yet in this series. They've been clinical but haven't been put under any pressure.'

England 233-7 (41 overs; Beaumont 61) beat West Indies 87-6 (28 overs) by 121 runs (DLS method).

CRICKETING DOGS XI

For one day during the World Cup, the BBC's live text commentary service on its website was somewhat distracted during the Australia innings as they tried to name a Cricketing Dogs XI. Here is the final result:

Graham Pooch

Quinton de Kocker Spaniel

Great Dane Williamson

Joe Rootweiler

Virat Collie

Puglas Jardine

Jack Russell

Moeen Alisation

Spaniel Vettori

Muttiah Muralitharan

Jimmy Hounderson

Umpires: David German Shepherd and Aleem Darlmation

Monday 10 June
South Africa v West Indies – ICC Cricket World
Cup – Match 15
The Hampshire Bowl, Southampton

Team *TMS*: Natalie Germanos, Fazeer Mohammad, Alison Mitchell, Ebony
Rainford-Brent, Graeme Smith, Tymal Mills, Sir Curtly Ambrose

The weather is the primary topic of conversation as the Hampshire hotel room is once again occupied by team *TMS*. It's not looking good for the day, but the rain is holding off for the time being. Play gets under way on time, but Alison Mitchell is already saying that 'It feels like there is rain in the air,' and after just 7.3 overs the players are led from the field, never to return.

In that time, Sheldon Cottrell is still able to take two wickets, underscoring the doom felt by the *TMS* South African contingent, who spend a lot of the free time given by the rain discussing their displeasure at the destabilising effect of A.B.de Villiers' apparent offer to come out of retirement to play for South Africa.

After another lovely conversation between Tymal Mills and Sir Curtly Ambrose about the differences in fast bowling between the modern era and the 1980s and 1990s when Ambrose ruled the roost, *TMS* decide to cut to commentary on county cricket, with occasional pundit Jimmy Anderson in action for Lancashire against Worcestershire.

As the button is pressed to transfer the commentary, it becomes clear the ground staff at Old Trafford are just pulling the covers on in Manchester too. It all rather sums up what has been an immensely frustrating day and when the game is called off at 4 p.m., that is simply that, and *TMS* troop off to a soggy car park and everyone's next stops on the constantly rotating World Cup carousel.

South Africa 29-2 (7.3 overs) v West Indies. No result.

Tuesday 11 June
Bangladesh v Sri Lanka – ICC Cricket World
Cup – Match 16
The County Ground, Bristol

Team *TMS*: Simon Mann, Charles Dagnall, Daniel Norcross, Vic Marks, Graeme Swann, Paul Farbrace, Athar Ali Khan

Team *TMS* arrive in plenty of time for the start, which is great news for Charlie Dagnall in particular as, when *TMS* were in Bristol earlier in the summer, he encountered a rather frustrating transportation issue. Arriving in good time and parking up in the 'park and ride' area as instructed, Dagnall locked up his car and walked over to the bus stop to catch his ride to the ground. Happily for him, an empty bus was there ready and waiting. Less happily, the driver refused to let him on. There then developed a stand-off, with Dagnall sat on the pavement, staring through the door, while the driver sat there and ate his sandwiches. This lasted for half an hour. Two lessons were learnt: firstly, always park within walking distance of the ground if you can; secondly, never underestimate the determination of Charlie Dagnall.

While Dagnall learns from his mistake, another transport misfortune sadly befalls *TMS* today. As Daggers demonstrated, and particularly so during the World Cup, a crucial currency in the media bubble is parking permits. Graeme Swann has been granted one of these for today's match but needs to collect it on arrival in Bristol. Henry Moeran, who obtained the pass and is in possession of it, arranges with Swanny that he will leave it under the front right wheel of an ancient green Renault Espace that he has located, parked just by the entrance to the car park. The reason he chooses this particular model of car is because they're not exactly prolific on the roads these days and should therefore be pretty easy to spot.

Swann arrives, pulls over and then spends the next 20 minutes searching the car and its near vicinity for his pass – to no avail. A quick call to Moeran then reveals the problem. There is a totally identical Espace parked just around the corner and Swanny has been searching the wrong car. The chances are slim, but by this stage in the World Cup, nothing should surprise you.

Sadly, today is another 'one of those days' where play looks unlikely from the off and never materialises. Nonetheless, it is another excellent day on air with particular highlights being a long discussion between Paul Farbrace and Swann about what cricketers and coaches do when it rains. Given the glint in both men's eyes, it becomes apparent that certain activities are not considered 'fair game' for the conversation!

The extended rain also draws the revelation from Farbrace that, in Galle on the south coast of Sri Lanka, the reason there are so many people available to pull on the massive sheets that cover the entire ground is because they're all prisoners from the local jail! Swanny is unable to balance his reaction in between delight at their determination to get a good game of cricket on and his concern that there might be a few escaped detainees running around Sri Lanka who would still be behind bars were it not for the need to get a Test match played.

In the context of the competition, it's desperately disappointing that another game has been ruined, particularly for the Sri Lankans, who have now lost consecutive games to miserable weather.

Match abandoned.

Wednesday 12 June
Australia v Pakistan – ICC Cricket World
Cup – Match 17
County Ground, Taunton

Team *TMS*: Alison Mitchell, Simon Mann, Daniel Norcross, Geoff Lemon,
Vic Marks, Ramiz Raja, Michael Vaughan, Andy Zaltzman

Shortly after *TMS* pitch up in Taunton, a group of cricketers emerge from the pavilion, each wearing one more layer of clothing than the next. This means two things: firstly that it's extremely cold; and secondly that it's finally dry enough to play cricket, which is extremely good for the soul.

Taunton is a wonderful ground – but relatively unused to hosting major matches and consequently *TMS* are using another converted facility for this game. It is a tremendously large room but does create a few issues for commentators. The view of the wicket and the fielders within the circle is perfect. Sadly though, to see any further towards the boundary at one end than that, you need to quickly stand up and peer downwards. Therefore, onlookers of the commentary on all games here must surely think that the entire *Test Match Special* team are constantly battling cramp in their calf and thigh muscles and frantically stretching them out so as to avoid yelping with pain on the air.

When the game gets under way, Aaron Finch and David Warner combine for a sensational partnership of 146, assisted by Asif Ali, who drops Finch on 26 and then, later in the game, also puts down Warner. It is described by Geoff Lemon, probably the first *TMS* commentator to be clad in a denim jacket with a picture of '90s American female rap trio Salt-N-Pepa on the back, as 'committing the cardinal sin'. It is also highly frustrating for the bowler, Wahab Riaz, who brings back memories of his incendiary duel with Shane Watson in Adelaide four years ago by furiously steaming in and whacking Finch amidships.

Finch survives Wahab's onslaught but goes in the 22nd over and Australia immediately start to struggle to keep up the momentum set by their opening pair. A promotion for Glenn Maxwell delights Lemon, who brilliantly says that 'Glenn Maxwell is doing exactly what he was put on this earth to do,' but he goes quickly and they end 307 all out, which is a challenging total but somewhere short of where you'd want to end having been 146 for no wicket at the start of the 23rd over.

The discrepancy in the Pakistan bowling is a hot topic of conversation in the box. During the innings Simon Mann described Mohammad Amir as 'playing a different game to the rest of the Pakistan attack', and at the end of the innings, his ten overs have gone for 30 runs and generated five wickets. Every other Pakistani bowler, bar Wahab Riaz, has gone for well north of 6 an over. Michael Vaughan, despite only being 44 years of age, thinks that Amir's spell 'should be a DVD on how to bowl in ODI cricket'. The point is excellent, but whether any aspirant young bowler would still possess a DVD player on which to watch said masterclass is a different matter.

Pakistan lose Fakhar Zaman early in the chase and while Imam-ul-Haq, Babar Azam and Mohammad Hafeez all make good starts and show the promise of anchoring the innings, they all fall at key moments. Fakhar, caught at third man by Kane Richardson, causes a nostalgic Vic Marks – proud to be commentating on a World Cup match at his home ground, having played in one here in 1983 – to wistfully remark that 'Third man used to be a lovely place to graze peacefully but now catches go there all the time, you can't relax anymore.'

Marks is further affronted when Andy Zaltzman points out that he has fallen 'off the podium' for World Cup bowling figures at Taunton. His five for 39 against Sri Lanka in 1983 has now not only been overtaken by Jimmy Neesham's five for 31 earlier in the week, but also by Mohammad Amir's five for 30 this morning. Combined with a five for 31 return for Robin Singh in 1999, Vic is down to fourth. Victor remains the World Cup's leading spinner in Taunton, although he is far too humble to point that out on air.

Australia captain Aaron Finch played very well with the bat during the morning, but when he introduces his leg spin there are eyebrows raised, none less than by Alison Mitchell, who recalls that the last time she saw Finch bowl was with his pads on in the nets at the MCG. However, it is the Aussie who has the last laugh, causing Hafeez to slap a rank full toss straight down the throat of Mitchell Starc on the boundary.

With Pakistan 200 for seven, it seems like it's all over for them, but – potentially still ticking after his spell in the morning – Wahab Riaz joins Sarfaraz Ahmed and something amazing develops. The crowd, vocally in favour of Pakistan throughout the day but quietened by the recent clatter of their middle order, spring back into life as Wahab in particular starts to find the boundary with regularity. Due to their strong scoring rate,

Pakistan have plenty of time to win the game but are lacking wickets. Riaz wellies a Nathan Coulter-Nile slower ball into the stands and, at 264 for seven with six overs remaining, the game is almost back in the balance.

While *TMS* utterly maintain their journalistic integrity on air, there is always a small part of the soul of an English cricket lover that likes nothing more than to see the Australian team under pressure. This is often manifested in playful badinage with self-confident alpha Australians, who are easily niggled by this, creating an excellent mix. Sadly for Daniel Norcross, who is a self-proclaimed expert in the provocation of Australians, *TMS*'s current resident Aussie Geoff Lemon is possibly the least patriotic Australian in the country. Off the air, Norcross is pulling out all his best moves to try to get a reaction out of Lemon, but Geoff's faultlessly sporting attitude and delight in the slightly manic brilliance of the Pakistanis ensures he retains equability at all times, dampening Norcross's lustre immensely.

Back on the field, Riaz aims a mighty swing at a quick one from Mitchell Starc and the ball flies through to wicketkeeper Alex Carey, who comes up with a huge appeal. It is given not out and attention immediately turns to Aaron Finch to see whether he will ask for the decision to be reviewed. The new 15-second 'DRS countdown clock' appears on the big screen and dramatically continues to tick as Finch discusses what to do with his team-mates. With just one second left, the Aussie skipper lifts his left fist to the point of his right elbow, making the classic 'T' sign to send the decision upstairs.

When UltraEdge comes through, it seems like Riaz has got the thinnest tickle on the ball and the decision is overturned. He forlornly returns to the dressing room and the Australians quickly wrap up the final three wickets, the last through a piece of fielding brilliance from Glenn Maxwell, to secure a 41-run victory. As the game is wrapped up, Ramiz Raja says that 'Every team is unpredictable to a certain degree, but Pakistan are even more. It is a term they do not like and the fans don't like.'

While they may not like it, Vic Marks says that, in his view, 'It is a typical Pakistan performance. There have been moments of chaos and moments of brilliance.' Michael Vaughan adds that already in this World Cup we've seen one Pakistan against the West Indies, another against England and today both sides have appeared in the same game.

A memorable day ends with a *TMS* sprint to catch the last quick train back to London. Approaching Taunton station, Henry Moeran, Simon Mann and Andy Zaltzman are making good pace but realise they have lost Daniel Norcross. Further investigation reveals he has ducked into a shop to pick up some wine for the journey. It is a high-risk decision, but just pays off as the train is caught by the skin of its teeth and the finer points of the game are dissected over a plastic glass of room-temperature Pinot Grigio on the 21.15 to Paddington.

Australia 307 (49 overs; Warner 107, Finch 82, Amir 5-30) beat Pakistan 266 (45.4 overs; Imam 53) by 41 runs.

DANIEL NORCROSS'S TOP FIVE TRAIN DRINKS

A cheeky New Zealand Sauvignon Blanc

An easy-drinking Pinot Grigio

A quarter-bottle of Prosecco (screw top) from the buffet car

Pre-mixed Marks & Spencer Gin and Tonic

Pre-mixed Marks & Spencer Mojito (for Diane Abbott)

Thursday 13 June
India v New Zealand – ICC Cricket World
Cup – Match 18
Trent Bridge, Nottingham

Team *TMS*: Jonathan Agnew, Bryan Waddle, Prakash Wakankar, Jeremy
Coney, Graeme Swann, Sir Alastair Cook, Phil Long

The day starts with more transport controversy, this time
involving Jonathan Agnew and the 'junior pro' of the *Test Match
Special* team, who is on his opening day and has not made a
great first impression on Aggers. At Trent Bridge, Aggers has
a particular parking space that he likes to use. It allows him to
make a quick getaway at the end of matches and he has a long-
term arrangement with the parking attendant that allows him
to guarantee it at every game.

This morning, Agnew – very much a 'senior pro' with 28
years' experience on the *TMS* roster – rolls into the car park
and, to his utter horror, the space has been filled. He pulls up and
the attendant sheepishly directs him to a different spot
and Aggers, despondently, acquiesces. Upon getting out, he
locates the attendant who greets him warmly and explains what
has happened.

Said new kid on the block has arrived before Aggers and, after
coming to their own arrangement with the attendant, taken
the spot and headed into the ground. The aggrieved Agnew
accepts the situation and trudges towards the ground, forlornly
anticipating the bun fight later on to get back on the road. In

the box, he takes up the situation with his colleague, politely explaining his arrangement. The new staffer, still wet behind the ears and keen to fit in at all costs, is hugely apologetic and mortified to have caused a scene on their first day in the job. They were totally unaware of the history of the Trent Bridge car park and simply parked where they were instructed, happily posing for a photograph with the attendant afterwards.

As popular and well-loved as *TMS* may be, it is unusual for new starters on the team to be stopped in car parks for selfies on their first day. However, on this occasion, it is possibly more because of the career this man forged before joining *TMS* – he's captained his country in 59 Tests, scored 23,455 first-class runs and had one of the most memorable Test match farewells in the history of the game last summer: it's Sir Alastair Cook – and Aggers might not be getting his space back anytime soon.

Sadly for everyone, today is another occasion where not a ball is bowled. Nonetheless, a broadcast is produced with Cook and Graeme Swann initially taking listeners' questions for two hours. Revelations from this session include former South African batsman Ashwell Prince being Swanny's favourite batsman to bowl at; Cook backing James Vince to bat at No 3 during the Ashes and revealing that he enjoyed fielding at slip to Swann's bowling because it meant Swann was at the other end of the pitch and he could get some peace and quiet!

Swanny also tells a brilliant story about when he was fielding for Northamptonshire in front of the pavilion at Eastbourne, where the Sussex physio was chatting to him in an effort to distract him from the game. This worked, with Swanny being late on a ball rolling towards him. Sadly for the physio, such was Swann's desire to atone for his initial error, he swooped on the ball, threw it in hard and true and got a direct hit, running the batsman out as they tried to use his distraction to turn a single into a two!

The match is abandoned at 3 p.m. without a ball bowled. Aggers trudges back towards the car park, slightly buoyed by the fact that many other users have abandoned the situation much earlier than he was able to. Pleasingly, the following morning, BBC listening figures indicate that despite the total absence of any cricket on which to commentate, *Test Match Special* was still the corporation's fourth most popular show that day, trailing just *TMS* accomplice Greg James on Radio 1, Zoe Ball on Radio 2 and the *Today* programme on Radio 4.

Match abandoned.

Thursday 13 June
England Women v West Indies Women – Royal London
One-Day Series – Match 3
The Essex County Ground, Chelmsford

Team *TMS*: Natalie Germanos, Ebony Rainford-Brent, Charlotte Edwards, Lydia Greenway, Henry Moeran, Isabelle Westbury

While rain washes out all play at Trent Bridge, down south in Chelmsford conditions are sufficiently improved for the final match in England women's series with West Indies women to go ahead. England already have the series in the bag after victories in the opening two games, but in conditions charitably described by Henry Moeran as 'brisk', the game starts on time at 2 p.m.

With England's record of played 13, won 13 at Chelmsford

and the series already gone, the West Indies are playing for pride in England's backyard, but even so, Natalie Germanos's early observation that 'It didn't really look like West Indies' players were into this game when they were warming up' doesn't bode well.

England bat first, Tammy Beaumont and Amy Jones continuing their good form at the top of the order with an 84-run opening partnership, split in two by an extensive rain break that causes the game to be shortened to 39 overs, as the West Indies make a series of errors in the field. Such is the lack of enthusiasm shown by the tourists, Ebony Rainford-Brent controversially wonders on air whether England wouldn't be better off playing England A to prepare for the Ashes.

England, inspired by a brilliantly aggressive knock from skipper Heather Knight, post 258 for four with the main incident of note in their innings a break in play for West Indies opener Britney Cooper to be sick while fielding at backward point. This is not something usually seen on a cricket field and the mess is rapidly dealt with by a pile of sawdust, which immediately becomes a focal point for the rest of the game with all commentators and summarisers constantly terrified the ball will land back in the pile.

DLS sees the West Indies require 267 to win and they are given little hope by anybody on the *TMS* team, an opinion underscored by an extraordinary piece of cricket at the start of their innings. England's Fran Wilson takes one of the catches of the summer in the covers, leaping full length to her left-hand side and taking the ball with both hands as her body is parallel to the turf. It is the match of Ben Stokes at The Oval, that's for sure.

Norcross explodes with joy on air, declaring, 'If we see a better catch than that in the covers this year, in men's or women's cricket, I'll be amazed!'

Sadly, that is by far the highlight of the innings, which drags out into a freezing cold night. Confusingly, the West Indies show no appetite for achieving the run rate required to conduct a meaningful chase and refuse to take any risks. Consequently, they end up 131 for nine from 37.4 overs. The innings comes to an end following a debate on the existence of the colour greige, which is claimed to be a grey version of beige and seems to be an apt description of the depressing hue of the Chelmsford sky.

The end of the game marks the end of the ODI series and, while they have won the series comprehensively, there is a feeling that they haven't been properly tested, well expressed by Norcross, who concludes, 'West Indies aren't putting England under any pressure when they're batting so we're not finding a lot out about the England bowlers ahead of the Ashes.'

Next time England women are on the field playing 50-over cricket, the opposition will be in canary yellow and the pressure will be on.

England 258-4 (39 overs; Jones 80, Taylor 70) beat West Indies 131 (37.4 overs) by 135 runs (DLS method).

CHAPTER 6

Curtly and the Judge

Friday 14 June
England v West Indies – ICC Cricket World
Cup – Match 19
The Hampshire Bowl, Southampton

Team *TMS*: Jonathan Agnew, Fazeer Mohammad, Charles Dagnall,
Michael Vaughan, Phil Tufnell, Sir Alastair Cook, Sir Curtly Ambrose,
Andy Zaltzman

At the site of his unexpected 5 Live hotel room walk-in last year, today marks Sir Alastair Cook's official *TMS* commentary debut as England look to continue their recovery from the shocking Pakistan defeat at Trent Bridge. Eoin Morgan wins the toss and bowls first, with the weather forecast showing a gloriously untroubled day full of sun and little fluffy clouds. There will be a game, but Aggers points out, more than fairly, that Sir Curtly Ambrose might need persuading that a mean temperature of 17 degrees is 'nice'.

The national anthems ring out and Cook immediately unveils

his first secret, revealing that – as England captain and a former St Paul's Cathedral choirboy – he would always try to lead the singing of 'God Save the Queen'. Sadly for him, though, he was often standing next to Stuart Broad, who is apparently tone deaf and consistently just sang the same note, hugely putting Cook off.

Although Evin Lewis goes early, the game starts poorly for England with Mark Wood uncharacteristically dropping an early chance offered by Chris Gayle and – more seriously from a long-term perspective – Jason Roy limping off after seemingly pulling his hamstring while chasing a ball to the boundary.

Similarly to other innings seen this week, however, West Indies struggle with consistency. After Gayle and Shai Hope both go in quick succession, only Nicholas Pooran is able to get past 40 and England take regular wickets to dismiss the West Indies for just 212 – with two more wickets for Joe Root's occasional off-spin – despite another uncharacteristic fielding error as Chris Woakes drops Andre Russell in the deep.

As ever, you can never tell what will happen next on *TMS*, and today's entry into that storybook is the unexpected appearance of former England footballer and manager Glenn Hoddle in the box. He is an impromptu but very welcome guest.

While the English commentators are relishing the fact it's not actually raining and are pretty realistic about the 17-degree temperature, conditions are not putting Sir Curtly in a good mood. His grumpiness is expanded during a session alongside Charles Dagnall, who tries to raise his dander by reporting predictions of 21 degrees next week, suggesting that such an occurrence might even lead to Curtly removing his ubiquitous thick black fleece. 'I don't like to take too many chances,' is the terse response received.

After losing Roy to his hamstring problems, the last thing any England fans want to see is captain Eoin Morgan also leaving the field, clearly in some discomfort after coming round to take a shy at the stumps and then quickly clutching at his thigh and hobbling towards the physio. 'He's gone! That's a proper "gone" walk,' says Tuffers, slumping mournfully in the summariser's chair.

With Roy and Morgan off the field and out of the game, Root is promoted to open the innings alongside Jonny Bairstow. The charismatic combination of Roy and Bairstow has been key to England's success over the past few years, but there is nothing to worry about today, as Root slips into Roy's shoes seamlessly and the two quickly amass an opening partnership of 95.

The confidence is delighting the Southampton crowd but, back in the box, it is causing Sir Curtly's mood to drop from 'cold and grumpy' to 'cataclysmic' as the West Indian bowlers are either banging the ball in short, to be cut or pulled, or landing it too full, allowing them to be driven and flicked. He didn't like the lunch either, which hasn't helped. Not even a long conversation with Phil Tufnell about the famous 1994 match where he took six for 24 as the West Indies dismissed England for 46 in Port of Spain can draw a smile.

Jonathan Agnew MBE, DL – who feels intimidated after following not one but two knights of the realm – is more polite, merely describing the bowling as 'ill directed', but as England gather momentum and another harsh West Indian defeat becomes more inevitable, the Ambrose mood moves from 'cataclysmic' to 'apocalyptic'. 'If they continue to bowl like this, the game will all be over very shortly. I don't know what the West Indies plan is – there is no plan from what I can see,' he rages, before taking a pregnant pause and adding, 'There is no plan to contain the batsmen.'

Strangely, when Bairstow falls, it is Woakes who walks out at No 3, but with the lacklustre West Indian bowling he is able to affirm his credentials as a genuine all-rounder, supporting Root excellently, who has just enough time to record his second century of the tournament as England saunter to a dominant eight-wicket victory with 17 overs to spare.

Ambrose is unrelenting in his onslaught, sucking his teeth hard and adding, 'The West Indies team look like a defeated bunch; there is no urgency, they are just waiting for this game to be over. That's not how you play – push to the end, every ball. Stranger things have happened. They have just about given up, I'm afraid.'

Fazeer Mohammad, also disappointed at the performance of his home team, adds, 'The West Indies have let themselves down in many areas. You can talk about the toss, but you have to be prepared for days when you have to defend a low total. They look comfortable losing, like it's all fun and games now. That's what hurts people like Sir Curtly Ambrose, who you know would go down fighting.'

From an English point of view, Michael Vaughan OBE is delighted with his team's performance. 'England have put in a really good performance,' he enthuses. 'When you think a couple of players had to limp off it was a wonderful display.'

On the field, the England performance has been a clear highlight of the day, but off the field, it feels like the finest *TMS* moment came away from the ball-by-ball commentary. During the innings break, Aggers was joined by former England batsman Robin Smith, who has just released an astonishingly honest autobiography, discussing his outstanding career but also laying bear the intense struggles he has suffered in his retirement, which culminated in alcoholism, depression and suicidal thoughts.

It is a remarkable interview, with Agnew clearly moved by his old friend's travails and Smith speaking in unflinching detail about his life. It feels incredibly special, partially because of another major factor that many would not consider: after his retirement, Smith moved to Perth in Western Australia and barely returned to the UK.

In the incredibly privileged world of *TMS*, the team is lucky enough to meet, work with or interview virtually all great former players. Even if their career goes in a totally different direction, it is rare for them to completely disappear from the cricketing world. While it is always a privilege to spend time with these people, it inevitably becomes, to a point, 'part of the routine'. However, due to his relocation to Perth, Smith has maintained an incredible mystique. Hardly any of the team have met him before and there is a real frisson of celebrity when he is in the box, with far more selfie requests than are usually issued when a guest is around. For the interview to then reveal such pain and traumatic experiences is a further shock and creates an amazing *TMS* moment.

West Indies 212 (44.4 overs; Pooran 63) lost to England 213-2 (33.1 overs; Root 100*, Bairstow 45) by eight wickets.

Saturday 15 June
Sri Lanka v Australia – ICC Cricket World
Cup – Match 20
The Oval, Kennington, London

Team *TMS*: Simon Mann, Geoff Lemon, Daniel Norcross, Ebony Rainford-Brent, Mel Jones, Jason Gillespie, Andy Zaltzman

Arrival at The Oval for the last time this tournament is slightly tinged with sadness. This great old ground has been an amazing venue for the World Cup, consistently delivering sellout crowds, memorable moments and incredible atmospheres. It has also had an astonishing streak of luck, with every match taking place under blue skies and unimpeded by the weather that has had such a deleterious impact on the past week of action.

TMS are joined by Australian legend and Sussex coach Jason Gillespie for the first time today – and he wastes no time in getting stuck into the Sri Lankans, who are frustrated at having two straight rainouts and have given some entertaining press conferences this week. Their World Cup organisational complaints include, but are not limited to: the quality of pitches, net facilities in Cardiff, a cramped single-decker bus and the fact that their hotel in Bristol did not have a pool.

'Sri Lanka are complaining for the sake of complaining – it's different level moaning,' is Gillespie's pragmatic take on the situation. 'Just crack on and do your jobs. Nobody can help the rain.'

Australia bat first and look ominous, with Aaron Finch finding excellent touch very early on and Ebony Rainford-Brent asserting, 'Finch has seen a lot of this ground from his stint with Surrey. He could be dangerous if he gets going.'

He continues to 'go' in an untroubled manner, but there is a distinct lack of fireworks, which distracts *TMS* into exploring other topics of conversation, firstly helping out Jason Gillespie with a domestic issue. Gillespie had put a wash on overnight but, rising early to get to London from his home in Brighton, discovered that something had gone significantly wrong and his family's clothes were merely resting at the bottom of the drum in a pool of stagnant water. With no time to do anything about it before he had to leave, Gillespie left the house and has been communicating with his family ever since, who have been trying to get a local engineer to pop round and take a look.

When Gillespie mentions this on air, the *TMS* inbox explodes with offers of assistance, but one listener, who happens to be a washing machine engineer, sends a stupendously detailed note, offering a number of courses of action for him to take. This email is kept from the Aussie until he is on air with Daniel Norcross, who adopts his best impression of the great English comedian Peter Cook to helpfully read the suggestions out on air.

Back on the field, Aaron Finch completes his century to warm applause and praise from Gillespie, who declares that 'This is one of Aaron Finch's best hundreds. It's been a great one.' Finch and Steve Smith then raise the temperature significantly, attacking the Sri Lankans to all sides. Finch goes for a brilliant 153, followed by Smith, but a brutal closing knock of 40 from 25 balls from Glenn Maxwell, with Simon Mann describing the Sri Lankan bowling as 'January sales time', allows them to reach 334 for seven.

The Sri Lankan response is initially brutal, with Dimuth Karunaratne and Kusal Perera laying waste to the Australian attack in spectacular fashion as they put on 115 from the first 15 overs. As the chase continues, more and more Sri Lankan support seems to reveal itself in the crowd, with Norcross speaking for them all when he says, 'This is rather fun, isn't it? I don't think any of us were expecting this.' Disappointingly for Norcross, who sees another opportunity to antagonise Australians, Jason Gillespie is a similar character to Geoff Lemon and refuses to engage in the traditional England–Australia cricketing conflict.

Mitchell Starc makes the breakthrough and when a second

wicket falls in the 23rd over, Geoff Lemon observes, 'Sri Lanka will now have to find a way to consolidate and keep that run rate going. It's not what they needed.'

The primary non-cricketing entertainment during the afternoon is provided by Ebony Rainford-Brent, who reveals a recent personal misfortune that has befallen her. Rainford-Brent, who lives in the Cambridgeshire countryside but is moving back to London, had driven to the railway station at the start of a week on the road. On her return home, she had a deal in place to sell her car, which would not be required in London. When she arrived at the station, she was in quite a rush and, when she encountered an issue with her automatic windows meeting the convertible soft top of her car, she made the decision to catch her train rather than hang around and fix the problem. What's the worst that can happen?

With the weather as it has been for the past week, the wind and rain combined to create a pool of water at least a couple of inches deep across the bottom of her car. Upon her return to the car park, she discovered this and, knowing she was to report to the garage to complete the sale the next day, realised she was in significant trouble. She duly reported to the garage and, characteristically, was somehow able to charm her way out of the situation. It is a story that certainly tickles her fellow commentators and generates significant listener emails too!

Sadly for the recently expanded Sri Lankan supporter base, 186 for three is as good as it gets, with Karunaratne dismissed just 3 short of what would have been a well-deserved World Cup hundred. After that, it all goes the way of Ebony's car quite quickly, with Sri Lanka losing their last seven wickets for 61 runs to lose by 87. A solid victory for Australia, who are beginning to look ominously efficient.

Australia 334-7 (50 overs; Finch 153, Smith 73) beat Sri Lanka 247 (45.5 overs; Karunaratne 97, Perera 52, Starc 4-55) by 87 runs.

Saturday 15 June
South Africa v Afghanistan – ICC Cricket World
Cup – Match 21
Cardiff Wales Stadium, Cardiff

Team *TMS*: Natalie Germanos, Charles Dagnall, Alison Mitchell, Vic
Marks, Jeremy Coney, Graeme Smith, Phil Long

In Cardiff, the day/night game is between two sides who are unlikely to be troubling the scorers come semi-final time, South Africa and Afghanistan, playing each other for the first time ever in one-day international cricket. The Afghans bat first and get off to a belligerent start, Hazratullah Zazai and Najibullah Zadran regularly finding the boundary before the rain that has bedevilled the western grounds in this World Cup returns to create a short break.

Hazratullah perishes, trying one bold shot too many, and the next major event is the unwelcome return of the rain – 'Frustrating for everybody!' according to Graeme Smith when questioned by Natalie Germanos as to which side will be most annoyed by the pause in play.

Upon the return to the field, the Afghans immediately lose a wicket and then quickly fall from 69 for two to 125 all out, failing Vic Marks's initial challenge – to at least bat through 50 overs – by a giant 95 balls.

'You would imagine that the chase will be relatively routine,' says Charles Dagnall in the innings break, and he couldn't be more right. South Africa score the required 131 runs from just 28.4 overs, Quinton de Kock and Hashim Amla nearly taking them all the way there with a 104-run opening partnership. It's a conservative effort, with de Kock and Amla prioritising securing the win over the chance to up their run rate, much to the frustration of Smith, who wearily wonders what would happen 'if South Africa won five from five, then their run rate let them down ...' The thought ended there, with a furrowed brow.

Afghanistan 125 (34.1 overs; Tahir 4-29) lost to South Africa 131-1 (28.4 overs; de Kock 68) by nine wickets (DLS method).

Sunday 16 June
India v Pakistan – ICC Cricket World Cup – Match 22
Old Trafford, Manchester

Team *TMS*: Jonathan Agnew, Isa Guha, Prakash Wakankar, Michael Vaughan, Ramiz Raja, Jimmy Anderson, Graeme Swann, Andy Zaltzman

Some people describe India v Pakistan as the biggest rivalry in sport – and this clash has certainly been billed as one of the headline acts of the Cricket World Cup. It is a rematch of the final of the 2017 ICC Champions Trophy and they've only played each other twice since then, India dolling out two hammerings to Pakistan in Dubai last September.

An incredible atmosphere is guaranteed and *TMS* are on site for 7 a.m. to ensure safe passage into the box through all the anticipated craziness. This is just as well when it is discovered that, on today of all days, the ICC have decided to entirely change their accreditation system without telling anyone and, therefore, nobody's passes work when they arrive. Fortunately, you have to get up early to get past the crack production team of Adam Mountford and Henry Moeran, who are able to solve the issues and prevent early calamities.

As well as *TMS*, there is a coterie of BBC productions coming live from Old Trafford, with *5 Live Sport*, *6-Duck-6*, BBC Asian Network and BBC World Service all broadcasting different takes on the game throughout the day. Before the start, Henry Moeran is dispatched outside to get interviews with some of the crowd and does a wonderful job getting across the nuttiness of the situation. First, he bumps into a Pakistani man who has decided to arrive on a white horse. Sadly, due to his sitting on the (extremely large) horse, the microphone won't reach up to allow him to provide further details.

There is also a wonderfully modern family of three, who are thoroughly confused by the whole situation. Mum is Pakistani, Dad is Indian and their daughter is very resentful at being made to choose a side. Similar tension abounds in the *TMS* box with both Prakash Wakankar (India) and Ramiz Raja (Pakistan) present as the resident experts for their sides. They have vowed not to fall out all day, no matter what the outcome.

Over the past week, the *TMS* inbox has left the team in no doubt as to the anticipation levels being felt for this game, and some of the potential viewing figures quoted in the build-up have been astonishing. Australian journalist Adam Collins tweets early in the morning that there have been 800,000 applications for the 25,000 tickets available and an estimated TV viewership for the match of 1.5 billion. Whichever way, it is decided that Jimmy Anderson – also on commentary duties today – will never have had more people see his End over the course of one 24-hour period.

The weather is shaky, but the toss goes up on time and is won by Pakistan, who choose to bowl first in conditions that could only really be described as 'classic Manchester murk'. The atmosphere is such that Virat Kohli practically has to yell at Ramiz Raja in the post-toss interview.

TMS goes on air and Aggers greets listeners around the world, saying he is surrounded by 'a raucous cacophony of cricket fans. They have worked themselves into a frenzy. Fierce rivals on the field, bitter enemies off it, this is much more than just a game.' With that, the match starts, Michael Vaughan pointing out that Sarfaraz Ahmed is already in trouble because Imran Khan, former star Pakistani cricketer and now the country's prime minister, has tweeted saying that if you won the toss you should definitely bat.

The atmosphere in the ground really is something else, unlike anything that would be experienced at an England match, and Aggers, already struggling to hear himself think underneath his headphones, suggests that 'There will be some weary people tonight if they carry on cheering at this rate.'

The Indians do continue cheering, although the Pakistanis would be forgiven for taking some time off, because the first 25 overs of the Indian innings could scarcely have gone worse for them. India openers Rohit Sharma and K.L.Rahul move swiftly through the gears on a trustworthy pitch, as Pakistan are loose in the field and inconsistent with the ball. The India hundred comes up in the 17th over and the two add 136 before

Wahab Riaz breaks through, Rahul chipping to Babar Azam at mid-off.

Sadly for Pakistan, that is as good as it gets for some time, with Virat Kohli coming out to an ovation that can comfortably be heard in Liverpool. He picks up where Rahul left off and, seven overs later, Sharma pushes the ball through the covers for a single that brings up his second century of the World Cup. Vaughan is full of praise for the innings, saying, 'He's a wonderful player; he has just found rhythm and timing early in the tournament. He knows how to deal with the emotions of the big stage.'

Kohli celebrates the century on the field and then drives on the up through the covers, piercing an astonishingly small gap in the field to get four runs, and Ramiz Raja admits that he is searching for a white flag. However, when Sharma goes for 140 and then Hardik Pandya follows soon afterwards, India start to slow up slightly. The great M.S.Dhoni goes second ball, shortly before the Manchester murk breaks out into full-on rain and the players leave the field with 3.2 overs left in India's innings.

With rain falling, the white horse from earlier once again becomes a topic of conversation in the box, Vaughan wondering where it is now. His top choice is 'just up the road at Old Trafford', where he decides it couldn't do much worse in central midfield than Manchester United's current occupiers of that position. Cue some inflamed emails in the inbox.

Play resumes and Kohli goes, feathering an attempted hook off impressive Mohammad Amir through to the keeper. Graeme Swann thinks that Kohli will win a lot of friends among Pakistani fans by walking for the dismissal but, once he is back in the dressing room and the replays rolled on the TV, it becomes apparent that there is no spike on the UltraEdge and Kohli wasn't actually out! 'There is no way Virat Kohli is going to walk off a cricket ground if he hasn't nicked that,' says Prakash Wakankar, but it does seem like that is what has just happened.

India end on 336 for five. 'With the platform they had, I'm sure 360–370 looked on the cards with Pandya and Kohli in earlier,' says Swann, but he also admits, 'Pakistan closed this innings out beautifully. This is going to be a good game of cricket.'

The innings break, shortened by rain, nonetheless brings the chance to discuss some of the marvellous Indian personalities at the match, with one of them, Bollywood actor Ranveer Singh, particularly taking Michael Vaughan's fancy – largely due to the incredible pair of sunglasses he is wearing. A competition is launched for members of the *TMS* team to have a selfie with Ranveer, who is currently in the UK because he is filming a new Bollywood film about the 1983 World Cup. His fantastic facial hair is a good clue that is he playing then captain Kapil Dev.

After a bit more toing and froing with the rain, the chase is under way and seamer Bhuvneshwar Kumar is forced off with an injury midway through his third over. What seems like bad news for India is given a silver lining when Vijay Shankar, who has never bowled before in a World Cup, is brought into the attack to finish off his over and takes a wicket with his first delivery.

Pakistan are struggling to keep the rate ticking over and Andy Zaltzman points out that they have the 'fifth slowest score after ten overs batting second in the tournament', adding that 'The difference with the other four is that they were not chasing 337 to win.' Shortly after this, Vaughan is the man receiving congratulations for winning the Ranveer Singh selfie competition, posting a brilliant Instagram picture in the Bollywood star's truly superb (huge) sunglasses.

Agnew is looking at the rain radar and thinking that Pakistan should be considering their Duckworth–Lewis position, while Ramiz Raja pegs Babar Azam as the key man, pointing out that the 'Pakistan batsmen have got starts before and thrown them away. A good-looking 40 is not going to win you the game, so it needs to be a 140 from Babar.'

'I just get the feeling we're going to see a great cracker of a game,' says Prakash Wakankar positively, shortly before Babar Azam is bowled by a ripping leg break from Kuldeep Yadav. Fakhar Zaman goes to the same bowler, top-edging a sweep to short fine leg, Mohammad Hafeez holes out off Hardik Pandya, and Shoaib Malik is bowled the very next ball. Pakistan have lost four wickets for 12 runs and are suddenly 129 for five.

Back on for his next stint, Wakankar admits that 'It's a bit of an anti-climax' after the wickets, and when Sarfaraz is bowled by Shankar, it's virtually all over. There are doom-mongering predictions of rain just around the corner and, when it does arrive, Pakistan are 86 behind on DLS. As the rain continues, the stands thin out and it seems like that will be that and the result is clear. However, with the stands almost empty, Aggers spots the umpires heading to each dressing room and giving the thumbs-up.

Graeme Swann, who got up at 5 a.m. to receive his Father's Day present and is mentally halfway back down the M1, is outraged by the suggestion that the game should restart. 'That would be a joke!' he exclaims. 'I think we should refuse to broadcast.'

Adam Mountford's eyebrows shoot skywards before Swann quickly adds, 'We won't. Don't worry, *TMS* listeners.' And, before you know it, the stumps are back in the ground and the game resumes. Swann warms to his theme, adding, 'They are not pleasing anyone by trying to have any more cricket now. I can't see any positive reason for going out. Oh, cricket, stop shooting yourself in the foot. This is just nonsense. We live in a world that has gone mad, so we might as well have cricket going mad as well.'

Agnew agrees, adding, 'Cricket is prone to farce – this is up there, this is a top-five moment.' Nonsense or not, Pakistan need 136 off 30 balls at a run rate of 27.2. As the players emerge and Pakistan, not wanting to risk damaging their run rate, knock the ball around rather than trying to hit every ball for six, Swann continues his rant. 'All the people that are a bit confused by cricket and think it's a bit daft will definitely be won over now! Surely Goochy and Botham would be doing bowling impressions by now, that would have been a good way to end,' he nostalgically speculates.

'They would have locked the umpires in their room,' Agnew corrects him.

The game ends, and India win by 89 runs. 'If you're at home and you are trying to explain this to children, just say that some-times grown-ups do things that don't make sense,' says Swann, before taking his headphones off for the last time and heading to the car park.

A day of surreal sights ends with a bobby dazzler as *Doosra* podcast host and Pakistan fan Aatif Nawaz, disappointed by Pakistan's abject end to the game, is comforted by Ranveer Singh, who is still wearing huge sunglasses despite the mizzle falling around them. It's been a fun occasion. India have looked very good, Pakistan capable of brilliance and Old Trafford has put on one hell of a show, rain regulations permitting, for however many billion people ended up being part of the India v Pakistan experience.

India 336-5 (50 overs; Sharma 140, Kohli 77, Rahul 57)
beat Pakistan 212-6 (40 overs; Zaman 62) by 89 runs
(DLS method).

BBC SPORT ALL-TIME INDIA XI

Rohit Sharma

Virender Sehwag

Virat Kohli

Sachin Tendulkar

Yuvraj Singh

M.S.Dhoni

Kapil Dev

Anil Kumble

Harbhajan Singh

Zaheer Khan

Jasprit Bumrah

BBC SPORT ALL-TIME PAKISTAN XI

Saeed Anwar

Shahid Afridi

Inzamam-ul-Haq

Mohammad Yousuf

Javed Miandad

Imran Khan

Moin Khan

Wasim Akram

Saqlain Mushtaq

Waqar Younis

Shoaib Akhtar

Voted for by readers of BBC Sport in the week leading up to India v Pakistan at Old Trafford.

Monday 17 June
West Indies v Bangladesh – ICC Cricket World
Cup – Match 23
County Ground, Taunton

Team *TMS*: Fazeer Mohammad, Simon Mann, Daniel Norcross, Vic
Marks, Mel Jones, Athar Ali Khan, Sir Curtly Ambrose, Phil Long

TMS are back in the 'Hokey Cokey Commentary Box' in
Taunton and everyone is praying for a better West Indies
performance. Impartiality is impregnable on air – but from a
practical point of view, being in a relatively confined space with
Sir Curtly Ambrose when he is physically seething with rage
is quite difficult, so a better show from the West Indies would
be appreciated.

Bangladesh win the toss and bowl under more heavy
skies, with Daniel Norcross nostalgically remembering Chris
Gayle's brief T20 stint with Somerset, attempting to identify
specific flats that he has seen the ball hit into and seeing if
the necessary repair works have been completed in the intervening period. Mostly, they have. Sadly for those who have
tickets – and happily for homeowners in the vicinity – there
is no repeat performance from Gayle today, who goes for a
13-ball duck.

Once again, the incredible Bangladesh fans have made the
trip to Taunton in large numbers – and once again they are
bearing large fluffy tigers. This is excellent for the atmosphere
but confusing for Brian, Somerset's resident ginger cat, who is

still spotted enjoying some welcome back-scratches from the friendly tiger owners.

Gayle's fellow opener Evin Lewis starts slowly and is just beginning to up the ante when he is caught at long-off, but Nicolas Pooran starts aggressively, damaging the white ball by smashing tiles on the roof of the Andy Caddick Pavilion. West Indies keep up their momentum, as Phil Long points out they've hit 32 from the first ten overs, 54 from the next and 65 from the third set of ten.

A fielding shambles from Bangladesh gives both Shai Hope and Shimron Hetmyer another life, and some sumptuous fireworks from Jason Holder lift his side to 321 for eight. It has already been pointed out that 244 is the highest successful chase so far in this World Cup, so when Ambrose says that 'West Indies need to win this game and win it handsomely to give themselves a chance in the competition,' there is a degree of hope and expectation in his heart.

His opposite number, Athar Ali Khan, is more circumspect in his appraisal: 'It's not going to be easy. If you get a good start, you need to push on and get a big score,' he says as Tamim Iqbal and Soumya Sarkar start the chase well, offering up a crowd catch to a Bangladesh fan who was carrying a tiger under each arm, 'which rather hampered his chances of catching it,' Norcross notes.

Soumya goes in the eighth over, but all that succeeds in doing is bringing Shakib Al Hasan to the crease, who has already taken two for 54 and then turns the rest of the game into a demonstration of all the reasons he is the ICC top-ranked one-day player in the world. West Indies are once again attempting to bounce a side out, seemingly ignoring evidence that the batsmen are dealing with aggressive treatment quite handily.

Ambrose starts to prickle, saying, 'I'm not happy with the lengths that West Indies are bowling. They've either been too short or too full, they haven't found the right length between the two.' It's not a meltdown on the scale of Southampton yet, but the seeds have been planted. A smile is briefly brought to the great man's face by Sheldon Cottrell, who executes a brilliant pick-up and throw to dismiss Tamim Iqbal – 'A fantastic bit of cricket,' he comments – and when Mushfiqur Rahim is strangled down the leg side, it seems possible that the 'angry Curtly' that all *TMS* personnel are terrified of encountering again could go back in the box.

However, Liton Das joins Shakib and the two form a sensational partnership, hugely helped by some buffet bowling from the West Indies. Every bad ball is dispatched for four or six – and there are a lot of them. As the partnership begins, Curtly is sitting in the back of the palatial Taunton commentary suite, headphones on, determinedly staring at his iPad as he simultaneously watches every ball and follows an advanced guitar tutorial on YouTube. Such is the glowering visage of rage he is wearing, the TV crew even train their cameras on the *TMS* box so as to pick him out.

While Simon Mann and Athar Ali Khan continue on air, Fazeer Mohammad – feeling similarly downcast – is sent over to Ambrose to try to get a true reading on his mood. The two engage in a brief conversation before an explosion that shakes the Mendips occurs and weeks of pent-up frustration come pouring out. 'FAZ! IT'S BRAINLESS, MAN! THEY'VE NO PLAN B. THEY'VE GOT TO CONTAIN!' thunders Ambrose before abruptly putting the headphones back on and returning to the guitar tutorial.

West Indies are finding it impossible to stem the flow of runs coming from the Bangladeshi blades. The ask gets to less than 100 and Fazeer admits that 'It has a look of going through the motions.' From a *TMS* perspective, the rota becomes a key document as the team try to work out whether Curtly is going to make it back on air before Bangladesh have successfully completed their chase. It seems likely and the man who will be tasked with marshalling him is Daniel Norcross.

Shakib's century comes up – giving him World Cup totals of 75, 64, 121 and now this unbeaten ton – 'You would want to cover your ears if you were in a rum shop in the Caribbean with some of the colourful language that would be coming out now,' adds Fazeer wonderfully.

Vic Marks is next in the summariser's chair and the Bangladeshi runs are still flowing. Then, with only around ten to go, Curtly's time is up. He stalks towards the chair and forlornly picks up his microphone to see through the dying act of his side's World Cup campaign. 'They can kiss their chances of getting to the semi-finals goodbye after this,' is his lamenting looser. 'I can't see them winning their remaining games and even so, they are going to need top teams to lose. All they can do is try to win to save face.'

A glorious straight drive from Shakib takes the Bangladeshis a step closer.

'Bangladesh have always been a team to show promise, they have come a long way,' he adds magnanimously. 'They have played extremely well and deserve to win this game but the bowling from the West Indies has been less than ordinary.'

With two required, Norcross steels himself and says, 'Curtly, you're looking really furious.' This opens the floodgates to an on-air emotional cleansing.

'This is a disaster. I've been saying this from before the World Cup started, with these bowlers we cannot contain and there you go. It has been an extremely poor performance from the West Indies from the very first delivery. The plan they had to bowl short and aggressively didn't work, but they never abandoned it. All I can say is it was a total massacre for the West Indies. Totally outplayed, well done to Bangladesh, but the West Indies bowlers were very ordinary.

'The 322 was a good score, but they came out and bowled absolute rubbish and the Bangladesh batsmen capitalised, took advantage and won this game handsomely. They murdered West Indies.'

And with that, the 6ft 5 Ambrose stalks out of the back of the commentary box to make his way into the night. On his way out of the ground, a still shell-shocked Norcross spots him holding court to a pack of Bangladeshi journalists, the most altitudinous of which must be 5ft 6 at the very most and describes it, off air, as like Gulliver addressing the Lilliputians.

West Indies 321-8 (50 overs; Hope 96, Lewis 70, Hetmyer 50)
lost to Bangladesh 322-3 (41.3 overs; Shakib 124*, Das 94*)
by seven wickets.

CHAPTER 7

Morgan's Maximum Effort

Tuesday 18 June
England v Afghanistan –
ICC Cricket World Cup – Match 24
Old Trafford, Manchester

Team *TMS*: Jonathan Agnew, Prakash Wakankar, Charles Dagnall, Alison Mitchell, Michael Vaughan, Graeme Swann, Vic Marks, Andy Zaltzman

The good news for England: it is sunny in Manchester and Afghanistan haven't won a game because of their misfiring batsmen. The bad news for England: Jason Roy has been ruled out for at least two games because of his hamstring issue sustained against the West Indies.

Eoin Morgan wins the toss, chooses to bat and declares it a really good pitch as Jonny Bairstow is joined by James Vince and the two get off to a solid start, helped by some Afghan fielding that would shame the lower levels of the Lancashire League, let alone Old Trafford. James Vince, continuing the theme of his international summer so far, top-edges Dawlat to Mujeeb and has to go for 26. 'It is a typical Vince innings,' says Vic Marks, slightly resignedly. 'He had looked threatening, had timed the ball nicely but has not got a great deal to show for it.'

Zaltzman then shocks the box with an absolute zinger. 'In 25 ODIs since the beginning of the 2017 Champions Trophy, this is England's second lowest score after ten overs,' he says, before following up with another pearler a few overs later when he proves the point of a disgruntled nation by offering: 'This is James Vince's ninth ODI innings and only once has he been out for less than 15 – but just once has he reached 50.'

The arrival of the Afghan president, who receives a standing ovation as he walks into the pavilion, is the highlight of the morning and, as England reach 139 for one at the halfway point in front of oddly empty stands for a 'sold out' game, there is a slight humdrum feel about today's match. Bairstow is caught and bowled by Gulbadin for 90. 'He's got some big guns on him!' cries Michael Vaughan as the former bodybuilder poses with both biceps in celebration.

As Morgan walks to the crease, concern abounding about his back spasms last time out, Vaughan's thoughts turn to the pitch, adding, 'You wouldn't want to be chasing 225-plus this afternoon. It's getting slower.'

'Morgan's back seems to have improved very rapidly!' chortles Vic as he kicks his innings off with two big sixes. He continues to hit for the ropes, causing a relatively simple chance to be offered to Dawlat Zadran on the midwicket boundary, who never looks comfortable, never gets in the right position and spills it. Aggers is unflinching in his criticism. 'That is a horrible effort. This is abysmal. If there were a shovel anywhere nearby, you'd be digging a hole and lying in it,' he says frankly. 'If there was a stinker of the tournament, that would be it.'

The next ball flies over the same fielder's head for six and Morgan quickly brings up his fifty, with five sixes struck from

36 balls. Root and Morgan bring up their hundred partnership from just ten overs before, astonishingly, Morgan's own hundred comes up. He has faced just 21 balls for his second half-century, pummelling an Afghanistan attack to every corner of Old Trafford.

FASTEST CENTURIES IN WORLD CUP HISTORY

Kevin O'Brien (Ireland) –
50 balls v England, 2011

Glenn Maxwell (Australia) –
51 balls v Sri Lanka, 2015

A.B.de Villiers (South Africa) –
52 balls v West Indies, 2015

Eoin Morgan (England) –
57 balls v Afghanistan, 2019

Similarly to Jos Buttler's onslaught at Southampton earlier in the summer, *TMS* largely becomes an interconnected series of wonderfully crisp leather-on-willow sound effects, followed by onomatopoeic gasping by whoever currently has the microphone. 'It's like a benefit match of days gone by,' laughs Aggers, temporarily regaining the power of speech.

Zaltzman, meanwhile, is putting all his pound coins into a jukebox of cricket records where every disc is a stone-cold classic. Morgan passes most sixes hit by an England player in a one-day match as Rashid Khan disappears for yet another maximum, the 13th of the innings, and when Gulbadin is dispatched summarily down the ground for the skipper's 17th, he gets the big one – most sixes ever in an ODI innings.

'There will be some stiff necks in this Afghanistan side after this innings,' says Aggers, shortly before Morgan eventually gets caught at long-off going for the 18th. It has been an extraordinary knock and the England captain is roared from the field by an appreciative crowd who are well aware they've seen something very special indeed. 'Whatever tablets he has taken since that back spasm, I want some,' adds Vaughan, correctly surmising that Morgan's back issues seem to be behind him.

Not satisfied with the statistical exuberance generated when Morgan was actually batting, Zaltzman then returns five minutes later for an encore, adding, 'From his drop onwards, Morgan scored 120 from 46 balls.' As if that isn't enough, Moeen Ali then comes in all guns blazing and hits 31 from nine balls with four sixes of his own. Hilariously, he is still booed back into the dressing room after only managing a single from the last ball of the innings and stranding England on 'just' 397.

'An incredible display of entertainment,' is Vaughan's quick-fire verdict on the innings and no one in the box can disagree with the sentiment as the players troop off the field, Afghanistan showing such laudable spirit that he further observes that they 'are walking off like a team who still think they have got a chance!'

The innings break sees Zaltzman whirling away feverishly, ensuring that no good stat has been missed. His favourite is that in today's innings Rashid Khan conceded 11 sixes – 'beforehand he had never conceded more than two in an ODI innings'. If you think a day like today is enjoyable for a fan, just try being a statistician!

Afghanistan return to the field, with Vaughan pointing out that their main fault in the World Cup so far is that they only know one way to bat and they've tried to hit every ball for six, preventing them from rotating the strike. 'Well, today they're allowed to try and hit every ball for six because they are going to need to!' he ends, beaming from ear to ear.

Noor Ali Zadran comprehensively plays on in Jofra Archer's first over and, although England are not batting anymore, Zaltzman is still coming out with some fabulous stats from their innings, the latest being that Morgan has today become the first Englishman to hit a double century of one-day international sixes. Wonderful.

With England sailing towards an easy victory, chat in the box turns to some old stories, with Swanny telling the tale of how he received his maiden Test cap, which are usually presented by an England legend present at the game. 'I was in Chennai and it is generally someone from the Sky commentary box,' he begins. 'Athers would be cerebral and talk about E. W. Swanton. Nasser Hussain would say "Don't mess it up." Beefy walks over and said to me, "I've seen the wicket, if you don't get a five-fer you're rubbish," threw me the cap and walked off.'

The game can only be described as 'pootling along' before a brief period shortly after the 30th over when Hashmatullah, who had just been brutally felled by a Mark Wood bouncer, suddenly starts to take the game to England, smacking sixes with abandon. 'We have seen today some amazing sixes hit and that has got to go to the top of the tree,' says Aggers after another bouncer from Wood is fired, cross batted, straight back down the ground for six. 'It was a bouncer to a man who has just been felled by a bouncer and he has smashed it straight down the ground, just missing the sightscreen it was so straight,' he concludes, with due respect given in the tone of voice chosen.

Asghar Afghan goes to Adil Rashid, but the new man, Mohammad Nabi, clobbers his first ball for another massive six, causing Zaltzman to again explode with delight, gleefully pointing out that 'with 32 sixes, this is the most sixes in a World Cup match, and the third most in any one-day match'.

One more maximum is wellied by the Afghans, and Zaltzman returns with the cracker that 'There have been more sixes today than there were in the first World Cup.' He's almost had a better day than Morgan, and that is one of the best of the lot.

England end up winning by exactly 150 runs, leaving them top of the pile and on course to cruise into the semi-finals with four wins and just a single defeat from their first five games. Vaughan is delighted with the confidence England are showing and, after backing Moeen for continued selection over Liam Plunkett, concludes by saying, 'The last three performances could have been banana skins for England, and they've hammered their opponents. Can England play to this fashion, with this aggression, when it matters in a semi-final? The semi-final, for me, is the big game.'

England 397-6 (50 overs; Morgan 148, Bairstow 90, Root 88) beat Afghanistan 247-8 (50 overs; Hashmatullah 76) by 150 runs.

Tuesday 18 June
England v West Indies – Women's T20 series – Match 1
The County Ground, Northampton

Team *TMS*: Henry Moeran, Natalie Germanos, Ebony Rainford-Brent, Danielle Hazell

'We could be in for a frustrating evening' is a very solid opening gambit from Ebony Rainford-Brent upon arrival in Northampton, as she takes her regular place alongside *TMS* debutante Dani Hazell, recently retired from an impressive career in which she won two Ashes series, the World T20 and the World Cup.

If there is action, hopefully it will be better than a game played elsewhere in the world today, where the Rwanda women's team defeated the Mali women's team by ten wickets after bowling them out for 6 and then knocking off the chase in four balls. Even more remarkably, out of Mali's six runs, there were two byes, two leg byes and a wide.

'The rain radar is a horrible sight, a big green and yellow splodge across the middle of the country,' admits Henry Moeran, who is something of an expert in these things and even captures a picture of a couple of ducks stood, mockingly, on the covers, before word comes shortly after 8 p.m. that the game had to be abandoned.

Match abandoned.

Wednesday 19 June
New Zealand v South Africa – ICC Cricket World Cup – Match 25
Edgbaston, Birmingham

Team *TMS*: Natalie Germanos, Simon Mann, Bryan Waddle, Jeremy Coney, Niall O'Brien, Pommie Mbangwa, Andy Zaltzman

A first World Cup game at one of the country's finest grounds starts a busy period of cricket in Birmingham, which will host more group matches, England v India, a semi-final and then the first Ashes Test at the start of August. *TMS* are always delighted to be in residence in the snug Edgbaston facilities, largely because the standard of catering is absolutely out of this world. The BBC – and members of the travelling cricketing media fraternity in general – are very lucky to be looked after in the way we are, but Edgbaston takes the biscuit (literally) in all areas.

A wet outfield delays the start until midday and – maddeningly – reduces the game to 49 overs a side. 'If you're going to do that, why not just play 50 overs a side? It just messes everything up!' says an incredulous Niall O'Brien to widespread agreement. South Africa bat first and only go at 4 an over, posting the second-lowest 20-over score of the tournament (Zaltzman back on form after a decent lie-down overnight).

They only move to 123 for three after 30 ('Only the fifth time in World Cup cricket that a team's top three have all been out bowled,' adds Zaltzman), but Jeremy Coney thinks that 250 'is a very defendable target on this surface'. The rate stays at 4 an over and South Africa's attempts to increase it don't bring them a huge amount of joy – but they do bring Simon Mann the opportunity to deliver the line of the day when he describes a 48th-over boundary by Chris Morris as 'like a drunk woodsman trying to take down a tree', but when Rassie van der Dussen hits 10 from the last two balls, they end on 241 for six, just 9 shy of Mystic Coney's required 250.

'It's not a belting pitch and it will be intriguing to see how New Zealand go,' says Mann as the players head for the innings break. 'They had a similar chase to this against Bangladesh and stumbled over the line.' South Africa know that, realistically, if they can't prevent New Zealand from scoring 242, their World Cup is over and are clearly delighted when Kagiso Rabada gets Colin Munro in the third over.

However, the dismissal does bring Kane Williamson into the

game nice and early and there is a general acceptance that the Kiwi skipper, who quickly settles into a good partnership with Martin Guptill, is going to be the key man. Things are going smoothly when Guptill attempts to pull Phehlukwayo and, after two full spins to the tune of 720 degrees, he loses his balance, slips to the floor and in doing so wallops his left foot into the stumps, sending the zing bails for a full monty. In a sign of the New Zealander's general geniality and good sense, it's clear that Guptill can see the funny side of what's just happened as he walks off.

Whether the smile remains after Zaltzman points out that he's the first ever New Zealander to be out hit wicket in the history of the World Cup (and only the tenth player ever) is unknown. Ross Taylor and Tom Latham both go cheaply to Morris and, as Coney says, 'Because of the wickets the control is coming back to South Africa.' Given the New Zealanders' easy success to date, his further point that 'suddenly we have got to that part of the line-up that just hasn't batted' feels very relevant indeed.

Jimmy Neesham is the next man, but the pitch is proving just as tricky for New Zealand as it was for South Africa and he struggles to get the ball away, allowing South Africa to continue exerting pressure before Morris angles one across him and Hashim Amla picks up the catch in the slips. 'That confirmed to me that South Africa are on top,' says Coney a couple of minutes later. 'Not only is the run rate escalating, but half of the team is out now.'

The power of new man Colin de Grandhomme combines superbly with the technical mastery of Williamson and quickly Pommie Mbangwa observes that 'I see the initiative shifting to New Zealand a bit now, especially with Imran Tahir running out of overs.'

Williamson hooks Phehlukwayo and is dropped on the fine leg boundary by Ngidi. However, the umpire raises his arm to the side, indicating a no-ball, and the drop doesn't matter so much. Nonetheless, the pressure seems to be getting to South Africa. A Morris over sees only one run scored from the first five balls before de Grandhomme swipes the final ball to the boundary to swing the pendulum towards New Zealand and bring up his half-century.

Ngidi bowls the 48th over for just five runs, leaving New Zealand needing 14 runs from the final 12 balls, and when de Grandhomme holes out to long-off that pendulum swings back towards South Africa. However, the ever-alert Williamson had ensured the batsmen crossed so new man Mitchell Santner heads to the non-striker's end.

'You don't want to leave too much to do in the last over,' says Jeremy Coney, masterfully ratcheting the tension. 'You'd like to get it down to a run a ball so, I'm afraid, folks, belt yourselves in – this is going to be a beaut!'

Williamson narrowly evades being caught and bowled, sneaking a single in the meantime, and then Santner hammers his first ball back into the stumps at the other end, the timbers saving South Africa three runs but bringing Williamson back on strike. Twelve are required from seven balls when Williamson plays one of the most superbly audacious shots of the World Cup so far, spotting a Rabada slower ball and deliberately guiding it in between the wicketkeeper and a slightly wide first slip for four. The Kiwis need eight from the last over, but Williamson is at the wrong end. As if the tension couldn't get any greater, Zaltzman quickly picks up his microphone to announce that 'Phehlukwayo is going at 7.45 an over – and New Zealand need eight to win.'

There is a long delay as South Africa plan their last over. 'If Santner can get off strike, I'm backing New Zealand,' says Coney, shortly before Santner masterfully pulls his first ball for a single to get Williamson, on 96 not out, to the striker's end. 'If the bowler can stay calm, South Africa may just edge this game,' says Coney, hedging his bets somewhat before Phehlukwayo sees his next delivery launched over mid-wicket for a huge six by Williamson.

Simon Mann captures the moment superbly as he says, 'What a brilliant innings that has been. He's had to sweat hard but it's been a monumental innings of patience, determination and skill. What a way to bring up a hundred – to level the game with a six. He's one of the world's best and he showed it today.'

The job is completed next ball as Williamson hits a victorious boundary to end on 106 not out and see his side home to another tight victory.

Thanks to his brilliance, Williamson's side hold onto their unbeaten record and head back to the top of the group. South Africa, who have lost five straight World Cup games against New Zealand, are virtually out. 'New Zealand were tested today, and they will be better for it,' concludes Coney.

South Africa 241-6 (49 overs; van der Dussen 67*, Amla 55) lost to New Zealand 245-6 (48.3 overs; Williamson 106*, de Grandhomme 60) by four wickets.

Thursday 20 June
Australia v Bangladesh – ICC Cricket World
Cup – Match 26
Trent Bridge, Nottingham

Team *TMS*: Jonathan Agnew, Jim Maxwell, Prakash Wakankar, Michael Vaughan, Graeme Swann, Mel Jones, Athar Ali Khan, Phil Long

TMS stay in the Midlands, moving over to Nottingham for Trent Bridge's final involvement in the competition and upon arrival the ground looks a picture, with Bangladesh fans once again arriving in numbers, once again accompanied by their legion of tigers (stuffed). There is a seasonal debutant in the team today – a man who has just arrived in England but will be staying for some time, also forming a key part of *TMS*'s coverage of the Ashes later this year – the voice of Australian cricket, Jim Maxwell.

It being his first game, Maxwell has to collect his official ICC accreditation in Nottingham, and does so more successfully than Sir Curtly Ambrose, who had to complete the same task at the same venue. With all of Nottingham's sports venues so close to each other, Nottingham Forest very kindly host the ICC's accreditation office at the City Ground, a hop, skip and jump from Trent Bridge. However, Maxwell has only been told to collect his pass from the 'football ground', and so spends a fruitless half-hour searching around Notts County's neighbouring Meadow Lane before someone spots a legend in difficulty and redirects him.

'It's lovely to be back although I don't have great memories of this place after four years ago . . .' says Maxwell as he comes on air for the first time, still trying to exorcise the demons of Stuart Broad's extraordinary Ashes spell in 2015. Maxwell's fellow Australian Mel Jones rushes into the box shortly before her first stint of the day and is gently warned by today's producer Henry Moeran that her first stint is with a relative newcomer to broadcasting, so she may need to be understanding and lead the way slightly. She nods as she puts the headphones on and stops with a start as she turns to her right and sees Maxwell, who sound-tracked both her childhood and career, smiling broadly, microphone in hand.

David Warner and Aaron Finch get Australia off to a good

start, with Warner dispatching Shakib Al Hasan into the top tier for a six measured by the television analysts at 94m. 'This is more like the Warner we know!' says Graeme Swann, referencing his uncharacteristically slower scoring to date. 'I was going to say we know and love, but I'll stick with just know.'

Finch goes in Soumya Sarkar's first over, the ground momentarily pausing in disbelief before exploding in delight at seeing the back of the dangerous Aussie captain. That's about the strength of it for Bangladesh though, as Warner goes through the gears and receives strong support from Usman Khawaja. 'You say you should be doubling your score after 30 overs, so 330 should be on,' opines Michael Vaughan. 'But Australia should be pushing themselves and aiming for 360 to 380.'

Despite Australia having lost only one wicket, there is still disquiet in the box at what is considered a relatively slow scoring rate, especially at a comparatively small ground like Trent Bridge and on the exact pitch that gave up England's world-record total of 481 for six against Australia last summer. As the final ten overs set in, the pace is picked up, with Warner playing with the abandon associated with his earlier career, and there are murmurs of a potential double ton for the New South Welshman.

'If you win the toss and bowl here you need to go for an MRI scan,' says Swann helpfully as the ball disappears once again. It should be pointed out that today's toss was won by Australia, who opted to bat, but his point remains, nonetheless.

Warner goes for 166 – the highest individual score of the World Cup to date – and is replaced by Glenn Maxwell, who thrills all and sundry for the ten balls he faces, belting an incredible 32 runs before being BBQ'd by Khawaja, who turns down a quick single to see Maxwell run out.

Steve Smith eventually emerges once Khawaja goes – to entreaties from Vaughan for him to bat at No 3, like his fellow greats Joe Root, Virat Kohli and Kane Williamson – but he is plumb LBW second ball. To Jim Maxwell's open-mouthed astonishment, he opts to review the decision. 'That is without doubt the most optimistic review I have ever seen. It is going to smash all three out,' says the great man. 'That is what I call using up a review.' Smith heads back but Maxwell (Jim) clearly hasn't got over his rage, calling for a team fine to be imposed on the back of such an outrageous decision.

Sadly, the next drama to arrive is rain, which starts falling heavily with just one over left to play in the Australian innings. Incredibly, once it has cleared off, they come back out and face one over, setting Bangladesh a total of 382 to win, before the powers that be insist that – despite the rain-enforced break that has been and gone – the full 30-minute break between innings is still taken.

As the Tigers head out for the chase, Vaughan expresses a view that has taken hold in the *TMS* box over the past few weeks as he says, 'I really hope Bangladesh get close to this total just for the atmosphere. There were a lot of their supporters at Taunton and a lot more here.' The passion of the Bangladesh fans – and the quality of a lot of their play – have made it hard not to fall in love with their team.

A solid start is made before disaster strikes in the third over, as Soumya Sarkar and Tamim Iqbal have an awful breakdown in communication as they both hesitate at the same time, before then both making the decision to run to the same end at the same time. Finch does the necessary with some style and Sarkar is the man who has to go. 'That is a real waste of a wicket,' says Maxwell, a slight smile flickering at the corner of his lips.

Shakib gets a leading edge off Marcus Stoinis and is successfully pouched by Warner at mid-off. 'That is a disaster for Bangladesh,' says Prakash Wakankar, which is both accurate and to the point. Tamim is then cleaned out by Mitchell Starc, getting an inside edge back onto his stumps, and suddenly the weight of the Australian runs looks very heavy.

Bangladesh enter the last ten overs requiring 138 to win and the game is all but over bar the swinging, but there is still time for Swanny to use the situation to tell an amusing personal story as he says that it's 'not an impossible task but pretty close to it. I hit four sixes in an over and I'm delighted to say the bowler was Kevin Pietersen – when he was still a South African.'

Bangladesh end up on 333 for eight, which is hugely creditable but not nearly enough for today. Australia replace their trans-Tasman cousins New Zealand at the top of the table and, appropriately, Jim Maxwell has the last word. 'The quality of the Australian attack most of the time will be enough to defend a score, but we will see what happens when they play England on Tuesday.'

Australia 381-5 (50 overs; Warner 166, Khawaja 89, Finch 53) beat Bangladesh 333-8 (50 overs; Mushfiqur 102*, Mahmudullah 69, Tamim 62) by 48 runs.

CHAPTER 8

Upset in the Farby Derby

Friday 21 June
England v Sri Lanka –
ICC Cricket World Cup – Match 27
Headingley, Leeds

Team *TMS*: Jonathan Agnew, Simon Mann, Charles Dagnall, Michael
Vaughan, Jimmy Anderson, Paul Farbrace, Andy Zaltzman

England are rolling towards the World Cup semi-finals; Sri
Lanka have struggled with weather and form and the sun is
beating down on Leeds. It's fair to say there is an air of expectation in the Yorkshire air this morning. The optimism is also
bubbling in the box. Paul Farbrace – a man with recent experience of coaching both sides – is back as a guest pundit; Jimmy
Anderson is on air – fresh from match figures of nine for 47 for
Lancashire against Derbyshire – and there is an international
film star booked as a guest in the innings break who claims
appearing on the programme is 'on his bucket list'.

However, while Michael Vaughan is not wanting to puncture

the jubilant pre-match mood, he does bring an element of caution to proceedings – this is still a World Cup after all. 'Sri Lanka do have talent in that team which can cause an upset,' he warns. 'They are street fighters. If there's one team which can leave everything else off the pitch and just put a performance together, it's Sri Lanka.'

His warnings are unheeded by a packed house, though, who explode when Jofra Archer nicks off Dimuth Karunaratne in the second over and Chris Woakes follows up, removing Kusal Perera in the third as Sri Lanka are rapidly 3 for two. Through Avishka Fernando, they then start to counter-attack, which pleases Vaughan who says, 'Sri Lanka have got to play like this – there's no point being conservative and posting 240. That won't be enough.'

Fernando goes but Kusal Mendis and the veteran Angelo Mathews – who has two ducks so far in this World Cup – double down and keep Sri Lanka moving. England's support from the massed ranks at Headingley is superb, with Farbrace revealing that 'the party stand at Headingley is the one which captures the players' attention more than any other in this country. They love it.'

With nearly 30 overs gone, England are firmly in control. 'The Sri Lankans just aren't doing any damage. England are controlling the game,' says Vaughan when Mendis tries to get a shift on and slaps it straight to mid-wicket. England are circling like a pride of lions. Jeevan Mendis then goes first ball – 'As soft a dismissal as you'll see,' according to Jimmy Anderson – and at 133 for five he adds that they 'are stuck between a rock and a hard place here'.

Farbrace is back on and, after catching Dhananjaya de Silva above his head, Joe Root takes some flak from his former coach, who alleges that 'he's milked it a bit at the end with a dive. It's a fantastic catch, though.'

It's 209 for eight when Isuru Udana mistimes a hoick and is caught by Root. 'That rather sums up Sri Lanka's misfiring innings,' says Aggers philosophically, as the Sri Lankans' effort ends on just 232 for nine. 'Fantastic from England,' says a buoyant Vaughan. 'They got all the combinations right. Sri Lanka look like they have no confidence. England will look to chase this down quickly.'

During the interval, Aggers is joined by the actor Matthew Lewis, who is most well known for playing the excellent Neville Longbottom in the Harry Potter films. While he has married a California girl, Matthew is still an avid *TMS* fan out in Los Angeles and describes the programme as 'the soundtrack to his childhood'. It is an excellent interview and ticks off another Harry Potter cast member on the ever-growing list kept in producer Adam Mountford's shirt pocket.

The programme's history with 'Potter' is long and dignified, with Daniel Radcliffe (Harry Potter himself) appearing on his 18th birthday. Over the years, there have also been interviews with alumni such as Draco Malfoy (Tom Felton), the Weasley Twins (James and Oliver Phelps), Professor Dolores Umbridge (Imelda Staunton) and Barty Crouch (Roger Lloyd-Pack). The films were full of cricket fans, in front of and behind the cameras, and Matthew tells Aggers that the cast meet up every year for a charity cricket match between Gryffindor and Slytherin.

England come out to chase down the total and secure their semi-final spot but, in an echo of the opening match against South Africa, lose Jonny Bairstow second ball for a golden duck. It is a disappointment to all but Andy Zaltzman, who takes full advantage of the occasion by rolling a crackerjack of a stat. 'The only opener other than Jonny Bairstow to be out first ball twice in one World Cup was Sri Lanka's Romesh Kaluwitharana in 1996,' he says. 'The good news for England is they went on to win the tournament.'

'Sri Lanka will need a lot more of that if they are to win this game,' points out Anderson realistically, adding after another couple of overs of observation that 'I don't think this will be as easy as everyone thought. It looks like the pitch is slowing up a lot.'

James Vince, having looked unsurprisingly elegant in the early going, then nicks off to slip leaving Eoin Morgan and Root to rebuild. 'In 49 matches at home since the last World Cup this is England's second lowest score after ten overs,' adds Zaltzman. It is a very similar stat to one he used shortly before Morgan's barrage against Afghanistan, for those interested in signs.

'Even though England are just knocking the ball around, they know if they bat the overs they will win the game. Sri Lanka need to be bold and get some catchers in,' says Farbrace before Zaltzman returns five overs later to add that 'since the last World Cup this is the lowest score England have had after 15 overs at home, and the second lowest anywhere.'

England are then 73 for three when Udana takes a superb caught and bowled chance from Morgan and they are beginning to fall a little behind the rate. 'Sri Lanka's fielding has been spirited for a team we were told was demoralised,' says Agnew, with Anderson adding, 'It's noticeable how they've got their best fielders in the most important positions.'

Root makes it to his fifty, but, 'at 78 balls, that is Joe Root's second slowest ODI fifty', says Zaltzman. However, Ben Stokes mows two massive sixes in an over, and stomachs are temporarily settled. Lasith Malinga then goes up hard, convinced he has got Root strangled down the leg side. 'I think that is worth a review. If they get this, it's huge,' says Farbrace, hedging his bets as the 'Farby Derby' in front of him turns into a classic. 'It could only be bat,' adds Simon Mann after watching a replay, and he's right – Root's shoulders droop as he is sent on his way when the thinnest of lines pops up on the UltraEdge.

Buttler is next in; 'Not a bad player to have coming in in this situation,' observes Mann, quickly adding that 'half an hour of Jos Buttler and that could be it.' He gets only 16 minutes, though, as Buttler is given LBW to Malinga, burning the review in the process. Charles Dagnall and Paul Farbrace are initially unconvinced, but Daggers immediately offers his apologies to Australian umpire Paul Wilson when the three red boxes appear on the replay.

Nerves can be palpably felt around the ground but, ever the optimist, Vaughan states, 'It's important before you get to a semi-final that you win a couple of tight games. It gives you belief you can get over the line.'

Zaltzman comes back in to reveal that, after 35 overs, Sri Lanka were 158 for five and England are 154 for five. There is nothing in it and Ben Stokes and Moeen Ali are crucial to the cause. Moeen drops to one knee to waft a flat sweep just over the boundary for six, but tries to repeat the trick off the very next ball and perishes, caught by Udana. 'That was stupid, daft,' says Vaughan, frustratedly taking his inspiration from another Yorkshireman that *TMS* will be welcoming for the Ashes later in the summer. 'Moeen had just hit the ball for six. There was no need for him to try and hit that boundary. That is dumb cricket.'

Woakes gets a thin edge and goes early, leaving Simon Mann to think that 'Sri Lanka are surely favourites now,' and then Adil Rashid follows four balls later, creating a carbon copy of the dismissal. Mann is now more certain, upgrading his statement to 'Sri Lanka will surely win this game from here.'

A dread has fallen over the ground, even infecting Jimmy Anderson who, despite having to potentially line up alongside Woakes and Rashid for the Ashes, describes the dismissals as coming from 'two nothing shots outside off'. The new man, Archer, sees off Malinga's penultimate over but falls into the trap set by Udana, cuffing a slower ball to long-on to go for 3 and leave England almost needing snookers. 'Not very sensible cricket from England. Give Ben Stokes the strike!' cries Anderson, disproving the theory that current players are sometimes unwilling to criticise their team-mates.

Interviewed in the mid-innings break after taking three for 40, Mark Wood said that 'If it gets down to me then we're in trouble.' It's fair to say that this comment is referenced as the Durham fast bowler walks to the crease – England requiring a final-wicket partnership of nearly 50 from him and Stokes to avoid a calamitous defeat.

Stokes is dropped before hammering back-to-back sixes, and every ball that Wood successfully defends is cheered to the rafters. 'That is the cheer of a tail-ender blocking out for a draw like Jimmy Anderson and Monty Panesar at Cardiff,' laughs Vaughan.

The over is seen off, Stokes hits two more fours off Pradeep and there is a real feeling that England can somehow do this if Wood can see off the last ball of the over and get Stokes back on strike. However, Pradeep finds Boycott's 'Corridor of Uncertainty', Wood can't help but poke a bat out and Kusal Perera completes a straightforward catch to hand Sri Lanka a famous victory and England a dreadful defeat. 'The World Cup needed an upset and it has got one,' says Dagnall through gritted teeth and with his hand pressed hard against his temples. 'The cat is among the pigeons!' adds Vaughan, clearly relishing the drama of the situation if not the reality.

Later on, as the game is summed up, the criticism of England is all about their failure to play the much-used phrase 'smart cricket'. 'England have not played with any smartness,' says Vaughan. 'The game was won when Moeen Ali hit a six and he tried to hit another. I hope we are not in an era where in the dressing room you can't say, "That is not good enough."'

That question is answered by Farbrace, the man with the most recent experience of the England dressing room, who says that 'They don't make excuses. Eoin Morgan will call it as he sees it.

There won't be any shouting or finger-pointing, but there will be some quiet conversations with some players about their modes of dismissals.'

The reality of the situation is England will most likely need to win two of their last three games to make the World Cup semi-finals. Those games are against Australia, India and New Zealand.

Sri Lanka 232-9 (50 overs; Mathews 85*) beat England 212 (47 overs; Stokes 82*, Root 57, Malinga 4-43) by 20 runs.

Friday 21 June
England v West Indies – Women's T20 series – Match 2
The County Ground, Northampton

Team *TMS*: Henry Moeran, Natalie Germanos, Ebony Rainford-Brent, Isabelle Westbury

On the tenth anniversary of England's glorious triumph in the 2009 World T20, England win the toss, and bat underneath skies of a far bluer hue than were in place on Tuesday evening. With Northampton one of the more intimate grounds in the country, *TMS* are situated just behind the families of the England players, which is a cue for Isabelle Westbury (a former county player for Middlesex) to reminisce about her mum's bizarre tactics when she came to watch her play.

'She used to bring the paper and coffee with her, and wouldn't watch until she realised I was batting,' she remembers. 'Then she wouldn't watch because she was too nervous. Not the greatest of sports watchers, but at least she was there.' It seems like the families of Natalie Sciver and Danni Wyatt are somewhat more engaged tonight.

Wyatt is opening for England and is the beneficiary of some outrageous strokes of fortune, cashing in her chips to blast a 55-ball 81 and lead her side to an imposing total of 180 for six. While it's clearly going to be hard for the West Indies to chase, it does somehow feel that there were more runs out there, especially with more poor ground fielding from their visitors. 'Underwhelming' is the word chosen by Westbury to express her feelings during the innings break.

However, when Hayley Matthews goes to Linsey Smith in the opening over, the West Indies are really up against it and only for a brief period when Stacy-Ann King and Chedean Nation are motoring in the middle overs do they look like they may pose a challenge. 'England have been clinical when they have needed to be in this series,' says Westbury. 'It was a very workmanlike win. But very satisfying knowing what England could achieve if they get everything right.'

England 180-6 (20 overs; Wyatt 81) beat West Indies 138-9 (20 overs) by 42 runs.

Saturday 22 June (Super Saturday)
India v Afghanistan – ICC Cricket World Cup – Match 28
The Hampshire Bowl, Southampton

Team *TMS*: Prakash Wakankar, Daniel Norcross, Scott Read, Mel Jones, Alec Stewart, Tymal Mills

Since the London Olympics of 2012, you don't get to call your-self an international tournament without 'Super Saturday', and so here it is. Two of the favourites against two teams that they should beat but that could equally cause them a few concerns. The opening encounter sees *TMS* back at 'L'Hotel Hampshire Bowl', accompanied by tens of thousands of light-blue-garbed, full-throated India supporters and slightly fewer, but nonetheless noisy, royal-blue-garbed Afghanistan fans.

Given England's recent summary dismissal of the Afghans, and some internal strife in their camp, when India win the toss and bowl on a sunny day on what looks a placid pitch, the discussion turns to World Cup records rather than who is going to win.

There is also a little more local difficulty with the hotel facil-ities today, as the *TMS* box has windows with a large partition in the middle, directly covering the wicket, and a TV monitor that blocks the view of a large chunk of the outfield. Anybody wanting to spot a *TMS* team member in Southampton today just needs to look for people with a neck badly cricked to the left-hand side.

Mel Jones and Alec Stewart also vocalise a growing frustra-tion that is being felt with the Afghans. 'Afghanistan probably want to drop the fairy-tale tag now, to be more contenders. They're top cricketers who have been around a good amount of time,' says Jones.

'Afghanistan's goal has to be more consistency and to be com-petitive,' continues Stewart. 'Nobody expects them to win, but they just haven't been competitive, really.'

'If Afghanistan were to win this, would it be fair to say it would be the biggest shock in World Cup history?' asks Daniel Norcross as the in-form Rohit Sharma and K.L.Rahul walk out to take guard for India. 'Yes, I think it would!' replies Stewart confidently.

To general shock and silence, Rohit is bowled for 1 by Mujeeb Ur Rahman and Afghanistan get off to a brilliant start, restricting the scoring rate. 'The spin of Nabi, Rashid and Mujeeb will be key for Afghanistan – if they can restrict India to anything around 300, they will be very happy with that,' says Tymal Mills, and Rahul and Virat Kohli have just set a platform for India when Rahul plays a reverse sweep he instantly regrets and lobs the ball to short third man.

'K.L.Rahul once again promising a lot but under-delivering!' says Prakash Wakankar ruefully as Vijay Shankar joins his skipper. Another relatively slow fifty partnership is constructed before Shankar is LBW to Rahmat and, after 30 overs, India are just 133 for three. 'India are not going to be satisfied with 260. They will want to get over 300,' says Prakash – and with M.S.Dhoni and Virat Kohli at the crease together, the whole of India would relish a big partnership.

The overwhelming joint celebrity of the two combatants is the only explanation for the almost total silence and shock that fills the Hampshire Bowl after the third ball of the 31st over. Kohli, on 67, rocks back to cut Nabi for a routine boundary – another stroke on the way to his almost inevitable century – but does not get on top of the shot properly and offers a chance to Rahmat at short third man, who times his forward dive perfectly to take a good catch. 'It wasn't quite there to cut. Virat Kohli is furious with himself. India are in a little bit of trouble,' says Mills.

Dhoni and new man Kedar Jadhav are not showing a huge amount of intent. 'At this rate India will be struggling to get past 220,' says Prakash, who is proven right as India total just 224 for eight.

'If Afghanistan pull this off, it will be one of the biggest shocks in World Cup history,' says Norcross, updating his earlier statement now they require only 225 to do so. 'India have limped their way to 224. If Afghanistan bat the majority of the

50 overs, they should win,' adds Mills. 'They have the opportunity to be heroes here.'

Early in the Afghanistan reply there is a guest appearance in the commentary bedroom by Indian legend Virender Sehwag, who is still confident in his side's chances of victory. However, as someone who has not been trained to broadcast, Sehwag is unaware of some of the unwritten rules of radio, including the golden rule of the summariser never speaking when the bowler is actually bowling, thus clearing the decks for the commentator to describe the action. The experienced Norcross is on air with Sehwag and slightly squirming in his seat, aware that *TMS* listeners are not being entirely appraised as to what is going on in the game – however, such is the intimidating visage of the great Sehwag, it is decided not to cut him off in stride.

Hazratullah and Gulbadin combine some plays and misses with the occasional solid boundary before Hazrat goes, bowled by Mohammed Shami. Afghanistan continue nicely though, reaching 50 with no further alarms and bang on the required run rate after 20 from Hardik Pandya's first two overs. The big all-rounder returns to the attack to dismiss Gulbadin, who top-edges a pull shot, but they continue onwards towards their target, sticking to the run rate and riding out the occasional moment of danger. 'These are slightly worrying signs for India,' says Scott Read. 'The body language and the sloppiness at times in the field.'

Away from the cricket, there is general happiness for Scott in the box. Of the many dedicated commentators who cover county cricket day in day out for the BBC, he is one of the finest, hence his promotion to the World Cup team. However, his early matches in the competition were ruined by rain, so to get the chance to describe a classic such as this is just desserts for his skill and dedication.

With India burning both their reviews in the early going,

there is significant controversy when Bumrah smacks a ball into Rahmat's pads and goes up with a huge LBW appeal that is turned down. Kohli reacts badly in the field, feeling his side have been wronged, and approaches the umpire with his concerns. 'Virat needs to be very careful there,' warns Alec Stewart from the summariser's chair. 'He is showing aggression towards the umpire. Whether it is out or not, you have to accept the umpire's decision. That is not good. It is the pressure.'

However, Kohli's frown turns upside down as the over continues with both Rahmat and Hashmatullah going to fine catches. It's a double-wicket maiden and there are two new batsmen at the crease. The body language that concerned Scott Read five overs ago turns around and backs are straightened in Room 426 (*TMS* commentary box) as well as on the field. 'You would say it is evenly poised, but I would rather be in India's shoes,' says Stewart.

The fifth wicket falls as Asghar is bowled by Chahal, but Mohammad Nabi is a very capable and experienced T20 batsman and is clearly the key man. Najibullah helps him add a further 36, but as Prakash Wakankar says, 'Just when it looked like Afghanistan would be able to pull this off, Najibullah is out.'

Rashid Khan is next in and, after settling at the crease, plays a brilliant reverse sweep off Chahal but falls the next ball, lured out of his ground for a cover drive before gazing helplessly back as he misses the ball and Dhoni whips off the bails.

For 'the greatest shock in World Cup history', 32 are required from 24 balls with just three wickets left and Jasprit Bumrah, one of the finest one-day international bowlers in the world, will bowl 12 of those deliveries. This equation favours India, but when Nabi slams Bumrah deep into the stands it becomes 25 off 21 and Prakash Wakankar, already pacing in the space left after the removal of Tufnell's favourite king-sized divan with Egyptian cotton, stiffens and increases his speed.

It's 24 from 18 and, if possible, the drama goes up another notch as Nabi successfully overturns an LBW decision before taking a single and stranding himself at the non-striker's end as 18-year-old Ikram Alikhil can't force the single. 'What a game of cricket!' says the normally phlegmatic but now breathless Stewart.

With 21 runs needed from 12 balls, Bumrah lives up to his billing, only allowing occasional singles, and Afghanistan go into the last over requiring 16 for a victory that would shake the very foundations of their nation. India are favourites, but Nabi is on strike and heaves Shami's first ball straight down the ground for a boundary. Twelve off five!

A single is available but not taken from the next ball before Nabi gets hold of the third ball and hits hard and high down the ground. Billions of Indian hearts are in mouths as the ball starts to drop. Will it clear the ropes or will it find the hands of Hardik Pandya just in front? The answer is Pandya, and the ground explodes in shattered relief as Nabi drags himself off, fully knowing that with him goes the game. Had it gone for six, he'd have remained on strike needing six off three balls. 'The whole ground is stood for Nabi,' says Stewart. 'That was a wonderful innings. It was a ball you could hit for six, but he didn't get under it enough.'

No 10 Aftab Alam sees his first ball crash into the base of the stumps before No 11 Mujeeb Ur Rahman is unable to prevent his first ball smacking his leg stump. Astonishingly, Shami has won the game with a hat trick and the ground explodes once again. 'That is how you win a game of World Cup cricket. What a thrilling, thrilling game!' says Norcross.

'This has been the game of the tournament so far – the ebbs and flows, the quality of the cricket,' adds Stewart. 'You can see what it has meant to the Indian players. They were odds-on favourites by a country mile. Going into the last over, we didn't know who was going to win, India didn't know who was going to win.'

Such would have been the national impact of a victory, for periods of today's game *TMS* were joined by BBC Afghanistan correspondent Emal Pasarly, who is brought back onto air in the aftermath of scenes at the end. 'I am emotional, but it was a great game,' he says. 'All of the Afghanistan fans wanted the team to fight and they did fight today. That is the main thing. Afghanistan will get a lot out of this game. If they can take this to the Bangladesh game, it will be even closer.'

The result is also not what England fans wanted, as an Afghan victory would have significantly eased England's passage to the semi-finals. All English eyes are now on Lord's on Tuesday – where the first 'must win' game will be played.

India 224-8 (50 overs; Kohli 67, Jadhav 52) beat Afghanistan 213 (49.5 overs; Nabi 52, Shami 4-40) by 11 runs.

Saturday 22 June (Super Saturday)
West Indies v New Zealand – ICC Cricket World
Cup – Match 29
Old Trafford, Manchester

Team *TMS*: Fazeer Mohammad, Kevin Howells, Bryan Waddle, Jeremy Coney, Michael Vaughan, Jimmy Anderson, Sir Curtly Ambrose, Phil Long

After a short amount of confusion when the great David Boon, now a match referee for the ICC, can't read the side the coin has landed on at the toss, it is determined that West Indies will have the option and they will field first. The weather is fine and, with Sir Curtly Ambrose and Jimmy Anderson on the team, you'd have to work hard to score against today's *TMS* summarisers in a Test match.

'It is always warm and sunny in Manchester. Always,' says Anderson, the closest thing to a Mancunian on the team, with a glint in his eye. 'I noticed that yesterday,' replies Bryan Waddle darkly, who as a New Zealander is used to a bit of rain, but ideally not around the cricket season.

Any late-arriving Martin Guptill fans are gutted after he is dismissed from the very first ball of the match, LBW to Sheldon Cottrell. It is pointed out that this is some contrast to the last time West Indies came up against Guptill in a World Cup, at the quarter-final in Wellington in 2015 when he hit 237 not out from 163 balls, a total that remains the highest individual score in World Cup history.

The next ball sees a rare but beautiful all-run four, as Carlos Brathwaite provides a Twitter meme for the ages by going down too early and in stages, flinging himself headfirst after the ball and missing it by about a foot.

Then, before the first over is done, New Zealand are 7 for two, with Colin Munro playing around a full, straight delivery from Cottrell and also going for a duck. The final ball sees Evin Lewis pick up an injury and Ross Taylor narrowly evade a run-out. There are 594 balls potentially left in this match and everyone is already a bit knackered.

Fortunately, it calms down quite a bit from there, other than Jeremy Coney saying that Kane Williamson has 'anesthetised' the ball as he deliberately tickles a boundary through a laboured-looking Chris Gayle in the slip cordon. There are differing perspectives in the box, as Waddle thinks that 'New Zealand need 30 to 35 overs of batting from Kane Williamson and Ross Taylor' and Curtly thinks that 'This is exactly what [West Indies captain] Jason Holder wanted – a couple of quick wickets and his bowlers continuing to put the pressure on Williamson and Taylor.'

It is Waddle who gets what he wants, as Williamson and Taylor bat together for 33.4 overs, adding 160 before the 39-year-old Gayle – who gets a huge cheer when he comes on to bowl in his *Top Gun*-style Aviator sunglasses – forces Taylor to miscue to mid-off and then hilariously shanks his shoulder after punching the air in celebration. The partnership has been broken and Curtly is 'quite sure New Zealand will want at least another 110, 120 runs. They've got the wickets in hand and Williamson – we know how dangerous he can be.'

This is proven when the Kiwi captain swivels Kemar Roach away for four to bring up his second century of the week. The appreciation for Williamson in the box is palpable, with Vaughan calling him a 'genius', Ambrose saying that 'He's carved a wonderful hundred out for his team', and Bryan Waddle, as ever the softly spoken professional commentator, simply adding 'Nicely played' behind a beaming grin.

Williamson continues unabashed, losing partners hand over fist as he alone ensures his team posts a strong total, eventually getting to a superb 148 with wonderful shots to all parts of the ground. After his unbeaten 79 against Afghanistan and 106 not out against South Africa, his runs today mean the New Zealander has scored 332 runs without losing his wicket, breaking Kumar Sangakkara's record of 326 from the last World Cup.

There is particular delight for one member of the *TMS* team when Cottrell becomes the star of the end of the innings as well as the beginning, removing Tom Latham, running out Colin de Grandhomme and then taking catches to remove Mitchell Santner and Jimmy Neesham. As delighted as Sir Curtly is to see the young man's success, it's actually Vaughan who reveals that 'My little boy is here and he's been wanting to see that salute in real life!'

New Zealand post 291 for eight, and it is agreed that given the pitch and the size of the outfield, it is a very good effort. 'This is a dry pitch, it's slow, it's not been easy, and we've seen a genius at work,' reckons Vaughan, while Bryan Waddle thinks that 'We're going to see something special if West Indies are to win this game. This is a challenging target.'

That is proven when Trent Boult benefits from two wild swings early on: firstly Shai Hope getting an inside edge on a massive drive and seeing his stumps splattered; and then Nicholas Pooran getting a top edge on a big swipe and being caught behind to leave West Indies 20 for two in the sixth over. Despite his excellent start with the ball, Boult can't capitalise in the field and spills a very hard chance offered by Gayle, who then smacks the next two balls into the stands for six, generating huge roars from a now well-oiled Manchester crowd who are clearly here to see some brilliance from the 'Universe Boss'.

'This is dangerous for New Zealand,' says Kevin Howells. 'Hetmyer and Gayle are striking it well and look like they're enjoying themselves.' The two need to score at a run a ball throughout the innings and are doing so. In a mirrored echo of previous West Indies performances, Sir Curtly is on the microphone, this time calling for the New Zealand bowlers to 'contain these batsmen', adding that 'It seems the quicker they bowl, the faster it goes to the boundary.' As an independent summariser, this is very true. As a proud West Indian, he is clearly delighted that Matt Henry has gone for 42 off his first five overs – a performance made worse when he drops a simple chance from Gayle at deep square leg.

'That should have been taken quite comfortably. He didn't have to move an inch,' says Ambrose, only just suppressing his delight as Gayle is dropped on a third occasion, this time by

Colin Munro at deep mid-wicket. True to form, in the next over Gayle again hits back-to-back sixes, causing Ambrose to reach for a little-used but terrifically effective trick in the summariser's handbook: the middle name. 'That is Christopher Henry Gayle at his best!' he exclaims – as Bryan Waddle and Jeremy Coney get increasingly nervous on the other side of the aisle.

'Shimron Hetmyer has to keep his composure, keep his head and not give it away. They're well in front of the required rate,' adds Ambrose after the youngster gets away with a top-edged slog that somehow bisects three fielders and finds the boundary and then brings up his fifty with a brutal pull shot off Lockie Ferguson.

'If you want Caribbean flamboyance, that's the shot,' says a clearly delighted Fazeer Mohammad. 'Lockie Ferguson is one of the fastest bowlers at this World Cup, but that one disappeared.'

The Kiwi paceman gets his revenge, deceiving Hetmyer with a leg cutter out of the back of the hand and bowling him for 54. 'With the rate required, the West Indies management will be thinking, *Did he need to take any risk at that stage?*' says Michael Vaughan, before Jason Holder is caught behind first ball to once again change the face of the game.

Gayle then aims to hit his seventh six but hangs the ball high in the air, down to long-on where Trent Boult makes some amends for his earlier error and pouches it. West Indies have lost three wickets for 10 runs in 12 balls. Williamson goes for the kill and brings back Boult to try to end the game early – and when Ashley Nurse is caught behind at the start of the next over and the clearly injured Evin Lewis at the end of it, West Indies are 164 for seven and all but out of the game.

'It's looking pretty dismal for West Indies now,' says Jimmy Anderson, 'Having been so good when Gayle and Hetmyer were at the crease.' They've now lost five wickets for 22 runs in

29 balls. Carlos Brathwaite is still swinging, though, and clears the Media Centre with an almighty smash down the ground that is measured at 96m and signals that the West Indians won't go down without a fight. Even the tail-ender Kemar Roach joins the party, carving it high and handsome over long-off for another six. 'Now would be the time for four consecutive sixes from Carlos Brathwaite,' says Fazeer Mohammad. 'He'll always be remembered for that World Twenty20 final.'

The eighth-wicket pair add 47 before Roach edges Henry behind, bringing Cottrell to the crease to join Brathwaite. There is an element of panic to their partnership, but it starts to build. Brathwaite reaches his fifty, overthrows are scrambled and, as Sir Curtly says, 'The runs are gettable, it's being eight wickets down that's the problem. New Zealand are in the driving seat.'

Cottrell hits back-to-back boundaries, one through fine leg and the next through a vacant slip cordon, being rewarded for his success with a bumper from Neesham that just causes the West Indian fast bowler to laugh in his face. Phil Long points out that both batsmen are on ODI best scores, and when Ferguson angles in a quick one to take Cottrell's off stump, it seems that that's that.

'Safe to say, it's all over,' says even Sir Curtly, before Brathwaite thunks Boult back down the ground for four more. Oshane Thomas is just able to see off Boult's final three balls, but with West Indies needing 40 from 23 balls, Ambrose admits that 'I do have faith ... but I'm also a realist!'

The next over sees Brathwaite hammer Ferguson for a big six before Thomas again sees off his final ball, meaning both New Zealand's best bowlers are out of overs. 'If anyone can do this, Carlos Brathwaite can. Cast your mind back to a couple of years ago with those four sixes,' says Ambrose, once again raising the spectre of 2015. Henry comes back on to bowl, as Mohammad adds that he 'will probably be bowling the final over if it goes that far. It could be a grandstand finish.'

Henry has been expensive today, but when the second (over long-on), third (beyond third man) and fourth (above deep cover) balls of his over go for six, Brathwaite has scored 18 from three balls. This becomes 22 from four, as he top-edges the fifth ball over Latham's head and it scurries away to the boundary. The final delivery is guided away for a crucial single as Brathwaite keeps the strike and, suddenly, West Indies need just eight from 12 balls.

The normally inscrutable Ambrose is almost breathless, but retains enough severity to deliver a critical warning to his side's potential match-winner. 'A fantastic innings by Carlos Brathwaite,' he growls. 'But don't take any unnecessary risks here – you've got more than enough deliveries.'

Neesham bowls the 49th over and the first three balls render no score before Brathwaite shovels him out to deep mid-wicket for two, reducing the ask to six from nine balls and also bringing up an incredible – and unlikely – century. 'He's played exceptionally well to put West Indies on the brink of victory,' says Ambrose, who is now officially breathless. 'They're one boundary away.'

The next ball is left alone by Brathwaite, who needs a single from the final ball of the over to keep the strike. However, Neesham serves up a delivery right in the slot and, true to the fashion of this match for the ages, Brathwaite has a massive heave and sends the ball out towards the long-on region. Will it clear the ropes, or will it find the hands of Boult just in front?

Exactly as happened with Mohammad Nabi just hours earlier in Southampton, the answer is find the fielder. Boult takes the catch, adding to the drama as he stumbles back just slightly but stays safely on the right side of the boundary. Brathwaite, defeated at the last, drops to the ground in tears, while the crowd, conversely, rise to their feet to applaud a stunning effort. Though clearly upset at not getting the victory, Ambrose is delighted that his side have shown the fight he feels has been lacking in their previous performances.

'It certainly is painful,' he says. 'When you look at the way West Indies played, they'll be thinking about what could have been. They were ahead of the rate, but kept losing wickets. Some people, myself included, thought it was all over, but Carlos Brathwaite had other ideas.'

After Williamson offers a typically level-headed take on an incredible game, it is time for the wrap-up, and Kevin Howells beautifully captures the essence of the occasion when he says, 'What a game of cricket that was. To hear Kane Williamson talk so calmly . . . that's why he's an international captain and I'm not. I'll probably lose sleep myself thinking about Carlos Brathwaite almost getting them over the line. I didn't realise it at the time, but that first over of the day, with ten runs and two wickets and an all-run four, set the tone for the rest of the day. Chaos.'

There is further praise for Williamson, but Jeremy Coney, not for the first time, strikes a slightly discordant tone when he adds that 'If you say how well Williamson has done as a captain, when there were seven overs left, he had two overs each left from Trent Boult, Matt Henry and Lockie Ferguson, and one from the fifth bowler. But he left it so that the last three overs had to be bowled by Henry and the fifth bowler. That was a decision that could have gone better.'

To simply call this game a tight one underestimates the drama that Old Trafford witnessed today, but, whichever way, New Zealand have once again snuck home and they now top the group. Super Saturday has delivered in spades. What a competition we are witnessing – and we haven't seen the Home of Cricket involved yet. Tomorrow, *TMS* – and the 2019 World Cup – go to Lord's.

New Zealand 291-8 (50 overs; Williamson 148, Taylor 69, Cottrell 4-56) beat West Indies 286 (49 overs; Brathwaite 101, Gayle 87, Hetmyer 54, Boult 4-30) by 5 runs.

Sunday 23 June
Pakistan v South Africa –
ICC Cricket World Cup – Match 30
Lord's Cricket Ground, St John's Wood, London

Team *TMS*: Natalie Germanos, Isa Guha, Daniel Norcross, Jonathan Agnew, Phil Tufnell, Ramiz Raja, Graeme Swann, Andy Zaltzman

The World Cup is well over halfway through, but this is the first time in 2019 that *TMS* have been in residence in the 'spaceship' that hovers above the Nursery End at Lord's Cricket Ground. While the World Cup is entering Lord's, South Africa are entering the last-chance saloon – defeat today would mathematically rule them out of the semi-finals, while a victory for Pakistan would keep their hopes alive and add to the pressure on England after their loss to Sri Lanka.

Pakistan bat first and race out of the starting blocks, Imam-ul-Haq and Fakhar Zaman taking the Powerplay overs for 58, while the chat in the box is about how you need to be careful with Twitter, leading Tuffers to admit that, on his first time using the social media platform, he gave his mobile phone number out!

A controversy over a catch sees Imran Tahir get what Aggers calls 'a big old boo' from the overwhelmingly

Pakistani crowd, before the South African leg-spinner strikes back and gets Fakhar in his first over, then takes a superbly instinctive caught and bowled to account for Imam, causing Graeme Swann to harshly proclaim that 'Imran Tahir is one of the worst fielders I've ever played cricket against, so that catch is phenomenal.'

After the abuse from Swann has concluded, Daniel Norcross turns to Andy Zaltzman, expecting some kind of stat to be proffered. Has the dismissal made Tahir South Africa's most prolific World Cup wicket-taker, for instance? Zaltz confirms that it has, before delving into a far more significant issue. Having observed Tahir's traditionally lengthy sprint in celebration, the statistician established that he had run around the edge of the fielding discs in a perfect semi-circle from where he took the catch (towards the Mound Stand and Kagiso Rabada).

Then, by dividing $2\pi r$ by two (halving the formula for the circumference of a circle to create one for that of a semi-circle), he has decided that, at 51 yards, the celebration was Imran Tahir's shortest ever. Whether or not it's true (and, knowing Zaltzman, it probably is), it is a truly fantastic piece of creative cricketing mathematics.

The final ten overs belong to Haris Sohail, who arrives at the crease with a 'licence to thrash' according to Norcross – and takes full advantage. Despite not playing for weeks, he plunders the bowling to all parts of north London, at one stage causing Aggers to state that he'd tried to hit the ball into Regent's Park, before quickly working out the capital's geography and suggesting the ball was instead bound for Edgware Road.

Such an impressive feat of calculation has clearly moved Zaltzman closer to the edge, because today sees the first 'venting' of the tournament. After Imad Wasim has been caught by J.P.Duminy for 23, the competition's resident cricketarist (a person with a guitar made out of a cricket bat, who, for some reason best known to the ICC, plays the batsmen back and forth from the crease, and has been present, in one incarnation or another, at every match), once again ponderously strikes up the riff from 'Livin' on a Prayer' shortly after the ball reaches the boundary.

Zaltzman, his tired countenance suffused with thunderous rage, rips his headphones from his ears and throws them to the ground, the catharsis immediately evident as he takes a deep breath before shouting at the world (off microphone), 'IS IT NOT BRILLIANT ENOUGH? DO WE NEED TO BE TOLD IT'S BRILLIANT?'

Outburst over, a second deep breath is taken, the headphones are retrieved, placed back on his head and business as usual is returned to, as he assiduously records the boundary in his scorebook.

Off the field, there is astonishment late in the Pakistan innings when, after a tweet received from Birdoswald Cheese in Ayrshire demonstrates love for *TMS* in the cheesemakers' community, it becomes clear that Natalie Germanos has never eaten Stilton! Shockwaves ripple through the box, particularly from Leicestershire-based Jonathan Agnew, who has enjoyed many a fine local cheese in his time. Fortunately, the Media Centre in Lord's is notoriously well stocked with rich foods and Tuffers quickly nips down to source some Stilton. The tasting is declared a success, with Germanos then quickly demonstrating mastery of her art by declaring that Imad Wasim 'was all over that like stink on cheese', as he dispatches one towards the boundary.

Pakistan end on 308 for seven and, with Zaltzman's words that 'Bangladesh's run chase of 322 for three against West Indies is the only successful chase of over 250 in this World Cup', South Africa embark on their innings, getting a stroke of luck in the first over when Quinton de Kock is dropped by

Wahab Riaz, the Pakistani making 'a pretty ordinary attempt', according to Swann, who is clearly taking no prisoners with his fielding analysis today.

However, Mohammad Amir successfully reviews an LBW decision in the next over to see the back of Hashim Amla and, although runs from Faf du Plessis help South Africa to 189 for four with 20 overs to go, they fulfil the prophecy of Daniel Norcross, who wonderfully says that 'South Africa have been drinking in the last-chance saloon for a long time in this World Cup. They're looking worse for wear because of it.'

A middle- and lower-order collapse sees them end well short, only reaching 259 for nine at the end of the 50 overs and crashing out of the competition in an ignominious fashion that well represents the mediocre tournament they've had. South Africa have put up a very poor show indeed and the criticism is unstinting. 'This is the worst South Africa team to play at a World Cup. What a shambles,' says Norcross before everybody clears out of the way and Natalie Germanos comes in off her long run.

'There was only once in this World Cup when South Africa showed a little bit of intent with the bat and that was against New Zealand, but even then it was a little bit too late,' she begins. 'That's what has been lacking, that ability to put their foot down. But, if you leave out 2003, they have made the knockout stages in every other World Cup they have played in and, going into the tournament, they were second only to Australia in terms of win/loss ratio in group stage games. So, they usually lose in the knockouts, but this time it was the preliminary stage.'

For South Africa to be eliminated when they still have to play two more matches is not what anybody thought would happen – and it underscores the fact that there may well be a few dead rubbers on their way over the next ten days. Not the England games, though.

*Pakistan 308-7 (50 overs; Sohail 89, Azam 69) beat South
Africa 259-9 (50 overs; du Plessis 63) by 49 runs.*

Monday 24 June
Bangladesh v Afghanistan – ICC Cricket World
Cup – Match 31
The Hampshire Bowl, Southampton

Team *TMS*: Prakash Wakankar, Scott Read, Simon Mann, Ebony
Rainford-Brent, Niall O'Brien, Athar Ali Khan, Andy Zaltzman

It's *TMS*'s final visit of the summer to Hotel Hampshire, for a
game between a Bangladesh side that have gained a lot of fans and
an Afghanistan side that has not really lived up to even the limited
expectations they brought with them. A victory for Bangladesh
would keep alive their hopes of a semi-final spot. Bangladesh
bat first and lose Liton Das early on but, as ever, can rely on the
superb Shakib Al Hasan. When he passes 40, he triggers a wonderful stat from Andy Zaltzman, who says that the all-rounder
has become 'only the second player to hit six consecutive 40-plus
scores in a World Cup', adding for context that 'Matthew Hayden
was the first – he hit seven in the 2007 World Cup.'

Simon Mann describes the scenes that unfurl when Shakib
reaches his fifty as 'like a home game in Dhaka', but the air is
sucked out an over later when he is given LBW to Mujeeb off
a delivery where he could well have been caught behind and
stumped as well, had the umpire decided not to give LBW.
Soumya Sarkar is given LBW on review to Mujeeb, with the ball

just clipping leg stump, causing Zaltzman to crack that 'You do have to ask, in the context of this tournament, "Would that nick on leg stump have been enough to knock the zing bails off?"'

While journalistic integrity is scrupulously maintained on air, Bangladesh have become a favourite of the *TMS* team during the competition because of the vivacity of their play and the passionate fanbase that has followed them around the country. During a press conference with Tamim Iqbal yesterday, it appears that the feeling is mutual. Niall O'Brien, who was listening to Tamim as part of his pre-match research, reveals that the opener admitted the Bangladesh team had been listening to *TMS* in their dressing room during a match and changing their tactics according to what the team was saying! It was said with a light smile on his face, so whether Tamim was being entirely serious is up for debate, but the boost to the programme's ego is very much appreciated, especially deep into a pretty intense World Cup.

Back in the game, Mahmudullah plays a memorable knock for Bangladesh, battling on through injury to partner Mushfiqur Rahim – including at one stage being forced to run a three when even a single seemed unlikely. They end up with 262 for seven, the highlight of the final over being Zadran – the man who dropped Eoin Morgan in the 20s last week – putting down a chance so simple that O'Brien refers to it as a 'goober'.

Afghanistan start well, giving themselves a chance of chasing the total down, but a mid-innings collapse sees them slide from a promising 104 for two to a potentially fatal 132 for six. The damage is being done by that man Shakib – 'a master of his craft' according to O'Brien – who is making a very convincing case to be named Player of the Tournament. He accounts for both openers, Gulbadin and Rahmat, before taking the dangerous Nabi and Asghar Afghan, who sums up the innings as he allows pressure to build before being caught at deep square leg attempting the big shot.

'Shakib is living up to his ranking as the number one all-rounder in the world,' beams Athar Ali Khan. 'Absolutely brilliant,' adds the Bangladeshi for emphasis. He now has four wickets and when Zaltzman points out that 'Only one man has taken five wickets and hit a fifty in the same game – India's Yuvraj Singh against Ireland in 2011', it almost sounds like a challenge.

If it is, it's a challenge that is accepted and completed in Shakib's next spell, as Najibullah charges down the pitch, misses his attempt to smack the ball back over the bowler's head and Mushfiqur whips the bails off to complete the stumping. Southampton rises to its hero and Zaltzman confirms the achievement, with Ebony Rainford-Brent adding that 'He'll still be hunting for these last three wickets if he can.'

The haul stays at five, with Mustafizur Rahman and Mohammad Saifuddin completing the victory, Mujeeb Ur Rahman failing to see out the final two balls of the 47th over and stranding poor Samiullah Shenwari on 49 not out, who chucks his bat away in disgust, marooned just one run short of a World Cup half-century.

'Bangladesh read the surface and conditions very well. It wasn't a 300 pitch and they made sure to put a score on the board that was beyond Afghanistan,' says O'Brien. The round-up is focused on the brilliance of Shakib, with Scott Read stating that 'It has been the Shakib show today.' Bangladesh are still alive, but will need to beat both India and Pakistan in their final two games to be in contention to qualify for a semi-final.

Bangladesh 262-7 (50 overs; Mushfiqur 83, Shakib 51) beat Afghanistan 200 (47 overs; Shakib 5-29) by 62 runs.

CHAPTER 9

England Hammered to the Brink

Tuesday 25 June
England v Australia – ICC Cricket World Cup – Match 32
Lord's Cricket Ground, St John's Wood, London

Team *TMS*: Jonathan Agnew, Jim Maxwell, Simon Mann, Isa Guha,
Michael Vaughan, Phil Tufnell, Alec Stewart, Andy Zaltzman

The summer of England v Australia starts here. Well, technically it started last month in Southampton, but this is the first time there's money on the table.

'There's a real tingle in the air this morning,' confirms Aggers as *TMS* comes on air to the sound of a nervous nation shifting in their seats. 'Is this a preview for the final?' wonders Jim Maxwell, as England bowl first and immediately benefit from a bit of nip under some early cloud cover as David Warner lines up with no fewer than three slip fielders for company. 'It's like the first over of a Test match,' adds Agnew as Chris Woakes fizzes one past the outside edge.

England have a tension about them that has not often been

seen in the past four years. 'They know they have to win,' explains Vaughan when asked about the atmosphere in the dressing room. 'Normally it's all jovial and playing football – not today though, you can see it in their eyes.'

It's not the most convincing start from Australia, although James Vince dropping a very difficult chance offered by Aaron Finch – 'He turned it around the post,' according to Tuffers – doesn't help England take advantage of some fantastic opening bowling. They are also disadvantaged by an extremely tight LBW referral, which sees the Aussie captain stay at the wicket by the skin of his teeth after the box turns orange instead of the expected red and it is judged as 'umpire's call'.

Simon Mann is concerned, though. 'I think England are better when they bat first,' he reveals. 'I understand the decision because of the overnight rain and the overhead conditions, but their troubles in this tournament have been when chasing.'

According to Andy Zaltzman, by 43 minutes into the game Australia have already recorded eight play and misses, but Jim Maxwell is seeing it very clearly. 'It's dangerous for England if these two get away again,' he warns. 'Australia have such a strong record when defending.'

Mark Wood cracks Finch on the hip with his first ball, but the rugged Aussie shakes it off and the openers continue, seeing off the first ten overs and really beginning to establish a partnership. 'We focus on England's frustrations, but you have to say that these two stayed calm when the ball was zipping around and they have weathered that storm,' says the sage-like Victor Marks. 'When you're in form you don't worry so much about what the ball is doing.'

With Australia looking ominous, attention turns to those surrounding us. Even by the normal standards of a big Lord's occasion, there is a serious parade of well-known people around the famous old ground. England football manager

Gareth Southgate, sitting in the row behind superstar comedian Michael McIntyre, is spotted greeting Hollywood actor Damian Lewis in a corporate box, while nearby the likes of Ed Sheeran (watching with his dad, John), former prime minister David Cameron, Muse frontman Matt Bellamy and even Prince Edward are present and correct.

Rumours abound that Australian tennis world number one and recent French Open Champion Ashleigh Barty – who previously played professional cricket for the Brisbane Heat in the Australian women's Big Bash League – is in the house, as well as her British compatriot Laura Robson. As Finch and Warner continue to plunder, assistant producer Henry Moeran is dispatched to pick up a big-name guest for half time.

Back on the field, it is going from bad to worse for England. 'Australia are cruising, the crowd are a bit stunned. This has not gone to script at all,' says Aggers shortly after Finch and Warner have both brought up fifties. Soon afterwards, Warner misjudges one from Moeen Ali and cracks it to Joe Root at point, who takes a juggling catch.

Although Moeran is still away trying to secure a celebrity interview, *TMS* are joined by cricketing royalty in the box as former Australian captain Allan Border drops in to give his perspective. 'The Aussie boys have done well today after the ball was flying about a bit,' he says. 'They have had to battle away.' There is also support from the legend for the under-pressure Usman Khawaja, who has just come in to bat at No 3. 'Khawaja has been doing reasonably well in the tournament, so I'd stick with him at three,' he adds. 'He's been a form player for the last 12 months or so.'

The two add 50, with a missed stumping by Jos Buttler for good measure, and there is a notable drop in morale among the *TMS* England contingent. Alec Stewart is still bemoaning the LBW referral earlier in the innings, returning to previous concerns he has expressed over the use of technology in cricket as he says, 'I think they should get rid of umpire's call. If it's hitting the stumps, it's hitting the stumps. As long as you've got the correct bails, they fall off!'

Tuffers, meanwhile, is concerned that it's not going to get any better, adding disconsolately, 'I think it might be harder to bat in the second innings. England just haven't been able to apply any pressure.' The times are changing though, as Ben Stokes whistles a 90mph inswinger through Khawaja's defence and there is wood all over the floor. 'It's just what England needed!' says a quickly rejuvenated Tufnell as Steve Smith comes out – again, loudly booed – and the atmosphere really picks back up.

Finch brings up his hundred off a misfield but, off the very next ball, he top-edges into the deep and Woakes takes a regulation high catch to leave Australia 185 for three with 15 overs to go. New man Glenn Maxwell plunders Jofra Archer over long-on for six, prompting Vaughan to point out that 'One thing is for sure – England have to get him out.' Five balls later and he's gone, attempting to paddle Wood to third man and instead nicking to the keeper. 'That's a huge blow for Australia and perfect timing,' says Vaughan, gleefully piping up again. 'He's such a frustration for Australia fans.'

Suddenly, the momentum is being sucked out of the Australian innings. Marcus Stoinis and Smith have a complete misunderstanding that sees them both at the same end of the pitch – never an ideal scenario. It is Stoinis who goes and suddenly Vic reckons that England are back in it. 'There's been a little flurry of wickets, the run rate has slowed, and Wood has bowled an excellent spell,' he tells the listeners. 'It's a fantastic game. There's that wonderful feel that no one quite knows which way it's going to go.' Smith goes soon afterwards and it's only thanks to some more late hitting from Alex Carey that Australia end up finishing with a little spurt and setting England 286 to win.

The summer gets underway on 3 May, with 136 days of cricket to follow. Niall O'Brien, Michael McNamee and Ian Bell were there to see an early England victory.

An unexpected visitor to the *TMS* box. Ramiz Raja and Simon Mann eye a giant spider heading for them at The Oval, as England prepared for the World Cup, taking on Pakistan.

Chas and James: Jimmy Anderson and Daggers warm up with the bass guitar at Southampton.

A brilliant ramp shot from Jos Buttler against Pakistan at Southampton, during his extraordinary innings of 110 not out.

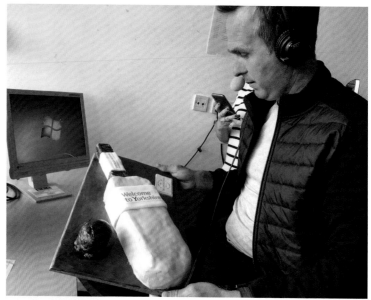

This Welcome to Yorkshire cake had suffered somewhat in transit, and the *TMS* team is accused of ball tampering.

Sam Curran, to the manner born – not only a great all-rounder in the making, but (at the age of 20) a superb summariser in the making.

Some of the World Cup *TMS* team: (Left) Sir Curtly Ambrose wrapped up against the cold as West Indies take on Australia; (right) Ramiz Raja and Prakash Wakankar. Unsurprisingly, Ramiz didn't try the same trick on Curtly.

Bangladesh's Athar Ali Khan and Zimbabwean Pommie Mbangwa were welcome additions to the *TMS* commentary roster.

Aggers poses with cricket legend Sir Viv Richards, one of his four Test victims, during England's defeat to Pakistan on 3 June.

Having already destroyed the Bangladesh attack, Jason Roy takes out umpire Joel Wilson during his brilliant innings of 153 that endangered the ducks on the River Taff.

'The biggest game in the world' – India v Pakistan at Old Trafford. Michael Vaughan poses for a selfie with Bollywood star Ranveer Singh (left), while in the stands a tremendous atmosphere built up, with friendly rivalry to the fore.

Eoin Morgan hits out against Afghanistan on the way to making 138, including a record-breaking 17 sixes along the way.

After Jonny Bairstow's complaints about media treatment, he delivered a match-winning innings of 111 against India to keep England's World Cup hopes alive. Meanwhile, Sundar Pichai, CEO of Google, delivered some appropriately branded cup cakes to the *TMS* team.

After New Zealand had been soundly beaten by England at Chester-le-Street, Jeremy Coney feared the worst for the knockout stages: 'There is a decline, there is a lack of skill and lack of intent.'

The vital moment: Trent Boult traps Virat Kohli in front for 1, and New Zealand are on the way to the World Cup final.

Jos Buttler runs out Steve Smith with a direct hit that nutmegged him during the World Cup semi-final.

An amazing cake sent in by the Duchess of Cornwall did full justice to the World Cup final.

The tension is visible in the *TMS* commentary box, as the World Cup final builds to an incredible climax.

A key moment in the last over of England's run chase: as Ben Stokes dives for safety, the ball deflects off his bat for four overthrows.

The England team celebrate winning the World Cup final. 'What a day it's been!' concluded Aggers, after it took a Super Over to decide the outcome.

PLAYERS' LUNCH MENU AT LORD'S FOR ENGLAND v AUSTRALIA

Starter

Roasted tomato and basil soup w/ freshly baked bread rolls

Main

Seared duck breast w/ braised duck leg, pancetta,
chestnuts and sprouts

Slow cooked salmon fillet w/ octopus salad and salsa verde

Ham, pea and mascarpone risotto w/ shaved parmesan

Chickpea tagine w/ coriander cous cous

Sides

Prawns w/ Marie Rose sauce

Cauliflower, mangetout, beans or mashed potato

Smoked chicken Caesar salad

Desserts

Apricot and almond sponge w/ apricot sauce

Bitter chocolate and peanut butter tart w/ crème fraiche

Fresh fruit salad

Selection of ice creams

While all that was going on, Moeran pulled a blinder and managed to secure Laura Robson for the lunch break. She is an excellent guest, recalling the time she spent in the nets at Trent Bridge with fellow British tennis star Heather Watson. Sadly, she wasn't trialling for Nottinghamshire at the time – she was helping to promote a local tennis event – but it's still fantastically surreal to imagine her and Heather firing serves down at Jake Ball, who was desperately trying to hit them with a cricket bat 22 yards away at the other end!

A successful chase for England would count as the joint second highest of all time at Lord's, but nobody is doubting their capability to deliver it. A defeat would not knock them out immediately, but would require them to beat India and New Zealand back to back. This is tough enough in normal circumstances but, off the back of two consecutive defeats and with a home World Cup on the line, it would be a very tricky ask indeed.

James Vince opens the innings with a lovely looking on drive for no run and then, second ball, receives an in ducker from Jason Behrendorff. Tragically, he allows the ball to pass between bat and pad and crash into the stumps. 'Jason Roy is proving a huge loss for England,' notes Tuffers as the scoreboard changes to show England 0 for one and everyone takes a very deep breath indeed.

Root hits two quick boundaries but is done for pace by Mitchell Starc and misses the ball as it smacks hard into his pads with a hint of late swing. 'That looked absolutely dead,' says Simon Mann, and when Root simply turns tail without even considering a review, he is proved correct. 'Disastrous start for England,' mourns Tufnell, sitting to next him.

Eoin Morgan produces a gorgeous straight drive off Behrendorff, and Vaughan, who slumps into the summariser's chair to replace Tufnell, immediately says that England 'just have to steady the ship. Just for a few overs.' His head is quickly in his hands as Morgan goes after a short delivery from Starc, but doesn't time his hoick and sends a swirling chance down to fine leg that is well taken by Pat Cummins.

Vaughan is frustrated by England's refusal to compromise, saying, 'Eoin Morgan said England would carry on playing the way they have played, but sometimes when you lose two wickets you have got to try and bat for a few overs. Morgan has gone for the big, big shot. I don't think you can win a World Cup playing just one way. You have to realise Australia are on top and nullify them for half an hour. It just required a bit of sensible batting, just for a while. But it is not the England way. They just keep going for it.'

With such a struggle on the pitch, Aggers decides that 'The only thing to do is to thank people for the various culinary delights we have received today to distract ourselves from the cricket.' While there are a significant number of culinary delights in the box, the suspicion is that there are many more that have not made their way up, with the Lord's branch of the ICC security operation just as intense as the Trent Bridge branch a few weeks earlier.

There is a lovely cake made for the team by the wonderful ICC Cricketeers, a volunteer force without whom the World Cup would undoubtedly grind to a crunching halt (and due to their passes they are able to bypass security!), and another that is baked with homemade honey, which can supposedly cure all ills, according to an attached note. 'Can it cure batting collapses?' asks Vaughan immediately, bringing the house down with his dry Yorkshire wit.

The doom is compounded by Andy Zaltzman, who says that 'England were 39 for three in the first ten overs. In 51 ODI matches in this country since the last World Cup, that is the joint third slowest in 51 innings – the second slowest was against Sri Lanka the other day.' His point is clear: the signs are not good at all.

They are even worse when Jonny Bairstow is the latest England batsman to get out in a horrible way, replicating Morgan as he tries to go aerial into the leg side, doesn't get all of it and is well caught by Cummins, who this time is patrolling the deep mid-wicket boundary. 'It was an ugly dismissal,' admits Vic, his trademark tact and delicacy preventing the rocket that might have been received from an angrier pundit. 'England are in the mire.'

Nathan Lyon comes on to bowl and immediately summons turn and bounce out of the surface, Carey's loud, classically Australian, entreaties of 'bowling, Garry!' after every ball echoing around a silent, shell-shocked Lord's. For those wondering why Lyon is known as Garry, it's all to do with a chap who played Aussie Rules Football to some success in the 1980s and 1990s and is now rather ubiquitous on Aussie sports TV.

Stokes is one of England's last big hopes but is visibly struggling with his mobility. 'Stokes will literally have to have a broken leg for him to walk off,' says Alec Stewart, visibly exhibiting that he was a cricketer not a physiotherapist in his former career. While, on one hand, hopes are lifted that Stokes may only have a bad case of cramp, they are dashed on the other as Buttler smacks a short delivery that really should have found the boundary straight to Khawaja to leave England 124 for five. 'Buttler should have hit that 20 rows back,' says a rueful Isa Guha.

Woakes does his best to accompany Stokes and the two add 50 in quick time, leaving Mann and Marks to majestically apply the curse to the England innings. 'You sense a bit of optimism around Lord's now,' Mann says, with Vic (attempting to cosset his curse by referencing the crowd) adding, 'You can sense the crowd are just beginning to think something might be on the cards ...'

That is the perfect cue for Starc to thunder a virtually perfect delivery into the base of Stokes's off stump, causing the all-rounder to drop his bat and then kick it away in frustration as he tried to jam down on the yorker. 'What a ripper!' yells Jim Maxwell, gleefully reaching for his catchphrase for the first time this summer in a tussle between England and Australia.

Moeen goes quickly and, while Adil Rashid provides a touch more resistance, it is all over with more than five overs left for England; Behrendorff – who Zaltzman disconsolately points out had just eight wickets in seven ODIs before today – collecting his five-fer on the way as they slump to a 64-run defeat. 'You wonder what damage this will do to England's confidence,' says Michael Vaughan. 'They had a brain freeze in that chase against Sri Lanka. But this is a hammering. This is on the big stage, in front of 28,000, all the England fans had come to see the comeback.'

Australia have become the first team to secure their place in the semi-finals, but for England it is little short of a disaster. 'England haven't felt that bristling presence today that they've treated us to for the last four years,' admits Aggers. 'They made everyone think they were invincible – but that's not their fate today.'

'I don't think England looked on it for the first 15 overs,' adds Vaughan. 'I don't think they looked the same England side in the warm-ups. They looked a team that arrived today knowing they could lose the game. I've not seen that for a few years.'

'Poor,' says Stewie, clearly wounded with what is described off air as a 'patriot's disappointment'. 'Very poor. It almost wasn't a contest. It felt bigger than a 64-run defeat.'

On the other side, the Aussies are buoyant. 'Australia just continue to grow in this tournament,' says Maxwell, plainly anticipating a long, successful English summer ahead of him. 'I think today they got their bowling better than in any other game.'

From a *TMS* point of view, it's a very long day. Oftentimes, the drama and elation the game can create will make time fly by. That is not the case today, with many parts of the BBC keen to discuss England's gloomy World Cup outlook long into the night. Therefore, after a 7 a.m. arrival, Michael Vaughan and Alec Stewart are still in the box at 8 p.m. discussing the importance of tomorrow's clash between Pakistan and New Zealand and England's trip to Birmingham on Sunday to play India.

Australia 285-7 (50 overs; Finch 100, Warner 53) beat England 221 (44.4 overs; Stokes 89, Behrendorff 5-44, Starc 4-43) by 64 runs.

Tuesday 25 June
England v West Indies – Women's T20 series – Match 3
The County Ground, Derby

Team *TMS*: Henry Moeran, Natalie Germanos, Ebony Rainford-Brent, Danielle Hazell

A return to *TMS* for Danni Hazell who is seeking to make her commentary debut for the second time after her previous efforts were wiped out by rain in Northampton last week. Sadly for her, conditions are, if anything, even worse than they were a week ago, and play is once again called off without a ball being bowled.

Match abandoned.

●

Wednesday 26 June
New Zealand v Pakistan – ICC Cricket World
Cup – Match 33
Edgbaston, Birmingham

Team *TMS*: Charles Dagnall, Bryan Waddle, Natalie Germanos, Jeremy
Coney, Ramiz Raja, Graeme Swann, Andy Zaltzman

After overnight rain there is a slightly delayed start and an
unseasonal chill in the air in Birmingham this morning.
However, the chill is certainly not enough to justify Jeremy
Coney's arrival in a scarf and a beanie. 'I had my hat on in
the car as I couldn't get the heating going, but it is cold!'
he argues after being immediately upbraided as soon as he
gets on air. 'If a New Zealander says it's chilly you know it
is a bit icy.'

This is a huge game for both sides. A win for New Zealand
will put them through to the semis; a win for Pakistan is
critical for their chances of advancement and would also
make England's life even more difficult. The crowd is almost
entirely behind Pakistan, and they get going very quickly as
Martin Guptill, Colin Munro and Ross Taylor are all dismissed inside the first ten overs. There are further positive
signs for Pakistan as Munro is taken cleanly at slip, causing
Ramiz Raja – who once again is working for a number of
different media outlets (leading to occasional moments of
high farce as different producers battle to locate him ahead
of a scheduled commentary stint on their network) – to

sarcastically announce, 'It is an event! A catch has been taken by Pakistan!'

When Taylor goes shortly afterwards, the great man rises instinctively from his seat to hail a glorious catch from Sarfaraz Ahmed, who makes a tumbling dive to his right-hand side after anticipating an outside edge. 'Magnificent! Magical! Sarfaraz with the full-length dive and this is up there with the best catches of the World Cup,' he says. 'Brilliant anticipation!'

'This is not what you want to see as an England fan!' adds Charles Dagnall nervously.

It all gets quite familiar as Tom Latham is caught behind, leaving a heavy weight once again resting on the shoulders of Kane Williamson. Chants of 'Pakistan! Zindabad!' are rocking the ground, and Graeme Swann – who has plenty of experience of a raucous Edgbaston – says, 'The noise in this ground when Pakistan take a wicket is phenomenal! I thought it was loud at Edgbaston during the Ashes but it's nothing on this.'

Any remaining rafters are ravaged when Williamson gets 'a villainous little edge' (Jeremy Coney) off Shadab Khan through to Sarfaraz, but the New Zealand innings is salvaged by Jimmy Neesham and Colin de Grandhomme adding 132 for the sixth wicket in just 21.2 overs. Their final total of 237 for six is particularly impressive given Andy Zaltzman's excellent observation that 'Their score of 94 for five after 30 overs is comfortably the lowest score at that stage so far in this tournament.'

Charles Dagnall thinks it's a winning total, Graeme Swann thinks it's a good total from where they were and Bryan Waddle and Jeremy Coney, constitutions already shredded from the numerous close shaves their side has experienced in recent weeks, are just very nervous. Pakistan start positively but lose Fakhar

Zaman in the third over. However, a star-making knock from Babar Azam guides them to one of the more famous wins in their recent history.

It is a brilliantly managed chase, with Pakistan adopting a game plan to bat out the overs and trust that will be enough to reach the 238 runs required. New Zealand are committed in the field and accurate with the ball, with Williamson generating yet another 'World Cup moment' by bringing himself on and taking a wicket in his first over of the tournament. Such is the tension generated during the chase that the knowledgeable Pakistan fans even cheer dead-batted defensive prods, to the great amusement of Ramiz Raja in the commentary box. However, Babar and Haris Sohail hit 126 together from 23.4 overs to secure the win. Zaltzman hits the nail on the head when he reveals that 35 runs came off their first ten overs together before the pair added a further 91 from the subsequent 13.4 overs.

It is a blow for New Zealand, but Coney is characteristically sanguine, easily admitting that 'Pakistan have deserved this.' They have now mirrored the results from the 1992 World Cup for seven consecutive games – and there is a significant momentum building behind their candidacy for a semi-final spot. 'Pakistan are like a snowball, rolling down that mountain . . .' says Swann. Dagnall adds, 'This really does blow this World Cup wide open,' before adding, with the combined verve of a quality broadcaster and a massive cricket fan, 'This is a really wonderful couple of weeks coming up. It's wide open.'

New Zealand 237-6 (50 overs; Neesham 97*, de Grandhomme 64) lost to Pakistan 241-4 (49.1 overs; Azam 101*, Sohail 68) by six wickets.

Thursday 27 June
West Indies v India – ICC Cricket World Cup – Match 34
Old Trafford, Manchester

Team *TMS*: Prakash Wakankar, Fazeer Mohammad, Isa Guha, Simon
Mann, James Anderson, Ebony Rainford-Brent, Sir Curtly Ambrose,
Andy Zaltzman

'I don't think West Indies have any chance of reaching the
semi-finals. I don't think it's even a slim chance,' says Sir
Curtly Ambrose as *TMS* get under way with Match 34 on
Day 29 of the World Cup. While the great man is expressing
an opinion, it is mathematically very unlikely that he's going
to be wrong.

In front of another overwhelmingly Indian crowd, Virat
Kohli chooses to bat first and his side produce a very steady
innings, with only Hardik Pandya scoring at more than a run
a ball. 'I experienced this atmosphere on a number of occasions
in India, but not in Manchester!' comments Jimmy Anderson.
'It's an amazing atmosphere. Even walking to the ground, the
sea of blue was phenomenal.' However, he adds with an air of
warning, 'This is a good indicator of how Edgbaston will be on
Sunday for the England game.'

Ebony Rainford-Brent agrees, adding, 'I am nervous a little
bit for England, I have to say. When you turn up for an India
match the ground is packed with their fans, and the whole
dynamic, the whole pressure, shifts a little bit.'

Pleasingly, there has been a breakthrough with the
incredibly vigilant ICC security regime to such an extent

that today sees the box garlanded with a wonderful 'Tailenders' cake, courtesy of listener Julie Hall. Not only is the cake delicious, it is decorated with edible versions of Greg, Felix and Jimmy and includes the show's 'Go Well ...' '... Cheers!' catchphrase and its patented hashtag: #tailendersoftheworlduniteandtakeover.

Hopefully it is a sign of a more delicious end to a World Cup that, thus far, has been disappointingly light in baked goods – at least for the *TMS* box (the ICC security guards have allegedly been spotted wiping their mouths sheepishly in the presence of *TMS* personnel).

Kohli continues in the theme of his World Cup so far, looking entirely untroubled before guiding an attempted pull straight to mid-wicket on 72, causing silence to break out for the first time all day. 'This is the first time since 2011 that Virat Kohli has failed four times in a row to convert a fifty into a century,' adds Zaltzman, proving he is more clinical with a stat this World Cup than Kohli is with the bat.

After his previous upbraiding of the entire attack, Sir Curtly is also pleased to see the West Indies bowlers produce a more controlled display, with Jason Holder bowling 46 dots during his ten overs as they restrict India to 268 for seven. The highlight of the innings is the final over, with M.S.Dhoni rolling the clock back by taking 16 runs, including a massive six into Old Trafford's gaping temporary stand from the final ball.

'I think we're in for a thriller,' says Ebony Rainford-Brent, who is due to be replaced in the summariser's chair by Sir Curtly Ambrose for the start of the West Indies innings. However, Ambrose – normally a picture of reliability – is not back in time to start his stint. Given the West Indies have put in one of their better bowling efforts of the tournament thus far, it is even more of a surprise. Eventually, a long arm pushes open the door of the commentary box, allowing a large Antiguan frame to stoop through it apologetically and head straight for the microphones. 'Let me apologise for being a bit late back. I was mobbed by the fans as I went outside,' he says brilliantly.

The West Indies chase does not start well as the 'Universe Boss' Chris Gayle goes first and Shai Hope follows quickly afterwards. The game is very slow going, but it's anything but in the box as former India captain, and 1983 World Cup winner, Kris Srikkanth joins *TMS*. His punditry style can best be described as 'caffeinated, bordering on the chaotic', but he is tremendous fun to have in the box and hugely enlivens what is turning into an uncharacteristically dull and utterly unsuccessful chase for the West Indies.

They reach 71 for two, but that is their highest of hopes and the innings quickly falls apart after that, descending to 143 all out and a 125-run defeat – another thrashing. 'India look ruthless, ready to win,' says Rainford-Brent, as all eyes turn to Sunday.

Having dispatched the bowlers previously, the West Indian efforts during the chase have built Ambrose back up to his bristling best and he returns to the airwaves for the reckoning, lining up to take down the other half of his national team. 'The batting was really poor,' he begins. 'Nobody got in and tried to get a big innings, they got out in a soft manner. West Indians in this team are big hitters and if they can't hit fours and sixes, they can't rotate the strike. You can't come into a game and expect to just wallop every ball to the boundary. If they continue like this, they are never going to improve.

'West Indies have a mindset that they are a power-hitting team and when it's not working for them, they can't manipulate the scores. They need to change their mentality and throw away this foolish notion. Anyone can hit a six or four, but the smarter teams manage to keep the scoring rate going.

Unless they change that notion, they will never be a force to reckon with.'

India 268-7 (50 overs; Kohli 72, Dhoni 56*) beat West Indies 143 (34.2 overs; Shami 4-16) by 125 runs.

●

Friday 28 June
Sri Lanka v South Africa – ICC Cricket World
Cup – Match 35
Chester-le-Street, Durham

Team *TMS*: Natalie Germanos, Charles Dagnall, Scott Read, Pommie Mbangwa, Mel Jones, Paul Farbrace, Phil Long

When the structure for the 2019 World Cup was revealed some time ago, it was pointed out that there were liable to be some dead rubbers at the end of the tournament. Today, in Durham, sees the first. While an Oxbridge mathematician could come up with a formula that sees Sri Lanka making the semi-finals, realistically it is not going to happen. South Africa are long gone, to great lamentations back home – and indeed in England, where their lack of quality has robbed this World Cup of one of its traditional gladiators.

Although the match action is in Chester-le-Street, today's off-field attention has been firmly centred on a primary school in south London where Jonny Bairstow has been conducting interviews after helping with a children's cricket session. He is clearly upset with the tone of the coverage that surrounds

191

England at the moment and he comments, 'People were waiting for us to fail. They are not willing us on to win, in many ways, they are waiting for you to get that loss, so they can jump on your throat. It's a typical English thing to do, in every sport.'

Eyebrows have been raised around the country, and among the highest of those have been from *TMS*'s Michael Vaughan, who took to his Instagram account to say, 'How wrong can Jonny Bairstow be ... Never has England team had so much support but it's you and your team that has disappointed Jonny ... WIN 2 games and you are in the semis ... With this negative, pathetic mindset I am concerned though ... it's not the media's fault you have lost 3 games ... !!!'

The syntax of his comments read better on social media than on the printed page, but nonetheless, the blue touch-paper has been lit ahead of Sunday. Back in Durham, Sri Lanka become the latest side to lose a wicket first ball and succeed only in posting 203 all out from 49.3 overs. Former England and Sri Lanka coach Paul Farbrace is back on *TMS* today and at the fall of the third wicket puts his finger on it when he simply says that 'Thirties don't win matches.'

The comment is made when Kusal Perera is dismissed for exactly 30, and no Sri Lankan batsman is able to score any more than that. Sri Lanka's timidity allows a good World Cup stat to crop up, and Phil Long does not miss out on the chance to point out that 'Dwaine Pretorius's three for 25 off 10 overs is the most economical spell of the Cricket World Cup.'

As South Africa wheel away with the ball, one of the World Cup's thorniest conundrums is solved by African duo Pommie Mbangwa and Natalie Germanos, both of whom have been holding seminars for commentators still struggling to pronounce the name of Andile Phehlukwayo. Mbangwa produces a slip of paper with PET-LOOK-WHY-OH written on it, generating great nodding of heads and silent mouthing of words from all around him.

The Sri Lankan innings is rolling to a nondescript end when suddenly something extraordinary happens, and all the players immediately drop to the floor in a 'synchronised belly flop' (Scott Read), lying flat on their stomachs. Only South Africa captain Faf du Plessis is still stood up. Initially, there is utter confusion until it quickly becomes clear that a swarm of bees has briefly engulfed the playing area.

'Should we shut the window?' asks Paul Farbrace before answering his own question and doing it himself, just in case. 'Not one spectator was stretched or bothered, and yet all the players were on the ground,' he later points out. 'There must have been some people wondering what on earth was going on! If you're new to that game, you'd go home going, "Not only do they stop for a drink, but halfway through the game they all lay down! Stressful game, cricket!"'

South Africa lose Quinton de Kock early on, but it is remarkably plain sailing after that, Hashim Amla rolling back the years to hit a patient 80 not out and du Plessis showing what might have been with 96 not out. 'It's not been a thriller,' admits Daggers, adding, 'South Africa have shown how to knock off a low total. They haven't been expansive, but they've been positive and pushed singles.'

There is now one less challenger for the last semi-final spot, and with Pakistan and New Zealand both playing tomorrow, England will have a much better idea of what situation awaits them on Sunday.

Sri Lanka 203 (49.3 overs) lost to South Africa 206-1 (37.2 overs; du Plessis 96*, Amla 80*) by nine wickets.

●

Saturday 29 June
Pakistan v Afghanistan – ICC Cricket World
Cup – Match 36
Headingley, Leeds

Team *TMS*: Fazeer Mohammad, Daniel Norcross, Alison Mitchell, Ebony Rainford-Brent, Ramiz Raja, James Anderson, Mel Jones, Phil Long

Today is the 31st day of the Cricket World Cup and if anyone on the Headingley end of the *TMS* team are starting to flag, the passionate din that awaits them inside the ground should put a stop to that. Despite a horrendous start, Pakistan are still very much alive in the competition, and such is the desire of their fans to get inside the ground for this match, two members of the *TMS* team were walking in the concourses when they saw a pair of Pakistan fans vaulting over the wall of the ground, landing perfectly on two electrical boxes on the other side before leaping off and running into the Kirkstall Lane End concourse.

The fevered atmosphere in the box is pierced by the famously dry wit of Kevin Howells, who is not on air today but is producing the game. Shortly before the action gets under way, he warns the commentators that 'I was once given a compliment – and it was the precursor to a lot of criticism. So be aware, if I give you a compliment it's likely to lead to criticism.'

Statistician Phil Long looks forlorn before replying, 'God, I've been doing a terrible job for you!'

Afghanistan bat first and Daniel Norcross comments that the cricketarist (a man with a guitar made out of a cricket bat who plays the batsmen back and forth from the crease and has been present, in one incarnation or another, at every match) choosing to play the riff from 'The Passenger' by Iggy Pop is richly appropriate given the Afghan skipper's contribution to the tournament thus far. Shortly afterwards, he is dismissed by Shaheen Afridi for 15, the first wicket to fall.

Afridi gets rid of Hashmatullah next ball, with Ebony Rainford-Brent worrying that 'This ground is literally going to go up in smoke if he takes a hat trick; it's already on fire.' Mercifully for the sold-out crowd, the hat-trick ball goes for four leg byes, but Pakistan are on top early.

Similarly to Shaheen's hat-trick ball, the Afghan innings occasionally sizzles – mostly when the enticing Asghar Afghan is at the crease – but never ignites and Pakistan end up need-ing 228 to win and put even more pressure on England ahead of tomorrow.

Sadly, for the first time this World Cup, there has been another side to today's game, with Pakistan and Afghan fans briefly fighting outside the ground and, during the Afghanistan innings, a plane flying over the ground trailing a political mes-sage. *TMS* report on the events as they happen, reading out a statement from the ICC on air, but it is never an easy or pleas-ant thing to do and hopefully there will be no more trouble going forward.

As the Afghans come out to bowl, the team give a guard of honour to Hamid Hassan, who announced prior to the World Cup that he will be retiring from international cricket at the end of the tournament. However, the Afghans still have to play the West Indies next week. It is presumed that Hassan has already been told he's not playing then but, not for the first time where this World Cup and Afghanistan intersect, confusion reigns.

Fakhar Zaman goes LBW second ball of the innings, Pakistan losing their review in the process and England fans start sniffing a potentially advantageous upset. The Hassan confusion is then extended as he opens the bowling, bowls two average overs for 13 and is removed from the attack, never to be seen again.

Babar Azam and Imam-ul-Haq settle things down, but Afghanistan are bowling very well and Pakistan are definitely not having things all their own way, with Imam tied down and then stumped after a rush of blood to the head takes him far too far down the pitch. Babar follows in the next over, bowled by Mohammad Nabi, and then the next three Pakistan batsmen make starts but are cut off in their prime just as they are about to play the defining knock the innings requires.

Afghanistan are really turning the screw and Pakistan's No 7 Imad Wasim is struggling, to the extent that Alison Mitchell asks, 'How is Imad Wasim not out? He's a walking wicket out there.' Rashid Khan goes up for a huge appeal for LBW against him that is turned down but unreviewable due to a poor decision from Gulbadin earlier in the innings – it turns out it would have been plumb.

Sarfaraz Ahmed is run out to leave them six down and Ebony Rainford-Brent can immediately see the upset. 'Pressure does crazy things. What a huge, huge moment,' she says as Shadab Khan walks in with the hopes of an incredibly passionate nation riding on him. With just four wickets in the hutch, they need 71 from the final ten overs and, as the time remaining ticks away, it becomes clear that this is going to be another excruciatingly tight one.

The din from this morning, which has been unrelenting at every Pakistan match so far, quietens to create an incredibly tense hush inside Headingley. Could Pakistan, having beaten England and New Zealand, be throwing it away by losing to Afghanistan? Not only are there nerves from the attendant Pakistanis and Afghans, every England fan – including a number in the commentary box – is on the edge of their seats, knowing what an Afghanistan win would do to England's semi-final chances.

Then, despite having enough overs in hand from his prime bowlers Rashid Khan, Mujeeb Ur Rahman and Samiullah Shinwari, Gulbadin decides to bring himself back on to bowl. The over is an utter disaster, goes for 18 and swings the match right back into Pakistan's hands. 'A calamitous over for Afghanistan. A potentially calamitous over for England as well,' bemoans Daniel Norcross, passionately wringing out the tension. Gulbadin then somewhat makes up for his bowling with a lovely piece of work to run out Shadab Khan, and Pakistan need 18 off 18 balls.

A superb turn from Mujeeb makes it 16 from 12 and the hush suddenly descends again as the upset is back on. Wahab Riaz, as he has done before this World Cup, throws caution to the wind and smacks Rashid Khan for a huge six before, to the utter astonishment of Mel Jones, tickling an audacious reverse sweep for a single. It's six off the last over for Pakistan to win.

Then, to overwhelming amazement from the entire ground, Gulbadin brings himself back on for the final over. His first ball is a full toss that somehow only goes for a single and his second is a mile down the leg side, but such is the heave that Wahab aims at the delivery, he somehow manages to get a glove on it to turn a wide into another single. Norcross, doing his best to take the listeners through this madness, is audibly stunned. 'At this stage everyone's brain is melted,' he says, almost laughing, such is the level of Gulbadin's decision-making. The next ball goes for a single, a poor throw from mid-on meaning the Afghans miss out on a sure-fire run-out.

Finally, the inevitable comes to pass as Gulbadin's fourth ball is another rank full toss. This time, Imad Wasim (who would have been long gone had the review not been burnt early on) thrashes it through the covers to secure the win for Pakistan.

A crazy scene is further enhanced by an unwelcome mass pitch invasion and it quickly becomes clear that there are not enough stewards to protect the players and the camera crews as they try to exit the pitch. Given the events earlier and the plane flying overhead, there is serious concern for some of the players' welfare, farcically confounded when one of the stewards who has made it onto the field mistakes Mohammad Nabi for a pitch invader and briefly tries to take him out.

Pakistan have the win, in their true fashion, and have climbed above England in the table, having played one more game. England's game in hand is tomorrow and it's against India. What a World Cup this is.

Afghanistan 227-9 (50 overs; Afridi 4-47) lost to Pakistan 230-7 (49.4 overs) by three wickets.

Saturday 29 June
New Zealand v Australia – ICC Cricket World Cup – Match 37
Lord's Cricket Ground, St John's Wood, London

Team *TMS*: Simon Mann, Jim Maxwell, Bryan Waddle, Jeremy Coney, Phil Tufnell, Isa Guha, Andy Zaltzman

Meanwhile, at Lord's, New Zealand are looking to finalise their semi-final spot by defeating an Australia side that have been growing ever more rampant over the past fortnight. Australia bat first and lose both Aaron Finch and David Warner inside the first ten overs – and Steve Smith follows them soon afterwards – Martin Guptill making amends for a couple of early drops with a magnificent snare 'around the corner' on the leg side to give New Zealand an early advantage.

'We have seen some magnificent catches in this tournament, but I think that is the best,' says Simon Mann, ranking it above efforts from Ben Stokes, Quinton de Kock, Sheldon Cottrell and Imran Tahir, all of which would have been worthy winners in their own right. 'WOW!' shouts Tuffers, again briefly rendered onomatopoeic by the quality of what he has seen unfold in front of him.

The great Allan Border drops in again and is in a very good mood. Firstly, he offers a positive take on the Australian position, saying that 'The top order was always going to miss out at some stage. This might be the test that Australia need.' Bearing in mind their semi-final spot is in the bag, the great man may have a point. He then claims that Australia have a '70 per cent chance' of winning this World Cup, which is a bold position to hold. Glenn Maxwell is also victim to a classic catch, Jimmy Neesham taking a sprawling caught and bowled from a shot that Jeremy Coney calls 'a cue-ender' and leaves Usman Khawaja and Alex Carey with some lifting to do.

Away from the cricket, there is all sorts going on elsewhere this weekend, with the Boston Red Sox and New York Yankees across town for the first Major League Baseball games to be played in England, and also, 125 miles west, the Glastonbury Festival is under way, attendance at which is certainly a more enticing prospect to Isa Guha than it is to Simon Mann, as their on-air discussion makes abundantly clear.

Carey goes for a well-made 71, Jeremy Coney throwing out a gloriously mixed metaphor when asked whether the dismissal will help New Zealand keep Australia to a gettable total. 'The horse has bolted,' he says, adding, 'I think when you get a team like Australia down, you must keep the foot on the throat.'

It's 241 for six going into the last over, which is entrusted to Trent Boult. Khawaja is bowled by the third ball, Mitchell Starc from the fourth and Jason Behrendorff plumb LBW from the fifth. The drama is slightly spoilt by Behrendorff pointlessly attempting to review the decision, but when red lights duly fill the boxes, the World Cup has its second hat trick.

'It makes you think that Boult could have come on at 92 for five. I think Williamson missed a wee trick there,' suggests Coney, well knowing that chasing 244 will not be straightforward and wondering whether New Zealand applying their star bowler earlier could have paid dividends.

While professionalism and commentary are maintained at all times, the start of the New Zealand innings is somewhat overshadowed by events at Headingley. Tuffers, in theory preparing to provide analysis, is in reality rooted to the spot at the back of the box, unable to find a picture or radio stream to follow events in Leeds, so is therefore reduced to simply repeating what people tell him, at twice the volume.

'GULBADIN?!'

'A FULL TOSS?!'

'OH! NOT ANOTHER ONE?!'

'NO! OH DEAR, THERE WE GO!'

When the Pakistan victory is confirmed, there is a general acceptance that England's recent form has not entitled them to do anything the easy way – and in any case, they now know that they simply need to win four consecutive matches against the best sides in the world to win the World Cup. When you put it like that it seems reasonable, and even, maybe, doable.

Back at Lord's, New Zealand lose Tim Nicholls – brought in to replace Colin Munro – cheaply, which sets the tone for their innings. Other than the inevitable resistance from Kane Williamson, they fold for just 157. Not only that, but legitimate concerns about their eventual run rate cause them to do so over the course of 43.1 overs, hardly offering a capacity crowd a very good show. It's a disappointing outcome for New Zealand, especially coming out so spectacularly on the wrong end of a trans-Tasman rivalry that Jeremy Coney says has always 'felt like you're playing an older brother that used to take you into his bedroom and give you a good old sharp punch'.

At 92 for two, requiring approximately a run a ball, and with Williamson and Ross Taylor at the crease, it felt possible for New Zealand. As has happened many times in the past though, Mitchell Starc and Pat Cummins made the key breakthroughs and it all went south pretty quickly afterwards. Chuckling to himself at his own dad joke, Tuffers delightedly says that it is 'more like a "run walk" than a run chase'.

Shortly before Starc completes a brutal five-fer, Coney – reflecting on his team's performance – thinks that 'There's been an element of self-abuse in the dismissals.' It's a wonderful expression from a superb commentator and, with New Zealand having such a dramatic World Cup, *TMS* are very lucky to have such a high-class Kiwi summariser to turn to. Australia have won five in a row and look extremely dangerous. New Zealand still have work to do. England are now playing knockout cricket. You've got to love the World Cup, haven't you?

Australia 243-9 (50 overs; Khawaja 88, Carey 71, Boult 4-51) beat New Zealand 157 (43.4 overs; Starc 5-26) by 86 runs.

CHAPTER 10

Bairstow Hits Back

Sunday 30 June
England v India – ICC Cricket World Cup – Match 38
Edgbaston, Birmingham

Team *TMS*: Jonathan Agnew, Prakash Wakankar, Daniel Norcross,
Michael Vaughan, Vic Marks, Isa Guha, Andy Zaltzman

With games yesterday in London and Leeds, it is a weary but adrenalised *TMS* team that assembles in Birmingham, late on Saturday night. Team Leeds are there first, allowing Daniel Norcross to purchase eight celebratory glasses of Baileys to herald the arrival of Team London at the hotel. They are gratefully sunk before a short rest ahead of the biggest game this World Cup has produced so far.

TMS arrive at the ground early, but there is still a hustle around the neighbourhood that makes it very clear something huge is happening here today. The loud boos that ring out after Eoin Morgan wins the toss and chooses to bat underscore suspicions that, despite Edgbaston's reputation for creating a nationalistic English cauldron, the crowd today will very largely be of an Indian bent.

'This feels like the biggest white-ball game England have played since the World Cup final in 1992,' says Aggers after welcoming listeners. 'It feels more like Bangalore than Birmingham,' he admits. 'I can see one England flag. The rest is a sea of Indian blue.'

There is confident Indian patriotism in the *TMS* box too, with Prakash Wakankar declaring to all and sundry that India are already through and their only purpose today is to destroy English hopes. Ire could be raised by such rags being offered, but the glint in Prakash's eye is large enough that it's impossible to take him too seriously, and he knows it.

The toss also reveals the answer to one of the more pressing questions of the past few days; Jason Roy is fit again and back in the side. It is a huge boost for players, fans and commentators alike. Further to this, there is a first start in a little while for Liam Plunkett, who is selected over Moeen Ali, a selection Michael Vaughan is slightly suspicious of.

Roy and this week's media assailant Jonny Bairstow walk out to open the batting and it's immediately clear what England have been missing as Roy rockets a boundary square through the off-side in the opening over. 'Welcome back, Jason Roy. We have missed you,' says Aggers with what is almost a nostalgic pang in his tone, even though the opener has only been gone for 16 days. 'You can just see Roy has the swagger. That is what England have lacked in the last couple of games,' adds Vaughan – and it is clear just what an intangible lift the Surrey opener gives this England side.

Bairstow looks less immediately confident at the other end, surviving a LBW shout in Jasprit Bumrah's first over, but the pair settle well and find the boundary with regularity throughout the powerplay overs. Graeme Swann replaces Vaughan and immediately goes in hard on the big selection decision of the day, taking a stand on behalf of his fellow off-spinner. 'Why on earth do England not have two spinners?' he asks. 'I do not see why Moeen Ali is the fall guy. He has been one of the reasons they have been so successful over the last four years.'

Roy then appears to get a slight glove on a Hardik Pandya delivery that goes down the leg side and, despite a strangled appeal, Virat Kohli opts not to review the not-out decision. When replays quickly reveal a small spike on the UltraEdge, it is clear Roy has been handed a second life and he immediately capitalises. 'The four deliveries Hardik Pandya bowled after he should have got the wicket of Jason Roy went for six, four, four, four,' Zaltzman points out soon afterwards. 'That is a shot of a guilty man. Lovely!' cackles Swann as England start to pick up the pace.

Bairstow starts to find his range too, bringing up the England hundred in just the 15th over, narrowly clearing K.L.Rahul on the boundary. 'It was close to a "why did he do that?" moment,' says Vic – but with Jason and Jonny back together at the top of the order, everyone is suddenly beginning to feel a bit more relaxed. Such is the partnership that is being built, for the first time in this World Cup the noise of the collected mass of India fans is being subdued. Pockets of seats appear as concession stands are sought out and horns are stowed. The England contingent even start to make themselves heard, cheering loudly as sixes continue to be struck with impunity.

Appropriately enough, given the battalion of maximums he has accrued this morning, Roy is dismissed for 66 to a superb catch from sub-fielder Ravi Jadeja. 'You felt it would require something special,' says a now slightly more subdued Wakankar. Bairstow continues undimmed and it's not long before Vaughan, his combatant of recent days, is lavishing him with praise. 'What an innings this has been from Jonny Bairstow,' says his fellow

Yorkshireman. 'This is what he can produce with a bit of fire in his belly.'

He reaches his century and, despite his protestations of last week, does not go 'full Nasser' as some have suggested, referencing the famous three-fingered salute offered to the press box by the then England captain in 2002, after disparaging questions about his ability to bat the position. 'A remarkable knock,' adds Vaughan, before adding, 'It's quite a muted celebration,' possibly slightly relieved that Bairstow has opted against making an angrier point.

England reach 200 in the 29th over, only the second team to reach the landmark before 30 overs in this World Cup, after Bangladesh did so against the West Indies – around the time Sir Curtly Ambrose was achieving 'full meltdown'. However, the India bowlers tighten up their lines and Bairstow is suddenly quelled. The slow-up in the scoring rate causes him to reach for the heave and he is caught at cover. 'It was on the cards, you could see it coming for the last 15 to 20 minutes,' admits Norcross.

Eoin Morgan comes and goes very quickly and the nerves that were prevalent at 10.25 suddenly resurface. Zaltzman reveals that overs 27 to 37 went for just 25 runs, with no boundaries, and Vic Marks says, 'You've got to give some credit to India for seizing the opportunity after those wickets and putting the squeeze on.'

Ben Stokes is a man in form, though, and hits an extraordinary six, changing the momentum of the innings at a stroke. Since Zaltzman's interjection about the slow scoring rate, England take 36 from four overs, although the India seamers are proving harder work than their spinners. Bearing in mind England selected Plunkett over Moeen, that may not prove to be a bad thing in the long run. Joe Root goes, but Jos Buttler plays very well in the limited time allowed and England reach 337 for seven. A chase of 338 would be the highest ever in a World Cup, but it's a measure of the Indian batting talent that Aggers only describes it as 'a challenging target' and very much does not rule them out.

To complement the cricketing excitement, there is an absolute crackerjack of a guest lined up for the innings break as Aggers is joined by Google CEO Sundar Pichai. As if any further points of emphasis were required to demonstrate the size of today's game, Sundar is one of the most influential men on the planet, running one of the biggest brands in the world. His firm employs nearly 100,000 people, is used by a large portion of the global population every day and is worth nearly $1 trillion. And he has flown over eight time zones to be here, just for this game.

Originally from Chennai, Sundar reveals that his introduction to cricket came via street cricket and short-wave radio in the late 1970s and early 1980s, listening to the great Brian Johnston describe iconic players like West Indian fast bowler Michael Holding. 'Short-wave radio brought the world to my house,' he tells Aggers, while dressed in a casual grey jumper and slacks. Were it not for the abnormal amount of heavies posted near the *TMS* box, you'd have no idea who he was.

Usually when Sundar submits himself to interviews by journalists, he will receive terrifically informed questions about the multifarious aspects of his business, the influence of big tech on the psyche of the world or any other intricate aspects of the Silicon Valley scene. At the start of today's interview, less so.

'Is it is possible to explain to someone who has absolutely no idea ... like me ... how the hell it works?' asks Agnew, to laughter from the rest of the box and an amused smile from Sundar, who replies with a wonderfully succinct answer about copying websites and using databases to match search terms with useful information. As the interview continues, Aggers grows in cyber confidence, eliciting a fascinating response from the tech titan when he asks what he thinks our phones will be doing in ten years' time. Will they literally be running our lives?

'I hope not,' Sundar replies, to Agnew's surprise. 'I always think technology should fade in the background over time and be there when you need it. Today phones aren't smart enough; they demand too much of your attention. It's not aware of what you're doing. Maybe you're with your kids and it shouldn't be disturbing you?'

The final part of his response is *TMS* at its finest, as the man who runs Google continues, 'I hope technology gets better, less distracting and puts humans first. We all need to work to get there,' before concluding, without taking a breath, 'Ah-ha, here are the cakes!'

For not only has Sundar come all the way from San Francisco, he's brought cakes with him. A whole tray of cupcakes in fact, all of which have the word 'Googly' written on them in perfect Google branding. 'Google is the only place where "googly" means something other than what people in cricket mean it as,' he laughs before disappearing down the corridor with Aggers, the man who earns $200 million a year nervously steeling himself to meet his childhood hero Sunil Gavaskar for the first time.

Rohit Sharma, currently in a Bradmanesque run of form, and K.L.Rahul emerge to herald the start of the Indian chase and Edgbaston explodes as Chris Woakes finds Sharma's outside edge in the second over. The nick flies straight to Root at second slip, goes into his chest and bounces straight out again. As soon as the ball hits the turf the ground explodes again, combined in two kinds of disbelief: jubilant for the Indians and agape for the English. If England go on to lose this game and don't make the semi-finals, it is a moment that will be replayed time and time again.

Woakes lifts the mood by removing Rahul with a tumbling caught and bowled and, as Kohli and Sharma inhabit the crease together, Vaughan concisely sums it up as 'Here is the game.' The two start to settle and, after seeing off the rest of Woakes's superb spell, build what can only be described as an 'ominous' partnership. 'We have got a good game on,' says Victor.

While the two Indian greats are able to resist English efforts, the bowling is relentlessly good and India start to fall well behind the rate. 'Rohit is just not himself today. He is not timing the ball,' says a worried Prakash shortly before Kohli brings up his fifty, his fifth consecutive half-century, to deafening roars from the assembled masses. As the innings approaches the halfway mark, Vaughan articulates the feelings of a nation when he worries that 'India are gradually sneaking their way back into this,' before upgrading it a couple of overs later to: 'I am officially nervous.'

Morgan calls for Plunkett, who has two habits that could prove terrifically useful to the situation in hand. Firstly, he frequently takes wickets in the middle overs. Secondly, he does seem to specialise in getting out high-profile, world-class batsmen. Thus far in the World Cup, he has dismissed: Quinton de Kock, Hashim Amla, Mushfiqur Rahim and Chris Gayle.

From the third ball of the over, Plunkett strikes. Kohli tries to cart a slower ball to the boundary but doesn't get over it, and James Vince, fielding in place of Roy who took a blow to the hand while batting, takes the catch. The ground falls silent, except for the *TMS* box, where Isa Guha says the dismissal is 'huge in the context of this game' and Vaughan, ever the captain, exhorts England to focus on removing Sharma too because then 'that could be game, set and match'.

Rishabh Pant is the new man, but although no more wickets fall immediately, England are able to turn the screw and dry up the runs, slowly raising the rate required to ten an over. Prakash is back on air and taking great joy in winding up England fans who are contacting the programme to explain how stressful they are finding this situation. 'You can't relax? Come on. England are in the driving seat,' he smiles, knowing full well what he's doing.

Rohit brings up a magnificent hundred, off 106 balls, and it is clear that he is the key wicket for England. A brief respite is provided by Pant swinging so hard at a delivery from Mark Wood that his bat flies out of his hands and almost travels further than the ball, but with time running out England are holding their nerve and staying on top. Woakes then produces the biggest moment of England's World Cup so far by putting down a slower ball, wide of the off stump, that Sharma tries to hit all the way to Coventry. He gets a noisy nick on it and the ball flies to Buttler, who takes a smart, head-high catch to end Sharma's innings and lighten the load on English dispositions.

'That is absolutely the wicket England wanted!' explodes Swanny, continuing, 'You'd think now that England are in a comfortable position. Oh, hang on, Hardik Pandya is coming in ...'

Pandya bangs three consecutive fours off Wood, bringing the crowd back to their feet with more chants of 'India! India! India!' The chants get even louder when Pant hooks Plunkett into the leg side for what seems like a big six. However, Woakes comes flying round the fine leg boundary and flings himself full length, plucking the ball out of the air low to the ground. 'I don't believe what I have just seen!' roars Norcross as Woakes is mobbed by his team-mates. 'I tell you how good that catch was – I assumed it was Ben Stokes,' adds Swann, who then again preaches caution as M.S.Dhoni, whom he describes as 'the best finisher in the game', is next man in.

Bairstow turns a seemingly guaranteed four into a two with another astonishing stop on the boundary, causing Swann to cheekily reference Bairstow's comments from earlier in the week. 'He's even got us wanting them to win – and we don't like England, do we ... ?!'

One hundred and five are required from the last ten overs, which is a figure described by cricket commentators the world over as 'eminently gettable' in the modern game. However, in one of his finest moments, Zaltzman reveals that in the history of ODI cricket, only two sides needing over 100 in the last ten overs have ever won. Gasps of astonishment are audible in a box that had assumed such a thing was easily possible.

'England just have to win. They have to find a way of making sure India do not get these 90 runs. It's as simple as that,' says Vaughan as Pandya and Dhoni continue to find the boundary with concerning regularity. However, when Pandya gets under a slower ball from Plunkett, and Vince holds his nerve to take a steepler of a catch at long-on, pulses start to calm a little bit. They are helped by an odd display by Dhoni at the end of the innings. While the great man may well be in his cricketing dotage, it is a strange innings as he wanders between the creases, turning down runs and allowing the rate to grow to an unmanageable level.

Edgbaston starts to resemble a Premier League ground when the home team are 4-0 down with ten minutes to go, as India fans realise the game is up and head for the exits. Even the India coach, Ravi Shastri, turns his back on the game on the Indian balcony, as England's crucial 31-run victory – one of their most important in World Cup history – somehow feels like a bit of an anti-climax. 'That was a tremendous performance,' says a relieved and beaming Vaughan. 'Early on England looked different with Jason Roy walking out there, great body language.'

As Bairstow is named Man of the Match, Vaughan continues, 'Bairstow coped brilliantly with the pressure that he had brought on himself in the last few days. He let his bat do the talking today. He's better at that.'

While England are not entirely out of the woods, this victory is huge both for them and the competition. Pakistan's match with Bangladesh on Friday is critical. If Pakistan win that, then it seems like England will still have to beat New Zealand to guarantee their place.

England 337-7 (50 overs; Bairstow 111, Stokes 79, Roy 66, Shami 5-69) beat India 306-5 (50 overs; Sharma 102, Kohli 66, Plunkett 3-55) by 31 runs.

Monday 1 July
Sri Lanka v West Indies – ICC Cricket World
Cup – Match 39
Chester-le-Street, Durham

Team *TMS*: Fazeer Mohammad, Charles Dagnall, Simon Mann, Graeme Swann, Jeremy Coney, Sir Curtly Ambrose, Phil Long

Sadly for the passionate cricket fans of the north-east, today's second match at the picturesque Chester-le-Street ground is another dead rubber, with neither Sri Lanka nor West Indies in the semi-final picture. Fortunately for the sold-out crowd – and everyone associated with *TMS* today – the arrival of Sir Curtly Ambrose has coincided with a beautiful summery day. While it may not be Caribbean temperatures, were one of those really chilly Durham days to have materialised there is a very real chance that Ambrose would have simply refused to leave the hotel this morning. As it is, he's still not in the best of moods with the West Indies. 'Are they going to turn up and put in a big effort or just go through the motions?' he asks. 'I have no idea.'

Sri Lanka, who Jeremy Coney points out are yet to bat

through 50 overs or even make 250 during this World Cup, are asked to set a target. They start well. The West Indies players allow the frustrations of a World Cup campaign that has not gone to plan to get to them and bowl poorly, to Ambrose's obvious chagrin. The fielding is also slack, and Avishka Fernando takes full advantage to post the Sri Lankans' first century of the competition, hitting some mighty blows in his run-a-ball 104 as Sri Lanka bat through and post a highly competitive 338.

West Indies lose a couple of early wickets, but the 'Universe Boss' Chris Gayle raises the temperature with a pair of sixes and the chase is on. Nicholas Pooran hits a brilliant century, dragging the West Indies closer than they would have imagined when they were 199 for six in the 34th over, but it's not enough and they lose by 23 runs.

The chief incident during the second innings is when international pop star Rihanna is spotted in one of the hospitality boxes, supporting the West Indies. While she is from Barbados and went to school with Carlos Brathwaite, it's not the sort of thing you expect to see at a dead rubber in Durham!

Graeme Swann is also highly amused by the accidental positioning of the ground's ambulance. There to provide immediate assistance to anyone who may require it while at the ground, it is repeatedly struck by sixes during the West Indies chase, leading Swanny to suggest issuing a public health announcement that 'If you're injured or ill, don't go in that ambulance!'

At the end of the game, a frustrated Curtly is in the middle of summing up – 'West Indies have the knack of getting into good positions and not finishing the job and that's not going to work' – when Rihanna is seen entering the West Indies dressing room. She stays for a little while before emerging with a signed bat over her shoulder. The image rather sums up an unexpectedly enjoyable day, where a dead rubber became a rather enthralling cricket match.

Sri Lanka 338-6 (50 overs; Fernando 104, Perera 64, Thirimanne 54*, Holder 2-59) beat West Indies 315-9 (50 overs; Pooran 118, Allen 51, Malinga 3-55) by 23 runs.

CRICKETERS IN POP SONGS

In honour of Fernando's century, the presence of Rihanna in Chester-le-Street, and the recently concluded Glastonbury Festival, BBC Sport spent part of the West Indies' reply gathering cricketers as pop songs. Here is an XI selected from readers' suggestions. Sadly, there are only really 30 overs of bowling so it seems like Joe Root's off-spin and Michael Bevan's left-arm spin may be required. Fortunately, with former West Indian all-rounder Carl Hooper at ten, the team bats very low down indeed. Due to Rihanna's presence, there would be bonuses awarded for playing 'Shut Up and (Cover) Drive'.

Ed Sheeran – 'Finching out Loud'

Stormzy – 'Blinded by your WG Grace'

Stormzy – 'Big for Your Roots'

UB40 – 'Virat in my Kitchen'

Abba – 'Gimme! Gimme! Gimme! (Amla After Midnight)'

Olivia Newton-John and John Travolta – 'You're Dhawan That I Want'

Abba – 'Knowing Me, Knowing Younis Khan'

Abba – 'Fernando'

Led Zeppelin – 'Stairway to (Michael) Bevan'

Abba – 'SuperHooper'

The Beatles – 'Bret it Lee'

Tuesday 2 July
Bangladesh v India – ICC Cricket World Cup – Match 40
Edgbaston, Birmingham

Team *TMS*: Prakash Wakankar, Simon Mann, Daniel Norcross, Vic Marks,
Athar Ali Khan, Niall O'Brien, Andy Zaltzman

Another full house of full-throated Indians, who know that a victory for their team would mathematically secure a semi-final spot that has seemed guaranteed for some time. With scores of Bangladesh fans also expected in attendance – who have consistently rivalled the Indians for noise generation – this is going to be an atmospheric Tuesday in Birmingham.

Before any action gets under way, there are ruffled feathers in the commentary box as Simon Mann, who is very much *TMS*'s sustainability tsar, upbraids the team for the use of disposable coffee cups. This has largely been caused by the delicious coffee machine provided by *TMS*'s kind hosts, but nonetheless he has a very valid point and heads off upstairs to the catering area to speak to the staff about making the machine work with reusable porcelain cups.

India bat first, with any India fans tuning in delighted to hear Andy Zaltzman report that '11 of the last 14 games have been won by the team batting first'. An opening partnership of 180 in 29.2 overs, the largest opening partnership to date in the World Cup, is duly constructed, with Rohit Sharma once again benefiting from an easy drop early on before going on to make a century, his fourth in what is becoming a truly memorable World Cup for him.

At one stage it seems that India are going to score a mammoth total, but an early dismissal for Virat Kohli – the first time in six innings he hasn't made at least 50 – as well as a second-ball duck from Hardik Pandya, slow things down somewhat and they end on 314 for nine, the highlight of the final ten overs being when Prakash Wakankar informs the listeners that, outside of cricket, M.S.Dhoni's twin passions are motorcycles and dogs.

One thing that can be guaranteed on a visit to Edgbaston is the quality of catering. Daniel Norcross describes the ground as '*TMS*'s favourite restaurant in England' and today feasts on a smoked salmon starter, a main course of roast turkey and chicken karahi with chapatis and poppadums, a dessert that consists of nine profiteroles and two miniature cheesecakes, and in between meals snacks of more smoked salmon, prawns and a decent-sized cheeseboard.

With the team extremely well fed and watered and now taking the medicinal coffee (this is the 40th match of the Cricket World Cup and *TMS* has now been on air for 33 straight days) out of porcelain cups, the Bangladesh chase commences. As has too often been the case in this World Cup, they are too heavily reliant on Shakib Al Hasan. The great all-rounder hits 66 but struggles for support around him as his side loses consistent wickets throughout the chase and end, two overs remaining, at 286 all out.

Roushan Alam, as he has for the whole tournament, is covering Bangladesh for 5 Live and is stationed in the commentary box next door to *TMS*. Throughout the day, he has been engaged in an ongoing debate with Prakash Wakankar about his side's chances of victory. Every half-hour, Prakash enters the box and goads Roushan into a prediction – at one stage even giving the Bangladeshis' chances at 51 per cent. Shortly before the end of the match, Prakash pops in for a final guess. Alam offers up 1 per cent. 'I would halve that,' responds the Indian with a sly smile as he slinks back into the *TMS* box.

India are now confirmed in the semi-finals, while that's it for Bangladesh. They have been an absolute joy for the tournament, with extraordinary fans, one of the players of the World Cup in Shakib, and a fighting attitude that has seen them produce some hugely memorable moments. Sadly for them, though, the final spot in the World Cup semi-finals will now be taken by either England or Pakistan – and tomorrow's game is rather vital in that equation.

India 314-9 (50 overs; Sharma 104, Rahul 77, Mustafizur 5-59) beat Bangladesh 286 (48 overs; Shakib 66, Saifuddin 51*, Bumrah 4-55, Pandya 3-60) by 28 runs.

Tuesday 2 July
England Women v Australia Women – Women's
Ashes – Match 1
The Fischer County Ground, Leicester

Team *TMS*: Natalie Germanos, Ebony Rainford-Brent, Charlotte Edwards, Mel Jones, Lydia Greenway, Henry Moeran, Isabelle Westbury

Not only do we have the climax of the men's Cricket World Cup, the Women's Ashes starts today in Leicester, kicking off a summer of competition for England and Australia. As before, the Women's Ashes are decided by a points system over the course of matches in all three formats: ODI, T20 and one Test match. Today is the first of three ODIs and England will be hoping that their annihilation of the West Indies in the warm–up series bodes well for their chances – although Australia are a far more well-drilled and professional outfit than the slightly lackadaisical West Indian one England encountered earlier in the summer.

From a *TMS* point of view, it's a slightly different set-up to the World Cup. Commentators' WhatsApp groups have informed the Leicester branch of the programme of the culinary riches on offer at Edgbaston, so when *TMS* slide into a Portakabin affixed to the roof of Grace Road to set up the kit ready for broadcast, it's clear that it's going to be a very different experience!

Australia choose to field first, and with the England Lionesses playing the USA in the women's football World Cup semi-final tonight, it feels like a significant day for women's sport in this country. 'England need to put the West Indies series out of their mind. This series is going to be vastly different,' says Alison Mitchell shortly before the first ball is bowled, and within six overs she's proved horribly right as England slide to 19 for four, with Amy Jones, Tammy Beaumont, Sarah Taylor and the skipper Heather Knight, who falls for a golden duck, all accounted for already.

'This is a nightmare start for England; Australia are all over them,' says wide-eyed former England captain Charlotte Edwards on commentary, adding, 'There will be a bit of panic in the England changing room. They are not put in positions like this very often, so it is an unknown. They've all got to dig in now.'

All-rounder Natalie Sciver starts the repair job and England are very grateful to her as she makes 64 to help them post a defendable total of 177. The highlight, certainly for a very excitable Ebony Rainford-Brent, is a wonderful catch from Rachael Haynes to dismiss Anya Shrubsole, leaping high at mid-off and taking the ball left-handed above her head. 'I think that's the greatest catch I've ever seen in my life!' says Ebony, leaping to her feet, breathless with excitement. 'I'm gobsmacked – we will see the standards of fielding going through the roof in this series.'

Sadly, there was a less memorable moment earlier when Fran Wilson was given out LBW despite the ball clearly hitting her glove first. It immediately brought home pre-Ashes worries about the lack of a decision review system (DRS) in this series and the criticism from the commentators is unsparing. 'It was a horror,' says Mel Jones. 'The umpire did everything right, apart from the first bit – did she hit it? It makes you ask why we don't have a review system in this competition. It's the biggest competition in cricket outside World Cups.'

'Umpires can make mistakes,' admits Henry Moeran. 'But the game is not served by decisions like that. Let's get rid of the horror decisions which can cost a team the game.'

The innings break gives the first opportunity to hear a lovely documentary by BBC Somerset reporter Charlie Taylor, looking at the history of the Women's Ashes, but when Australia start their chase, the early loss of Nicole Bolton aside, there is an ominous feel to it.

As the game continues, Aussie men's fast bowler Mitchell Starc is spotted in the crowd, relatively incognito in a grey hoodie. It's a very common sight to see wives supportively looking on while their husbands play, and Starc's presence is an excellent reversal of that tradition as he backs his wife, Alyssa Healy, who leads the way at the start of the innings.

Meg Lanning is dismissed and then Ellyse Perry comes and goes cheaply, superbly stumped off a leg-side wide by Sarah Taylor, and when Haynes goes too, England are keeping themselves in the game by taking wickets at the other end. So when Healy is caught by Wilson on the boundary for 66, the game is absolutely on.

Australia move clear but again are pegged back when Ashleigh Gardner is LBW and Moeran admits that 'This is a better game than I thought we might see when England were 19 for four.' The same thing happens 25 runs later, with Australia almost securing the match before Beth Mooney is bowled, momentarily foxing the *TMS* team, who assumed another brilliant stumping from Taylor. Despite one final wicket for England, Australia just about cling on to record a two-wicket win and take a two-point lead in the Women's Ashes. 'It shows these two sides are closely matched. Australia have come out the blocks today though,' says Rainford-Brent. England will be keen to bounce back in two days' time when *TMS* will be back in the rooftop Portakabin for game two.

England 177 (46.5 overs; Sciver 64, Perry 3-43) lost to Australia 178-8 (42.3 overs; Healy 66, Ecclestone 3-34) by two wickets.

CHAPTER 11

Riverside Stroll to the Semis

Wednesday 3 July
England v New Zealand – ICC Cricket World
Cup – Match 41
Chester-le-Street, Durham

Team *TMS*: Jonathan Agnew, Charles Dagnall, Bryan Waddle, Michael
Vaughan, Jeremy Coney, Graeme Swann, Andy Zaltzman

So, it's come down to this. Four years of preparation and five weeks of World Cup have resulted in England reporting to Chester-le-Street for what is effectively a World Cup quarter-final, knowing that victory over New Zealand would see them into a home World Cup semi-final. A loss is not terminal, but it would remove control from England's hands.

The night before, a selection of the *TMS* team, including Michael Vaughan, Charles Dagnall, Eleanor Oldroyd and producer Adam Mountford, gathered together in Durham to watch the end of the Women's Ashes and the subsequent women's football World Cup semi-final. What was supposed to be a relaxing evening before the big match actually ended up being quite stressful, with VAR, missed penalties and the like, and the team walk back to the hotel in a philosophical mood. 'It makes you think, doesn't it?' Mountford asks the team. 'What it could be like over the next few days if England can reach the cricket semi-final and even the final? I wonder what this summer will be remembered most for, the football or the cricket?'

Oddly, despite the size of the game, there are fewer nerves present than there were in Birmingham at the weekend. This is possibly down to the locale, with Durham having a naturally more laid-back vibe than Edgbaston, but also possibly down to the opposition. While they are a fiercely competitive sporting nation, New Zealanders certainly don't travel with the numbers and atmosphere the blue-shirted Indian army have been bringing to this World Cup.

England get off to another sensational start, again showing how crucial the return of Jason Roy from his hamstring strain was for the resurrection of their World Cup chances. He and Jonny Bairstow see off some fine early bowling from Trent Boult and Tim Southee, playing in place of the injured Lockie Ferguson, before once again imposing themselves on the opposition, finding the boundary relentlessly. 'Jason Roy's return has just reset England's World Cup,' says Aggers. 'He and Bairstow love batting together and they've got back to how we've been used to see them playing over the past three years.'

Meanwhile, Kiwi Bryan Waddle is less convinced about the state of his side. 'I think New Zealand, without Ferguson today, are severely depleted,' he says. 'Their selection policies are also being exposed. Southee shouldn't really have to wait until the ninth game of the competition to get a go.'

As England reach 100 off 15 overs, Jeremy Coney has almost written the game off. 'I'm afraid for New Zealand, the train has left the station,' he says. 'It's hard in cricket to pull things back at this stage. Batting has seemed like a grand pianist, rehearsing – it looked very easy, in other words.'

Roy goes for 60 but Bairstow carries on gloriously, reaching his century, jumping into the air and letting out a primal roar as the ball makes it to the boundary. 'It's a leap of triumph from Bairstow. He's at his bristling best now,' reports Aggers, with Graeme Swann immediately calling for England and *TMS* team-mate Michael Vaughan to be knighted, purely for his contributions to winding Bairstow up at just the right time.

Buttler is promoted to No 4, with Swann applauding the positive intent, saying, 'I think England will definitely be thinking more than 350. If Jos Buttler stays at the crease, then the sky is the limit.' However, when Bairstow is bowled by Matt Henry, New Zealand start to fight back and end up limiting the total to 305 for eight.

'It is not as many as it looked as if England were set for. New Zealand will be happy to have come back, but will that prove to be too many?' asks Aggers during the innings break. 'Three hundred has been difficult to chase in this World Cup. They should have enough if they bowl well.'

The crucial game is in the balance, but morale is boosted in the box by a visit from an Englishman with two world cups in his family: Ben Cohen. He, of course, was the barrelling winger in England's 2003 Rugby World Cup triumph, but his uncle, George Cohen, was famously a member of the 1966 England squad that won the football World Cup. Ben has never been to cricket before and is loving his first experience. He is also excited by the prospect of another contingent of English sportsmen adding their name to the rarefied 'World Cup winners' list that his family so proudly features on. Before the Rugby World Cup final, he spoke to his uncle, who told him that 'Most games for your country are important, but a win tomorrow will change your life.' It's advice that England's cricketers may need to avail themselves of in the days and weeks to come.

As he did against India, Chris Woakes gets the England bowling off to the best possible start, trapping Henry Nicholls LBW in the first over. 'The fourth golden duck by a New Zealand opener this tournament,' Zaltzman reveals shortly afterwards.

While pleased with the comeback his side made with the ball, keeping England to 111 for seven in the last 20 overs, Jeremy Coney isn't convinced by the batting. 'If New Zealand persist with the same batting order, they will get what they have done all tournament, i.e. not to 300,' he remarks, shortly before Martin Guptill gloves down the leg side and they slip to 14 for two.

Kane Williamson and Ross Taylor are the key men for England, but Williamson falls in desperately unlucky fashion, run out by dint of Mark Wood getting the thinnest of fingers on a straight drive from Taylor that goes on to hit the stumps. Even Swanny, a paid-up member of the bowlers' union, says, 'I don't have much time for batsmen saying they are unlucky, but on this occasion, it was very unlucky.'

Taylor then becomes the second run-out, calling through a dangerous second run but being gunned down by Adil Rashid in the deep, producing a superb throw straight over the stumps. Again, Swann is uncharacteristically magnanimous to the batsman. 'To be fair to Ross Taylor, I had no idea Rashid had an arm like that on him,' he says, barely suppressing a smile as the second dangerman returns to the Paul Collingwood Pavilion, bat under his arm. 'The two people England would have had meetings about how to bowl to, where to restrict them, I doubt if they'd have said, "Let's run them both out!"' adds Swann gleefully.

New Zealand recover to 123 for four at the halfway mark, but Jimmy Neesham chops Wood onto his stumps and Coney continues his criticism, saying that 'New Zealand have been hesitant, in the field and in their decision-making.' Ben Stokes is introduced into the attack on his home ground and gets rid of Colin de Grandhomme first ball, but New Zealand's negativity – presumably to protect their net run rate in the event of ending up on the same points as another team – is not creating a great spectacle.

Other than basking in the relief of England's assured semi-final status, something that seemed a long way away a few days ago, the primary amusement towards the end of the game is when a streaker invades the pitch. *TMS* has a long history with streakers, with John Arlott memorably describing a pitch invader as a 'freaker', adding slowly, ' . . . and it's masculine. And I would think it's seen the last of its cricket for the day.'

These days, streaking incidents are few and far between – and are generally dealt with relatively swiftly and brutally – but today the man in question makes it all the way to the middle, converses with the New Zealand batsmen and performs a cartwheel before eventually being collared by five stewards and marched towards the boundary. Despite it being a five-on-one scenario, he then manages to wriggle free and continue the performance before finally being more comprehensively apprehended and removed from the field of play. 'He's put the coat over his shoulder. That's not really the bit they are trying to cover up,' says Swann, laughing at the surreal situation unfolding in front of him. 'It was a lethargic effort from the stewards.'

With England bowling Joe Root and Rashid in an effort to ensure their captain doesn't get banned from the semi-final for over-rate infractions, Andy Zaltzman adds drily, 'It's not doing the over rate any good.'

New Zealand continue their negative batting, causing frustration in the commentary box that England's heroic comeback is not being completed with more panache. 'It's a shame because you have a good crowd, a beautiful afternoon and no contest,' says Aggers, with Swann considering his route back to Nottingham and adding, 'I'm never one for leaving before the end of a sporting fixture, but I think I'd be trying to beat the traffic now.'

England eventually dismiss New Zealand for a lachrymose 186 all out from 45 overs, a thoroughly underwhelming way to confirm their hard-won status as World Cup semi-finalists. 'Four days ago, we were all concerned about England, but they have steamrollered India and now New Zealand, and it's the Kiwis who are staggering into the semi-finals,' says Vaughan. It seems highly likely that England will be back at Edgbaston playing India a week tomorrow.

Although Pakistan can mathematically deny New Zealand their semi-final place, the outcome of Friday's match at Lord's would have to be so extraordinary as to rewrite almost every cricketing record that has ever been set. Fortunately, comedian Aatif Nawaz, a friend of *TMS* and the host of the BBC Asian Network's *Doosra* podcast, has done the maths, tweeting, 'To qualify, Pakistan must: Beat Bangladesh by 311 runs after scoring 350; Beat Bangladesh by 316 runs after scoring 400; Beat Bangladesh by 321 runs after scoring 450. Incidentally, the biggest ODI win in history was by 290 runs.' Andy Zaltzman helpfully adds, 'The absolute key for Pakistan is to win the toss because if they bowl first – even if they bowl Bangladesh out for nought – they couldn't overtake on run rate.'

Although they're almost certainly through, Jeremy Coney is very concerned with the look of the New Zealand team after their last two losses. 'New Zealand are overcome with lassitude at the moment. I have never seen a New Zealand team look like they do,' he says. 'There is a decline, there is a lack of skill and lack of intent. I have seen lack of skill before but not lack of intent.'

The final word is left with Michael Vaughan, who at times has been England's biggest critic and at times their biggest cheerleader. 'If England win the next two tosses, then I think they will win the World Cup,' he says. 'If they are in a chase, I doubt whether they can play the right intelligent cricket under pressure. Can they win four tosses on the trot? Of course they can.'

England 305-8 (50 overs; Bairstow 106, Roy 60, Neesham 2-41) beat New Zealand 186 (45 overs; Latham 57, Taylor 28, Wood 3-34) by 119 runs.

Thursday 4 July
Afghanistan v West Indies – ICC Cricket World Cup – Match 42
Headingley, Leeds

Team *TMS*: Fazeer Mohammad, Prakash Wakankar, Simon Mann, Michael Vaughan, Jeremy Coney, Vic Marks, Sir Curtly Ambrose, Andy Zaltzman

Another dead rubber featuring the West Indies today, but a big match for Chris Gayle, who equals Brian Lara's record by playing his 295th one-day international in what could be his last-ever game for his country. He also only needs another 18 runs to break Lara's all-time run-scoring record of 10,348.

As ever, Sir Curtly Ambrose – who has suffered one crushing disappointment after another at this World Cup – is hoping the

West Indies remain motivated. 'It's still a game; West Indies should still come out with intensity,' he says at the start as Gayle walks out to open the batting. He manages only 7 before going for a big shot and edging it behind to the keeper. 'Gone!' shouts Fazeer Mohammad. 'In possibly his final innings for West Indies! He departs typically – a big effort, a big heave and a thick edge to the keeper. Not the glory he would have wanted with this final innings.'

The West Indies, enlivened by fifties for Evin Lewis, Shai Hope and Nicholas Pooran, record a highly commendable 311 for six, posting 12 sixes along the way as they continue to follow the 'swing for the ropes' tactics that have served them so poorly so far in the World Cup.

For a game that has no bearing whatsoever on the competition as a whole, the atmosphere in Leeds is sensational. Following a conversation with an ICC volunteer 'Cricketeer' this morning, Andy Zaltzman reveals that is partially because over 3,000 tickets have been doled out to local schoolchildren, who are enjoying one of the better school trips of their educational careers.

It's another big day for fans of enraged Antiguans as Lewis ('poor, poor cricket'), Hope and Shimron Hetmyer are all caught in Curtly's crosshairs at one stage or another as the innings ends with another moment from Gulbadin that is bound to entertain people on social media for some time. Carlos Brathwaite – attempting to end the innings with a six – swipes the ball down the ground, offering what should be a straightforward catch to the Afghan skipper. However, he gets the sun in his eyes, completely loses sight of it as he turns his head away, and the ball simply lands next to him and runs off for four. 'That's the strangest thing I have seen on a cricket ground,' says Prakash Wakankar, who has watched more cricket than most people have had hot dinners.

As on a number of other occasions over the past five weeks, the Afghans flatter to deceive when it comes to their response. Gulbadin is the latest to attract the wrath of Ambrose, dismissed as 'naïve' by trying to hit a second consecutive boundary off Kemar Roach and giving it away. Rahmat and teenager Ikram Alikhil put together a good partnership for the second wicket and, with Afghanistan on 167 for two with 18 overs to go, Vic Marks admits, 'I'm suddenly getting excited by all this, I am going to have to write something about this!'

The next *TMS* team member to get excited is Andy Zaltzman, who is able to cross off a very exciting landmark when Ikram makes it to 85 and breaks Sachin Tendulkar's long-standing record to become the highest scoring 18-year-old in the history of the World Cup. He only manages one more before going LBW to Gayle, a man more than double his age who is once again bowling in *Top Gun*-style aviator sunglasses.

Sadly, after that, the innings is the converse of the West Indian effort, with the Afghans going backwards in the final ten overs, losing their last seven wickets for 99 runs – Fabian Allen adding to the shortlist for 'Catch of the World Cup' off the final ball of the innings – and ending the tournament without a win.

While Zaltzman points out that 'This is Afghanistan's highest score in the second innings of an ODI and their highest score against a top-nine nation,' that probably won't be the primary emotion in their dressing room at the end of another World Cup game where they had a chance to get their elusive win and didn't manage it.

Allen's catch – against all the odds – also means that Sir Curtly Ambrose wraps up his West Indian commentary duties in a good mood. 'It was a brilliant end to an entertaining match,' he says, beaming. 'Most players wouldn't have been bothered to take that catch, but Fabian Allen did. Well done!'

West Indies 311-6 (50 overs; Hope 77, Lewis 58, Pooran 58, Holder 45, Dawlat 2-73) beat Afghanistan 288 (50 overs; Ikram 86, Rahmat 62, Brathwaite 4-63, Roach 3-37) by 23 runs.

Thursday 4 July
England Women v Australia Women – Women's Ashes – Match 2
The Fischer County Ground, Leicester

Team *TMS*: Natalie Germanos, Ebony Rainford-Brent, Charlotte Edwards, Mel Jones, Lydia Greenway, Henry Moeran, Isabelle Westbury

On the morning of the second Women's Ashes ODI, Henry Moeran receives a text message from Ebony Rainford-Brent saying how much she's looking forward to working on tomorrow's game. While it is surprising that the normally hyper-organised Rainford-Brent has made such a basic error of calendar misman-agement, that is not Moeran's primary concern as he takes a deep breath before immediately reaching for the *TMS* little black book to try to find someone who can enlighten listeners on the game – and make it to Leicester within a three-hour window.

Just before the first SOS goes out, his phone flashes again. It's Rainford-Brent, revealing that she is well aware the game is tonight and Moeran has just been pranked. It takes a few minutes but, eventually, the producer/commentator's sense of humour is restored, and preparations continue.

Later, after telling the story on air, Moeran reflects on a

not-too-dissimilar incident that happened before an episode of 'TMS @ T20' a few years ago. He had arrived at Grace Road and met up with Leicester native Charles Dagnall ahead of a commentary assignment on a big Leicestershire T20 evening. With time ticking down towards the start of the game, they were sitting in the Portakabin waiting for their third wheel, Rainford-Brent, to arrive. With about 20 minutes to go before the match was due to start, Moeran's phone buzzed and up popped Ebony's name on the screen. Assuming she required directions to the commentary box, Moeran answered, thinking his colleague was cutting it slightly fine but no harm done.

The panicked voice at the end of the line immediately set his nerves jangling and very quickly it became clear that Rainford-Brent was not at the Fischer County Ground (formerly known as Grace Road) at all. Given that the game was only 20 minutes away, this was problematic. Ebony explained that she was standing on Grace Road, in Leicestershire, but was thoroughly confused as she could not see a cricket ground for love nor money, but was close to a very large reservoir; indeed, one of such a size that it was highly unlikely to be found within the metropolitan boundaries of the city of Leicester.

After a quick check of Google Maps (other digital mapping services are available), it turned out that she had allowed her satnav to direct her to Grace Road in Sapcote, a small village still within the county of Leicestershire but approximately 20 minutes southwest of the actual city of Leicester itself. The error was pointed out, the satnav reprogrammed, and she arrived, breathless, halfway through the first innings.

On the field, England bat first and hopes are raised when they get off to a decent start and build a solid platform. Charlotte Edwards calls for a total of 250 or more, thinking it will deliver an England victory that will level the series. Opener Tammy Beaumont bats superbly to make 114, her first Ashes hundred, and the commentary box, many of whom have played with and covered Tammy for some time, are clearly moved by her success. 'There's a lot of people very proud of her today,' says Ebony, while Natalie Germanos urges Beaumont to 'soak it up, you've deserved it'.

She lacks support, though, with Delissa Kimmince – who, like French Open champion Ash Barty, once again in attendance today, is a multi-sport professional, having played for the Brisbane Lions Australian Rules Football team – taking a five-wicket haul to reduce them to 217 all out.

This is chased down straightforwardly by Australia, who survive a wobble at the top of the order to see first Ellyse Perry and then Beth Mooney and Jess Jonassen marshal the innings home as they complete a professional win by four wickets. 'This puts a huge weight of pressure on England for the final ODI,' admits a forlorn Rainford-Brent before she heads for the car, hopefully plugging in the correct destination address on her satnav.

England 217 (47.4 overs; Beaumont 114, Kimmince 5-26) lost to Australia 218-6 (45.2 overs; Perry 62, Shrubsole 3-37) by four wickets.

Friday 5 July
Pakistan v Bangladesh – ICC Cricket World
Cup – Match 43
Lord's Cricket Ground, St John's Wood, London

Team *TMS*: Jonathan Agnew, Simon Mann, Daniel Norcross, Ramiz Raja, Alec Stewart, Athar Ali Khan, Phil Long

This is going be a very different day from what you normally encounter at the Home of Cricket, and you know it immediately coming out of St John's Wood station this morning. Pakistan and Bangladesh are in town – and it's loud. While it is basically a dead rubber, there is still the chance that Pakistan can qualify for the semi-finals. It's very straightforward. To do so, they need to win the toss, bat first and then beat Bangladesh by 316 runs. The current world record is a victory by 290 runs for New Zealand over Ireland in Aberdeen in 2008, so it's definitely possible. Sadly, *TMS* can't find the man who arrived at Old Trafford on a white charger to ask him his opinion.

When Sarfaraz Ahmed wins the first battle, as Mashrafe Mortaza calls the toss incorrectly, and immediately chooses to bat first, he does so with a broad, knowing grin on his face. Pakistan make a fine effort with the bat, racking up 315 for six with Imam-ul-Haq scoring a century and Babar Azam, who has been one of the players of the tournament, falling just four short as he breaks Javed Miandad's record for most runs by a Pakistani in a single World Cup.

As well as a superb caught and bowled by 'The Fizz', Mustafizur Rahman, the moment of the innings comes off the very last ball. Pakistan are 314 for six with one ball left to face and Sarfaraz, who had previously retired hurt after being smashed on the elbow by a vicious drive struck by Imad Wasim, heroically comes out to face the last ball, with Mustafizur on a hat trick. Loins were girded and superlatives prepared as the story, surely, was going to be the skipper smashing a six off the final ball to open up the possibility of Bangladesh being bowled out for 4 and Pakistan going through. Astonishingly, to the squawking consternation of Daniel Norcross, he merely blocks the final ball and jogs through for a single.

Initially their total of 315 doesn't seem to be mathematically enough to even have a shout at qualification, but there is a dramatic development during the innings break when, actually, *TMS* are told that, should Pakistan bowl Bangladesh out for 7 or below, it will be them in the semi-finals rather than New Zealand. Game on.

'I remember at primary school we bowled a team out for 10,' says Simon Mann, trying to build the narrative while also generating a personally nostalgic glow for his halcyon cricketing days. Even if that happened though, it wouldn't be enough. More references to primary education come during the innings break as *TMS* are joined by some of the youngest guests in the programme's history: a selection of the 250 children from local state schools that the MCC have invited in to enjoy today's game. In fact, not only have they been invited in, they have been given seats in the Lord's Pavilion! Naturally, they've been instructed to wear school uniforms, but it's still an extraordinary sight to see them sitting amid the MCC members.

It is the first time such an initiative has ever been trialled, and it further underscores the feeling that Lord's has had a very different vibe during this World Cup. Safe to say the children are having a wonderful time and are not too engaged in the question of net run rates and whether Bangladesh may get bowled out for less than 7.

Somewhat inevitably, they don't. Indeed, New Zealand can start planning for the semi-finals by the end of the second over. Sadly for Bangladesh, a memorable tournament – which could easily have seen them reach the semi-finals had a couple of close finishes gone their way – ends on somewhat of a downer as they are bowled out for 221 in the 44th over.

This is largely down to the efforts of teenage seamer Shaheen Afridi, who celebrates 'like the Redeemer on the top of the hill in Rio', according to Aggers. He underlines his stratospheric potential with six for 35, his wickets including Shakib Al Hasan, who bows out of the World Cup with 606 runs, becoming just the third man in history to achieve 600 runs in a single World Cup after Sachin Tendulkar and Matthew Hayden – and also joining Sachin as the only man to score seven fifties in a single World Cup. To emphasise his achievements over the past six weeks, as Lord's rocks to chants of '*AF-RI-DI, AF-RI-DI, AF-RI-DI!*', making it sound like 2006 all over again, Phil Long points out that only one of the eight innings Shakib played in the tournament didn't deliver a half-century for his side.

As the game comes to end, Aatif Nawaz joins *TMS* to discuss how he feels about his side's performances in the World Cup. Nawaz is positive, saying that 'These performances will be the highlights Pakistan take from the World Cup. It is very easy to think about not qualifying for the semi-finals, but it has not been all doom and gloom.'

With the semi-finalists decided, Michael Vaughan is sad that he's seen the last of Pakistan for the summer. 'I enjoy watching Pakistan play. They bring life and they have played the kind of game you really enjoy. Babar is a wonderful player to watch and I have to say it's a real shame they have not made the semis,' he says, with Norcross adding, 'If you'd told them they'd win five they'd have expected to go through.'

Roushan Alam, who has come a long way from his corridor creeping during the victory over South Africa at The Oval, is also around, and the bonhomie between the two rivals is wonderfully reflected in the stands. Although neither side reached the semi-finals, both their players and fans have contributed hugely to the tournament and they leave with their heads (and, in the case of Bangladesh, cuddly tigers) held high, throats raw and their green shirts ready to be donned another day.

Pakistan 315-9 (50 overs; Imam-ul-Haq 100, Azam 96, Mustafizur 5-75) beat Bangladesh 221 (44.1 overs; Shakib 64, Afridi 6-35) by 94 runs.

Saturday 6 July
Sri Lanka v India – ICC Cricket World Cup – Match 44
Headingley, Leeds

Team *TMS*: Prakash Wakankar, Fazeer Mohammad, Charles Dagnall,
Jeremy Coney, Vic Marks

Two more games to go and the group stage of the 2019 World
Cup ends with the competition's final Super Saturday. Neither
game will change the identity of the teams duking it out in next
week's semi-finals, but there is a chance the results could affect
who will play who. The first game out of the blocks is between
India and Sri Lanka in Leeds, and it will be the scene for a
number of farewells – with the great Lasith Malinga likely to
be playing his final World Cup match and umpire Ian 'Gunner'
Gould, a hugely popular veteran of 140 one-day internationals,
also bowing out of the international scene at close of play.

Sri Lanka bat first and post 264 for seven, with Angelo
Mathews taking the on-field plaudits with a hard-earned century. The off-field plaudits are handed entirely to *TMS*'s Jeremy
Coney, though. Coney, a former captain of New Zealand, has
had a long and tiring World Cup – and, with his side confirmed in the final stages, he still has a few more laps to go.
In retirement, Coney struck up a friendship with the cricket-
obsessed playwright and Nobel Prize-winner Harold Pinter
and is known by listeners and fellow commentators alike for his
striking and sometimes literary turns of phrase.

On this occasion, he absolutely outdoes himself by

lackadaisically describing the shot played by Dimuth Karunaratne, in being caught by M.S.Dhoni off Jasprit Bumrah, as 'a little like Boris Johnson herding geese into the abattoir'. Such is the off-kilter nature of the reference, the box is briefly stunned into gawping silence before deciding the best course of action is to carry on like nothing has happened.

Coney, a long-term friend and contributor to the programme, has come a long way since his first appearance on the airwaves this summer – on a commentary of the warm-up match between Afghanistan and Pakistan at Bristol. Stationed to summarise alongside Charlie Dagnall, disaster struck when the ISDN line that was handling the broadcast went down, taking all the commentary kit with it.

Dagnall's emergency BBC training immediately kicked in and he instantaneously opened the iPad (other desktop tablets are available) app that allows a back-up broadcast to be fired up, inserting his headphones into the socket as instructed. However, the app is only designed to support a single-person broadcast and while Dagnall's voice was being picked up by the microphone on his iPad, it was harder for Coney to make himself heard. Realising that the brand of headphones being used had a microphone on the cord (which was hanging down his chest so the iPad could be positioned close to his mouth), Coney's first analytical utterances to listeners this summer were spoken directly into his colleague's chest, his mouth millimetres from Daggers' pectoral muscles. Rather like Coney himself, it was unorthodox, but brilliant.

Today, after kicking off with his Boris Johnson line, Jeremy is in a rich vein of form. A mistimed trip down the wicket from Ajantha Mendis is 'like dancing. Keep your head steady, get to the length of the ball. Ballroom dancing – keep your eyes level. The biggest step is always the first step.' M.S.Dhoni, in taking a low catch in front of him, is described as having 'to fall over like a grandfather to take that'. On Jasprit Bumrah's run-up: 'It's only the last three or four steps where you'd go, "Oh, you're a cricketer."'

Another highlight of the Sri Lanka innings is the appearance of the great Mahela Jayawardene in the *TMS* box. He is not perhaps as upset as one would expect him to be, given that Sri Lanka's World Cup campaign lies in tatters before him. 'In patches Sri Lanka have played some really good cricket,' he says politely, 'but there has been inconsistency with both the batting and bowling.'

The Indian chase is brilliant, efficient and uneventful. K.L.Rahul hits his first century of the World Cup while Rohit Sharma, incredibly, hits his fifth. Once the two have added 189 runs in 30 overs for the first wicket, it's all over baby blue, and the runs are duly chased down in the 43rd. Words like 'clever', 'shrewd', 'glorious', 'gorgeous', 'toying', 'marmalised' and 'elegance' are thrown around with ease, but when Rohit hits his hundred, Coney once again produces a uniquely brilliant description as he talks about the 'terrible ease' that Sharma has batted with, adding, 'It's been a wonderful hundred. He hasn't had any chances at all. He's played with an unhurried venom.'

India end the group stages with 15 points and will top the pile and play fourth-placed New Zealand at Old Trafford on Tuesday – if South Africa beat Australia in the later match today. If Australia win in Manchester, India will finish second and play England at Edgbaston on Thursday.

Sri Lanka 264-7 (50 overs; Mathews 113, Thirimanne 53, Bumrah 3-37) lost to India 265-3 (43.3 overs; Rahul 111, Sharma 103, Rajitha 1-47) by seven wickets.

Saturday 6 July
Australia v South Africa – ICC Cricket World Cup – Match 45
Old Trafford, Manchester

Team *TMS*: Natalie Germanos, Jonathan Agnew, Jim Maxwell, Sir Curtly Ambrose, Graeme Swann, Pommie Mbangwa, Andy Zaltzman

Game 45 of the World Cup is something that has been on the mind of the *TMS* team for some time. Not necessarily because anybody thought it would be crucial (although if South Africa hadn't failed to perform so spectacularly, it could have been). No, this game has been anticipated for so long because it means, for the first time since Thursday 30 May, *TMS* will be getting a short break from the World Cup. The programme has been on air every day for 38 straight days, broadcasting 44 World Cup matches. During this time there has also been commentary on every ball of every county match, England women's series against West Indies and the start of the Women's Ashes.

Just considering the World Cup, and accounting for some matches that finished early and some that were rained off, that's well over 300 hours of live broadcasting at an average rate of nearly eight hours a day. Not one member of the *TMS* team has complained for one second of one broadcast and, given the wonderful messages that have continued to flood into the inbox, it seems like the listeners have enjoyed it, too. Everyone is excited by the prospects of the semi-finals and the final, but the two-day break (from the World Cup at least; the third match in the Women's Ashes is tomorrow!) will certainly be appreciated.

At Old Trafford, South Africa bat first and, frustratingly for all their fans, show exactly what might have been. Quinton de Kock, a batsman with an ODI average of 45, hits just his third fifty of the World Cup and – even more astonishingly – skipper Faf du Plessis hits the first South African century of the tournament in their very last match, as they end up with 325 for six.

During the innings, the aura of Mitchell Starc, who looks set to be the leading wicket-taker in the competition, is somewhat dented by Graeme Swann, who admits that he can 'never look at Mitchell Starc without laughing because Jimmy Anderson said to me once that he looks like the policeman from 'Allo 'Allo!' Search engines are consulted, pictures passed around the box and hilarity ensues for some time.

As South Africa play a game they have not brought to this tournament until now, Aggers says that 'Whoever plays Australia in the semi-final will enjoy Starc and Co. being put to the sword here' – Sir Curtly Ambrose adding that 'Australia don't look like the Australia we've become accustomed to.'

After de Kock and Aiden Markram had added 79 for the first wicket in the South African innings, Andy Zaltzman revealed a statistic that cut through a lot of the conversation on paths to success in this World Cup: 'This is the 17th opening stand over 50 in this tournament when batting first – and of the previous 16 only one has ended in the team losing,' he said. 'Throughout the tournament we have seen the importance of starting well when you are batting first.'

This is underscored as Imran Tahir – another great bringing the curtain down on his ODI career at this World Cup – dismisses Aaron Finch before Dwaine Pretorius traps Steve Smith LBW and Australia are suddenly 33 for two. David Warner plays a brilliant innings, hitting his third century of the World Cup, but wicketkeeper Alex Carey is the only other player able to make more than 22. De Kock is superb behind the stumps, firstly athletically running out Marcus Stoinis and then taking an incredible one-handed catch to remove Glenn Maxwell.

Carey hits an excellent 85, but when Warner is caught by

Chris Morris, South Africa are able to just about see off the Australian tail for a win that will make their flight home more enjoyable but, in the wider scheme of things, merely underlines the frustration of what might have been.

The biggest news of the evening is what it does to the semi-finals. England have avoided the rampantly in-form Indians and will play a newly fallible Australia at Edgbaston on Thursday. India will now travel to Manchester to play New Zealand on Tuesday. As Aaron Finch describes it to Aggers afterwards, England v Australia in a World Cup semi-final is a blockbuster. Also, with the remainder of the summer to look forward to, it seems appropriate that there is a proper curtain-raiser for the Ashes.

As for the World Cup, four teams remain, there are three games to be played and in eight days' time, the trophy will be lifted.

South Africa 325-6 (50 overs; du Plessis 100, van der Dussen 95, de Kock 52, Lyon 2-53) beat Australia 315 (49.5 overs; Warner 122, Carey 85, Rabada 3-56) by 10 runs.

Sunday 7 July
England Women v Australia Women – Women's
Ashes – Match 3
St Lawrence, Canterbury, Kent

Team *TMS*: Natalie Germanos, Ebony Rainford-Brent, Charlotte Edwards, Mel Jones, Daniel Norcross, Henry Moeran, Isabelle Westbury, Alison Mitchell

Results have conspired for England to play Australia in the semi-final of the men's Cricket World Cup. Meanwhile, the two sides are still going hammer and tongs in the women's game for the Ashes – and England could really do with a win today. The normally ebullient Ebony Rainford-Brent is not confident, worrying that Australia have 'worked out' the English batting, but it's the English bowlers who need to perform first and they find that, as before in this series, Alyssa Healy is quite a tough nut to crack. 'At the moment, she is playing a different game of cricket to everyone else,' says Henry Moeran. 'She looks in the mood.'

Without the injured Katherine Brunt, there is something missing in the England attack, and Healy and Meg Lanning add 109 for the second wicket. Healy is caught in the deep off Natalie Sciver ('a fortuitous dismissal', admits Daniel Norcross), but Lanning – who a statistically inclined listener tells *TMS* has not been dismissed between 50 and 99 since February 2016 – looks ominous.

Despite this stat, she goes to Sciver, who follows up by dismissing in-form Ellyse Perry, and England retain their discipline and restrict Australia to 269 for seven. It's a lot – though less than it might have been – but should England get what they need, it will be the fourth highest women's ODI chase ever. 'England showed real character after the first 25 overs,' says Rainford-Brent, 'but they will need more than Tammy Beaumont to come to the party with the bat today.'

Sadly for England, nobody comes to the party with the bat. In fact, if there is a party, the only guests are Australian. Six wickets fall in the opening nine overs, with Australia precipitously reducing Heather Knight's side to a truly desperate position of 21 for six, Perry taking five of the first six wickets. 'It has been an abysmal start and it feels so urgently necessary for England to win this game,' says Norcross after four wickets have fallen.

With six wickets down, the schedule brings Ebony back onto commentary. 'What are your thoughts, Ebz?' asks Moeran. 'Ugh ... ' she replies. It is not the first time this summer she has gone onomatopoeic, but it is the first time it has happened in a negative cause.

Fran Wilson is next to go and Moeran adds that 'We really are looking at a memorably horrible defeat for England.' Laura Marsh and Anya Shrubsole prevent total embarrassment for England, but they are bowled out for 75 and lose by a giant 175 runs. 'It has been a demolition of England today,' admits Norcross afterwards. 'I don't know what the bright sparks are. Searching for the positives today is a needle in a haystack.'

Australia 269-7 (50 overs; Lanning 69, Healy 68, Sciver 3-51) beat England 75 (32.5 overs; Perry 7-22, Schutt 2-21) by 194 runs.

CHAPTER 12

The Final Countdown

Tuesday 9 July
India v New Zealand – ICC Cricket World Cup –
Semi-Final
Old Trafford, Manchester

Team *TMS*: Jonathan Agnew, Bryan Waddle, Prakash Wakankar, Isa
Guha, Jimmy Anderson, Michael Vaughan, Jeremy Coney, Andy Zaltzman

There has been a lot spoken in recent years about home
advantage in cricket. Whether it's lightning-quick decks in
Western Australia, big turners in Hyderabad or green tops in
Nottingham, the discussion among experts has been how to
leverage your home conditions to provide the best possible
chance of victory. As *TMS* arrive at Old Trafford today, the
feeling could not be more Mancunian if Noel Gallagher himself
was sat at the back of the commentary box playing an acoustic
rendition of 'Blue Moon'. The sky is grey, the clouds are low
and there is an omnipresent, intangible threat of rain in the air.

The conditions are made for Jimmy Anderson and Stuart

Broad to take a fresh Duke's in hand and hoop it onto the outside edge of David Warner. But there are still a few weeks to wait for that and today there is no chance for England to take advantage of their home conditions as India and New Zealand will fight it out for the right to play in the World Cup final – and Anderson is in the *TMS* commentary box, wondering what might have been.

The day starts outstandingly well as *TMS*, up with the lark, spot New Zealand arriving at the ground and Henry Moeran, ever the master of a leftfield observation, notices that Trent Boult is carrying some of his kit in a 'Bag for Life' from the Co-op. This somehow perfectly represents both the unprepossessing charm of this New Zealand team and the beautiful difference between cricket and football that many listeners cite as part of their reason for persisting so passionately with their devotion to this beautiful sport.

On the other side of the coin, Amy Lofthouse – covering the game for the BBC Sport website today – arrived at the ground at the same time as the India team bus inched slowly through a fog of blue and orange shirts, all simultaneously chanting '*KOH-LI*'. There is very much the feeling of old versus new today. It is by no means a battle for the future of the game, but there is a definite clarity between the two sides.

Kane Williamson wins the toss and opts to bat first. Zaltzman has no need to point out the stat that 16 of the last 20 teams to win the toss at this World Cup have gone on to win, because it has been so well rehearsed over the past 48 hours that everyone knows it already.

New Zealand are happy to welcome back the raw pace of Lockie Ferguson, with Tim Southee missing out; India bring Yuzvendra Chahal back at the expense of Kuldeep Yadav and Ravi Jadeja holds onto his spot over Mohammed Shami. Brilliantly, it's not even the first time Williamson and Virat

Kohli have captained against each other in a World Cup semi-final, as the two led their respective nations into the semis of the 2008 Under-19 World Cup. On that occasion, India won by three wickets and Kohli dismissed his opposite number with his medium pacers, which were a little less occasional back in those days.

Martin Guptill survives a review off the very first ball of the match, but not much longer as he is caught by Kohli at second slip. The combination of the importance of the game, the release of the nervous tension and it being Kohli that takes the catch almost lifts the *TMS* box off its moorings and into space.

After ten overs, New Zealand are only 27 for one. It is the lowest score of the entire tournament at this stage and Michael Vaughan thinks Williamson misstepped at the toss. 'Teams are so obsessed with batting first because of the tournament trend,' he says. 'They are not thinking of the conditions on the day.'

However slowly they do it, though, New Zealand fight back, and when Kohli turns to spin in the tenth over of the day, Prakash Wakankar's comment that 'There's been a lot of surprise and conversation about India's selection today within the India media' is brought up again. The conditions are perfect for seamers, and Shami, with 14 World Cup wickets to his name already, would have loved to be bowling out there this morning.

This becomes an even bigger concern when Hardik Pandya starts grimacing and pointing at his upper thigh before leaving the field, clearly in some discomfort. Were Pandya to not be able to complete his overs, India would need to find 36 balls out of their remaining six players. Of those, only three (M.S.Dhoni, Kohli and Rohit Sharma) have ever bowled in ODI cricket, and they have bowled a total of 211 overs in more than 800 combined matches. Kohli last bowled in 2017, Rohit has bowled one over since the last World Cup and Dhoni is the wicketkeeper.

Henry Nicholls goes to Ravindra Jadeja and, after half their innings, New Zealand are just 83 for two. Williamson has a strike rate of 58 and new man Ross Taylor one of just 30. 'I think New Zealand are being tentative,' says Anderson. 'It's as if they know these two are so crucial, and they need to bat for the majority of the 50 overs.'

There is relief for India – and a stop to Zaltzman-led rampant speculation as to who would take up the bowling slack – as Pandya returns to the attack and, in the following over from Chahal, Williamson bends low and sweeps the first boundary in 13 overs. Vaughan is calling for New Zealand 'to go old school', with Williamson batting through and the others attacking, but the skipper goes in the 35th over, looping an attempted cover drive to Jadeja at point and going for 67 off 95 balls. It is described as 'a strange little shot' by a crestfallen Jeremy Coney, but attention quickly turns elsewhere as new man Jimmy Neesham is just getting started at the crease.

Almost as one, the *TMS* team get a series of notifications on their mobile phones, warning of impending downpours in the local area. The burgeoning skies that have hung claustrophobically above Old Trafford all day look set to burst and conversation turns to what that means for the game. The common thought is that if the target ends up being adjusted by the Duckworth–Lewis–Stern method, it's not going to be good for New Zealand. As Neesham is next to go, BBC Weather's Nikki Berry gets in touch with the programme, adding her impressive meteorological qualifications to the strong instincts garnered by the team's years of experience, and it becomes clear that Old Trafford is set for some disruption.

Suddenly, Taylor takes Chahal for 18 off an over – hitting the first six of the innings in the process – and New Zealand are looking a little livelier. 'That is what happens when you try and put bowlers under pressure,' says Anderson, who adds more forebodingly that 'It does look pretty grim where the rain comes from here.'

Colin de Grandhomme comes and goes and then, with just 23 balls of the New Zealand innings remaining, the weather turns from disgusting mizzle into much heavier rain and the umpires withdraw the players from the field. Discussions immediately turn to overs lost, DLS and cloud patterns over the Pennines, while Anderson is also grilled on air about the Ashes. *TMS* are also joined by outgoing ICC chief executive Dave Richardson, while off-air entertainment in the commentary box is provided by Johanna Konta's sadly unsuccessful efforts in the women's quarter-final at Wimbledon.

Nikki Berry stays in touch, offering a professional overlay to the constant checking of rain apps, but only ever seems to be bringing bad news as the following four hours and 21 minutes bring nothing but the utmost frustration, as covers are repeatedly inched off before being rushed back on. India would need to face a minimum of 20 overs for the match to be completed today, but, as time drags on, it becomes increasingly clear that this is not going to be possible and the reserve day is going to come into play. Aggers, ever the experienced old owl, calls it two minutes before the announcement is made when he spots the umpires leaving the field and heading into separate dressing rooms.

'India would prefer coming back tomorrow rather than having a truncated 20-over game tonight,' says Prakash. If he's right, and there's no reason to suspect he's not, then it's just as well, because that's what's going to happen.

Wednesday 10 July
India v New Zealand– ICC Cricket World Cup – Semi-
Final (Reserve Day)
Old Trafford, Manchester

Team *TMS*: Isa Guha, Bryan Waddle, Prakash Wakankar, Jimmy
Anderson, Jeremy Coney, Andy Zaltzman

Mercifully, the day dawns brighter in Manchester and it's clear that the game will be played to a finish today. For a second day the eyes of the world are on Old Trafford, and nerves are being felt all over the globe, not least by New Zealand cyclist George Bennett. He will be going from Saint-Dié-des-Vosges to Colmar today (175.5 km), racing in the Tour de France. Yesterday he went from Reims to Nancy (213.5 km) and was unable to follow the cricket, so today, innovatively, he is calling on roadside fans to keep him updated with a network of signs, promising to reward them with an official Tour de France bidon from his bike!

The game restarts with New Zealand facing the 23 balls they had remaining last night. 'If they can add another 15 then that would be average,' says Jeremy Coney. 'If they add 20 to 30 then that would not be bad – that is possible. If they get 40 or more then you are into bonus territory.' Despite losing three more wickets, they eventually add 28, firmly in Coney's 'not bad' zone, and he is backed up by Jimmy Anderson, who says that 'I don't think it is too bad for New Zealand. They would have said 240 minimum, maybe 250 if everything went well, but it didn't. They will take that. India will be very confident, but you never know with the pressure of a semi-final. It completely depends how New Zealand start with the ball.'

However, Isa Guha thinks that 'India will be pretty delighted by that,' and if the gods of cricket had offered them the chance to chase 240 for a place in the World Cup final six weeks ago, you can bet they'd have taken it. Any remaining positivity that may be felt by the New Zealand contingent listening in is sapped as the players walk onto the field and Andy Zaltzman plays his statistical trump card.

'The 15 times India have had to chase a score between 220 and 270 they have won 14 and tied one. They haven't lost a chase in this bracket in the last three years,' he reveals, as Bryan Waddle narrows his eyes surreptitiously in the rear of the box and Jeremy Coney stiffens in the chair next to him.

India start poorly though, with five-time centurion Sharma nicking off fourth ball to Matt Henry. 'That is exactly what was required for New Zealand,' says Coney as Kohli comes to the crease, underscoring the challenge his side still face. Kohli's first ball drops short of second slip and then, from his third, he is drawn into a big drive, wafting majestically outside off stump as the ball flies past his edge. 'That was nerves from Virat Kohli,' says Prakash Wakankar, betraying signs of them himself. His fourth ball is defended stoutly but his fifth is lobbed into the air, a tantalising distance from Guptill at short mid-wicket.

It's the sixth ball that will go down in World Cup history, though. Boult fires in a swinging delivery that raps the Indian captain high on the front pad as Kohli plays around it. Boult and the small minority of his fellow countrymen in the ground explode into an appeal they know could change the course of this World Cup and – as umpire Richard Illingworth slowly raises his finger – the team embrace as Kohli immediately reviews the decision.

'It was a swinging ball that beat the edge. It will probably be pitching in line,' says Coney, rigid as he watches the third umpire decision play out on the monitor in front of him. 'Very big moment.' Coney is almost disbelieving of what he is seeing, and preparing himself for the inevitable comedown if Illingworth is overturned – 'It is too high?' is his next utterance. The final, crucial, replay is shown and the boxes gradually are all filled red. The ball was going on to hit middle and leg and Kohli has just been dismissed for 1 in a World Cup semi-final.

'New Zealand are on fire here at Old Trafford!' says Prakash, fully aware of the scale of what is unfolding in front of him. 'They have got the two big wickets. India are in all sorts of trouble.'

'That just shows you what a bit of movement does,' replies Coney. 'It got Virat Kohli just to fall away with a heavy head.' The disbelief becomes even more stark when K.L.Rahul replicates Sharma's dismissal from the first ball of the next over and India fall to 5 for three. 'This is a terrific start for New Zealand,' says a wonderfully understated Coney before quickly warning that 'It is not over, folks.' Zaltzman adds, 'This is India's worst start ever in a World Cup match,' before revealing that, amazingly, in the entire history of the game, 'it is the first time in all international cricket, men's and women's, that the top three have all been out for 1.'

Dinesh Kartik, who took 21 balls to get off the mark – 'the third-longest it has taken a batsman to get off the mark in ODI cricket since 1999,' adds Zaltzman, who is relishing such a fiesta of stats – is the next to go, falling to an extraordinary catch from Neesham at point. Neesham, whose cricket was in such a state 18 months ago that he had taken a part-time job with a company in New Zealand who dealt in electronic collars for the remote herding of cows, dives low to his left and grabs the ball millimetres above the ground to give Henry his third wicket in five overs.

'Brilliant from Jimmy Neesham! He has taken a miraculous catch,' explodes Bryan Waddle, while Anderson, a Lancastrian not known for overstatement, adds, 'You are not going to see many better catches than that. It has not got above knee height all the way and he has caught it with his weaker hand. Incredible, incredible catch.'

As if to underline the unpredictability of this World Cup, Neesham then drops a far simpler chance offered by Rishabh Pant, allowing India to start to rebuild. 'New Zealand can't allow India to stage a recovery. Either Neesham or Santner need to come on,' says Coney, and Williamson listens, bringing both of them back into the attack almost immediately.

As if to reward him, Coney then reaches deep into his box of tricks and pulls the most perfect commentator's curse you could wish for. 'These two look set now,' he says. 'They've been there long enough to know the pace of the pitch.' Virtually the next ball, with India only having scored one from the previous 16 deliveries, Pant loses his patience and tries to smash Santner into the stands beyond mid-wicket. Instead, he picks out the man and the partnership is broken. 'Pant just couldn't wait to play the big shot,' says a beaming Coney, quietly aware of the role he played in his country's success.

The man striding to the crease, though, is M.S.Dhoni. 'In the whole world of cricket, M.S.Dhoni would be my choice of man to walk to the crease now,' says Graeme Swann on Twitter, following along at home with everyone else. 'This is amazing stuff to watch.'

Just like New Zealand yesterday, India are getting stuck in the middle overs – and the extent of the muddle is laid bare by Zaltzman when he points out that 'There have been 13 runs off the last eight overs.' The run rate has gone up to 7.38, with the accuracy and class of the New Zealand bowling meaning India's scoring rate is below three an over. 'We're again seeing that the pace of the pitch is making it difficult for batsmen to find their timing,' diagnoses an increasingly agitated Bryan Waddle.

With 20 overs left, 148 are required, and when Pandya skies

to Williamson to leave India 92 for six, many are calling the game over. However, Dhoni and new man Jadeja refuse to be cowed and start to form the genesis of a partnership that could make this game very tight come the death. Possibly for reasons of emotional protection, the boots are on the wrong feet in the commentary box, with Prakash certain the game is over and Coney far less convinced.

'You can just sense that India are coming back into the game after a nice little period of play,' says Coney, as the Indian crowd once again find their voice and start cheering every single like it was a Kohli six. 'If they can go run a ball for a while, India still have an outside chance,' adds the former New Zealand captain, well aware that there is still work to do as chants of '*DHO-NI, DHO-NI*' echo around Manchester, despite the fact that it's Jadeja who is seemingly playing the key innings.

With ten overs to go, 90 are required. Jadeja reaches his fifty and suddenly it's 72 from eight overs and Waddle is calling the game '50/50 now'. To emphasise the all-rounder's brilliance, Zaltzman says that 'Jadeja now has the highest score by anyone batting at seven or lower in a World Cup knock-out match,' and India continue.

India need 62 from six overs and when Jadeja smashes his fourth six of the innings, Kohli involuntarily leaps off the chair he has occupied on the balcony and punches the air. It's now 52 from five overs. Jadeja is the dangerman and Dhoni is doing brilliantly at delivering him the strike, belying his years to run hard twos and even leaving the occasional ball to ensure that Jadeja is at the right end for the start of the next over.

With 42 needed from four overs, Henry overcomes Jeremy Coney's fears that he is 'not a multi-dimensional bowler' by only conceding five runs to make it 37 from three overs. Boult bowls another superb over to continue to build the pressure. The ask is 32 from 14 balls when Jadeja tries to go again but hits the ball straight up in the air. The ball should come down with snow on it, but Williamson keeps his cool and pouches the catch.

Now 31 runs are required from the last two overs. When Ferguson goes fast and short to M.S.Dhoni, who jumps into the air and upper-cuts him over deep cover for a six that seems destined to feature in every World Cup highlights montage for the rest of time, it seems like the penultimate chapter of a story is being written. Two balls later, Dhoni shovels the ball into the leg side and comes back for a second. It's tight but the run should be there until Guptill, who has barely scored a run for New Zealand at the top of the order, gathers the ball smoothly and produces a perfect throw to hit the stumps directly and run out the Indian great by inches.

As the word 'Out' appears on the big screen, it's as if some-one has punched a hole in the side of a passenger jet at 30,000 feet. There is an audible 'whoosh' as the Indian fanbase realise their last hero has departed and, with him, go their chances of a World Cup many thought was inevitable. Later in the over, a slower ball is too good for Bhuvneshwar Kumar and it's all over soon afterwards as a review reveals that Chahal has got a slender nick on a delivery from Neesham and the party can start for the Kiwis.

'India are absolutely dejected, but it's been a fantastic match,' says an enraptured Coney. 'It just emerged – everyone thought New Zealand would win comfortably after those early wickets, but Ravindra Jadeja and M.S.Dhoni changed the game. There are always twists and turns in these games. Players can't continue at that level without making errors.' Coney even offers a hint of emotion, explained away when he says he is just 'thinking about the people back home who will be so pleased. The ICC won't like it, but I don't care – we're through!' he ends, with the glint that indicates his independent nature shining through in New Zealand's great moment.

The two-day one-day international ended at 2.55 p.m. on Day 2. Nobody could claim they successfully predicted what was going to happen, but that is the beauty of sport, world cups and life itself.

New Zealand 239-8 (50 overs; Taylor 74, Williamson 67, Kumar 3-43) beat India 221 (49.3 overs; Jadeja 77, Dhoni 50, Henry 3-37, Santner 2-34) by 18 runs.

●

Thursday 11 July
England v Australia – ICC Cricket World Cup –
Semi-Final
Edgbaston, Birmingham

Team *TMS*: Jonathan Agnew, Simon Mann, Jim Maxwell, Isa Guha, Sir Alastair Cook, Michael Vaughan, Phil Tufnell, Andy Zaltzman

Whether the extraordinary scenes at Old Trafford have heightened or reduced nerves is gloriously unclear, but nobody quite seems to know what to do this morning in Edgbaston. While everyone has long gone into autopilot mode to do all the tasks required to get *TMS* on the air, little things that previously would have occupied people's minds – like where to find the best coffee, which well-known people are in attendance, what's on the menu at Ristoranti Edgbaston, or where the owners of any particularly well-thought-through fancy dress outfits are located in the crowd – are not discussed today.

Even Jim Maxwell is worryingly softly spoken as he discusses

Australia's prospects. 'Australia may yet win a fifth World Cup in six attempts, but they are not a great team,' he suggests. 'They have good players, but the performances of the likes of Warner are papering over some cracks. Will Warner continue to weigh in with that amount of runs? If he does, as he gets to the back end of his career, people will say, "He might not always have been the best bloke, but boy he could bat."'

The toss, as demonstrated in recent weeks, will be crucial, and Maxwell, a noted equine enthusiast, adds an excellent sheen to proceedings by describing it as 'the most important toss since 1799, when the Earl of Derby won the toss to see what the horse race would be called ... '

Aaron Finch wins the toss and bats – and the silence that greets the announcement indicates that avoiding India in the semi-finals has at least garnered England a more supportive Edgbaston crowd to play in front of than last time they were here, nearly two weeks ago. The toss is a bad sign – but a good one comes from the studios of BBC Radio 1, where 'Alan the Psychic Robot' has predicted an England win by immediately hoovering the Australian flag off the floor of Greg James's studio. For those who think such things are pointless fripperies, it was refereed by former England captain Michael Vaughan and World Cup-winner Ebony Rainford-Brent, so it was definitely legitimate.

Vaughan is with the hoover, enthusiastically telling anyone who'll listen that England have nothing to fear from chasing. 'This is why England have done the work for four years,' he says. 'It is why Eoin Morgan created the culture around this team. I don't think it'll be the kind of chase where "crash, bang, wallop" will win it. Australia have been very good at defending in this World Cup. It is going to be a nipper.'

The teams emerge for the anthems, with Aggers pointing out that – sportingly – Australia have allowed England to use their regular (home) dressing room at Edgbaston, despite their higher group finish qualifying the Aussies as the 'home' team and giving them the option to turf England out, should they wish.

With expectation levels and nerves set to a maximum, Chris Woakes – on his home ground – runs in and delivers the first ball of the game. It is crashed through the covers for four by David Warner and eyebrows go through the roof. The other five balls are bang on the money and, with that, the game is under way and there is suddenly something for everyone to focus on.

Jofra Archer stands at the end of his run to bowl the second over. It is impossible to remember an era when people were arguing against his inclusion in the World Cup, but such a time existed only a couple of months ago. He flies in, whacks Finch on the pads and goes up for a huge appeal, which is granted! Finch immediately reviews the decision, but it is quickly clear that there is no bat and when Aggers delivers what has become almost a catchphrase in this World Cup, 'Red, red … red! OUT!' the ground erupts. 'What a start for England,' says a gleeful Tufnell, involuntarily rubbing his hands together with excitement.

Woakes returns for the next over and again gets whacked for four by Warner before coming back and finding his outside edge off the very next ball. Australia's divisive opener fends to Jonny Bairstow in the slips, who makes no mistake. Woakes then thinks he's trapped new man Peter Handscomb LBW, referring the decision to the DRS but – only just – seeing an orange light for umpire's call. 'That was probably worth the gamble,' agrees Aggers – and Mel Jones is delighted to see Handscomb survive to fight again, if only because his dad was her first cricket coach and geography teacher.

Sadly for Mel, but incredibly for England, he doesn't last much longer, inside-edging a fuller length delivery into his middle stump to send Edgbaston into paroxysms of jubilation and leaving Australia in trouble. 'Fourteen for three against Australia in a World Cup semi-final? It doesn't get any better,' says Tuffers, once he has bent down and retrieved his jaw from the floor. 'There are shades of Trent Bridge,' adds Simon Mann, referencing Stuart Broad's extraordinary burst for England in 2015.

Although he's beaming with delight, Andy Zaltzman is ever the voice of realism. 'This is the second worst start any team has made in a World Cup semi-final,' he says mischievously. 'Australia were 8 for three in Mohali in 1996 and went on to win.'

As they have done on more than one occasion in the World Cup, Steve Smith and Alex Carey start to salvage matters for Australia – but not before Carey has a bizarre moment when an Archer bouncer cracks him right on the side of the head and knocks his helmet clean off his head. It is falling towards his stumps – and a seriously unlucky dismissal – when he instinctively sticks out a hand and catches it. His chin looks like he's had a bad shaving accident and Jim Maxwell, shaken for both Carey and the situation, says, 'I feel like I'm watching the Ashes but with a white ball.'

After 15 overs, Australia are just 47 for three but Alastair Cook says that will not concern them. 'The score will be irrelevant in Australia's eyes at the moment,' he says. 'They will want these two to be at the crease in the 35th over, and even if they are only 140 for three then they can launch.' Ten overs later, the hundred has been brought up and England's position of total dominance is slipping.

Smith's mannerisms cause the imperturbable Simon Mann to suggest the Aussie would be a terrible poker player, shortly before *TMS* are joined by hard-nosed former Australia captain Steve Waugh, who is the polar opposite. Waugh is confidently beaming, saying, 'This has been a brilliant recovery from Australia.' It is impossible for anyone to tell what he's really thinking.

As the quiet recovery continues, Waugh is questioned as to whether one of cricket's favourite stories – dating back to Headingley in 1999 – is true. Waugh responds, 'Did I say "You've just dropped the World Cup" to Herschelle Gibbs? Well, it was something like that. Let's not ruin a good story!'

The distraction from on-field affairs is only momentary, however, as Carey, out of nowhere, plays a poor shot. He tries to take on the long-on boundary off Adil Rashid and only finds the fielder on the rope. Sub James Vince takes another crucial catch and Australia lose their fourth wicket. Their fifth goes before the end of the same over, Marcus Stoinis not picking Rashid's googly, playing around it and getting trapped right in front.

It's an obvious LBW decision and he turns tail and leaves the crease almost as soon as he's arrived, with a flea in his ear from Jim Maxwell to boot. 'Marcus Stoinis had no idea how to play that. Totally deceived,' he says disappointedly. 'A lack of concentration from Stoinis. You have to prepare for Rashid's wrong 'un,' agrees Waugh, the two Aussie greats combining for a stinging dissection of the departing all-rounder.

Glenn Maxwell, called to the crease by Waugh suggesting that it 'could be the defining moment of his career', combines with Smith to some effect before lobbing a gloriously disguised Archer knuckle ball to extra cover and soon after another googly from Rashid is more than enough for Pat Cummins. It gives Rashid final figures of three for 54 (three for 25 in his final six overs, Zaltzman points out) and he is given a standing ovation.

Such is the buzz around the falling Australian wickets, occupants of the box almost fail to notice one of the most extraordinary elements of the *TMS* summer unfolding in front of them. Assistant producer Henry Moeran, a fine musician as well as talented radio man, has somehow been granted the honour of being a temporary 'cricketarist' and is grinding out a bit of 'Sweet Child O' Mine' as Mitchell Starc walks to the crease.

Not only that, the whole exercise is being covered by the enormous big screens that overlook the stands at Edgbaston, with Moeran beaming into the camera, clearly having the time of his life. Even Zaltzman, who has been moved to physical rage by the exploits of the cricketarists in the past, is able to raise a smile at the ever-enterprising Moeran and his moment of glory.

Starc sticks around but is unable to help Smith raise the rate and confidence is growing in the box, with Sir Alastair Cook boldly stating, 'I just think England will be comfortable chasing 220, 230.' Smith is beginning to find his range when he fluffs an attempted pull shot into his body and tries to sprint a single to the wicketkeeper. Before you can blink, Jos Buttler has whipped off a glove, gathered the ball cleanly and thrown down the stumps at the bowler's end. It's only in subsequent replays that it is made clear that, fantastically, the ball has actually nutmegged Smith, perfectly bisecting his legs as it flew towards the stumps.

Starc goes next ball and when Mark Wood gets one down the other end that is far too quick for Jason Behrendorff, Australia have been bowled out for 223 and England will need only 224 to beat them and make the World Cup final. 'It doesn't get any better than that,' beams Tuffers. 'A 90mph yorker to finish off the Aussies! That was brilliant from England – everyone came to the party.'

Oddly, such was the quality of the England bowling per-formance, it has created nerves around the chase. There are mentions of the difficulties faced back in Malahide at the very start of the summer, of the performance against Sri Lanka – and, by those with long memories, Australia's performance at this very ground in the 1999 World Cup semi-final.

There are nerves about the state of Jason Roy's fitness, nerves about what happens if England lose early wickets and nerves about whether the nerves are self-perpetuating. Tuffers is still buoyant though. 'Half an hour of Jason Roy could put England in a great position,' he is saying. 'He doesn't seem to feel any pressure; if the ball is there he'll hit it. Just the chap to open the innings.'

He says this at 2.43 p.m. – by his stated check-in time of 3.13 p.m. England have rock and rolled their way to 31 for no wicket, the undisputed highlight of which is Roy taking a ball from Starc that is almost yorker length and flicking it off his legs, high and handsome over deep fine leg for six, one of the shots of the World Cup.

After ten overs, England are 50 for no wicket and everyone is breathing a lot easier. There is some unsettled movement in chairs when Australia bring on Nathan Lyon for the 11th over, but this quickly dissipates when Roy takes his first ball and smacks it back impudently, straight over his head, for six. This is followed up by a reverse sweep for four and, by the end of it, 13 runs have come from the off-spinner's over. 'It is absolutely fantastic to watch,' beams Cook. 'They have obviously spoken about how they are going to play Lyon. They are not going to let him settle.'

As Roy and Bairstow carry on gloriously, Zaltzman – working his penultimate *TMS* game of the summer, as Andrew Samson will be coming in for the Test matches – has plenty of choice for impressive partnership statistics generated by the pair. He opts for the following, which gets across the scale of their achievements very neatly. 'This is the 32nd time Jonny Bairstow and Jason Roy have opened the batting together and it is the 18th time they have reached 50,' he says. 'They have ten hundred partnerships among those, and their average opening stand is 69. That is comfortably the best of the 113 pairs who have batted together 15 or more times in ODI cricket.'

There is trouble ahead, though, when Bairstow appears to

damage an ankle while running. *TMS* turn to the programme's expert summariser, Sir Alastair Cook – hoping the great batsman can offer some experienced thoughts on what might be wrong. The response is unsatisfactory. 'I am no expert here,' he begins, to general surprise from people who thought that was exactly what he was being paid to be, before unveiling his killer line, 'I didn't run fast enough to pull something,' and immediately bringing the house down.

Bairstow recovers and England keep piling on the runs. Vaughan suggests Australia could try bowling barefoot as they seek to buy a wicket and the hundred is brought up in the midst of three giant sixes that Roy smashes off no less than Smith – who is asked to supply some of his part-time leg spin as part of Australia's 'try everything once' strategy. 'It's fair to say that gamble to bowl Steve Smith didn't work,' says Vaughan, who has now thoroughly relaxed and is truly living his best life in the summariser's chair.

There is a slight concern about some nearby rain dampening proceedings, but Zaltzman immediately points out that England are 81 ahead of the required DLS total 'and Australia need an asteroid strike not rain', and everyone just goes back to enjoying the spectacle. 'Sweet Caroline' is sung – certainly not for the first time this World Cup, but probably with the most gusto – and the only reason Simon Mann can find to be grumpy is that it's hard for his microphone to compete with the glorious, celebratory din generated by the England fans.

Bairstow is dismissed LBW to Starc, for whom the dismissal collects the record for the most wickets in a single World Cup, with 27, beating Glenn McGrath in 2007. While the milestone might look good one day, he'll probably take a while to appreciate it.

With 83 still to go, 'Sweet Caroline' is replaced by 'Hey Jude' and Vaughan officially declares victory. 'England were favourites to win this game, but Australia just haven't arrived,' he says. 'They have been marmalised. It has been a wonderful display.'

'I don't think I have enjoyed a day quite so much,' adds Paul Farbrace, who has popped in for a chat, and not even an odd dismissal for Roy, given out gloved down the leg side off one he didn't touch, can puncture the atmosphere.

The game passes 20 overs, meaning it will definitely finish today, and appropriately England's captains Joe Root and Eoin Morgan take it home. There's a party mood everywhere, especially in the *TMS* box. 'It has been a day full of tension. I just sighed and released some of that tension,' says Tuffers, stretching out for a stint on the home straight. 'Jason Roy and Jonny Bairstow were fantastic, and it was all set up by the bowling. It has been one of those dream semi-finals. England have grown from their dips in this tournament. The game against India here was one of the biggest games they have had since 1992. You felt if they won that it'd go on an upward climb and that's what has happened.'

As the game runs towards a conclusion, Tuffers is insatiable. 'I think Merv Hughes's moustache is even more droopy now!' he cracks when his former adversary is shown sitting in the stands looking particularly morose. 'The Cat' then calls for Sherlock Holmes to immediately be brought to Edgbaston because 'There have been 10 or 11 murders here today.'

'This is beyond all imagination, let alone expectation, of what might happen today,' adds Aggers, brought in to call the victory home. 'It has been an absolute hammering.'

'I can't stop smiling,' says Tuffers, explaining his face for the benefit of listeners, but he doesn't need to. Such is the jubilation in his voice there is no chance anyone listening at home cannot tell he is wearing a grin from east to west. Aggers, who has been in place for many a worse day than this, even starts to get wistful. 'Think of all the lows there have been in English one-day cricket,' he says. 'What a day to be here!'

With two required, outstandingly, the rain arrives. 'Shall I check the DLS par score?' asks Zaltzman, before pausing with the poise of an experienced stand-up comedian and delivering the perfect punchline: 'England are 114 ahead.'

Morgan smashes the winning boundary and, after some firm handshakes are exchanged, they dash off, allowing the weather to have its way. Despite the size, nature and import of the victory, England know there is an even bigger game to be played on Sunday, and today is more a case of 'job done' than cause for wild celebrations. 'England have answered all of those questions we had this morning,' says Aggers. 'Would the occasion be too much? Would the pressure be too much to bear? They have come out looking like world champions and if they play like this on Sunday they will be.'

As the rain hammers down, soaking Edgbaston through, the praise comes from all quarters. 'Is there a better opening partnership in the world than Jonny Bairstow and Jason Roy? I can't think of one,' asks Tuffers. 'I can't believe I have just watched that,' adds Cook. 'You always think there will be a twist in the tail, but there was no twist. England were so good.'

'England are so big and strong that they might do this to New Zealand on Sunday,' wonders Vaughan. 'Don't rule out New Zealand, but if this England team arrive and play to the same standard on Sunday, they could do the same again.'

Forty-seven matches down, one more to go. And England will be playing in it. It's going to be a big day at Lord's on Sunday.

Australia 223 (49 overs; Smith 85, Woakes 3-20, Rashid 3-54) lost to England 226-2 (32.1 overs; Roy 85, Root 49*, Morgan 45*) by eight wickets.

BBC SPORT LISTENERS' TEAM OF THE WORLD CUP

Rohit Sharma (India)

David Warner (Australia)

Virat Kohli (India)

Kane Williamson (New Zealand)

Shakib Al Hasan (Bangladesh)

Ben Stokes (England)

Alex Carey (Australia)

Chris Woakes (England)

Mitchell Starc (Australia)

Jofra Archer (England)

Jasprit Bumrah (India)

Voted for by readers of the BBC Sport website and revealed on Friday 12 July, two days before the final.

CHAPTER 13

The Greatest Final

Sunday 14 July
England v New Zealand – ICC Cricket World Cup – Final
Lord's Cricket Ground, St John's Wood, London

Team *TMS*: Jonathan Agnew, Simon Mann, Isa Guha, Bryan Waddle,
Michael Vaughan, Phil Tufnell, James Anderson, Jeremy Coney,
Andy Zaltzman

Florence Welch was standing on the street when a harp player pulled up and got out of a taxi, carrying his instrument. The singer invited him to play a song and, to this day, he's still an integral part of Florence and the Machine. Fifteen years later, Jimmy Anderson is sat backstage at Hyde Park, enraptured with this story of random fortuitous chance and generally enjoying the relaxed rock 'n' roll vibe that is present at one of London's biggest gigs of the summer. Stubbornly ignoring repeated polite suggestions to call it a night and head back to his hotel, England's all-time leading Test match wicket-taker is having a ball.

The following morning, a slumbering Lancastrian is rudely awoken at 8.30 a.m. by a phone call from his hotel receptionist asking if he would like to speak to a 'Mark Sharman'. His heart falls and a quick glance at the clock on the wall confirms his worst fears: Anderson is due on air at the World Cup final in less than half an hour – and he's been woken up by a 'Hail Mary' phone call from his producer, known affectionately as 'Sharky'.

Following an 'Australian shower' and liberal dashings of aftershave, 'the King of the Swingers' sprints out onto the street, flags a passing taxi and asks to be taken to Lord's as quickly as humanly possible. Upon arrival at the Home of Cricket, Anderson encounters more disaster as the required road is closed. Abandoning his cab, he sprints up the street towards the North Gate, realising halfway up that it's actually quite a good fitness test on a recalcitrant calf muscle that is currently threatening his participation in the forthcoming Test match against Ireland.

Passing rapidly through a mandatory bag search purely on the basis of his 575 Test match wickets, Anderson pelts across the Nursery Ground, dragging his wheelie suitcase right across the square and barely acknowledging England captain Eoin Morgan, who is preparing for the biggest game of his life with coach Paul Collingwood. Getting to the lifts that take you up to the ground's iconic Media Centre, Jimmy pushes past five waiting journalists and jumps in, hoping the notoriously unreliable Lord's lift mechanisms will not let him down on this of all occasions.

They do not, and he sprints through the written press box, up the stairs to the broadcast centre. At 9.01 a.m. he exhaustedly flops into his chair, pulls on a set of headphones and is seamlessly introduced to listeners by his *Tailenders* cohort Greg James, beginning what will become an 11-hour *TMS* takeover of BBC Radio 5 Live.

Why? Because it's the World Cup final. And England might win.

Next door, in the *TMS* box, Phil Tufnell has his lucky underwear on. In fact, it turns out that Tuffers has selected every item from his wardrobe that he deems to have any sort of fortune attached to it whatsoever. While never the most traditionally sartorial member of the team, it appears mere happenstance that his outfit even has any semblance of order.

Meanwhile, Jeremy Coney has been called onto *Tailenders* to give a typically humble, creative and funny tale of 'General Cricketing Sadness'. Donning a fisherman's beanie to help adopt the character, Coney regales the team with a wonderful story from his playing career.

Soundtracked by a heart-breaking improvised acoustic coda from Felix White, Jeremy tells of a time when he was bowling for New Zealand against India at the Gabba in Brisbane. Coney recounts how he initially bowled well before being recalled for a second spell when all-rounder Kapil Dev was dominating the crease. He wonderfully describes how he 'disappeared over the hills', his deliveries 'panel-beating the top of the stands'.

'I swore at him and gave him the best slower ball,' continues Coney. 'They all disappeared. Three overs later, I found a white handkerchief in my pocket – and waved it. It fluttered gently in the Woolloongabba breeze. A New Zealand selector caught up with me later behind the stands. "Don't ever let me see you do that again," he said.'

As expected, the combination of Coney and *Tailenders* is a winner, and as Greg hands over to Jonathan Agnew, one of the most anticipated editions of *TMS* in its 62-year history is under way. The overriding feeling is one of nervous tension, because while a World Cup final is clearly an iconically important game in its own right, it feels somehow like there is something more insistent resting on this game. As ever, this unconstructed

thought hanging in the air of the commentary box is vocal-
ised by Aggers, who says, 'There's so much anticipation and
excitement. It's more than a cricket match. I know that sounds
ridiculous, but you just feel like this is such an important day
for English cricket. There's a lot hanging on this day. Cricket's
future possibly?'

Part of this feeling is the recent announcement that today's
match will be the first since September 2005 to be broadcast live
on free-to-air television in the UK – with Channel 4 carrying
Sky Sports' coverage of the game. 'This is a massive day because
anyone can stumble across cricket today,' says Michael Vaughan.
'Huge credit to Sky for letting the final be on Channel 4.'

Classically for a big day of English cricket, there is enough
rain in the air to cause a slight delay to the start and the coin
is tossed at 10.15 a.m. Somehow, the result feels less important
than it did at Edgbaston on Thursday and everyone seems to
be happy in the end when New Zealand win it and opt to bat
first. Eoin Morgan – unaffected by his early-morning run-in
with a speeding Anderson – claims he'd likely have bowled
first anyway.

Former England all-rounder Derek Pringle has been recruited
to commentate on the game for an overseas broadcaster and,
superbly, arrives in the Media Centre clad in his original shirt
from the 1992 final. 'There is no way that still fits him,' states
Aggers reasonably. 'The '92 shirts were very, very large,' points
out Alec Stewart, who is covering the game for BBC 5 Live and
was also on the field in 1992 – the last time England reached a
World Cup final in this format. He is wearing a bespoke modern
version of the shirt, especially made by the ECB and given to
all members of the 1992 squad this week.

The national anthems are as loud as anyone has ever heard
them and, as Chris Woakes runs in to bowl the first delivery,
Agnew strains to be heard over the passionate din of support

that is being raised. 'It's not a typical Lord's atmosphere; this is an ICC World Cup,' he almost shouts – just before Martin Guptill takes a massive swipe at first ball, eliciting nervous peals of laughter from Tufnell, whose analysis of the shot is simply: 'Wow!'

With that, we're under way, and, despite the massive build-up, the fans outside asking over £2,000 for a ticket, the Red Devils parachute display team landing on the Nursery Ground and the presence of virtually every legend of cricket you could want to see, it quickly settles down into a classical 'nip and tuck' limited-overs international.

There is certainly something in the pitch, and when Henry Nicholls is whacked on the pads, seemingly right in front of all three stumps, and given out LBW, he consults with Guptill at the other end and decides to review the decision. This generates the following, rapid-fire conversation between Aggers, Tuffers and Coney, all of whom are convinced that Nicholls has made a terrible, adrenaline-fuelled mistake:

Agnew: 'That's a hoping-I've-got-away-with-it review.'

Coney: 'That is not going over the stumps.'

Aggers: 'If that's not out I'll eat Geoffrey Boycott's hat!'

Tuffers: 'That's a big hat, that is!'

Aggers: 'That is plumb. Nicholls is in so much trouble.'

The review is then rolled out on the TV coverage and the big screens in the ground and, astonishingly for everyone, shows the ball just passing over the top of the stumps. Somehow, Nicholls is safe to bat another day.

Aggers: 'It's going over! What?!'

Tuffers: 'I've fallen off my chair! He's 4ft 10! That looked absolutely plumb!'

Coney: 'It's a very calm review, gentlemen!'

Tuffers: 'How's that gone over?!'

Coney: 'It did look out. The three of us were wrong.'

Aggers: 'I think the three of us were right. Well, we didn't say anything naughty.'

The game continues, and two minutes later Aggers announces that 'A certain Geoffrey Boycott has messaged me, asking where to bring his hat and a knife and fork.'

'Okay, Geoffrey, fair enough.'

New Zealand crack on, and Guptill, who has done very little with the bat all tournament, is bristling with intent. 'He looks like a man with nothing to lose – he looks dangerous,' observes Tuffers, shortly before he upper-cuts Jofra Archer over third man for six. Soon, though, he is wrapped in front by Woakes and, despite the LBWgate that has just transpired, Tuffers is once again straight on his feet, declaring, 'If he's not hit that out, he's out!' Isa Guha, wisely withholding any promises with regards to Geoffrey Boycott's headwear, simply says it looks 'plumb'.

Given not out, it is England who make the referral and, when the three red lights all illuminate, Guptill's race is run and he trudges disconsolately back to the Pavilion. 'A beautiful piece of bowling by Mr Dependable,' adds Tuffers, happy to have been proven right on this occasion.

The key man, Kane Williamson, is at the crease and backs straighten across the ground with the knowledge of how much New Zealand have relied on his runs to get them to the point they're currently at. Archer keeps him honest early on with a gem that flashes past the outside edge, eliciting loud reactions from both Guha and Michael Vaughan. Williamson and Nicholls slowly start to build a platform and Anderson – partially recovered after being granted time for a sit-down and a large breakfast – goes so far as to say that 'New Zealand will be the happier side.'

TMS are joined on air by former Australian captain Steve Waugh, who says New Zealand 'are looking at 250 to 270 at least and then they can rely on their bowlers and are an exceptional fielding side'. Jonny Bairstow then makes a wonder stop on the boundary, causing Waugh to add, 'It is no coincidence the two best fielding teams are here in the final.'

Liam Plunkett, expensive in an initial three-over spell, is brought back into the attack and off just his third ball goes up hard, thinking he has Williamson caught behind. The batsman is unmoved, the umpire is unmoved. Morgan is anything but, immediately punching his arm in the time-honoured motion and sending the call upstairs. Aggers nervously manages listener expectations by saying that he didn't hear anything in his headphones but – when the pictures are rolled – it's clear that Morgan was spot-on and Plunkett's ability to get batsmen out in the middle overs has paid off with the biggest wicket of his career. 'Plunkett does this so often!' roars Agnew over a cacophonous din at the Home of Cricket. 'In these middle overs he comes in and takes a key wicket, and this is *the* key wicket.'

A couple of minutes later, Andy Zaltzman chips in with an absolute gem, adding, 'Liam Plunkett has only taken nine wickets at this tournament, but every single batsman has been a top-five player. Eight of those wickets, the batsman has been on 30 or more.'

'He gets out good players, who are well set,' ends Zaltz, hammering home the unique quality that Plunkett brings to this England side. As if to thank Agnew and Zaltzman for their praise, Plunkett then repeats the trick, sending down a cross-seam delivery that draws Nicholls – who had just raised his bat for a fifty – into a loose shot that sees the ball fly through and send the zing bails flying. The only note of concern for England comes from Jeremy Coney, who adds that Plunkett's wickets 'suggest the pitch is a little slower than the players thought', something that could benefit the Kiwis in time.

However, there is no implosion, and when Phil Tufnell says that 'New Zealand will be thinking that if they get 250 then you're always in the game. If you aim for that score you always manage to find another 20 runs from somewhere,' there is some concerted nodding from those around him.

Mark Wood returns and gets rid of the dangerous Ross Taylor, who has to walk due to Guptill burning New Zealand's one review earlier in the innings. Shortly after he has left the field, it becomes clear the ball was not going to hit the stumps after all. Unremarkably, Vaughan is unsympathetic to his problem, laying it firmly at Guptill's door. 'If you make the wrong decision of whether to review it can cost a key player their wicket,' he says with a slight air of amusement.

Just as Jonathan Agnew is reeling from hearing 'Who Let the Dogs Out?' at Lord's for the first time, Plunkett strikes again, removing Jimmy Neesham, and as the last ten overs of the innings start, Jimmy Anderson backs up Tuffers' earlier point, adding, 'Watching how the pitch is playing, I don't think England will want to chase more than 250. New Zealand's bowling attack likes the challenge of defending low totals and they are good at it.' He adds ruefully, 'The pitch looks similar in pace to the one for the Old Trafford semi-final. New Zealand got to 240 against India in that game and managed to defend it.'

Tom Latham helps his side continue to tick runs over, despite an odd innings from Colin de Grandhomme, who struggles to get the ball away. 'De Grandhomme is wearing a few,' chuckles Anderson. 'He has been early on the slower bouncer and late on the fast bouncer.'

The magical figure of 250 is the topic of much discussion as the final overs play out. Coney thinks that 'New Zealand are a little short of where they would like to be', and a well-directed last over from Archer sees the final reckoning sit at 241. England will need 242 to win the Cricket World Cup.

As if today hasn't been extraordinary enough, the *TMS* team then get one of the shocks of a lifetime as a cake that leaves everyone virtually lost for words is ferried into the back of the commentary box during the break between innings. Remarkably, it consists of perfect replicas of both the England and New Zealand helmets, with the Cricket World Cup in the middle, a pair of bails under one helmet and – perhaps to signify we still have the Ashes to come? – a perfectly constructed red ball, with a white seam, under another.

There are also miniature versions of Kane Williamson and Eoin Morgan and the flags of the ten teams competing in the competition. On a programme that has been privileged to sample the finest of world baking over the years, it is one of the most beautiful creations any of us has ever seen.

Aggers is MCing the cake presentation and interviews the wonderful Julie Brownlee, from Stroud, who had started baking the cake a week ago but – with the semi-finalists only confirmed on Thursday – had her work somewhat cut out to complete the finer details in time. This in and of itself would have been amazing enough, but there is also a note included with the cake, and it becomes clear that this hasn't been a solo project from Julie. In fact, she has been commissioned by no less than Camilla, Duchess of Cornwall, who reveals herself as a *TMS* fan.

She has been closely involved in the design of the masterpiece and specifically requested the elderflower and lemon sponge flavour. The final part has to be taken entirely on trust because it is so beautiful that nobody dares go anywhere near it with a knife. The note itself says, 'I hope this cake will bowl you over! With my best wishes, Camilla.'

It is an utterly remarkable gift and, for once, everyone is quite lost for words. It is also not the first time that a cake has been presented to *TMS* by the royal family. Back in 2001, *TMS* – then represented by Aggers, Henry Blofeld, Christopher Martin-Jenkins, Peter Baxter and Bill Frindall – were summoned to the Committee Room to be presented with a fruit cake by no less than Her Majesty the Queen. 'They tell me people give you cakes,' she said to then producer Peter Baxter, who confirmed the tradition that was started by Brian Johnston in 1974.

After some royal chit-chat down the receiving line, Aggers was the last to meet Her Majesty. 'Ma'am, did you bake it yourself?' he asked.

'No,' came the immediate and firm reply. 'But it was made under strict personal supervision.'

Fortunately, in the intervening 18 years, Aggers has learnt better royal protocol, and thanks the Duchess far more properly on this occasion. The cake is stowed at the back of the box – almost a museum piece for fellow media members to come and inspect during the rest of the game – and with Jason Roy and Jonny Bairstow making their way out to the middle, there's a World Cup final to get on with.

Immediately, Trent Boult comes flying in with the new ball, swings one back into Roy and offers up a huge appeal as it smacks him on the pad. The decision is not out, and New Zealand send it upstairs. It's a remarkably similar scenario to what happened to Nicholls at the start of the New Zealand innings and, as before, the inner third umpires in the box – in this case Tuffers and Bryan Waddle – immediately give their verdict.

Tuffers: 'Oooooahhhh! That looked close! It might have done too much?! That's a banana! He's bowled him a banana! Swung big! Swung big!'

Waddle: 'Now, the front-on will decide. It was a beauty of a delivery! It's come back in and . . . Ooooaahhhh.'

Tuffers: 'Oooaoahhh, 'ello!'

Waddle: 'It's been given not out. It might have done too much?! It might have missed the leg stump or be umpire's call?'

Tuffers: 'Yeah, umpire's call. Going down the leg side.'

Waddle: 'Oooooh no, that's hitting! I reckon that's hitting!'

Waddle and Tuffers (in harmony): 'Oooooh no! Umpire's call, it's umpire's call!'

Waddle: 'How's that not out?!'

Tuffers: 'Oof, wow, wooooahhhh. Wow. Wow.'

Waddle: 'That was hitting all three!'

Tuffers: 'Wow. It wasn't hitting all three, but it was certainly hitting one.'

Waddle: 'That's one that's gone England's way. If that was given out, I wouldn't have moaned. That's unlucky for New Zealand.'

Boult is bowling like a man possessed, at one stage nutmegging Roy with a yorker, but it is Matt Henry who makes the breakthrough, forcing Roy to edge behind – and the quality of bowling simply does not let up. Joe Root, despite being England's highest run scorer in the tournament, is just unable to get his innings going, and Tufnell, still on commentary and quickly turning a whiter shade of pale, adds, 'If you think you are 20 to 30 runs short of a target, this is the sort of opening bowling you want from your side.'

England continue to toil as the great Brian Lara arrives in the back of the box for a visit and stands chatting with Alec Stewart. Despite the collective weight of experience, all that their 48,321 first-class runs can agree on is it's likely to be very tight indeed.

Root goes, with Bryan Waddle slightly gleefully pointing out that his forced shot – caused by the continued build-up of pressure by the singular lack of bad balls – 'is very unlike Joe Root'. At the other end, New Zealand's top 'trundler', de Grandhomme – identified as a weakness in the bowling battalion at the start of the game – is bowling one of the most abstemious spells in the history of the World Cup, and England are starting to panic.

'I can't take this. I'm going to go home,' gasps Michael

Vaughan, becoming the highest-ranking member of the England fanbase to publicly admit to not being able to take it – shortly after his Sheffield Collegiate CC protégé Root was dismissed and the new man, captain Morgan, takes a wild swipe at one of his early deliveries.

Vaughan remains on commentary, working with Bryan Waddle, when Lockie Ferguson takes the inside edge of Bairstow's bat and bowls the England opener. 'PLAYED ON!' shouts Waddle as the bails fly, leaving a perfect cogitation gap afterwards. Quite often that gap would have been filled with an involuntary noise from a summariser or 'noises off' from elsewhere in the box; on this occasion there is nothing, the box stunned into silence as the realisation hits that England, after everything they've been through, could be messing this up.

De Grandhomme continues to be England's torturer in chief, bowling his medium-pace deliveries with such metronomic consistency that Zaltzman reveals it has taken until his 39th delivery for him to concede a boundary. With such success of that style from one end, New Zealand call for Neesham to bowl at the other end (on commentary, Isa Guha wonders 'whether Trent Boult might have been a better option for these two early in their innings?'). Disappointingly for his side, Neesham's first ball is a short, wide long-hop to Morgan.

However, the England captain opts for the up-and-over approach and, instead of slotting it into the Lord's Grandstand for six, offers up a very tough chance to Lockie Ferguson in the deep. The fast bowler sprints in, eyes focused intently on the ball, times his dive perfectly and claims what seems to be a world-class – and potentially World Cup-winning – catch. Umpire Kumar Dharmasena sends the decision upstairs and breath is collectively held as the replay is shown. Initial impressions are that the catch has been cleanly taken, and when these are confirmed, Guha's voice drops an octave and sums up the deathly dread that has just encapsulated a nation.

'Yeah, that's just poor cricket all round really, apart from the catch!' cries Jimmy Anderson dispiritedly as Morgan becomes the latest to trudge back.

Jos Buttler and Ben Stokes are the men at the crease – the last of England's recognised batsmen – and there are still 147 runs required to become world champions. The spectre of the Sri Lanka defeat a few weeks ago is beginning to haunt this game and New Zealand are everyone's favourite, a position under-lined when Zaltzman pipes up with the gem that 'there have been 107 dot balls in the first 25 overs of this innings. That is the most England have played out in the first 30 overs since the last World Cup.'

However, slowly but surely, Buttler and Stokes combine to move the game forward. They tick through the landmarks: firstly, de Grandhomme's final over is seen off without further damage and then they make it to the drinks break together. Vaughan, who is on the rota to take the game home in the summariser's chair, attempts to dispel his nerves by tweeting positively, 'England starting to play the smart game. Don't get bowled out and they win the World Cup methinks.'

Henry has a huge shout for LBW against Buttler turned down and, after taking it to the third umpire, New Zealand lose their review. 'Something has to give!' says Tuffers. 'It's bubbling up beautifully. You get the feeling there will either be an over where England score 18 or there's a wicket ... ' Then, with the final ball of the 39th over, Buttler pulls out his famous ramp shot and flicks Henry over his shoulder and away into the Pavilion for four.

As the game enters the last ten overs, the tension in the com-mentary box – and the wider world – is becoming unbearable, but Stokes and Buttler are seemingly unafflicted. 'The two guys out there are cool as cucumbers,' gasps Tuffers shortly before he has to be prised out of the summariser's chair for the last time in this World Cup. 'We're all a mess up here, but those two look as calm as you like!' His replacement, Michael Vaughan, replies, 'All good captains are good actors. There's no way that Eoin Morgan on the balcony and Kane Williamson at mid-off are calm!'

Buttler and Stokes bring up their fifties in the same over, but Buttler miscues a big drive in the next over and is well caught by the substitute fielder, Tim Southee. It's a 'magnificent grab in the context of the game', says Vaughan.

With Woakes walking to the wicket, it would be safe to assume that the tension in the box could not be punctured. Think again. Vaughan's phone vibrates in his pocket, he reads it, and you can see a weight, at least temporarily, lift from his shoulders. 'I've just had a text from my dad saying Yorkshire have got 520 and Somerset are 76 for four!' he reveals. 'You have to love parents.'

Neesham continues to bowl and Stokes flicks his final ball through mid-wicket for a vital boundary. The roar is such that you can barely hear a puce-faced Jeremy Coney screaming, partially off microphone, '141kph. BOWL. SLOWER.'

As the players prepare for the next over, 'Sweet Caroline' by Neil Diamond is played through the Lord's PA system and the crowd – somehow finding a vocal memory for the famous old tune – sing along, almost out of instinct and a certain level of duty. This astonishes Agnew, who emphasises the extraordinary situation in front of him, and dispels some of his own personal tension by laughing, 'This is Lord's! This has never been played at Lord's before!'

Woakes is dismissed off the first ball of the next over, but Plunkett, a hero with the ball earlier, comes in and finds the boundary, a feat matched by Stokes off the first ball of the next over. With two overs to go, England require 24. Wonderfully, despite his desperation for a New Zealand victory, Jeremy Coney has a magisterial take on the situation as he simply says, 'It's going to the last over and that is fitting for a World Cup final.'

Vaughan, more nationalistically, adds, 'This over's got to go. This is the one. This is England's over.'

Agnew feels a buzz on his wrist and looks down in case it's producer Adam Mountford passing him a key message. It's not; it's his very modern watch – which contains a heart rate monitor – buzzing to tell him that there is 'a minute of slow breathing needed' for his ticker to return to a normal state.

Two singles come from the first two balls and then Plunkett goes, caught trying to go down the ground for the six required. Crucially though, the batsmen cross, so Stokes retains the strike. 'England need a boundary in the next three balls, of one sort or another . . . ' says Coney.

Stokes crunches the next ball into exactly the same area where Plunkett has just been caught. He hits it harder though, and Boult steadies himself underneath it. 'Ohhhhhh, he's fallen over! The catch is taken, and this will be a replay,' wobbles Aggers.

'It's six,' replies Coney stolidly.

'He thought he was a metre inside, he was dead casual and stepped back straight onto the foam roller,' explains Vaughan.

'He caught it by the way, everybody!' adds Coney, defending his countryman despite his lack of awareness.

As the next ball is about to be bowled, Neesham pulls out of his run-up as Stokes walks away from the crease, seemingly seeing someone moving behind the bowler's arm. 'It's probably some poor old member having a heart attack!' speculates Aggers.

'He's probably leaving; it's not exciting enough,' suggests Vaughan, who has clearly been the victim of some opinionated MCC members in the past.

The next ball is a single, effectively giving new man Archer a free hit off the final ball of the penultimate over. He swings mightily but is bowled. It almost doesn't matter because Stokes is at the right end to take the strike for the final over. Adil Rashid is at the other end, with his sprinter's boots on. England need 15 off the last over to win the World Cup.

'For England to win this game, you feel like Adil Rashid doesn't have to face a ball,' says Vaughan. 'You need to deal in even numbers: two, four or six.' Referring back to 2017 – and identifying the potential for one of cricket's greatest-ever redemption stories for Stokes, Agnew adds, 'He has the chance to redeem himself, but what a tall order he faces.'

The first two balls are dots, with Stokes first turning down a single and then hitting straight to cover. 'What bowling that is,' says Vaughan, gently starting to come to terms with a New Zealand victory. The next ball is on a length, though, and Stokes heaves it high and mighty over the leg side. 'That's going to go for six! What a shot!' shouts Agnew as Phil Tufnell's instinctively loud clapping in the back of the box gets picked up by the microphone and comes over on the broadcast far louder than the 28,000 people roaring in the stands below. Nine off three.

The next ball is a full toss, swiped into the leg side by Stokes.

Agnew: 'They want to get two here, surely. Come on, Adil Rashid, run! Stokes to the far end, he's desperate to get in there – he dives!'

Vaughan [yelping]: 'It's going for four!'

Agnew: 'That came off Stokes! If it goes for four there's nothing they can do about it!'

Vaughan: 'That's four!'

Agnew: 'There's nothing they can do about it! Stokes is saying to the umpire, "Don't let it count!" But it does count! There's this silly little thing in cricket where if it deflects off a tailender and goes for a run, the sportsmen don't run – but that's gone for four, there's nothing they can do about it, it's not a dead ball.'

Vaughan: 'Ben Stokes here is almost saying to Kane Williamson, "I'm sorry, I've not meant that," and he didn't. He's just got a full dive on and the ball has hit the bat.'

Agnew: 'That was thrown in from the deep, Stokes was diving for his ground, the throw hit him – absolutely accidentally – and ricocheted to the boundary.'

Coney: 'It hit his bat, it hit his bat – as he dived to get in!'

Agnew: 'Had it just gone for one more, Ben Stokes might not have run. He'd have said, "Well no, we don't do that." That has flown down to third man. It's like in Wimbledon, that net cord and that horrible little bounce. That is just a freak. *That. Is. A. Freak.*'

England need three runs from two balls.

Agnew, somehow managing to sound simultaneously adrenalised and exhausted, declares that 'I've never heard a noise like this at Lord's. Poor old Old Father Time has turned away; he can't bear it. Look at him there, up above the scorers' shed. He's never heard a din like this before!'

Coney, still believing his men's ability to get the job done, adds, 'Get up, New Zealand, you've still got two balls to go!'

Stokes hammers the next ball down the ground and Rashid sets off like a racehorse, desperate to run the two that would guarantee at least a tie. The throw comes in and Rashid is run out, but it doesn't matter because Stokes is on strike.

Agnew: 'We're going to have a tie here.'

Vaughan [uncomprehendingly]: 'Hahahahahahahahahahaha hahahahahahaha.'

England need two runs from one ball.

Wood walks to the crease, knowing his job is one of three things: to run, to celebrate or to commiserate.

'What a game!' says Vaughan, clearly disbelieving the situation that this wonderful sport has thrown up in front of him. 'Mark Wood is getting his horse out here.'

'If they win, I expect to see it!' answers Agnew.

'It's one of those games where you almost don't want a winner – in a sense,' says Coney.

The last ball is delivered, a perfect low full toss on leg stump, and Stokes pushes it back down the ground. They secure the single for the tie and then turn to run the victory run. Neesham hurls the ball in from deep mid-on, and Wood is caught two metres short. England have scored one – and the game is tied and going to a super over. The rules of the super over are quickly produced by Andy Zaltzman, who has been an astonished, squawking, off-air presence for the entirety of the England innings.

RULES OF A SUPER OVER

Only nominated players from playing XI may participate. Three batsmen and one bowler.

Team batting second will bat first.

Fielding side will choose end to bowl.

Team scoring more runs in the super over will win.

Loss of two wickets ends the team's super over innings.

If the super over is tied, the team hitting more boundaries in their innings and the super over win.

'I've never commentated on a super over,' says Agnew, to general amusement. With a gap while the teams prepare, Anderson, who has a huge sweat on (not for the first time today), is called onto the air to give his thoughts.

'Not good. I'm not enjoying this at all,' he gasps.

'If you're just joining us,' says Aggers, summarising for any new listeners who may have recently arrived, 'the World Cup final has tied between England and New Zealand. There will now be a super over bowled by either side – most runs wins it. I'm not sure what happens after that – we go to one of those Newton's Cradles or something, I don't know, what'll we do?!'

'Sport does this,' says Jeremy Coney. 'Sport does this – time and time again.'

'I've never experienced a super over before,' admits Anderson. 'I wonder whether it's like a penalty shoot-out where the coach and captain go to the person that looks like they want it? It's pressure like they've never experienced before.'

Agnew reads out the rules of the super over – answering his own question about what happens if it's tied. The team that has hit the most boundaries in the game and super over combined win. 'I'm queuing the statto boffin to our left,' he says as Zaltzman is called upon to provide the key piece of information.

'That will be England. They hit 22 fours and two sixes. New Zealand, 14 fours and two sixes,' he dramatically confirms.

Stokes and Buttler are chosen as the two England batsmen to face the first over, with Roy waiting to come in should a wicket fall. Boult will bowl it for New Zealand, from the Nursery End.

'What a finale! What a climax!' says Agnew, brilliantly relaying the unique experience unfolding in front of him at Lord's. 'Six balls from each team decide this World Cup final. It's a total lottery, but my word it's an exciting one. You just can't beat this for a World Cup final. All the miles driven, the balls bowled. Everything else. I mean, for goodness sake, it comes down to this. Absolutely incredible. We could have done this six weeks ago.'

'Cricket needed this drama. It needed a day like this,' replies Vaughan.

'I hope MILLIONS are watching. I hope MILLIONS are listening,' adds Agnew. 'Just everywhere, because this is the best game on the planet and it's given a great account of itself today.'

Stokes takes first strike and sends the first ball to third man for three, sinking to his knees in exhaustion as he makes his ground at the Nursery End. Something suddenly strikes Vaughan. 'Do these runs count in the history of the game?' he asks Zaltzman. 'I think they just dissolve into the ether,' replies the mind-boggled statistician.

The second ball is a single, returning Stokes to the strike, and the all-rounder, astonishingly, goes down on one knee and sweeps the fast bowler through the leg side, perfectly finding the gap as two deep fielders converge but are unable to stop it going for four. England have eight runs from three balls. As Boult runs in for the fourth ball, Agnew almost wistfully recalls the moment that 'someone, sometime ago, told me cricket was a boring game'.

'I hope he's watching.'

The fourth ball is a single to the edge of the circle and the fifth a two deep into the off side, Henry Nicholls allowing an extra run because he had the sun right in his eyes and couldn't initially track the path of the ball correctly. 'What a horrible moment for him,' Agnew sympathises. The final ball is chipped into the leg side by Buttler – and timed so beautifully there isn't even the time for a despairing dive as the ball crashes into the boundary. England have scored 15 off their super over.

'They've set New Zealand 16 to win the World Cup,' says Agnew, 'and in case you're just tuning in and thinking, *That's not very many*, we have actually had a game up to this point!'

'It's going to be heart-breaking for one side or another after the full seven hours we've had here or whatever,' says Jeremy Coney, as 24-year-old Archer bowls a final few warm-up deliveries and readies himself to deliver what will be a defining experience for many generations of English cricket fans.

Agnew addresses Anderson directly, saying, 'Come on, Jimmy, this is an interesting call. The faith they're putting into someone who's only just started off an international career. Think of the experience there is up there in that England dressing room. It's an incredible call, isn't it?'

'It is, it is,' replies Anderson. 'But I don't think Eoin Morgan would trust him with this over if he wasn't 100 per cent sure he was the man for the job. If he didn't want it, you'd be able to see it in his eyes.'

'He must have impressed them so much,' continues Agnew.

'Absolutely,' says Anderson. 'I just hope he's keeping it together better than me and Tuffers at the back of the box, because we're not enjoying this!'

'Poor old Tuffers, he shot his bolt about 20 minutes ago!' says Agnew. 'Look at him in the back there, it's a terrible sight!'

'You can't say that!' responds Vaughan.

'Well, he has,' counters Aggers. 'He's just blown it. He's gone, hasn't he? He's just gone!'

Guptill and Neesham are the two men facing the super over for New Zealand. They need 16, or 15 for another tie, and as they stride out to face their destiny, Coney posits a more sporting solution to Aggers.

Coney: 'Do you like the idea of a tie-breaker?'

Agnew: 'Yes, I think so.'

Coney: 'I think I'd rather share. It's such a long part of the day.'

Agnew: 'It's great tension, isn't it? The drama!'

Coney: 'Well, the day's been tense, hasn't it?'

Agnew: 'Yes.'

285

Coney: 'Look at you, you've lost weight.'

Agnew: 'Do you think so? God, I hope so!'

'The sun is fully out now, but the lights are on and the shadows are creeping onto Lord's. A sunlit evening. What a perfect stage for this dramatic finish,' says Agnew as Archer comes in to deliver his first ball.

He starts with a wide outside the off stump and the second ball is thumped down the ground, substitute fielder James Vince gathering cleanly and keeping it to two. Combined, it means New Zealand have scored three from the first ball. The next ball is on a length and Neesham's eyes light up. He heaves the ball into the Mound Stand for a giant six, swinging the game back New Zealand's way and causing Vaughan, almost involuntarily, to mutter, 'What a shot that is!'

Neesham works the next ball into the leg side and a slight fumble from Roy allows them to return for a second, meaning New Zealand require five from three. It's not lost on anybody that this is New Zealand's second consecutive World Cup final, and when Vaughan remembers that 'Neesham was in the crowd at the MCG four years ago, supporting New Zealand,' Agnew replies simply, 'Well, he's on strike now to win them the World Cup.'

The fourth delivery sees the ball once again dispatched into the leg side, and this time, although he collects the ball cleanly, Roy throws the ball to the wrong end and the two is completed. Three runs from two balls. Incredibly, it's exactly the same ask England had in the final over of the game itself.

Archer goes back of a length for his fifth ball and Neesham can only get an under edge to his cross-batted swipe, sending the ball straight into the ground as he dashes a single. Archer does the fielding from his own bowling and cocks his arm as if to attempt a run-out at the non-striker's end.

'DON'T THROW IT! DON'T THROW IT!' shouts

Agnew, his voice breaking with stress before quickly adding, 'He didn't throw it. Sorry.' Somehow, this moment of pure fandom from Agnew, followed by his quick realisation and apology, manages to break the tension in an utterly packed *TMS* box, which is grateful to briefly dissolve into fond, terrified laughter before quickly righting itself and regaining rigidity.

The single means that Guptill is facing his first ball, the last of the super over. He needs two to win the World Cup for New Zealand. A dot ball or a single will deliver the trophy to England. 'Where do you bowl it?' asks Agnew.

'Guptill is quite good on the cross-batted shot, so you'd think he'd have to go for the yorker,' replies Vaughan.

'Yes,' says Coney, before returning to wondering how on earth you can separate the two teams in a situation like this.

'Why is Rashid in the slip cordon?' asks Vaughan suddenly, seeing the leg-spinner well out of his normal position. Suddenly, off mic, there is a garbled noise from the back of the box as Tuffers attempts to express his agreement with Vaughan's befuddlement.

'What? Well, he hasn't got a third man?' suggests Coney, desperately searching for a reason for such an odd fielding placement. Rashid then retreats to the edge of the circle, causing a full-throated laugh from Vaughan, who nervously repeats himself, 'Yeah, you don't need a slip!'

'Three slips and a gully,' replies Coney mischievously.

As Archer runs in, Agnew takes over and Vaughan brings his hands together in prayer. 'Here's the last ball of the World Cup final. Archer bowls it and it's clipped away into the leg side, they're going to come back for the second! The throw is picked up. THEY THROW TO THE WICKETKEEPER'S END. HE'S RUN OUT, IS HE?! I THINK HE'S RUN OUT!'

While the decision is subject to third-umpire approval, England disappear in wild celebration and everyone's cricketing instincts tell them that Guptill has indeed been run out and England have done it. The ground and commentary box erupt in pure delight, with Tuffers just grabbing anyone close to him, Anderson removing his head from hands and hugging all and sundry, and the atmosphere descending into bedlam and delirium. The decision is confirmed and that is it: England have won the World Cup.

In a slightly surreal motif, the royal cake – which no one has yet dared to cut into – sits untouched as bodies are flung past it, left and right, up and down, almost as if Julie had baked a powerful forcefield into her elderflower and lemon sponge. Amid everything, assistant producer Henry Moeran's reaction is the most professional of the lot. While England may have just won the Cricket World Cup, he remembers that his job is to get onto the outfield as quickly as possible and get reaction from the players. So, ducking under Tufnell's elbow, narrowly avoiding Anderson's right knee and sliding out of the way of a Graeme Swann bear hug, Moeran retrieves his 'pitch access' bib and broadcasting equipment and makes for the door.

Elsewhere, fireworks erupt from the roof of the Grandstand, Archer sinks to the hallowed turf and beats the ground before getting up and quickly being engulfed by his team-mates. 'Well done, young man. My word!' says Aggers. 'What an effort that is, what an effort. It's been an absolutely brilliant game of cricket – and I'd have said that if they'd got those two runs there. What a day it's been.'

Simon Mann takes over on air as Aggers and Vaughan are dispatched to join Moeran on the pitch, and celebrations unfurl wherever you look. They gather up reaction from England players before taking their spot behind the official cordon to describe the moment this has all been building towards – which, on top of witnessing the trophy being lifted, gives Aggers one last memorable moment to take home with him.

'Eoin Morgan has clasped the trophy in his hands,' roars Agnew. 'He's shaking hands with the fella that's giving it to him, and in a moment you're going to hear a tremendous roar from this crowd here at Lord's as Eoin Morgan stands on the podium in front of his team – there it goes!'

The trophy is lifted skywards, setting off more fireworks and yet another round of celebrations across the country, which will last for some time. Later in the evening, Aggers is mortified to discover that 'the fella' who has just given Morgan the trophy was, in fact, the Duke of York.

The broadcast goes on long into the night and as the final member of the *TMS* team heads out onto the Wellington Road at around midnight, celebrations are ongoing all over the place. New Zealand have apparently turned the Long Room into a disco, England have been on the field with their wives and children, and there is talk of a party for players, fans and everyone else at The Oval tomorrow.

As ever, after such a massive high, there is an inevitable comedown, which must be overcome when there is still work to be done. Fortunately, *TMS* had the perfect strategy to deal with this. Thank you, Your Royal Highness, your cake was delicious.

New Zealand 241-8 (50 overs; Nicholls 55) tied with England 241 (50 overs; Stokes 84*, Buttler 59). Super over: England 15-0, New Zealand 15-1. England win by most boundaries scored.

CHAPTER 14

Perry Rules in Somerset

Thursday 18 July
England v Australia – Women's Ashes – Test
Match – Day 1
County Ground, Taunton

Team *TMS*: Alison Mitchell, Henry Moeran, Natalie Germanos, Isabelle
Westbury, Melinda Farrell, Charlotte Edwards, Lydia Greenway, Mel Jones

Just three days after 'The Greatest Match in the History
of Cricket'®, the Women's Ashes reconvenes at a buzzing
Taunton for the only Test match in the series. For everyone in
the *TMS* team, the past few days have been a mess of regaining the ability to think straight, taking a long lie-down in a
darkened room and celebrating the fact that England are now
world champions in both men's and women's one-day international cricket.

The 'darkened room' was, in fact, taken literally last night as
there was a *TMS* team outing to the cinema in Taunton, with
Alison Mitchell, Mel Farrell, Natalie Germanos and producer

Adam Mountford forsaking the delights of *The Lion King* and *Spiderman* to watch cricketing documentary *The Edge*. The film was made by a good friend of *TMS*, Barney Douglas, and features a brilliant soundtrack by *Tailenders* co-host Felix White. It was thoroughly enjoyable and, when the lights came up, it was immediately clear it wasn't just the *TMS* team enjoying a pre-Ashes trip to the flicks – the cinema was full of cricket journalists, England coaching staff and even some players, with Tammy Beaumont enjoying some popcorn to help ease the Ashes nerves.

The England women, after 'going viral' in a wonderful video of their celebrations on Sunday evening, need to get their heads back in the game, as anything but a victory in this week's only Test match will see the first Ashes of the summer head straight back to Australia at the earliest possible opportunity.

An early *TMS* pitch inspection encounters a spinning deck and an Australia team that has won the toss, batted first and given a debut to Tayla Vlaeminck, which the collected team unanimously agree is very kind of them from a pronunciation standpoint, especially with Andile Phehlukwayo having only recently left the country. Mitchell Starc is around again, helping out with fielding practice beforehand, and Aussie all-rounder Dan Christian is also here to present a cap to another Test debutant, Ashleigh Gardner – a lovely touch as both are indigenous Australians.

While there are significant hopes invested in the England win that will keep the series alive, *Telegraph* journalist and former Middlesex captain Isabelle Westbury is also hoping for a quality game for other reasons. 'Every girl, every boy wants to play Test cricket,' she says. 'We want to see the multi-format across more series so this is an important game. Test cricket is the pinnacle, but it's not reflected in women's cricket.'

Henry Moeran is in early trouble as play is initially delayed by a couple of minutes due to a drain that has not been covered, causing a small puddle on the outfield. The allegation in the box is that he was responsible for stepping on it and breaking it earlier in the day. It is an accusation he vehemently denies, but fortunately the Taunton ground staff are able to quickly make the necessary amends before Hercule Poirot is dispatched to the West Country, and the action gets under way.

England grab an early breakthrough when Katherine Brunt bowls Nicole Bolton but, as Mel Farrell says, 'They have to restrict Australia to under 200 as it's going to be very difficult batting last.' This looks increasingly unlikely as the day wears on, with England turning to the first of their front-line spinners, Sophie Ecclestone, less than an hour into the first day. 'You sense Sophie Ecclestone is going to bowl a lot of overs in the next few days,' says Moeran.

However, it's the left-arm spinner Kirstie Gordon, who played her first multi-day match only last year, who gets the next breakthrough, bowling Alyssa Healy on the first morning of a Test career that has started very well indeed. Gordon's morning seems to improve when she thinks she has Meg Lanning caught at cover, the Aussie skipper turning to walk off before realising that her opposite number, Heather Knight, has in fact dropped the catch.

The problem for England is that the removal of Healy brings the immovable object, Ellyse Perry, to the crease. She has been in good form in the ODI series, and the last time she played an Ashes Test match, at the North Sydney Oval in 2017, she got a relentless double century.

TMS are joined by the great Belinda Clark, captain of Australia from 1994 to 2005 and a double World Cup-winner and double Ashes-winner, during the lunch interval. As expected, she is spectacular company, talking excitedly about her role on the board of the 2020 T20 World Cup in Australia and the aspiration to sell out the Melbourne Cricket Ground's 100,000 capacity for the final.

The afternoon continues much as the morning session before Ecclestone bowls Meg Lanning – but Mel Farrell's ambition for England to keep Australia to less than 200 is looking unlikely at 160 for three, with Rachael Haynes the new woman at the crease. 'It's like Medusa's heads,' mourns Westbury in a wonderfully classical reference to the Australia batting line-up. 'You cut one off, and another one grows in its place.'

Throughout the day, an on-air debate rages about the correct culinary vernacular for poor deliveries (Mel Jones says 'yum yums'; Natalie Germanos swears by 'doughnuts'; and Lydia Greenway flies the flag for 'pies'), but there aren't many such balls in an evening session that Mel Farrell suggests has turned into 'a war of attrition'. Perry is continuing much as she did in Sydney, defending the multitude of good balls she's presented with and dispatching the occasional bad one to the boundary to keep the scoring rate ticking over. By the end of the day, she is 84 not out.

Australia close on 265 for three. It's difficult to see how England can win the Ashes from here and, as Natalie Germanos says, 'There are going to be some tired bodies and some hurt bodies out there. And England must be feeling mentally drained.' After the World Cup he has just worked through, culminating in the final of all finals on Sunday, Henry Moeran can relate. However, he has the perfect tonic to pep him up tonight. Complete with his date Ebony Rainford-Brent, Henry is off to see *An Evening with Aggers* at the Brewhouse Theatre, Taunton, and couldn't be more excited by the prospect.

Friday 19 July
England v Australia – Women's Ashes – Test
Match – Day 2
County Ground, Taunton

Team *TMS*: Alison Mitchell, Henry Moeran, Natalie Germanos, Isabelle
Westbury, Melinda Farrell, Charlotte Edwards, Lydia Greenway, Mel Jones

While Moeran is buzzing around the commentary box even
more effervescently than usual, full of tales of his 'Evening with
Aggers', the general feeling around Taunton this morning is
one of concern. Concern for England's Ashes chances (slim at
best, given their position in the match), concern for the weather
('thundery showers' have been predicted and BBC Weather's
Simon King has been called onto air to confirm that 'there is a
lot of rainfall on the radar'), and concern for England's chance
of getting 17 more wickets in the match.

'Perhaps when no one is looking, they should send someone out with a crowbar and prise Ellyse Perry out?!' suggests
Mel Farrell. It's not intended to be serious, but it sums up
the issue staring England in the face. 'It's 297 runs and 579
balls since Ellyse Perry was last dismissed in Test cricket,'
says grim-faced statistician Phil Long. England can possibly
count themselves unfortunate that she's even playing in this
series. Up until 2011, she was another dual international,
playing both cricket and football for Australia and even scoring in a World Cup quarter-final. Eventually she decided
to choose cricket – and yesterday England perhaps wished
she hadn't.

A nice battle opens up between Brunt and Perry. 'You
couldn't get two more contrasting characters,' laughs Charlotte
Edwards, who is enjoying watching the steaming Brunt take

on the metronomic Perry. Shortly after the increasingly put-upon Moeran is accused of stealing Mel Farrell's last wine gum, Haynes is dropped by Ecclestone in a similar way to how Knight dropped Lanning yesterday. It rather sums up England's Ashes so far and is quickly followed by Perry reaching her inevitable century. The depth of the Australia batting line-up is discussed again, with Moeran saying, 'Even if England get a wicket, it's almost like a cat toying with a mouse.' It's not got the gravitas of yesterday's Medusa reference from Issy Westbury, but it makes the point.

A wicket does indeed come, Perry being dismissed from the 655th ball she's faced since her last Test dismissal. 'What a player. What an innings!' says Natalie Germanos simply, and the appreciative Taunton public give her a standing ovation as she leaves the field after adding a surely Ashes-clinching 162 with Haynes, who goes next, LBW to Laura Marsh.

The dreaded rain arrives in force during the lunch break, eventually falling with such force that a replay of the commentary of the final hour of the World Cup final is deployed as the *TMS* equivalent of full covers. Two restarts are attempted during the afternoon session but, sadly, no play is possible as the rain comes back with a vengeance. However, a spirited 'state of the nation' conversation about women's cricket breaks out among the team. Many topics are covered, with concerns expressed by many about a growing gap between Australia and England, fuelled by the increased investment in Aussie domestic cricket and concern about the brand-new Hundred competition that will be the primary source of English domestic women's cricket next year.

Saturday 20 July
England v Australia – Women's Ashes – Test Match – Day 3
County Ground, Taunton

Team *TMS*: Alison Mitchell, Henry Moeran, Natalie Germanos, Isabelle Westbury, Melinda Farrell, Charlotte Edwards, Lydia Greenway, Mel Jones

'There is nothing to lose for England. That is the approach they have to take,' says Issy Westbury, resolutely encouraging them to be bullish at the start of the day, despite still bowling in the first innings of a game they have to win. A sunnier day brings a bigger crowd but little more hope for England. 'What score do we need to get where we back ourselves to get 20 wickets in a day and three quarters?' asks Australian summariser Mel Jones. 'That is the question for Australia.'

Jess Jonassen goes early in the day, but Australia turn more aggressive than they have been for the past two days and start setting up a declaration that comes 25 minutes before lunch. To stay in the Ashes, England need to get far enough beyond 420 for eight to set Australia a target and then bowl them out tomorrow afternoon.

'It's not going to be easy batting out there,' warns Alison Mitchell as Amy Jones and Tammy Beaumont walk out into the middle. 'These two batters are really going to have to apply themselves.' They prove to be wise words as Perry – who else? – fires one full, fast and straight at Beaumont, who goes for a duck just before lunch. 'We are very lucky to be watching Perry live,' adds Mitchell. 'As an English supporter, you appreciate her greatness but just wish she was one of ours.'

England come out to start the afternoon session facing 'the mother of all uphill challenges', according to Henry

Moeran, and start okay. Knight and Jones form a partnership as Charlotte Edwards, on air with Mel Jones, reminisces about running out her commentary colleague during an Ashes Test at Guildford in 1998. 'I was at point and could only see one stump at the non-striker's end and threw it down,' says Edwards immodestly. 'That's how I'm selling it to everyone!'

The afternoon continues with the dual outrages of the kleptomaniacal Moeran once again stealing the last wine gum, and the discovery that a box of fairy cakes has been mistakenly delivered to the Sky commentary team rather than the intended *TMS* box. With some of the *TMS* team working on both TV and radio this week, a picture emerges on social media of Charlotte Edwards tucking into one of these delicacies in the Sky box. Producer Adam Mountford considers an immediate termination of her contract, but she saves herself by arriving shortly afterwards with the rest of the cakes under her arm, having liberated them from the Sky team.

As the day wears on, it all starts to go wrong for England, though. Knight is LBW to Australian debutant Sophie Molineux, and the rest of the day sees Australia building on their advantage. The turning pitch provides some engrossing Test cricket, but any prospect of an England victory is ruled out by the end of the day when they close on 199 for six. At stages, despite the presence of the free-scoring Natalie Sciver and Brunt at the crease, England seemed to almost 'shut up shop' at times – including a spell when their pair played out 33 straight dot balls, much to the consternation of Issy Westbury.

An excellent day of commentary almost goes horribly awry towards the end, when there is a potentially mortifying linguistic misunderstanding between Natalie Germanos and Lydia Greenway. The South African is about to tell listeners all about Lydia's pants when Greenway, terrified of what is about to unfold on air, immediately jumps in, rapidly adding,

'For the sake of our British listeners, we're talking about *trousers!*'

As well as the cricket and Lydia's pants, the afternoon is notable for Moeran's passionate advocation of the Somerset Space Walk, an eight-mile trek starting in Taunton that takes you past perfectly scaled models of all the planets in the solar system, ending up with the sun. 'Pluto is less than the size of a pea,' he says, full of wonder, 'and when you get to the sun at the end, it's the size of a house!'

Sunday 21 July
England v Australia – Women's Ashes – Test
Match – Day 4
County Ground, Taunton

Team *TMS*: Alison Mitchell, Henry Moeran, Natalie Germanos, Isabelle Westbury, Melinda Farrell, Charlotte Edwards, Lydia Greenway, Mel Jones

With the final day of the Test match dawning in Taunton, England are stuck in an invidious position. To have any chance of winning the Ashes they need to go for the victory. However, they are starting the day 231 runs behind with four wickets remaining in their first innings. In a series with a different structure, England could bat for a face-saving draw and move onto the next match – but with the Women's Ashes being decided on a points system, that isn't good enough.

The only option, realistically, is to make it past the follow-on mark of 271, declare and then attempt to bowl Australia out for as a low a total as possible. It sounds straightforward, but Henry Moeran puts his finger on it when he says that 'England need a miracle today to possibly force a victory.'

However, given some of the passivity on show in the final session last night, Issy Westbury doesn't see that even as a possibility. 'England's hashtag for this series, which we keep seeing on the screen, has been #GoBoldly,' she says. 'For this match, it might as well be #GoMeekly.' Further reflecting on the recent World Cup – and England's match against India in particular – she neatly describes it as 'doing a Dhoni'.

England also receive stinging criticism from former captain Charlotte Edwards, who adds, 'If this was a normal Test match, I would have no problem with England doing what they are doing. But England are 6-0 down and have to win this Test match. That frustrates me as an England fan. I would rather lose the game trying to win it.'

Anya Shrubsole goes early but Marsh, who is subject to a detailed on-air examination of her furniture-making skills by former house-mate Lydia Greenway, sticks with Sciver and the pair move closer to the magic number of 271. As England get closer and closer, pre-cricket careers become a topic of conversation and Mel Farrell wins the day by a good few lengths when she admits to having made her professional on-stage debut in Australia as 'Princess Primrose', taking to the stage with no less than a magical watering can. 'I was never a princess,' says Natalie Germanos bluntly. 'I had normal jobs like working in a clothing store and a pet shop.'

Suddenly, Sciver is dismissed, 12 short of her ton, and a really exciting period of cricket breaks out as Marsh and Sophie Ecclestone battle towards 271, with Vlaeminck bowling genuinely quickly from one end and Jonassen probing her left-arm spin from the other. 'This is proper Test cricket,' says Germanos, as the tension continues to build with a number of near-misses before Marsh hits the crucial boundary that avoids the follow-on.

England declare and it effectively becomes a one-innings game with Australia starting on 145 for no wicket. There are 84 overs remaining in the day and while the Aussies have no need to push for the win, if they want to secure the Ashes whitewash that has been discussed, that is what they need to do. 'The big thing for Australia is to decide how many they need to be safe,' says a very happy Mel Jones. 'The Ashes are in their pocket; they don't need to give England a sniff. Their first job is to win the Ashes, not to play exciting cricket.'

After a panel discussion at lunchtime where Issy Westbury allows England to have their #GoBoldly hashtag back following the morning's positivity, England pay back her faith by quickly reducing Australia to 15 for two, getting rid of both openers and, as Natalie Germanos puts it, 'All of a sudden England can put their money on the table and have a bet.'

Knight stuffs four fielders around the bat and, for the first time in the game, forces Australia onto the back foot. Strong appeals for LBW and caught behind against Perry and Lanning are turned down and Ecclestone is adding an excellent sense of theatrics with her pained reactions to every delivery. When Lanning drives to cover and is caught, Westbury and Moeran make increasingly desperate entreaties for them to declare and set England a chase during the afternoon, but Mel Jones's comments about having the Ashes in their pocket clearly have more influence and they decide to bat on remorselessly. They declare at 5.37 p.m., shaking hands with the England fielders and securing the draw that hands the first Ashes prize of the summer to the tourists.

Perry ends the second innings 76 not out and is named Player of the Match, and Issy Westbury offers the take that 'Australia's big guns outperformed England's big guns. Heather herself hasn't had a great series perhaps, Sarah Taylor hasn't performed with the bat and Shrubsole maybe hasn't bowled well. But the ramifications of this Test match will take a little more time to sink in.'

England women trail 8-2 in the series and the Ashes are lost – but there are still three T20 internationals to come – and wins in all three would allow the series to be drawn and Australia only to retain the title as its current holders. As the players gather on the field for presentations and interviews, the day ends on a rather surreal note, as Moeran notes that 'Georgia Elwiss is holding a sausage dog in one arm.'

Australia 420-8d (154.4 overs; Perry 116, Haynes 87, Healy 58, Lanning 57, Mooney 51) and 230-7 (64 overs; Perry 76*) drew with England 275-9d (107.1 overs; Sciver 88, Jones 64; Molineux 4-95).

CHAPTER 15

Murtagh in St John's Wood

Wednesday 24 July
England v Ireland – Specsavers Test Match – Day 1
Lord's Cricket Ground, St John's Wood, London

Team *TMS*: Jonathan Agnew, Michael McNamee, Isa Guha, Daniel Norcross, Phil Tufnell, Niall O'Brien, Vic Marks, Sir Alastair Cook, Michael Vaughan, Andrew Samson

Lord's, the Home of Cricket, is renowned as a very traditional place. However, classical Lord's days have been in short supply thus far in 2019. From noisy World Cup carnivals with Pakistan and Bangladesh to mass singalongs of 'Sweet Caroline' in the dying embers of the World Cup final – just ten days ago – to today, the first four-day Test to take place in England in decades and the first time that England have played Ireland in a Test match.

After his extraordinary World Cup, Jason Roy has been handed his England Test debut and there is also a maiden cap for fast bowler Olly Stone. There are four members of the World

Cup-winning XI pressed back into action immediately, with Roy and Root joined by Chris Woakes and Jonny Bairstow, while Ben Stokes and Jos Buttler are given a rest and Mark Wood and Jofra Archer sit out with injuries.

For Ireland, Middlesex stalwart Tim Murtagh is achieving his ambition of playing a Test on his home ground and there is a debut for Mark Adair. Root wins the toss and, with two spinners in the side, opts to bat first in England's first Test match since 13 February in St Lucia.

For former Ireland international Niall O'Brien, making a special early morning appaearance on *TMS* – whose brother Kevin is on the other side of the ground preparing to play – the sun has risen on an emotional morning. 'I never thought this day would happen,' he says, looking out of the Lord's 'spaceship' perched above the Compton and Edrich Stands. 'I didn't think Ireland would play Test cricket in my lifetime. But I'm here – my brother is playing, and my mum and dad are here.'

The shaky status of Lord's traditions is exemplified as the day starts with Jonathan Agnew and Sir Alastair Cook broadcasting from the outfield – and Cook is wearing pink shorts and trainers. It is a hot day, but it does not go down well with the traditionalist Aggers, who chidingly mocks the former England captain for his breach of protocol throughout the day, describing his sartorial decision-making as 'an absolute disgrace'. On the other side of the coin, Isa Guha is having clothing issues of her own, having to use Gaffer tape purloined from the *TMS* engineers to stick her dress to her legs, such is the gusty breeze present out in the middle on what is otherwise a baking-hot day.

Tim Murtagh, who averages 23.9 with the ball at Lord's, opens the bowling for Ireland and breaks through immediately, spoiling Roy's debut as he snicks off to slip for just 5. 'Jason Roy has not opened in the first innings of a first-class match since 2013,' says Andrew Samson drily. Andrew will be the *TMS* statistician for the rest of the summer, attempting to build on the incredible work of Andy Zaltzman and Phil Long during the World Cup.

Samson is delighted – as is everyone else on the team, to be fair – when the first cake of the Test match summer arrives. Certain *TMS* commentators (who shall remain nameless for fear of withheld accreditations at future tournaments) have taken to renaming the ICC the 'International Cake Concealers', such was the lack of baked goods during the World Cup, so to receive one so early now they've left town is deeply reassuring. This particular cake, supplied by a very kind listener, has been made on board a narrowboat and, very appropriately given today's opposition, contains a full bottle of Guinness.

Just as a cake-infused Daniel Norcross is settling into his chair and talking about how much 'it's lovely to be back in the rhythm of Test cricket', the comfortable pace that he is referring to is blown apart. Joe Denly is LBW to Adair before Murtagh has Rory Burns caught behind, Root goes the same way as Denly, Bairstow is bowled by Murtagh, Woakes is LBW to Murtagh and Moeen Ali is caught behind to complete the Middlesex seamer's five-fer and send England to 43 for seven. 'This is astonishing stuff,' gawps Michael McNamee, while Vic Marks warns, 'Tim Murtagh could well bowl England out in a hurry here. He's got five for 11 at 75mph. Amazing stuff.'

'I have no idea what is going on,' says a dumbfounded Alastair Cook. 'Just ten days after the high of the World Cup to this. Tim Murtagh has bowled beautifully, but England just needed to get through the first hour and I think this will have turned out to be a good wicket to bat on.'

Sam Curran makes a resourceful effort to counter-attack, but the damage is done as Stuart Broad is caught behind, Curran himself grabbed at short leg, and Olly Stone (who is compared to Wally Hammond by Norcross by dint of hitting one boundary) bowled as England troop off at lunch, astonishingly, 85 all out.

'No matter where England are playing, if the ball does something, you feel they will get bowled out,' mourns a crestfallen Michael Vaughan, whose phone is seriously racking up the missed calls and unanswered messages as a result of having an Irish wife. 'I'm not sure what is more remarkable – that amazing World Cup final or England being 67 for eight on the first morning of a Test match at Lord's. This is an embarrassment. No other word can describe what we've seen.'

Looking ahead to what's to come later this summer, Norcross simply says, 'Cummins. Starc. Pattinson,' before taking a pregnant pause and adding deeply, 'Oh dear.'

'Maybe the extra pace will help England?' suggests Vaughan. 'They'll at least edge a few down to third man.'

As the final Irishmen disappear into the Lord's Pavilion for a lunch they have been anticipating for generations, a jubilant, disbelieving McNamee says, 'England are clattered and shattered and all out for 85. This is not a dream! It's Irish delight! This is surely up there with Ireland's finest moments in cricket. They are embarrassing the hosts at Lord's.' Charmingly, he then adds, 'I never thought I'd live to see the day where Michael Vaughan is peering at one of my son's exercise books where I've scribbled down England being bowled out for 85 inside a session by Ireland!'

Incredibly, due to the proliferation of one-day cricket around the World Cup, *TMS* has been on the air since early May, and it's not until today that the first of the much-loved 'View from the Boundary' interviews is taking place. Today, the first guest of the year is the legendary Northern Ireland footballer and manager Martin O'Neill. As a player he won the then First Division and two European Cups with Nottingham

Forest and captained his country before, as a manager, leading Wycombe Wanderers, Norwich City, Leicester City, Celtic, Aston Villa, Sunderland, the Republic of Ireland and Nottingham Forest.

Despite growing up in Ireland at a time when cricket was not widely popular, O'Neill reveals to Aggers – who he once bought a flat off in Leicester – that he fell in love with the game by watching it on television and, although he played Gaelic Football at school, happily discovered that the McAllister family a few doors up were able to provide solid cricketing opposition as he learnt the game on the streets outside.

It is clear from the attention with which he is watching the action that he is a keen student of the game and O'Neill declares himself a passionate Ireland fan. One of his opening gambits is that 'Lots of cynics were saying this game could be over in two days. Well, it could be!' As 'View from the Boundary' draws to a close, the Ireland batsmen are walking out of the pavilion to start their first innings – still a staggering sight considering Root won the toss and chose to bat – and it will become clear whether O'Neill is right or not.

England start poorly, but Curran makes a breakthrough with what O'Brien terms 'a 74mph drag down' that gets 'clothed' by William Porterfield to mid-wicket before bowling James McCollum later in the spell to put Ireland under a bit of pressure at 45 for two. That pressure is then expertly dispelled as Andrew Balbirnie and Paul Stirling get on top of the bowling and slowly start to accumulate.

'What started out as disbelief among Ireland fans at what was happening has turned into belief at what they could do from here,' says Norcross shortly before tea, which duly arrives with Ireland 127 for two. 'They are well on top.'

'I don't think it could have gone any better for Ireland,' says Tuffers. 'Root has to tell the bowlers to pull their fingers out.

Ellyse Perry, not content with causing the bowlers grief during the Ashes, nearly takes out Amy Jones during the drawn Test at Taunton.

An unlikely hero emerges. After 20 wickets fell on the first day, nightwatchman Jack Leach celebrates with Jason Roy after reaching fifty against Ireland in the Test at Lord's. He was the first since Paul Allott in 1981 to do so while wearing glasses.

The view from the *TMS* box at the start of the Ashes, which, as Aggers said, always creates a 'really special feeling'.

Steve Smith's unorthodox style and brilliance would become a major feature of the entire series. Here he hits out on the first day of the Ashes at Edgbaston, on the way to a superb 144 that changed the momentum of the Test.

Mitchell Johnson and Michael Vaughan quiz Aggers on just how red his red shirt is on the Ruth Strauss Foundation day at Lord's.

Meanwhile, Henry Moeran has gone the full Rocketman.

One of the best cakes of the summer is delivered by Issy Batey, aged eight and a half, with a special request that Tuffers didn't eat it all. As the rain fell on Lord's, she brought some sunshine into the *TMS* box.

Jofra Archer hits Steve Smith with a sickening blow to his neck, during one of the greatest spells of fast bowling ever seen at Lord's. Smith suffered from concussion and missed the next Test at Headingley.

No prizes for guessing who the bowler is. Marnus Labuschagne, Smith's concussion replacement (a Test first), gets the same treatment from Archer, but battled on to make a valiant 59.

A gift from Betty's Tea Room in Harrogate, Michael Vaughan contemplates a Fat Rascal at the start of the Headingley Test.

As England slump to 67 all out, Geoffrey Boycott's mood didn't match the sunshine outside in Leeds.

A familiar story as Stuart Broad celebrappeals as David Warner is LBW in the second innings at Headingley and England begin their fightback.

Matthew Wade is out; Ben Stokes is out on his feet after a monumental spell of bowling late on Day Two at Headingley.

'I CAN'T BELIEVE WE'VE SEEN THAT!' Stokes and Jack Leach celebrate England's stunning one-wicket win that kept the Ashes alive.

Getty Images

Jim Maxwell proudly displays his Shipping Forecast t-shirt, while Joe Root is on the receiving end of an unplayable delivery from Pat Cummins that leaves England facing defeat at Old Trafford.

Getty Images

Tim Paine leads the celebrations after Josh Hazlewood has trapped Craig Overton LBW. Despite the Somerset man's review, he's out and the Ashes are on their way back to Australia.

Joe Denly bats on at The Oval to help put England in a winning position – and definitely not to avoid changing the nappies of his newborn baby, as Tuffers suggested.

Alec Stewart and Isa Guha give their support to two police officers, who seem to have Tuffers surrounded.

Aggers looks wistfully across The Oval outfield after England's win to square the Ashes series, at the end of one of the most brilliant summers of cricket anyone could remember.

They haven't bowled well – England will be having a stern talking-to, I think.'

As the final session of the day gets going, Stuart Broad pulls out his patented 'celebrappeal' as Stirling is struck on his front leg. It is sent upstairs and is only just successful as the 'umpire's call' confirms that it was going on to clip leg stump. Ireland are then quickly rocked by Stone's first and second Test wickets as Balbirnie plays across the line before turning to see his off stump in mid-air behind him and Gary Wilson then follows up in the same over, caught by Root at slip.

'England need to be batting tonight if they want to get control of this match,' says Vaughan, and when Stuart Thompson leaves one from Broad and is bowled, that prospect draws closer. 'There are two types of leave – and unfortunately for Thompson that was a bad one,' is Cook's concise analysis of his unfortunate situation.

While Thompson's dramatic dismissal may have roused a few fans out of a post-tea slumber, it caught the attention of Andrew Samson for a very different reason. 'The Nos 6 and 7 batsmen today have got four ducks between them – Moeen Ali and Chris Woakes, and Gary Wilson and Stuart Thompson,' he reveals. 'That is the first time it has happened in a Test.'

The final four Ireland wickets do indeed fall before close of play – with Murtagh raising his cult status at Lord's even higher by hitting 16 off ten balls, with every run coming via boundaries. By the skin of their teeth, England have answered Vaughan's call and are batting again. Night-watchman Jack Leach sees off the over – with Burns standing statuesque at other end – and, when the crowds start making for their evening plans, Aggers just about sums it up as he says, 'An amazing day. One you couldn't possibly have predicted.'

As for Murtagh? 'I'm there for a good time, not a long time,' he replies when asked about his day. He has made it onto the Lord's honours board, but when he returns to Middlesex duties next week, he will not be able to sit down and gaze at it, as his name will be listed in the away dressing room rather than the home.

'What is the record for the least wickets in a day the day after 20 wickets have fallen?' asks Sir Alastair Cook as *TMS* head out of the door. 'It might happen tomorrow.' Will there ever be a 'normal' day of cricket again?

Thursday 25 July
England v Ireland – Specsavers Test Match – Day 2
Lord's Cricket Ground, St John's Wood, London

Team *TMS*: Jonathan Agnew, Michael McNamee, Isa Guha, Daniel Norcross, Phil Tufnell, Niall O'Brien, Vic Marks, Michael Vaughan, Sir Alastair Cook, Andrew Samson

There are hot and sweaty days – and then there is today. It is 37 degrees in London and, although the *TMS* team have plenty of experience working all around the world, this is something different. As in quite a few grounds, the *TMS* box in the Lord's spaceship is the only one that has an opening window. This is because, while there are plenty of microphones that can be used to tap into the atmosphere around the ground for listeners at home, the programme likes to feel truly a part of the ground, which is sometimes difficult when you are inside a hermetically sealed structure.

This policy occasionally causes a few problems and occasionally has its benefits (like earlier this summer when Andy Zaltzman and Charles Dagnall had champagne passed through the window at The Oval), but today something is happening that has never been seen before. The Media Centre itself is a climatic delight, beautifully air-conditioned to create a fine working atmosphere compared to the Saharan mug outside. However, the open window is uncomfortably blowing what feels like the backdraft from a tumble dryer into the *TMS* box.

Given the weather, there is collective astonishment – and admiration – when Niall O'Brien shows up for work in a full suit. 'My feet are a bit sweaty; I'm not going to lie!' he admits, but after 'shortsgate' from Cook yesterday and Isa's Gaffer tape adjustments, he has set out to raise the standard and will suffer for his art if needs be.

Elsewhere at Lord's, when Boris Johnson – he of Jeremy Coney's 'herding geese into an abattoir' fame – became the UK's new prime minister yesterday, it gave former incumbent Theresa May more time to spend on her hobbies. It is thus that she, accompanied by some other former ministers, decides to follow in the tradition set by Sir John Major when he attended Surrey v British Universities in the Benson & Hedges Cup on 2 May 1997, and spend her first day without the stresses of office watching cricket. Although the opportunity of an unlikely political exclusive is tantalising, it is unanimously decided that now is probably not the right time to ask her for another inter-view and she is left alone to enjoy her day.

Jack Leach – pressed into action as a night-watchman last night – and Rory Burns stride to the crease to resume England's second innings with the words of Vic Marks ringing in their ears. 'Jack Leach won't hang around very long, I suspect!' he says, shockingly disloyal to his Somerset brethren. 'I'm not sure he's in great nick, actually . . . '

Leach and Burns start solidly, with the spinner progressing

his innings to such an extent that Daniel Norcross jokes, 'Jack Leach is in danger of becoming England's highest-averaging opener since Alastair Cook at this rate.'

'If England can't bat 90-odd overs in these conditions, then you can say it's going to be quite difficult for them next week,' adds Michael Vaughan, speaking frankly as ever and, shortly after Leach has asked the umpire to clean his glasses for him, England lose their first wicket. However, rather than No 11 Leach, it is in fact Burns who is first to go, prodding at a good line from Boyd Rankin and going for 6. He is replaced by Roy, who starts to form a very profitable partnership with Leach, who is still there after an hour's play, wonderfully outperforming Victor's expectations.

'It's amazing how what position you bat in determines how you play,' says Alastair Cook insightfully. 'Leach is opening so he plays like an opener. When he bats at No 11, he looks like a No 11!' Roy and Leach keep going, with Cook almost seeming to talk Roy through his innings. Chat turns to high scores from lower-order batsmen – with memories of Alex Tudor's iconic 99 not out in July 1999 being warmly embraced – but, as it should be when No 11 batting is being discussed, it's Phil Tufnell who is centre stage.

Soon after admitting that he used to get Mike Gatting to change his bat grip for him because he was unable ever to master the art, Tuffers says, 'I got a half-century at Lord's. I raised my bat to all four corners, but I didn't quite know how to do it. I stood in the middle and pointed at one corner, then the other . . . it looked a bit awkward. And I got there all in boundaries!'

Sadly for Tuffers, Andrew Samson is sat next to him, and it's literally his job to investigate such claims. It turns out his final score in the match (against Worcestershire in 1996 for those keeping records) was actually 67 not out, so while he stuck a superb 15 fours and deserves huge credit, seven of the runs did come from other means. Brilliantly, the great man seems irritated to this day that he was 'declared on' by Mike Gatting before he had a chance to advance his innings any further. The fondness in the heart of the English cricketing public for tailender heroics is underscored by a pronounced spike in the *TMS* inbox, with many people who claimed to have seen Tuffers' landmark knock in person immediately sending in fond recollections of the day 23 years ago.

Leach reaches his fifty – the first Englishman to do so wearing glasses since Paul Allott at Old Trafford in 1981. 'It's been a rare fifty by an England opener in the last few years,' says Norcross, a mischievous glint firmly in his eye. Shortly before lunch, Leach passes the milestone of having faced more deliveries than the entirety of England's top seven the previous day and he reaches the break 60 not out, with Roy also reaching his fifty in the morning session – off 47 balls, it is 'the fastest fifty on debut for England', says Samson.

The scores are exactly level at lunch and England continue unabated in the second session. Leach passes his all-time first-class best and serious nerves start to grip the box as he gets closer and closer to what would rank as one of the most unlikely Test centuries of all time. He loses Roy, bowled by Thompson, but then thumps a cover drive for four to surpass England's first-innings total all by himself. 'If you close your eyes, but not quite tight, you can see a bit of Trescothick in Leach,' Victor, a man who has watched a lot of cricket in the West Country, says lovingly.

It is not to be, however, as Murtagh finally finds the outside edge of his bat, to a strangled 'urghhh' from a rapt Tuffers – and indeed everyone else in the box and 27,000 outside in the stands. The standing ovation is prolonged and superb, and Leach will come to love this innings one day, however glum he looks as he walks off eight runs short of the ton. 'Listen to that applause as he goes up the stairs,' says Tufnell. 'I feel for the lad. Eight more runs . . . Just imagine, it could have been Compton, Graveney, Gooch, Vaughan . . . Leach on that honours board.'

England are effectively 60 for three when Leach is dismissed, a complete turnaround from yesterday's horror show, and as the two Joes – Root and Denly – try to add to it, Tuffers pulls another blinder when talking about the last dinner party he hosted at his house. 'Someone drove into your house, didn't they?' asks Agnew. 'Yeah!' replies Tuffers. 'They said their goodbyes and next thing they reversed into my house! I was on the black as well and suddenly there was a car in my pool room. They were terribly apologetic.'

Root then utterly sells Denly down the river, calling his partner through for a run before deciding, with Denly halfway down the track, he didn't actually want the single after all. Unsurprisingly, Denly is barely in the frame of the replay and has to go, Root smashing his bat into the turf in frustration.

A collapse begins as Bairstow completes a horrible pair by being trapped LBW by Adair, and as the day moves on, the air gets considerably stickier, the ball gets softer, Ireland start to fight back and the collapse intensifies. 'The minimum England require from here is another hundred,' says Vic, furrowing his brow shortly after tea with the score on 218 for five and the lead at just 96.

As soon as he says it, Moeen is next to go, caught behind, and then Root is out, playing what Niall O'Brien merrily terms 'as loose a shot as you can see', to fall in the same fashion. Norcross is less merry, clasping at his throbbing synapses and admitting that 'England are in terrible trouble'. Woakes goes just nine runs later as Samson reports England have lost their last seven wickets for just 77 runs, crashing from 171 for one to 248 for eight. Only some terrific biffing from Curran, supported by Broad, allows

England to breach the 300 barrier that at one stage they were serenely sailing towards.

Broad and Stone are in the process of wringing out every last run when a very dramatic lightning strike and some booming thunder in the distance causes all number of *oohs* and *aahs* from the crowd and, eventually and much to the noisy aggrievement of Sir Alastair Cook, the players are withdrawn.

'I still think England are favourites,' says Vaughan as the reckoning is under way. 'The Irish will be so proud of the way they've performed, but England have to be honest. The way they batted from 171 for one has been poor. In today's conditions for batting, there's no complaints. Today, they've made mistakes, and that's the vulnerability of this Test line-up. Who would have thought that we'd be saying at the end of Day 2 that Jack Leach had saved England's batting with 92? They have to start to understand that they are making too many mistakes, too consistently.'

HIGHEST ENGLAND TEST SCORES BY NIGHT-WATCHMEN

99* – Alex Tudor – v New Zealand – Edgbaston – 1999

98 – Harold Larwood – v Australia – Sydney – 1933

95 – Eddie Hemmings – v Australia – Sydney – 1983

94 – Jack Russell – v Sri Lanka – Lord's – 1998

92 – Jack Leach – v Ireland – Lord's – 2019

Friday 26 July
England v Ireland – Specsavers Test Match – Day 3
Lord's Cricket Ground, St John's Wood, London

Team *TMS*: Jonathan Agnew, Michael McNamee, Isa Guha, Daniel Norcross, Phil Tufnell, Niall O'Brien, Vic Marks, Michael Vaughan, Sir Alastair Cook, Andrew Samson

'Given that in 1882 when England lost a Test to Australia, such was the shock they burned the bails, if England lose to Ireland today, they'll need to burn down the MCC Pavilion.' Jonathan Agnew is in dramatic social media form on the third morning of a four-day Test that is now unlikely to make the fourth day. It makes the ECB's controversial experiment with the new format rather null and void, but such is the hand dealt by elite sport.

'If England can get another 30, that makes a huge difference in this game,' says Vic Marks as some early-morning mizzle delays the start by ten minutes. Anybody who has still not had time to get their coffee then immediately gets ten minutes more as Stone is utterly bowled by Thompson from the first ball of the day. Ireland need 182 for a victory that would see the MCC posting some heavy security guards around the pavilion and asking the Crown Prosecution Service to consider charges of incitement to arson against Aggers.

However, the floodlights are on, the clouds are low and there is optimism being preached by Alastair Cook. 'It feels like a Stuart Broad day,' says the man with more experience of

'Stuart Broad days' than most. 'With the game on the line and when England need a performance, that's when Stuart Broad turns up.'

'If England win, this would be the lowest total they have defended at Lord's,' adds Andrew Samson, offering a tabasco shot of realism into Cook's early-morning Bloody Mary of positivity. Sadly for Broad and Woakes, the perfect bowling conditions deteriorate after just one over and the mizzle returns, delaying things by an hour or so, but allowing *TMS* to be on air, with no cricket to commentate on, while the Australian Ashes squad is revealed. Michael Vaughan describes them as 'a team of street fighters' and thinks Peter Siddle will be picked for the first Test. Vic says he 'would be amazed' if Siddle lined up in Edgbaston. The debate adds yet another interesting point of contention to a fascinating series.

When play resumes an hour and a half before lunch, Ireland proceed to 11 without loss before Porterfield goes to a lovely take behind the stumps from Bairstow off Woakes. 'Stunning grab – absolutely stunning,' rhapsodises former wicketkeeper Niall O'Brien. Balbirnie, top scorer in the first innings, is squared up by Broad and well taken by Root at first slip and, in the commentator's chair, Michael McNamee senses what for him is a deeply unwelcome change in momentum. 'England are getting on top,' he says. 'The visitors are under real pressure.'

The stakes are raised when, amid the constant flurry of corre-spondence in the *TMS* inbox, a note is spotted from an English listener in Northern Ireland who recently became a father. He reports that a bet has been made with his Northern Irish fiancée whereby if Ireland win this match, the child will be allowed to support Ireland in all sports throughout their life. If England win, it goes the other way. That pressure deepens when Stirling is bowled second ball and, despite and possibly because of his desire to call home a historic Irish victory, the normally placid McNamee is unsparing. 'That is a shocker,' he says as Stirling walks back. 'Ireland are all at sea.'

New man Kevin O'Brien is then hit hard on the side of the head by Broad. Once it has become clear that he's okay, Tuffers decides to offer up his impression of the sound the ball made as it struck O'Brien's lid. It's hard to replicate in written word, but can best be spelt as '*waaaaaaaaaaaaaaaaaaaaaarghhhhhhhh*'.

Woakes forces McCollum to slice to slip three balls later and completes Wilson's pair with an LBW two balls after that, Andrew Samson pointing out that, in another amazing statistic to be generated by this bizarre match, not a single run has been scored by a wicketkeeper during the Test. 'Ireland might not make lunch at this rate,' worries Tuffers before another Broad celebrappeal comes out as O'Brien is fundamentally LBW. While England's collapse yesterday was pretty stark, Ireland have now lost five wickets for six runs in less than half an hour.

'Lunch is in jeopardy,' agrees Norcross, and when it is revealed that the menu offered up in the Lord's Media Centre today is planned to be sea bass, Tuffers is visibly mortified. Adair becomes the second Irishman to take a hefty blow but, off the very next ball, floats Broad for a huge six. Sadly for him, the fun then immediately ends as a loose drive combines with a bit of nip-back off the pitch and his stumps are rearranged. 'Stuart Broad gets the final say,' laughs Aggers as the England bowler fixes the departing Irishman with a trademark glare.

Woakes encounters a similar situation in the next over, getting tonked down the ground by Thompson before, later in the piece, having him caught in the slips as Ireland slip to 36 for eight. 'This is a really strange Test match,' says Aggers almost ethereally. 'England could win it before lunch on the third day, having been bowled out for 85 batting first.'

Root then takes his fourth catch of the morning before everything is wrapped up in the following over as Woakes claims his sixth scalp, bowling Wednesday's hero Murtagh to call time on an extraordinary game. Ireland have been skittled for 38 and, as Aggers said, England have won a match in which they scored 85 in the first innings by 143 runs before lunch on Day 3. 'Irish eyes were smiling on the first day, but Irish hearts are bleeding now,' says Aggers. 'This has been ruthless. What do you say about this Test match? To be blown away like this will be devastating for Ireland.'

'This is sad,' admits Cook. 'Ireland really stood up and competed for two days, but to crumble like this leaves a bad taste.' Leach is named Player of the Match ('bowling three overs for 26 and I've got Man of the Match – I didn't see that happening' is his characteristically self-deprecating reply) while Murtagh receives the Brian Johnston Champagne Moment for his bowling on the first day.

Michael McNamee, who has now seen his side throw away two winning positions against England in one summer, laughingly calls for a best of three, but England have other concerns now. The World Cup has been safely stowed in the trophy cabinet and the Ashes are just six days away. Australia await.

England 85 (23.4 overs; Murtagh 5-13) and 303 (77.5 overs; Leach 92, Roy 72) beat Ireland 207 (58.2 overs; Balbirnie 55) and 38 (15.4 overs; Woakes 6-17, Broad 4-19) by 143 runs.

Friday July 26
England v Australia – Women's Ashes – First T20
The Essex County Ground, Chelmsford

Team *TMS*: Henry Moeran, Isabelle Westbury, Ebony Rainford-Brent,
Danielle Hazell, Phil Long

At a sold-out Chelmsford, England women are playing for Ashes pride after Australia's clean sweep of the one-day international series and the drawn Test match. Fortunately for Dani Hazell's chances of future employment with *TMS*, her status as a rain curse is officially lifted when the Essex evening dawns bright and breezy and it is clear there will be a full game. It's never ideal for the start of your commentary career to be marked by two consecutive rain-outs, so she is doubly excited to see some cricket tonight.

The ground is known to the players as 'Fortress Chelmsford' and England have 14 straight wins here, including one earlier in the summer over the West Indies. Another win today would set them off on the right track for a moral victory as they aim to square the series, at least from a points perspective.

'If Australia come out and run over England in these T20s, it will show what a gulf in class there is,' warns Ebony Rainford-Brent early on, but when Kate Cross removes Alyssa Healy in the first over it seems like a more even contest is upon us. As during the ODI portion of the series, though, even taking a wicket against this Australian side brings its challenges, and Healy's opening-over departure means that Meg Lanning arrives at the crease nice and early.

With Lanning and Beth Mooney getting down to business, Dani Hazell's face turns white when a black cloud is spotted in the distance. 'It can't be! I've come all the way down from the north on a boiling-hot train!' she laments. Fortunately, the danger passes, and the Australia innings continues unaffected.

When Natalie Sciver has a stumping appeal against Lanning in her first over, Henry Moeran immediately turns his head to the monitor in front of him to describe the third umpire's deliberations. Normally this is a straightforward process, but today there is quite a major issue. Instead of showing the required feed from Sky Sports, the monitor is somehow tuned to a repeat of classic BBC sitcom *Last of the Summer Wine*. Undeterred, the resourceful Moeran is able to stick his head out of the open window and narrate the (unsuccessful) appeal from what is being shown on the big screen.

Lanning has another let-off when she is dropped by Tammy Beaumont in the 13th over and she then makes England pay. She hits the quickest ever T20 century by an Australian woman, from 51 balls, and then goes into overdrive, slamming 30 from the final 12 deliveries she faces. 'This is one of the best T20 innings I've seen,' says the experienced Hazell as Lanning ends on 133 not out, the highest individual score in the history of international women's T20 cricket. Australia's 226 for three is the fifth highest score ever, or the second if you discount scores achieved when batting first against Mali in the very odd series that has recently been concluded in Rwanda.

'This is an uphill task,' admits Rainford-Brent. 'England have already lost the series, I'm not expecting them to win, but I don't want this to look like the World T20 final: 180-plus is a minimum.'

By the middle of the third over, England are already 12 for three, and even 180 is looking like a pipe dream. 'Fortress Chelmsford, I'm afraid, is creaking a little,' says Moeran. 'Australia have not just dominated England, they're pulverising them.'

'You have to give credit to Australia,' adds Hazell. 'For England, apart from the word "disappointed", there's not a lot to say.'

England end up 133 for nine, losing by a giant 93 runs, their biggest defeat in T20 history. As is to be expected, the post-match analysis is not kind. 'This has been an absolute hammering,' says Moeran bluntly, with Rainford-Brent expanding by adding, 'There is a gulf at the moment. If England say there isn't one, they're fooling themselves.' The series is now 10-2 to Australia, who have guaranteed victory as well as retaining the Ashes.

Australia 226-3 (20 overs; Lanning 133*, Mooney 54) beat England 133-9 (20 overs) by 93 runs.

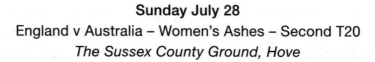

Sunday July 28
England v Australia – Women's Ashes – Second T20
The Sussex County Ground, Hove

Team *TMS*: Henry Moeran, Daniel Norcross, Isabelle Westbury, Ebony Rainford-Brent, Phil Long

The latest venue where England will attempt to halt Australia women's rampantly winning ways is Hove on a sunny Sunday afternoon, and it is difficult to imagine a more halcyon venue. England bat first and Amy Jones goes to the second legitimate ball of the match, spooning a catch to cover. 'It looked like the shot of someone chronically out of form with a scrambled mind,' says Daniel Norcross, with Phil Long adding that 'Ellyse Perry has bowled ten balls to Amy Jones in white-ball cricket in this series – and she's got her out four times.'

Beaumont, a regular opener who is batting at No 3, plays the totemic innings for England, hitting 43, despite being dropped twice by Beth Mooney, once off a chance that was so easy the big-screen operator had already put up the slide saying 'wicket'! Sadly for England, Beaumont is bowled with seven overs of batting remaining. 'Her stumps were splayed like a hillbilly's teeth,' says Norcross, turning a few heads in the box with his excellent, but slightly off kilter, turn of phrase.

To the distress of Norcross, who has commentated on this England team for some time but has not been present for much of the recent Ashes travails, England are able to post only 121 for eight from their allocation. 'This is 70 per cent Australia's game,' adds Rainford-Brent, 'but if England can get in early, they've got something to work with.'

After a chastened Clare Connor, the head of women's cricket at the ECB, is interviewed by Moeran at half time, Issy Westbury is even more certain of England's impending fate, thinking that 'it will take a hell of a bowling and fielding display by England – which we didn't see two days ago – for them to win here'. For a time it seems like England are in the game, with Australia only 30 for two after five overs, but after Ashleigh Gardner is caught at third man off Cross once again, England are undone by the pair Norcross refers to as 'Bradman and Bradman – in other words, Lanning and Perry'.

'If I could come back in another life, I'd come back as a cat, as they live the dream,' says Rainford-Brent suddenly. 'But after that, I wouldn't mind coming back as one of these two – Lanning or Perry.' Heads nod as her second sentence explains the confusion briefly generated by the first.

The pair sail Australia to another commanding victory, this time by seven wickets, with 2.1 overs to spare. As well as the brilliance exhibited on the field, the highlight of the second innings was a visit to the box from World Cup hero Jofra Archer, whose injured side came through a Sussex T20 game on Friday night (a tie against Surrey) and is being mentioned as a possibility for the second Ashes Test at Lord's. 'Meg Lanning has now scored 333 runs in T20 cricket against England without being dismissed, since she was run out in 2016,' says Phil Long as the game ends. Sometimes a statistic is all that's required to sum up a situation – and this feels like one of those occasions.

England 121-8 (20 overs) lost to Australia 122-3 (17.5 overs) by seven wickets.

●

Wednesday July 31
England v Australia – Women's Ashes – Third T20
The County Ground, Bristol

Team *TMS*: Henry Moeran, Daniel Norcross, Isabelle Westbury, Ebony Rainford-Brent, Phil Long

The day starts at Edgbaston with preparations for tomorrow's men's Ashes opener kicking into overdrive. There is demand for *TMS* interviews and previews from every corner of the BBC and it is terrifically exciting to remember the special feeling the word 'Ashes' generates in English sports fans. However, the real business is in Bristol, where England women wrap up their summer with one final attempt to get a win over Australia and, as a starter for ten, having sat through two dismal rain-ruined World Cup matches, Daniel Norcross is delighted to see the sun finally shining on Gloucestershire CCC.

To say the women's Ashes have not quite gone to plan thus far is somewhat akin to suggesting that Geoffrey Boycott is only slightly fond of a forward defensive shot. However, a victory in the final game of the series would be hugely welcomed by all. With Beaumont restored to the top of the order, England start well but slide to 84 for five in the 13th over. A 55-run partnership between Lauren Winfield and Katherine Brunt sees them to 139 – their highest total so far in the series – and 'England have a sniff here', says Ebony Rainford-Brent positively.

Opener Mooney goes early for Australia and then England actually dismiss Lanning, as she prods forwards uncertainly against Sophie Ecclestone's left-arm spin and is given LBW. Debutant bowler Mady Villiers gets through her first over with just two conceded, although she does miss a caught and bowled chance from Healy, but she returns for her second over and, as can so often be the case in T20, gets her reward with the worst ball she's bowled, Healy obligingly lifting a full toss to Ecclestone at long-off. She then has Ashleigh Gardner stumped first ball to start her international career with figures of two for 4 from two overs.

With Perry there, England are always staring defeat in the face. However, they are able to come up with a cunning plan to negate her Bradmanesque brilliance – 'get everyone else out and leave her stranded'. The scoring rate is already being squeezed and, when Rachael Haynes goes, Australia need 43 runs from the last three overs. A fine effort from Cross in the antepenultimate over means 37 are needed from the last 12 balls.

'Perry will believe it's still possible, that's the sort of character she is,' warns Rainford-Brent, but after smashing a huge six, the dominant all-rounder takes a single, strands herself at the non-striker's end and can only watch on as first Jess Jonassen and then Delissa Kimmince are trapped LBW from the last two balls of Ecclestone's over.

Australia need 28 off the final set of six, but Perry is on strike and such is the emotional scarring she has caused over the past month, nobody will rule it out. 'Five sixes here would make Ellyse Perry the greatest human to walk this planet!' says Ebony. But, when Perry takes a single from the first ball and Georgie Wareham sees out a dot ball and is then caught at mid-on, England have done it.

They win by 17 runs and can hold their heads high at the end of what has been a pretty trying summer. 'After getting drubbings throughout the series, England won't get too carried away. But at least they've been able to win one game in this series,' adds Ebony in the aftermath. 'Australia have been ruthless, clinical and opened up questions about the international game and where it's going.'

In the easiest decision made all summer, Ellyse Perry (Test century, seven for 22 in an ODI, match-winning T20 innings, leading run-scorer and leading wicket-taker from both sides) is named Player of the Series, and that is that for international women's cricket this summer. Tomorrow, after everything we've been through already this summer, it's the turn of their male team-mates to compete for the urn.

England 139-5 (20 overs) beat Australia 122-8 (20 overs; Perry 60*) by 17 runs.

Before the Ashes started, the Test Match Special *team were asked to make their predictions on how they thought the series would pan out. Here is what they said . . .*

Michael Vaughan – 3-2 either way

Sir Alastair Cook – 3-2 England

Glenn McGrath – 5-0 Australia
(only committed to scoreline after the first Test)

Jonathan Agnew – 3-2 England

Phil Tufnell – 2-2

Jim Maxwell – 3-1 Australia

Paul Farbrace – 3-2 England

Isa Guha – 2-1 England

Ebony Rainford-Brent – 3-2 England

Vic Marks – 3-2 either way

Daniel Norcross – 4-0 Australia

Alison Mitchell – 2-2

Simon Mann – 2-2

Geoff Lemon – 2-2

CHAPTER 16

Smith Takes Down
Fortress Edgbaston

Thursday 1 August
England v Australia – The Ashes – First Test
Match, Day 1
Edgbaston, Birmingham

Team *TMS:* Jonathan Agnew, Daniel Norcross, Jim Maxwell, Alison
Mitchell, Phil Tufnell, Michael Vaughan, Geoffrey Boycott, Glenn McGrath,
Andrew Samson

The early risers within the *TMS* team are sitting in the commentary box at Edgbaston at around 7.30 a.m. on the morning of the first day of the Ashes. Beside producer Adam Mountford and assistant producer Henry Moeran, there is absolutely no reason for most of them to be at the ground so early. However, today is a day that will excite even the most seasoned of seasoned pros. The traditional hum of expectation that buzzes around a cricket ground on the morning of a big match is loaded with a vital tension. Such are the levels of glory that can be attained, so large are the legends of the past written, and so loaded is this one series that the final few hours before battle commences are something nobody wants to miss.

Many is the quiet conversation that has been had at the back of a commentary box, in the lunch room or even in a hotel bar late at night that went a bit like this:

'If England could win the World Cup or the Ashes, which one would you choose?'

'I don't think you need to choose; they're definitely good enough to win both.'

'Yeah, but if you *had* to choose one – which one would it be?'

[Quieter, as if it's something hard to admit] 'I'd have to go with the Ashes.'

As *TMS* quietly anticipate what's to come, crews from the *Today* programme and *5 Live Breakfast* go about their business, garnering opinion on key topics. Will Jason Roy be able to stand up to the Aussie pace attack with a red ball in their hand? Which Australians will form that pace attack? Just how good is the Test return of Steve Smith going to be? What's the status of Jimmy Anderson's calf muscle? How loud will the booing be? All will be answered, but not for a few hours yet.

While all this is going on, Jimmy Anderson – of the *TMS* box earlier this summer but now back in the thick of the action on the field – is in the team hotel a short distance away, gathering his thoughts. After suffering a calf injury that caused him to miss the recent Test match against Ireland as a precaution, Anderson bowled a good spell in the nets at Jos Buttler earlier in the week and is excited to get cracking on the field.

Such is his positivity that the discovery that his car, parked up in the hotel car park, has been badly crashed into overnight ('By what I can only assume to be a tractor,' he later tells his BBC *Tailenders* podcast) puts but a tiny dent in his *joie de vivre*.

Even the realisation that his insurance company is open only from 9 a.m. to 5 p.m. – hours in which his phone will be securely locked away in an ICC-guarded locker, meaning he will have to wait five days to deal with the incident – is quietly taken in his stride.

Outside, the people of Birmingham go about their morning routine, and inside the last preparations are made. The ground staff buzz about deliberately, completing final checks, and before you know it, the 570 days have elapsed and the designated hour comes. Adam Mountford presses the button and *Test Match Special* is live around the world with the programme's final assignment of the summer: 25 days of Ashes cricket.

'There's that really special feeling that you have on the first morning of the Ashes,' says Aggers, neatly distilling the wonderful morning into an opening gambit – and with that, the practised routine sets in.

The game is previewed, the toss anticipated, and the players interviewed. 'I think you'd bat first – just,' says former batsman Michael Vaughan, grateful it's not him who has to make the decision. 'Whatever you decide, you'll need to do it very well.'

'I just like this breeze for bowling. I can just feel it's going to swing,' says former swing bowler Jonathan Agnew. 'It's not a bad toss to lose if it means you're going to be bowling first.' Which is exactly what happens: Joe Root spins the coin up, Tim Paine calls a head and it falls with Her Majesty staring back at her subjects. They're going to have a bat. 'I don't think England will be too upset about that,' says Aggers immediately.

The outcome of the first of the 'key topics' from earlier is revealed when Josh Hazlewood and Mitchell Starc are the two seamers to miss out and, in the final minutes before 11 a.m., the denizens of the Hollies Stand and the wider body of Edgbaston prepare themselves to welcome David Warner to the crease for his first Test innings since a fateful day in Cape Town in March 2018.

Back in the dressing room, Anderson is excited that England are bowling first, allowing less time for any potential nerves to build. As he walks out and lines up for the national anthems, 'God Save the Queen' is blasted out powerfully by the fervent crowd and all thoughts of the World Cup triumph are locked away until 17 September. Now, it's the Ashes.

The first over is bowled to a wall of noise emanating from the England supporters. The volume has been heard before from fans of Pakistan, Bangladesh and particularly India during the World Cup, but it was never as febrile as this, never so aggressive or tribal. 'The reaction to the sandpaper scandal showed how Australians have a love affair with cricket and don't want anyone to tarnish it by doing something stupid,' says Jim Maxwell insightfully. 'Bancroft, Smith and Warner will want to show they've moved on. But the crowd has not moved on.'

As Warner and Cameron Bancroft walk to the crease, the reception is astonishing. 'It's like a zoo – listen to the noise!' says Aggers as the boos turn to incessant cheers the instant Anderson is announced as bowling the first over. His first ball shapes away outside off stump and is left well alone by Bancroft.

'I actually saw David Warner out shopping in Birmingham yesterday,' says Agnew, chatting to Tuffers in the early going. Quick as a flash, the Cat replies, 'DIY shop, was it?!' The lengthy guffaws induced in the commentary box, from English and Australians alike, dispel any lingering pre-match tension.

Stuart Broad's first ball flies down the leg side, passing close enough to Warner to generate a huge yell from players, fans and commentators alike. 'I think he's nicked that!' says Tuffers, but Root decides against the review. When the replay comes back a minute later, it turns out Tufnell was spot on and Root was wrong. Warner got a tickle on it and would have been a goner had it been reviewed. Could it be a crucial moment? 'David Warner could have walked, I suppose?' concludes Tuffers, not entirely seriously. 'I think we'd have been sitting in the wreckage of Edgbaston if that happened,' replies Aggers.

Then, as if to pacify his bowler, Root does review an LBW decision in his next over. 'This didn't look good,' says the sage of Middlesex. 'It just didn't feel out,' agrees Aggers, and indeed it isn't out. However, later in the same over Warner is defeated again and the crowd explodes into yet another massive yelp. This time the finger is raised and, after a brief consultation with Bancroft, Warner opts to walk.

'I can see bits of sandpaper being waved as David Warner trudges off. What an exit!' says Aggers. As Usman Khawaja walks to the crease, the replay is rolled and it turns out that, had Warner reviewed, it wouldn't have been out. 'Add that to the twist of the tale!' says Alison Mitchell, revelling in the drama. 'That's karma for not being out when he nicked it,' replies Tufnell bluntly.

Although Broad got the breakthrough, Anderson is bowling superbly from the other end, causing Bancroft in particular some huge problems outside his off stump. 'I think that's called turning the man into an S,' says Tuffers after one of many agonised flashes past the outside edge. 'He's completely can of beans'd him! He looked like something out of *Strictly Come Dancing*.'

Broad then reaps the benefits of Anderson's tenacity, Bancroft nicking one to Root, and Australia slip to 17 for two. After just 40 minutes of action, nobody in the crowd is tired yet and Steve Smith is welcomed to the Ashes with a chorus of boos unlike any heard in an English cricket ground before. 'This is perfect for England to get Steve Smith out so soon,' says Vaughan. 'Though it's probably best for Smith as well to get that first big boo out of the way early on. For Australia to compete over here in these conditions, Smith at No 4 is the key.'

Anderson bowls his first four overs beautifully, with three maidens, conceding just one run before Chris Woakes replaces him. The early change raises a few injury suspicions, not helped by Olly Stone coming out to field in his place shortly afterwards.

On the field, World Cup hero Ben Stokes bowls his first Ashes overs and, in the box, listeners get their first taste of Glenn McGrath. Stokes immediately goes up for an LBW shout and the Aussie legend garrulously replies, 'Pitched outside. Going down. But apart from that it was pretty close!' McGrath is clearly starting as he means to go on, afer being introduced as 'Glenn McGrath, a man who's taken 563 Test wickets, the most for an Australian seam bowler . . . Obviously not the leading seam bowler ever, though . . .'

Khawaja is next to go, the latest beneficiary of a review of a poor umpiring decision, which gives Daniel Norcross his first Ashes wicket of the summer. 'He's got it! He's got the edge! The crowd go wild,' he yelps over yet another bombastic Edgbaston cheer.

With England on top and the nation entranced, the traditional *TMS* conversations break out about the programme's negative contribution to Great British productivity. This is underscored when the following message is received in the *TMS* inbox, offering precise guidelines for how people can follow the BBC Live Text commentary while also still using Microsoft Excel (other spreadsheet software is available).

'*Open Excel, Data tab, on right-hand side external data, click on From Web. Press yes to all the script errors. Copy and paste the BBC commentary web address into the address box. Click the yellow arrow in top left (if it doesn't work, refresh the page). When it turns into a green tick, press import. Voila, now you are simply looking at an Excel file that just so happens to update with all the live text commentary once you press refresh.'* TMS listeners (and now readers, too) are truly a wonderful bunch.

England opt for a change of pace, bringing Moeen Ali into the attack, and *TMS* match them with a change of pace in the commentary box. It's the moment many listeners have been waiting for all year: on Yorkshire Day, Geoffrey Boycott is back on the air.

'We missed you, Geoffrey,' says Agnew, referencing Boycott's extended break for the first part of the summer.

'I've had my heart check-up,' he responds testily.

'Oh, they found one, did they?' asks Aggers immediately. And they're off.

Australia go into lunch at 88 for three, with serious concerns about the missing Anderson, who has bowled only four overs all morning. 'If Joe Root is being sparing with James Anderson because of his calf injury, that is not a good recipe,' warns Boycott. 'If you're not confident he can bowl 20 overs in the day, then he shouldn't be playing.'

During the lunch session, news breaks that Anderson is leaving the ground for a scan on his right calf muscle this afternoon, after feeling tightness during the morning session. It's the same muscle he injured earlier in the summer that kept him out of the Ireland Test and, as Aggers says, this is 'not good news at all'.

While the news at lunchtime is bad, the radio is excellent as *TMS* join a lap of honour being done by England's 2005 heroes, with Aggers chatting to Michael Vaughan OBE, Simon Jones MBE, Ashley Giles MBE, Andrew Strauss OBE, Steve Harmison MBE, Ian Bell MBE, Paul Collingwood MBE and Matthew Hoggard MBE. As ever, the six revel in being back in each other's company, with Vaughan candidly discussing which members of his pace attack could get through a few overs today, admiring Simon Jones's chiselled visage while casting accusatory glances at Hoggard and Harmison's retirement physiques in particular. The lap of honour is crowned with a selfie and provides some lovely memories for listeners to indulge in during the first lunch break of the series.

After lunch, Smith and Travis Head continue to drag Australia back into the game, causing concern to the extent that Tufnell wonders about 'Joe Root and Jonny Bairstow having a whirl'. However, out of almost nowhere, Woakes blisters one through Head and, despite a dramatic call to review with just one second on the timer left, England have the decision upheld to set Australia back to 99 for four.

Matthew Wade – 'resuscitated and reborn as a Test cricketer', according to Maxwell – is the new man, but it's Smith who survives the latest moment of DRS drama, being given LBW playing no shot to Broad but successfully overturning the fatefully raised finger. Wade then goes the other way around, being given not out but having to walk when England review the shout, as Andrew Samson says that the game is already at five reviews within the first 34 overs. There is no requirement for the next one to be reviewed, though, as Paine makes a bizarre decision and hooks Broad to Rory Burns at deep square leg, who accepts the gift gratefully. 'A soft dismissal,' mutters McGrath, as Broad gives Paine the wide-eyed, hand-over-mouth treatment he patented when taking eight wickets in a morning at Trent Bridge in 2015.

James Pattinson (who should have reviewed his LBW decision because it would have been not out) and Pat Cummins follow along soon afterwards, leaving Australia 122 for eight and Boycott suggesting, 'If you've bought a ticket for Sunday, I'd be thinking about a pub to go to for Sunday lunch.'

England are flying and Edgbaston is utterly jubilant, making a determined mockery of Paine's pre-match statement that he can think of 15 more intimidating grounds in world cricket. New man Peter Siddle is given LBW but overturns it on account of a huge inside edge that was missed by the umpire and Smith reaches an excellent half-century, the landmark brought up by more loud boos, much to the chagrin of Geoffrey. 'The boos ... it's water under the bridge now,' he says. 'They know what they did, they've been punished for it, it's been and gone.'

Siddle and Smith form an adhesive partnership, hitting tea with the loss of no further wickets and the score on 154. During the second break, *TMS* are joined by former Aussie all-rounder Andrew McDonald, the newly announced coach for the Birmingham-based side in next year's Hundred competition. 'It's a rare opportunity to build something from scratch' is his take on his new appointment, although the deluge of correspondence received during and after the interview indicates that some cricket fans are yet to be convinced of the need for The Hundred.

As well as McDonald, there is another splendid arrival in the box as an incredibly complex cake in the shape of the SS *Great Britain* is delivered. The ship was engineered by Isambard Kingdom Brunel and launched in 1843, being considered the world's first great ocean liner. In 1861, she carried the first ever 'All England' cricket team, including W.G.Grace's brother E.M.Grace, to tour Australia. The ship is now docked in Bristol and offers a fascinating exhibition of memorabilia from those tours.

A short rain break follows tea, but when the players head back out again, Smith and Siddle still won't budge. 'This is becoming a little infuriating for England,' observes Tuffers, and the fifty partnership comes up.

'I've given up assuming that there's any chance of Steve Smith being out ever again. Peter Siddle, meanwhile, looks like a right-handed Jack Leach,' says Norcross morosely, as the two grind on remorselessly.

Boycott, naturally, is calling for patience and a nagging line outside off stump; Tufnell for a team talk to remove the hands that have made their way to England hips – and when umpire Aleem Dar, completing an action-packed day for him, is unfortunately stung by a wasp, at least Tufnell's idea can be put into practice.

'This is a very good position from where Australia were,' remarks Maxwell, and while Moeen finally gets Siddle – caught off an inside edge at short leg by Buttler – another 74 are then added for the final wicket.

'Smith was booed out to the middle, booed back after lunch, booed after tea, but now he is two short of a hundred,' says Aggers, before a rare show of crowd respect at least partially breaks out when he does bring up three figures. 'There are people applauding around Edgbaston,' continues Agnew. 'There is the occasional boo, but you have to admire a man who bared his soul. He was in a horrible place in the full glare of the publicity.'

'I don't think there are enough superlatives to describe Steve Smith,' says Norcross as the New South Welshman continues to dominate his partnership with Nathan Lyon. 'Steve Smith has wrestled the momentum back from a rampant England,' laments Tuffers, who continues his body-language analysis by adding, 'England's shoulders are drooping. They are scratching their heads.'

With Smith on strike, Root dispatches every fielder to the boundary, causing more disquiet in the box. 'This field is embarrassing for the bowler. I would not bowl to this. Every fielder is on the boundary,' says Maxwell. Tufnell, so jubilant earlier in the day, describes the tactic as a 'white flag from England'.

Broad eventually ends things – claiming his 100th wicket against Australia and one of the most under-celebrated Ashes five-fers of his career – when he bowls Smith for 144, but the damage is long done. 'It has been one of the great innings,' says Vaughan, with Maxwell adding, 'This has been one of the finest innings you will see.' As more boos ring out as Smith leaves the field, the pair agree that they are now entirely undeserved.

England still have two overs of the day to face, but there is no sign of a Lord's-style night-watchman, with Root entrusting the new opening pair of Roy and Burns to see them out. They do so with little alarm, ending the day on 8 without loss. It has been a very long day indeed, and for *TMS* the (hugely welcomed) continued interest from around the BBC means there is still quite some time to go, but there is no doubt as to who today belongs to.

'It seemed a long day because the cricket has been enthralling,' says Vaughan after play. 'It is Ashes cricket. It is great cricket. The greatest format delivers once again, and the greatest cricketing contest, in my eyes, delivered once again. Sometimes you have to accept greatness is in front of you. Today we saw one of the great, great innings.'

Friday 2 August
England v Australia – The Ashes – First Test
Match, Day 2
Edgbaston, Birmingham

Team *TMS*: Jonathan Agnew, Daniel Norcross, Jim Maxwell, Alison
Mitchell, Phil Tufnell, Michael Vaughan, Geoffrey Boycott, Glenn McGrath,
Andrew Samson

While the *TMS* team might have enjoyed a medicinal glass
of something strong after a long and eventful day yesterday, it
is the ground that feels hungover today rather than the commentators. If Day 1 of a new Ashes series is the first day at a
new school, Day 2 is the first day of the rest of your life. The
routines are becoming established, the faces more familiar, the
new kit acclimatised to and the rhythms comfortable.

Although remnants of the (delicious) SS *Great Britain*
and a beautiful gin and tonic cake that was also sent in still
litter the box, the team warmly greet BBC colleague Karthi
Gnanasegaram, who brings an early-morning delivery of yet
more cakes. 'Is 9.52 a.m. too early for a cake?' asks Norcross,
who knows the answer to his own question as he breaks the
baked goods seal quite magnificently.

'What's in store today?' asks Aggers as Rory Burns and
Jason Roy stride out, bats in hand. 'I don't think anybody has
got any idea whatsoever.'

'Phil Tufnell told me this England side need "mental flex-
ibility" today,' reports Michael Vaughan. 'I'm not sure what
that means and I'm not sure Tuffers does either.'

With both Burns and Roy representing the same county
(Surrey), Andrew Samson poses Agnew and Vaughan a
question: who were the last England opening pair to repre-
sent the same county? The two spend at least five minutes
cycling through almost all 18 sides before Vaughan's phone
surreptitiously buzzes in his pocket and he magically guesses
Graham Gooch and John Stevenson, who opened for Essex
and England in 1989. Subsequent questioning reveals the

surprisingly badgerish Alec Stewart to be the man bailing him out from afar.

Roy is the first wicket of the day to fall, caught well by Steve Smith at slip, shortly before the Barmy Army's 'Ben Stokes Tribute Day' reaches a whole new level. Having already handed out many thousands of Stokes masks to the crowd, a plane buzzes across Edgbaston. Rather than trailing an incendiary political message, as was sadly often the case during the World Cup, this one simply says 'Arise Sir Ben Stokes – Barmy Army', and receives a warm round of applause.

England bat through to lunch but do ride their luck on a couple of occasions. First, Burns survives a half-hearted LBW shout from Nathan Lyon, who would have been out had Paine made the fateful 'T'. Secondly – miraculously – Joe Root is given out caught behind but immediately reviews and it turns out that rather than flick his outside edge, the ball has in fact kissed the top of off stump before flying through to Paine, with the bails still intact.

Keenly aware of the ability of woodworking products to affect international sport, Paine even picks up the bails to make sure they haven't been nefariously glued down, but Root simply looks at the Aussie skipper, beaming from ear to ear, making maximum use of his cherubic features. 'That happened five times in the early stages of the World Cup,' remembers Andrew Samson. 'Then it stopped happening and the bails started falling off!'

After the conversation about Karthi's cakes earlier, more 'is it too early' chat is entered into when Geoffrey Boycott produces a bottle of no less than 'Boycott's Best Beer'. 'This must be the flattest, lowest-alcohol beer of all time,' suggests Aggers before going on to recount the story of Boycott's 150th first-class hundred, scored against Agnew's Leicestershire at Middlesbrough in July 1986.

'You were caught gully and didn't walk,' he begins, to plenty of Yorkshire caterwauling down the other microphone. 'You didn't play a shot all innings!'

'That's because I broke my finger!' protests Boycott. 'Yes,' replies Aggers, anticipating the comeback, 'you broke it gloving the ball to gully and then not walking. That innings was so boring that people were running out of the ground, screaming! I've seen the picture of you celebrating your hundred and there wasn't a single soul behind you in the stands. That says all you need to know about your batting!'

Samson is called in to referee the debate and, when it turns out the innings took 337 balls, the case is closed. For an encore, which receives a standing ovation from the box, Aggers reveals that in the picture of Boycott batting on the front of his own beer bottle, there is also no one watching.

Phil Tufnell replaces Geoffrey for the final stint before lunch and enquires what all the commotion is about. 'We're talking about Boycott's Beer, Tuffers,' Agnew replies.

'Boycott's got a beer named after him?!' says an astonished Tufnell. 'It must be bitter, surely?'

'Oh it's bitter. Very, very bitter,' confirms Aggers.

Following another outstanding Edgbaston lunch, Burns snaps into the afternoon session by reaching his half-century. 'He has just arrested Australia's momentum,' says Norcross, who then has to commentate on another overturned umpiring decision when Root is once more out, given LBW. 'That's the fifth overturned decision of nine reviews in the game,' says Samson. 'It's getting to the stage where, if you're given out, you just review it,' adds a dumbfounded Vaughan.

As the game meanders along beautifully, the *TMS* inbox fills with correspondence from listeners delighted to get a bit of Test cricket back in their life. The general consensus is that, while yesterday was excellent, the atmosphere could at times be considered a little frantic for a 'classic' Test and Steve Smith then spoilt it for everyone by being brilliant. Today's slow pace and gradual accumulation is just what the doctor ordered.

Glenn McGrath couldn't agree more, 'These two English batsmen have done the hard yards. Now they're starting to cash in a little bit more,' he says respectfully. 'That's old-fashioned Test cricket.'

Such is the pace of the game, a long conversation is able to break out during the afternoon session about the different regional names for bread rolls around England, caused by Tuffers being unable to communicate his desire for 'a nice bap' to a Brummie. It turns out his misunderstanding has opened a Pandora's box of different names, with cobs (East Midlands), stotties (North East), batches (Coventry), huffers (Essex), breadcakes (Sheffield and Leeds), banjos (the military), scufflers (Castleford and Rotherham), barm cakes (Lancashire and Manchester), baps (South East), bin lids (Blackburn), Dorset knobs (Wimborne), splits (Cornwall, where the domed top is known as a church and the flat bottom as a chapel), oven bottoms (more Lancastrians), huffkins (Kent) and muffins (Bury) all being sent in as alternative correct answers. Tuffers is flabbergasted but makes a note to pitch a feature to *The One Show*.

Root reaches his fifty but goes soon afterwards, Peter Siddle sticking out a hand into which the ball nestles after an uppish drive has been sent straight back down the pitch. Joe Denly joins Burns, and Boycott has some unsurprising words of wisdom for the new man: 'Just grind the runs out, that's what matters,' he says. 'It's five days of Test cricket.'

The characteristic comments are a mere warm-up for his headline act, though, as Boycott uses the tea interval to claim some delightful revenge on Aggers. He instructs the engineers to play back a clip of *TMS* from the World Cup final, where

Agnew is so convinced that Roy will be given out, he says that if he's not, he will 'eat Geoffrey Boycott's hat'.

He then calls Daniel Norcross to the front of the box to present Aggers with a ceremonial straw hat, complete with a Boycott-signed beige ribbon around the base. 'A big mouthful, please!' he requests. 'I need something else, it's dry – some rhubarb sauce, maybe?' replies Aggers, before stuffing a large part of the brim into his mouth and ripping into it like a hungry lion – creating a hole with his teeth.

'DON'T RUIN ME HAT!' cries Boycott, who has handed Agnew his actual hat and didn't expect the challenge to be taken so literally.

'It was tougher than old boots; I might have known that,' says an aching-jawed Aggers later on.

Shortly after tea, the Australians successfully petition the umpire to get the ball swapped, and suddenly everything changes. The 'new' old ball is hooping around corners, seaming around the place and generally making the England batsmen's lives a misery. Denly misses a scrambled seamer from James Pattinson and goes LBW and Tufnell shouts: 'IT'S THAT BALL!', as Jos Buttler begins his knock by creaming an overpitched wide ball through the covers for four.

'Everything about this ball is so much more dramatic,' says Norcross, conscious that the temperature in the middle has risen exponentially since tea. 'Australia just sniff an opening here.' Burns gets stuck on 92 for over half an hour and Buttler nicks to third slip and is taken by Cameron Bancroft.

Stokes is roared to the crease by a well-oiled Barmy Army – those who have still got their masks from earlier in the day, creating a very surreal sight indeed as they are worn en masse – but it's Burns who gets them on their feet next, scrambling home with a dashed single to reach his maiden Test match ton.

'Burns's hundred came in 319 minutes, from 224 balls with 14 fours. He was in the nineties for 54 minutes,' recounts Samson. 'Since Adam Lyth scored a hundred in 2015, England have had 15 opening batsmen. Alastair Cook scored six hundreds, Keaton Jennings two and Rory Burns is the only other one who has got a hundred.'

'It has been a proper Test hundred from Burns,' says Aggers reverentially. 'He has fought hard. It is terrific. It shows what you can do in a week since the Ireland Test.'

Burns and Stokes successfully negotiate the last of the new old ball before Australia take the actual new ball and call for yet another review, this time for an LBW that has actually been rejected correctly because it pitched a long way outside leg stump.

As the day draws to a close, crease occupation becomes the key. 'This is a situation of real strength for England. They have to keep playing the same way and keep showing the same discipline,' says Vaughan before returning to the much more fun art of commentating on whether a man in the Hollies Stand dressed as the Queen is leaving yet or whether he wants to stay and mock the Australians a little bit longer.

Burns walks off to the acclaim of a hero, having battled all day for his 125 not out. Stokes, on 38 not out, has had bigger days this summer – and will probably have more important moments to come this series – but, alongside Root and Denly, he has played a key role in England's adaptation back to playing 'proper Test cricket'. 'That was the best day of Test match batting I have seen from England in a long, long time,' says Vaughan as he merrily leads *TMS* towards Birmingham's Curry Mile for another installation of the now traditional 'Friday Night Curry Club'.

During the lunch interval on Day 2, John Holder appeared for another edition of the popular TMS *segment 'Ask the Umpire', where listeners can contact the programme to have their umpiring queries professionally resolved. This was the first email he dealt with:*

I was playing in a big game for my team earlier this summer, with the match heading for a tight finish. With nine needed from three balls, the batsman, a red-headed fellow who'd dug his side out of a bit of a hole, hit the ball straight to me at midwicket. I picked up as they turned for the second run and threw to the far end . . . As the batsman dived for his ground, the ball struck the outstretched bat and bounced away. To my horror, it headed away down the hill (the ground we played at doesn't have a very even surface) and went straight to the boundary. The umpire signalled for six runs, getting our opponents closer to their target. Suffice to say, it wasn't our day and we went on to lose the match. Should it have been five or six? – *Martin in Auckland*

John Holder: *In any match, when batsmen are running, the umpires are looking first at the creases to make sure batsmen ground properly. They are also looking to make sure batsmen don't run on the pitch. They cannot also be watching the action behind them – so the law needs to be changed.*

Strictly speaking, as the law stands now and with the evidence I've seen, that should have been five not six. Either umpire could have asked for the decision to be reviewed using the cameras but what probably deceived them, for want of a better word, was that the ball was live, and you've got to be watching the batsmen running as well. I agree totally with the decision that it was six runs, even though according to the law it was wrong.

Only when the ball is dead can you not score runs. As long as the ball is live you should be able to score runs.

Saturday 3 August
England v Australia – The Ashes – First Test
Match, Day 3
Edgbaston, Birmingham

Team *TMS*: Jonathan Agnew, Daniel Norcross, Jim Maxwell, Alison
Mitchell, Phil Tufnell, Michael Vaughan, Geoffrey Boycott, Glenn McGrath,
Andrew Samson

On the morning of Thursday 4 August 2005, Glenn McGrath was stalking the outfield at Edgbaston Cricket Ground, focused on the second Ashes Test that was due to begin within the hour. So focused was McGrath, he was not concentrating on where he put his feet and trod on a practice cricket ball that had been left on the outfield. He turned his ankle over, went a ghostly shade of white live on international television and was ruled out of the Test match. The rest is Ashes folklore.

On the morning on Saturday 3 August 2019, one day away from 14 years later, McGrath is bestriding that same outfield, focused on a conversation with his *Test Match Special* broadcast partner Alison Mitchell. So focused is McGrath, he is not concentrating on where he puts his feet. However, on this occasion he is far too smart to be burned twice and – at the last minute – sees what is about to happen and takes evasive action. His first thought is to blame Michael Vaughan for rolling one in his direction, but he quickly realises that the offending item had actually come from slip practice nearby, and that Ashes lightning had nearly struck twice. Elsewhere on the same outfield,

Jimmy Anderson is going through some mild warm-ups and England tell *TMS* that he will bat if required. There is still no news on whether he will be bowling in the second innings.

While the first two days have seen their share of French Maids, chefs and '80s wrestlers, the fancy dress on the Saturday of the Edgbaston Test is always on a different level. 'I saw a few carrots walking to the ground this morning,' says Jim Maxwell drily in the early going, and as the ground fills up there are a barbershop quartet, a Mexican mariachi band, an inflatable Donald Trump and, shortly before midday, the Pope arrives, followed by his band of cardinals, and passes out blessings in front of a group wearing hard hats and hi-vis jackets branded with 'Smith & Warner Carpentry Services'.

Rory Burns and Stokes look good in the early going, with Stokes in particular being talked up by Tuffers to such an extent that he is almost caught behind. 'I might stop talking up Ben Stokes,' he self-admonishes. 'I was saying how well he was playing and then he nearly got out!'

The all-rounder brings up his half-century to warm applause but fails to add another run, nicking behind to Tim Paine before being replaced by Jonny Bairstow at the crease. Andrew Samson points out that Bairstow is, almost certainly unwittingly, participating in a record at the moment as he has one of six first names in the England side that begin with a 'J'. It is a record for any letter, he adds, to general mild astonishment that he can come up with such a stat.

Drinks are taken before England suffer a disastrous late morning. Burns's marathon ends with a little nick behind off Nathan Lyon, Moeen Ali leaves one from the same bowler and is bowled fifth ball and – shortly after being described as 'the key' by Geoffrey Boycott – Bairstow edges to slip. Despite all of yesterday's hard work, England are eight down with a lead of just 16. 'That's a really, really poor shot,' says Boycott, frustrated at Bairstow's dismissal. 'That's the difficulty for some players coming from a lot of one-day matches. Jonny wants to try and hit every ball.'

Local hero Chris Woakes and Stuart Broad survive until lunchtime, when *TMS* are joined by the actor Keith Allen for the second *View from a Boundary* of the summer, this time hosted by Daniel Norcross. As expected, he is tremendously good value, telling tales of his days playing for a side called The Ruffians, blagging his way into The Oval to watch England play the West Indies, and being painted naked by Phil Tufnell (yes, that happened – on BBC television, in fact).

He also reveals that the last time he was at Edgbaston was to play in a charity game where he claimed to have dismissed the man who is now prime minister of Pakistan, Imran Khan, for 3. It turns out the reality of the situation is that he thought he had the great all-rounder LBW and turned to umpire David Shepherd to appeal for the dismissal. 'Not out' came the firm response. As a livid Allen returned to his mark to try and do the impossible for a second time, Shepherd had a quiet word in his ear, admitting that the dismissal should have been given but also reminding the actor that 'These people are here to watch him, not you!' Later in the day, Allen is spotted joyfully conducting the Barmy Army in a rendition of 'Vindaloo', the song he wrote for the 1998 Football World Cup with his band Fat Les.

The beginning of the afternoon session is marked by the return of Jonathan Agnew to the commentary box, who missed the morning so he could accompany his wife to the hospital. Aggers' wife Emma has recently waged a quite public battle against an aggressive form of breast cancer, and today is the day she received the results to indicate she is fully in remission. It is wonderful news for them both and hugely raises everyone's spirits.

Woakes and Broad carry on for over an hour after lunch, and the atmosphere continues to build. David Warner is sent down to field in front of the Hollies Stand, where he receives the predictable torrent before turning around and blowing a kiss to his tormentors. Later, as the deluge of comments continue, he is seen turning out the pockets on his whites to prove they are empty, which receives a good-humoured cheer.

Broad is eventually bounced out by Pat Cummins and another huge ovation is given to Jimmy Anderson, who walks out to bat not noticeably limping. There are no quick singles taken, however, and it appears clear that he won't be bowling in the second innings as England close on 374, a very useful 90-run lead.

TMS are lucky to be joined by another high-profile guest during the tea interval, with England rugby coach Eddie Jones coming on the programme ahead of a big autumn where he will try to match the feat of the cricketers and bring a World Cup back to these shores. Just like England head coach Trevor Bayliss, Jones is an immensely proud Australian charged with guiding England to World Cup glory. Was he pleased when the cricketers won the World Cup? His reply about liking the players and being pleased individually for them about their success is a triumph of media management but, as ever, his genuine passion for the game shines through and there are many preliminary selfies taken ready for posting should the World Cup deliver what it is hoped it might for England.

The Warner v Edgbaston relationship takes another turn at the start of Australia's second innings when the opener attempts to leave one from Broad but ends up getting a huge edge off the bottom of the bat. 'He's nicked the cover off it!' exclaims Aggers, as all fielders behind the stumps erupt in an appeal. The review makes it abundantly clear and even Glenn McGrath admits that 'Looking at the replays it was a regulation caught behind.'

With the ground railing at Warner and further delighting itself in cheering the exploits of a group of guys in England football shirts carrying their mate around, who is dressed in all gold as the 1966 version of the Jules Rimet Trophy, the roar when Cameron Bancroft loops Moeen Ali to short leg is something to behold – as is the chorus of boos that soundtracks Steve Smith to the crease, with the crowd now well aware of his potential impact on the game.

Smith and Usman Khawaja partner together ominously, but Ben Stokes, called into the attack, demonstrates his wicket-taking knack and gets a tiny nick from Khawaja through to Jonny Bairstow. Talk on air is all about the size of the chase England will be facing. 'England certainly have enough talent in the side to chase 200, but history tells you it will not be easy,' says Vaughan. 'This is the session. If England win it, they will win the game.'

Boycott is unimpressed with England's tactics, though, calling for more aggression and bigger variation in bowlers, reaching for the classics to express his point of view. 'Smith could have played that with my favourite stick of rhubarb,' he says after Australia have passed 90 and moved into the lead. 'He could have done it with a Blackpool stick of rock.'

The crowd receive a boost as Jofra Archer comes on as a substitute fielder, but Smith carries on implacably. 'I've been asked how to get Steve Smith out a lot,' says Glenn McGrath. 'I've given two answers so far: 1) I don't know; 2) I'll only tell you after the Ashes is over (which is probably because I don't actually know)!'

The volume from the Hollies Stand increases and Smith, described as 'an extraordinarily expressive man' by Daniel Norcross, gets clonked on the head by a Stokes bouncer, but is cleared to carry on, and as the umpires end the day due to bad light shortly after 6 p.m., Australia are effectively 34 for three, with Smith 46 not out and Travis Head 21 not out.

'A brilliantly balanced match,' says Aggers. 'I can't say which team is on top at the moment – it all hinges on that first half-hour tomorrow morning,' adds Vaughan. 'If England can remove Steve Smith then they will go on to win the match.'

Even Mark Ramprakash, who comes on after play to analyse the state of the game, has had it up to the back teeth with the Australian batsman. 'I'm sorry to disappoint you, but I don't know how to get Steve Smith out,' he admits. 'I'm sick to death of talking about him.' He may have to be patient, though, because this Ashes has a long way to run yet.

Sunday 4 August
England v Australia – The Ashes – First Test
Match, Day 4
Edgbaston, Birmingham

Team *TMS*: Jonathan Agnew, Daniel Norcross, Jim Maxwell, Alison Mitchell, Phil Tufnell, Michael Vaughan, Geoffrey Boycott, Glenn McGrath, Andrew Samson

As Phil Tufnell arrives in the *TMS* commentary box on the fourth morning, he is dragging something behind him. 'Is that your suitcase, Tuffers?' asks Alison Mitchell, and Tufnell confirms that it is. So convinced is he that this Test match is finishing today, he has checked out of his hotel and taken his suitcase with him to facilitate an easy departure at the end of play. It's a patriotic decision if nothing else, as Australia's next move will likely be to bat all day, should they be able to.

Strolling on the pitch before play, Michael Vaughan takes advantage of a quiet moment to slip in and have a chat with Steve Smith. 'Are you bored of batting yet?' is Vaughan's opening gambit. 'Not at all, mate,' replies Smith in his chirpy

Australian vernacular. Reporting the conversation back on air, Vaughan agrees that it's not a good sign.

However, there are shards of light elsewhere. Glenn McGrath thinks the game 'is on a knife edge' and puts the odds '52/48' in England's favour, and Tuffers, possibly with half an eye on his suitcase stashed under Adam Mountford's desk, reminds listeners that 'If you gave England Australia being 30 for three in the second innings they would have snapped your hands off.'

An early conversation about how to get Smith out is passed over to Andrew Samson for some statistical support, and it transpires that Smith's key weakness is against left-arm spin. As Tufnell heads for the corridor to start turning his arm over, Samson reveals that, oddly, South African batsman Dean Elgar has dismissed Smith twice in international cricket.

England run in hard but have no success to speak of, other than the occasional play and miss. 'It feels like Steve Smith thinks he has a year's worth of runs to make up for,' says Mitchell, and it's hard to argue with her take. Travis Head – 'a Yorkshireman' according to Geoffrey Boycott by dint of one first-class match he played for the county in 2016 – reaches his fifty but falls half an hour before lunch, nicking Ben Stokes to Jonny Bairstow. The bowler turns around and gees up the crowd while Tuffers, without minding one bit, decries the ball as 'a terrible delivery'.

As the conversation on ways to get a wicket had veered towards the surreal, the Cat had just been suggesting handing out whoopee cushions to short leg fielders in an attempt to put the batsmen off, and his triumphant cry of 'THE WHOOPIE CUSHION'S DONE IT!' is liable to confuse the inattentive listener quite significantly.

A dispiriting session for England ends with Smith on the brink of a ton and a lead of 141 in the bag. Then, as if listeners haven't had enough of jubilant Aussies, the lunchtime entertainment allows them to put their questions to Glenn McGrath and Mitchell Johnson. Referencing the atmosphere generated towards Smith and David Warner in this match, one listener asks Johnson how he dealt with treatment he frequently received from the Barmy Army. The response is possibly not what was expected. 'The way to block it out was to sing an alternative song in my head,' he admits, before revealing that at the time his young daughter was watching the Disney film *Frozen*, and it was the song 'Let It Go' he chose to play on a loop in his head while flying in to bowl his left-arm rockets at the England batsmen.

McGrath, meanwhile, chooses a perfect yorker to Aamer Sohail at the Gabba and a ball that missed Brian Lara's outside edge but hit the top of his off stump at Old Trafford in 1999 as the joint greatest balls he ever bowled.

The afternoon begins with Smith reaching his second hundred of the game. 'He is the greatest Test batsman I have seen in my time,' declares Vaughan, not pulling his punches. Over the course of the four days, Smith's brilliance has meant that more respectful applause can be heard than the towering cacophony of boos that he has become used to, which is reward enough for an astonishing performance.

England keep on coming in, but the ball is doing nothing. 'The ball looks like a fat rascal in Woakes's hand. It's soft and flabby,' says Tuffers, referencing a favourite cake of his, and Jim Maxwell agrees, describing the ball as like 'a pricked balloon'.

All 20 sets of Smith's gloves are laid out by the boundary rope, ready for action when called upon, and, remembering past tricks, Tuffers' creative mind comes up with another wicket-taking scheme. 'Peel some bananas and stick them in his gloves!' he suggests, before adding, 'I did that to Ian Botham once at Lord's. He wasn't very happy.'

Wade gets his fifty and Norcross and McGrath are reduced

to discussing where umpires are able to buy the tools of their trade. The flight of fancy continues for some time, with Norcross imagining a full umpire superstore stocked to the gills with white coats, light meters and broad-brimmed hats. Just as another overturned decision (the eighth in this match) sets the record for a Test in England and the crowd are starting to drift away into their own fun, Smith actually gets out. Chris Woakes, who did not bowl a ball all morning, gets a hint of away movement and Smith tickles it behind to a tumbling Bairstow.

Maxwell, a man not given to overstatement, remarks that 'We've seen some of the best ever Test match batting from him in this game,' while Boycott ominously thinks Smith getting out might be a good thing for Australia. 'That's the best thing that could have happened to them,' he adds. 'Otherwise they would have batted all day and only given themselves a day to bowl out England.'

Tea comes with Australia 266 ahead, which most of the team already view as a winning lead. Maxwell – aware that brevity can often cause more damage than verbosity – merely describes the return from the session (125 for one) as 'healthy for Australia'. The interval sees Aggers attend the opening of a new gate at Edgbaston that has been named after the great M.J.K. Smith, one of Warwickshire's favourite sons. In attendance is his son-in-law, Lord Sebastian Coe, who tells an excellent story about a recent meeting he had at Lord's.

Arriving at the North Gate on the Wellington Road, Lord Coe said he had a meeting at the ECB offices (three minutes' walk from the gate). He was told by the Lord's security, however, that all visitors had to enter via the Grace Gates (which is ten minutes' walk from the North Gate and then a further ten minutes from there back to the ECB offices). This back and forth continued for a while before Lord Coe reached for his trump card.

'I'm really sorry, and I hardly ever do this at all, but I'm Lord Sebastian Coe,' the double Olympic gold medallist pointed out. 'Oh! Are you?' replied the truculent Lord's security guard. 'Well, you can get to the Grace Gates nice and quickly, then, can't you?!' With his tail between his legs, and now late for the meeting, Lord Coe headed off around the corner.

If the first session was poor for England and the second session was bad, the third session almost defies description. First Tim Paine and then James Pattinson join forces with Wade as Australia pile on run after inexorable run. 'It's been a long day,' comments Tuffers after being sledged by Norcross for opening an ice cream too close to a microphone. Aggers prefers a strawberry pavlova that has been sent into the box, but Tufnell is mentally gone and simply replies, slightly manically, 'They think it's pavlova ... it is now!' The laughter echoing around the box has more than a hint of desperation to it as a long rendition of the theme from *The Great Escape* floods out of the Hollies Stand.

Wade gets his ton and Australia declare on 487 for seven, setting England 398 to win. More pressingly, they have seven overs to survive tonight. 'This game is dependent on how England play Nathan Lyon,' says Vaughan, as Paine calls on his off-spinner to open the bowling. Rory Burns and Jason Roy gut it out until the end of play, when attention immediately turns to tomorrow's weather forecast, which looks pleasingly unsettled. Vaughan, however, is positive. 'England should have enough, in terms of quality and strength, to see out 90 overs if they play Nathan Lyon well,' he says as evening becomes night and Phil Tufnell retrieves his suitcase and heads back to the hotel, hoping that his room has not been booked by someone else.

Monday 5 August
England v Australia – The Ashes – First Test
Match, Day 5
Edgbaston, Birmingham

Team *TMS*: Jonathan Agnew, Daniel Norcross, Jim Maxwell, Alison Mitchell, Phil Tufnell, Michael Vaughan, Geoffrey Boycott, Glenn McGrath, Andrew Samson

'I've got a feeling at about 5.49 p.m. England will be wheeling James Anderson onto the pitch to try and save the game. England don't do boring draws,' says Michael Vaughan, who has got out of bed the right side and thinks England can escape 'Fortress Edgbaston' with pride intact. Speaking before play, Mark Ramprakash adds, 'There'll be a few boys in the dressing room thinking they can knock these off today. There's a few, remember, who were in the one-day team who have had so much success.'

This is exactly what is worrying Geoffrey Boycott, though. 'What I'm concerned with, if I was an England supporter, is the comments coming out this morning from England sources about playing your normal game,' he says. 'I'm going, woah, hang on a minute. This is not normal. You're trying to save a Test match on a worn pitch.'

Australia make a disconcertingly early breakthrough when Pat Cummins accounts for Rory Burns, and then Joe Root is given LBW, but successfully reviews what turns out to be a horrible decision. 'That's nine decisions overturned now,' counts Samson. 'Seven of them have been against Joel Wilson.' Root is LBW again, reviews again, and this time he has got a huge inside edge onto his pads and it's the tenth overturned decision of the match. 'I'm finding it hard to believe Joel Wilson will be standing in the next Test,' says Jim Maxwell.

'He's not up to standard, no doubt about it. He's had a very bad game.'

Drinks arrive with nine wickets still in hand for England, but shortly afterwards Roy skips down the track, attempting to put pressure on Nathan Lyon, but misses the ball completely and is bowled through the gate. 'Oh, that looks terrible,' gulps Daniel Norcross, with Glenn McGrath adding, 'That was ugly, ugly decision-making by Jason Roy in the context of the match.'

'I'm putting up some iron gates so Geoffrey can't get into the commentary box after that shot from Roy,' says Aggers shortly afterwards, as Boycott warms up for his next stint, which will inevitably include an evisceration of Roy. Joe Denly is then caught off Lyon at short leg, wasting a review in the process, and Root finally has to go soon afterwards, falling to the same combination, leaving England four down at lunchtime.

'England have got it all to do – a mountain to climb,' says Tuffers as Ben Stokes and Jos Buttler walk out to resume after lunch. 'Mountains are there to be climbed, Philip,' says Norcross, almost giggling at his own positivity, any last trace of which evaporates when Buttler is bowled by Cummins in the first over of the session.

'You'd think this game will be over some time in the next couple of hours. England have to show some stickability to keep Australia in the field,' says Maxwell as Jonny Bairstow attempts to review a decision from Joel Wilson that he has been caught in the slips. This one turns out to be correct.

Stokes goes in the next over and, although Chris Woakes and Moeen Ali make Australia wait a short time, Lyon takes two in two to force Anderson to the crease. The injured Lancastrian blocks away the hat-trick ball and manages to remain unbeaten, the Test ending when Woakes – appropriately enough – is caught by Steve Smith. England fall for 146, losing a match where Australia were 122 for eight in the first innings by 251 runs, 35 runs less than Steve Smith scored across the entire match.

Maxwell describes the 'sought-after' victory as 'gratifying and memorable', while Boycott simply says, 'England should've done a lot better than they managed.' Vaughan expresses concerns about Moeen, Bairstow and Buttler, saying the trio 'look shot' after the World Cup, but, as ever, is preaching positivity: 'England can still come back and win this series,' he adds. 'I don't know what percentage chance they have, but it's not a lot.'

Australia 284 (80.4 overs; Smith 144, Broad 5-86) and 487-7d (112 overs; Smith 142, Wade 110, Head 51) beat England 374 (135.5 overs; Burns 133, Root 57, Stokes 50) and 146 (52.3 overs; Lyon 6-49, Cummins 4-32) by 251 runs.

Jimmy Anderson had one of the worst weeks of his professional life during the first Ashes Test. Not only was he able to bowl only four overs before the recurrence of his calf injury, subsequently ruling him out of the rest of the series, his car was crashed into in the hotel car park on the morning of the match.

The day after the game, with his car having been towed 24 hours earlier, he was forced into taking a train home from Birmingham to Manchester. Wanting to relax and listen to some music, he put his phone playlist onto shuffle. Possibly sensing his downbeat mood, this is the overtly depressing playlist it came out with.

Coldplay – 'The Scientist'
Stereophonics – 'Graffiti on the Train'
The Maccabees – 'No Kind Words'
Lewis Capaldi – 'Someone You Love'
Theme from *Phantom of the Opera*
T'Pau – 'China in Your Hand'

CHAPTER 17

Archer Fires Up Lord's

Wednesday 14 August
England v Australia – The Ashes – Second Test
Match, Day 1
Lord's Cricket Ground, St John's Wood, London

Team *TMS*: Jonathan Agnew, Simon Mann, Jim Maxwell, Isa Guha,
Phil Tufnell, Michael Vaughan, Geoffrey Boycott, Mitchell Johnson,
Andrew Samson

As *TMS* make their way from the Jubilee Line to the Lord's Media Centre, conditions for cricket are, at best, reasonable.

As *TMS* make final preparations for a day of broadcasting the second Ashes Test from the Home of Cricket, conditions for cricket start to deteriorate.

As *TMS* go on air, statistician Andrew Samson decides to wear his bright blue rain jacket inside the box. 'It's a mooching-around day,' confirms Aggers.

Sadly, the first guest to come on is BBC Weather's Simon King, who is a lovely man but an unwelcome presence on *TMS* because he is generally only around when there is bad weather that needs to be described. 'We've got a little window of a few drier spells, but behind it there is more rain,' he reports. 'It's going to rain for most of the day. If we want to clutch at straws, there may be some drier periods at three, four o'clock this afternoon, but it could still be quite drizzly. In all honesty, it looks pretty dismal for the whole day.'

Inspections come and go, but *TMS* carries on regardless, debating the make-up of the England XI, which Joe Root has not named in advance. Michael Vaughan is advocating the selection of Sam Curran over Joe Denly, arguing that he will give England more over the course of four innings. Mitchell Johnson, stepping in to replace an India-bound Glenn McGrath for this Test, is particularly disappointed with the conditions but always happy to discuss previous Ashes campaigns, telling stories of battles with Kevin Pietersen, some of the difficulties he faced with long tours and his incredible series in 2013-14, since dubbed the 'pomnishambles'.

The venerable Alec Stewart, working next door for BBC 5 Live, is brought in to discuss potential batting call-ups for England, with names like Dom Sibley and Zak Crawley mentioned. Stewart, also director of cricket at Surrey, is full of praise for his man Rory Burns's century in the last game, describing it as 'the perfect example of what an ugly hundred can look like'.

A bit of brightness transpires around 2 p.m., but Agnew admits it could be what he terms 'a sucker's gap'. The toss is scheduled for 3 p.m. and England form a huddle, allowing Jofra Archer to be presented with his Test cap. He has asked for his best friend, and Sussex and England team-mate, Chris Jordan, to present to him. Jordan is tracked down, brought on air and is glowing about Archer. 'I knew Jofra back in Barbados and he is like a brother to me,' he says. 'I view him as family now and, if the moment comes, I will be more than happy to do it.'

The moment does arrive and it's clearly emotional for the pair of them as Jordan stands in the middle of the huddle, gives a short speech and hands the cap over.

However, five minutes before the toss is due, it starts to rain again and that is that. Play is eventually abandoned for the day a little after 4 p.m. and everyone concerned will try again tomorrow, when the forecast looks much more promising.

Thursday 15 August
England v Australia – The Ashes – Second Test
Match, Day 2
Lord's Cricket Ground, St John's Wood, London

Team *TMS*: Jonathan Agnew, Simon Mann, Jim Maxwell, Isa Guha, Phil Tufnell, Michael Vaughan, Geoffrey Boycott, Mitchell Johnson, Andrew Samson

There is always something special about the queue outside the Grace Gates on the morning of an Ashes Test match, but today is a little different. Normally, the preponderance of MCC blazers, ties, boaters and socks means red and yellow (or 'bacon and egg') are the overwhelming colours to be spotted on a north London Test match morning. Not today, though. Today there is a feast of red as far as the eye can see.

The reason for this is that today's play is being staged in remembrance of the late wife of former England captain and director of cricket Andrew Strauss, Ruth Strauss, who tragically died from a rare form of lung cancer in December, aged just 46.

Today marks the launch of the 'Ruth Strauss Foundation' and everyone has been asked to wear red in her memory, similar to the annual 'Turn it Pink' day at the Melbourne Cricket Ground that honours Glenn McGrath's wife, Jane McGrath, who passed away ten years earlier after suffering from breast cancer.

The *TMS* team have absolutely got behind the initiative, every member of the team wearing some kind of red top (although Michael Vaughan and a red-socked Mitchell Johnson ask some serious questions as to how red the 'red' shirt that Aggers bought online for the occasion really is).

Most of the team are fortunate enough to have some kind of professional-looking red clothing in the back of their wardrobe, but Henry Moeran – who claims to own nothing suitable – comes to work wearing a red shirt that was bought for a fancy-dress party last year. By itself, it would do the job nicely. However, the word 'Rocketman' spelt out in buttons on the front and 'Captain Fantastic' and a large star on the back indicate that it has been customised to make the wearer look like Elton John. It is fabulous and raises many a smile.

Before today, Aggers recorded a wonderful interview with Strauss and McGrath, the three men openly and emotionally talking about their experiences with cancer. The response to the interview, which was played yesterday because of the rain and has also been released as a podcast, is extraordinary. Listeners from around the world share their own stories and explain how much it means to them to hear the three being so honest about what they've been through.

The most unexpected response to the interview comes via *Tailenders* host Greg James, who retweets a post about it and draws the attention of one of his followers, former WWE wrestler and now one of the world's biggest film stars, Dwayne 'The Rock' Johnson. The Rock rather neatly describes the interview as 'beautiful/heartbreaking and inspiring'. A reply is dispatched, inviting him onto *View from the Boundary* at his convenience, with the hashtag #canyousmelltherockcakescooking added as extra bait to secure the booking.

England, bedecked in some splendid special red caps, lose the toss and are asked to bat by Australia. Jofra Archer is confirmed as making his Test debut, stepping in for the sadly re-injured Jimmy Anderson, and Jack Leach comes back into the side in place of Moeen Ali. Despite Vaughan's protestations, Joe Denly plays ahead of Sam Curran and, after Andrew Strauss's two sons, Luca and Sam, ring the five-minute bell, the match is under way.

Rory Burns sees off the first over with no alarms, but Jason Roy goes for a huge cut shot off his first ball and completely misses. 'Have a look, Jase!' exhorts Tuffers, and Isa Guha, aware of a sudden change of temperature in the box, adds, 'Alec Stewart is stood behind us and he looks like he can't believe what he's just seen from Roy.'

The next ball he receives is a jaffa of the highest order. He plays and misses at it, but then nicks the third and Tim Paine takes a regulation catch behind the stumps. England then struggle with some more excellent Australian bowling early on, but take 13 from Peter Siddle's opening over before Joe Root is trapped LBW by Josh Hazlewood.

Leading into the lunch break, Burns and Denly add 50, but not without a few scares – Burns being quite poorly dropped by Usman Khawaja – and England go in at 76 for two to enjoy their choice of ribeye steak, chicken stir-fry, Cajun grilled swordfish or veggie paella, followed by treacle sponge, lemon meringue pie or a fruit salad.

During the break, *TMS* are joined by two pairs of special guests. Firstly, Dan Bowser and Chris Edwards, who were the winners of the 2018 Christopher Martin-Jenkins 'Spirit of Cricket Award'. Players for the England Learning Disability team, the pair were involved in a game against the Denmark

Under-17s last summer and appeared to have claimed a tight seven-run win when a caught-behind decision was given. However, fielding at first slip, Bowser could clearly see the batsman hadn't hit the ball and informed his captain, who then told the umpire and the decision was rescinded. The game was restarted and England went on to win by three runs.

The 'Spirit of Cricket Award' was created in 2013 by the MCC and the BBC in memory of the great 'CMJ', a former MCC president and *TMS* commentator whose passion for promoting the 'spirit of the game' was infectious and brought huge positivity to cricket and the commentary box. Dan and Chris are perfect winners and the interview is a lovely opportunity to reminisce about a much-missed old colleague.

Dan and Chris then give way to Tim Murtagh and his wife Karina, who are in the box for a dual purpose. Great friends of the Strauss family, they have been deeply involved in the organisation of today's day for the Foundation, but Tim also has a prize to receive: the 'Brian Johnston Champagne Moment' for the recent England v Ireland Test, awarded to recognise his five-wicket haul in the first innings. The final act during lunch is an attempt to unearth a thief in the box. The most delightful cake has been delivered during the early going, garlanded wonderfully with some very delicate macarons. One of them has been purloined, though, leaving a visual discordance that is not what the baker intended. An investigation is launched.

Denly goes soon after lunch, but Burns is dropped again and then brings up his fifty. There is high praise from Mitchell Johnson, who says that the Surrey opener 'in some ways reminds me of Alastair Cook, just playing to his strengths, waiting for the bad balls'. If the Australian's intent was to issue a 'commentator's curse', then he can consider himself successful, as Burns departs soon afterwards to a brilliant catch from Cameron Bancroft at short leg. Jos Buttler doesn't last long, offering a classic Boycott 'nothing shot' to Siddle and being caught behind before Ben Stokes goes too, LBW to Lyon. 'This is big trouble for England,' worries Simon Mann, sat next to a still-ruminating Boycott with the scoreboard reading 138 for six.

Jonny Bairstow and Chris Woakes stop the rot and settle into their new partnership, and as Steve Smith comes on to bowl his part-time leg-spinners, a new noise is heard among fans at the Home of Cricket. 'That is definitely not the crowd shouting "Roooot",' observes Isa, who has been identified as the perpetrator in 'Macarongate', much to the surprise of the *TMS* inbox, most of whom were convinced that Tuffers was responsible.

Mitchell Johnson comes back on air and talk once again turns to his battles with the Barmy Army. Asked if he can remember the words to the famous song written in his honour, he replies, 'Yeah, I remember the song: *He bowls to the left / He bowls to the right / That Mitchell Johnson / His bowling's all right.*' Hilarity ensues, both in the box and, as ever, on social media and in the *TMS* inbox.

Bairstow and Woakes reach tea with England 201 for six. It's not what the plan would have been at lunchtime, but Johnson argues that they should be happy with the situation, saying, 'I think England pegged that back in the last 40 minutes or so. Australia came out hard after the lunch break and they might have been feeling a little flat towards the end.'

Andrew Strauss joins *TMS* at tea-time, with the man of the hour adding to a theme of the day by saying how good it was of Aggers to turn up wearing purple on the day his new Foundation turned Lord's red, and suggesting he might do better next year. More personally, he reflects on the moment he watched his sons ring the bell at the start of play today: 'That was an incredibly special, poignant moment. I am very proud of them. It is not easy to stand there in the public when everyone knows the story.'

After tea, the Bairstow and Woakes show continues. Woakes then clonks Pat Cummins for six but pays the price, ducking into a short ball offered as retribution and needing a concussion check-over. He is ruled okay to continue, but Cummins gets even sweeter revenge soon after, as Woakes gloves one down leg side and has to go.

The England tail wags enough for Bairstow to complete a morale-boosting half-century, with Archer's first Test action being marked by a barrage of short stuff from Cummins, demonstrating that the days of the old unofficial 'Fast Bowlers' Union' are well and truly done for. 'They are going to face a barrage from Jofra Archer at some point so may as well get in there first,' reasons Johnson.

Leach once again carries his bat, Bairstow holing out as England are all out for 258. 'It doesn't look enough to me,' says Aggers ruefully, 'but at least there has been something of a lower-order revival.'

'It might be all right if England bowl well and catch everything, but Australia ought to be able to get more than 258,' adds Boycott. Vaughan is even blunter than his fellow Yorkshireman. 'You can't tell me 258 is a par score on that,' he says simply.

After an over from Stuart Broad, Archer (whose debut increases England's alphabetical world record from Edgbaston to no fewer than seven players whose forenames begin with a 'J', causing Andrew Samson almost to burst with excitement) is handed the new ball and the ground crackles with excitement to see what he's capable of. His first ball is an 86mph loosener, but the second flies through Bancroft, beats absolutely everything and sails away for four byes. 'That seemed to go a long, long way after hitting the pitch, but it defeated everything,' says a flustered Jim Maxwell, as the World Cup hero's sky-high red-ball potential is underlined in one delivery.

As the clouds draw over and the close nears, England take a wicket when Broad nips one back up the famous Lord's slope and bowls David Warner, dismissing the opener for the third consecutive time as the crowd fires up and starts getting behind Broad and Archer. Khawaja and Bancroft endure a torrid time, with Archer cranking his pace up to 92mph and Broad finding good movement both into and away from the batsmen. The two survive, though, ending a good day for their side on 30 for one.

'I think the day goes to Australia,' admits Tuffers, who has half an eye on tomorrow's weather, which doesn't look as good as it might. 'I think it's going to be another great Test match. Hopefully we won't lose too much time tomorrow, there is still enough time for a winner.'

Friday 16 August
England v Australia – The Ashes – Second Test
Match, Day 3
Lord's Cricket Ground, St John's Wood, London

Team *TMS*: Jonathan Agnew, Simon Mann, Jim Maxwell, Isa Guha, Phil Tufnell, Michael Vaughan, Geoffrey Boycott, Mitchell Johnson, Andrew Samson

BBC Weather guru Simon King is once again a disappointingly key man in the early going, saying that rain will be arriving between 12 p.m. and 2 p.m. So certain is he of the prediction, he even offers his social media followers a friendly sweepstake as to exactly when it will show up. The merest droplets of rain are present as Shane Warne, who will coach the MCC team in The Hundred next year, rings the bell to get things under way. His old rival Alec Stewart is unimpressed, however, describing his campanological efforts as 'limp'.

Clouds are dark and low and the floodlights on full beam as the action kicks off, Stuart Broad and Jofra Archer picking up where they left off last night. However, the bowling is not quite on the money, and while Australia don't run away with things, there are no chances being created. 'You feel here that England are wasting the conditions,' says Simon Mann, adding, 'It's not really happening for Jofra Archer.'

Yet, not long after Mann has issued this criticism, Archer, drawing towards the end of his spell, gets one to nip back and hit Cameron Bancroft in front. The opener reviews but Tuffers is spot on when he reckons 'This is trimming the bails.' Archer is mobbed by his team-mates as Steve Smith emerges from the Long Room to find the Lord's crowd slightly less spiky than their Edgbaston counterparts but by no means free of boos. 'Tuffers, didn't you say if Steve Smith got out for a duck, you'd walk around St John's Wood naked?' asks Isa Guha. 'Come on, Steve,' replies the Cat as Archer fires a 93.5mph delivery past Smith's off stump first ball.

Chris Woakes then joins the party, Usman Khawaja driving at a full, swinging delivery and only finding Jonny Bairstow behind the stumps. The rain continues to fall gently, and all residents of the St John's Wood area are grateful to Archer for offering one that Smith can tickle down to fine leg and get off the mark, removing any danger of them seeing more than they might want to of Philip Clive Roderick Tufnell.

Conditions marginally clear up and England's bowling is suddenly a lot more threatening. 'In the first eight overs this morning there were 30 runs, the next six just one run and two wickets,' says Andrew Samson, with Broad then adding a third (after appealing, not seeing the finger rise, reviewing and then celebrating again) as Travis Head is sent back. 'I don't know why Aleem Dar didn't give that out. It's hitting middle stump,' says Aggers, summing up some general perplexity in the box, particularly from a vocal Boycott, as to that specific decision.

The gentle rain then returns and Woakes tries to bounce Smith but only succeeds in providing a long hop he can pull for four. 'You'd have bowled that, Jonathan. You were good at bowling long hops,' says Boycott, tail up from the recent clatter of wickets, as the sun briefly makes a confusing appearance before once more giving way to the soft rain that has characterised the session and eventually forces the players off, three minutes before lunch.

England's World Cup-winning captain Eoin Morgan receives a solid silver cap on the outfield during the break for becoming the first ever England player to receive 200 ODI caps. He captained the side in 100 of those and the presentation is also to honour his role in England's World Cup victory. Speaking to Aggers afterwards, Morgan admits, 'It took me some time to process the game, given how the result was calculated and there being two ties. It took a couple of weeks actually. I've watched the game back twice in full, and there's a lot of mistakes by both sides. That's what makes it beautiful, in some ways.'

From the weather centre in Salford, Simon King reports that 'a miracle would be required' to get any more cricket played in St John's Wood today and, although it takes until after 5 p.m. for the final call to be made, he's absolutely spot on. Although the rain is unwelcome, it doesn't stop *TMS*, with chat continuing all afternoon. A particularly special visitor is Issy Batey, who is eight and a half years old and delivers one of the best cakes of the summer (a Milne Chocolate Biscuit Cake, no less) to the box alongside a wonderful letter, in which she specifically requests that Tuffers isn't allowed to eat all of the cake.

Her chat with Aggers and Boycott (with many listeners commenting that exposure to such a sweet young girl made Geoffrey sound almost human!) is a beautiful piece of radio and demonstrates perfectly the idea many listeners have discussed, that *TMS* doesn't need cricket to make good radio.

At the other end of the age spectrum, the programme is invited into one of the hospitality boxes to speak to the great Neil Harvey. Now 90 years old, Harvey is the only survivor of Sir Donald Bradman's 1948 'Invincibles' side and has travelled from Australia to England for this Test match. As well as some wonderfully historic recollections, he tells Jim Maxwell that comparisons being made between Smith and Bradman are off the mark. 'You can't compare anyone with Bradman, I'm sorry. He's twice as good as anyone else,' says Harvey, who is nonetheless delighted to have such a wonderful cricketer to watch in his dotage.

Saturday 17 August
England v Australia – The Ashes – Second Test
Match, Day 4
Lord's Cricket Ground, St John's Wood, London

Team *TMS*: Jonathan Agnew, Simon Mann, Jim Maxwell, Isa Guha, Phil Tufnell, Michael Vaughan, Geoffrey Boycott, Mitchell Johnson, Andrew Samson

The day dawns brightly and conversations this morning centre around two things: what the prospects of forcing a result are and what a superstar little Issy Batey was yesterday. While her cake has (long) gone, she made quite an impression on everyone and, with the sun shining brightly over north London and conditions set for a long day of cricket, life is good on planet *Test Match Special*. Alec Stewart, still on 5 Live duty next door, is positive of a result, but, Michael Vaughan says, 'Realistically, to get a result in this match, one team needs to be bowled out in 50 overs.'

'The batting of both teams is so unreliable, really anything could happen,' adds Aggers, to general agreement. It may not be one for the connoisseurs, but it's likely to provide excitement and entertainment aplenty.

The ground is subsumed with nervous energy as Steve Smith flicks, jabs and jolts his way through the opening session. 'He should definitely go on *Strictly*,' says Tuffers, a man with experience of such things. 'He'd be brilliant.'

TV cameramen are monitoring the crowd for well-known faces and quickly pick up former England captain Mike Gatting watching from a hospitality box on high. 'He is turning into Henry VIII,' observes Tuffers straightforwardly. Aggers simply replies, with not a scintilla of doubt or surprise in his voice, 'Oh he is, yes.'

Then something amazing happens. At 11.14 a.m. on Saturday 17 August 2019, Smith plays and misses at a good delivery from Stuart Broad. 'It feels like something absolutely cataclysmic and remarkable and extraordinary has happened,' says Aggers, breathless. 'Like an eclipse of the moon or something!'

An eventful morning continues when Geoffrey Boycott nearly falls through the floor of the commentary box. Nobody is entirely sure how this happened, but it certainly caused a commotion on air that would have awakened any listeners having a Saturday morning snooze. Fortunately, a bag of builders' sand that has been posted outside the commentary box since during the World Cup (nobody knows for what purpose) comes in handy and Yorkshire's finest is once again safe to summarise.

Matthew Wade edges Broad to Rory Burns in the slips, who does well getting his fingers underneath the delivery, but Tim Paine and Smith start to take the game away from England. An on-air conversation rages about *Scooby Doo* – and whether Smith looks like blonde-haired American animated dreamboat 'Fred', but is interrupted by a visit from Peter and Alastair from the Lord's Taverners, who have decided that what *TMS* need are more cakes. They are, of course, right on the money.

Jim Maxwell is called onto air specifically to undertake one of his favourite jobs, introducing the *Shipping Forecast* for listeners on BBC Radio 4 Long Wave, and then Smith brings up his fifty – his seventh consecutive Ashes half-century, another record to delight Andrew Samson – and Australia go to lunch at 155 for five, with the game right in the balance.

Lunch sees *TMS* joined by the third *View from the Boundary* guest this summer: actor and comedian Miles Jupp. He is returning to Lord's for the first time since watching the World Cup final from the Compton Stand, where – with no *TMS* earpiece in place – he says he missed the surety, camaraderie and expertise provided by the commentary. Rather wonderfully, he describes Aggers (to his face) as 'a grown-up in someone's ear, telling them what's going on'.

An England fan going back some time, the feats of brilliance and athleticism demonstrated in the World Cup have shocked Miles to the core, making him feel like a time traveller as he watched the likes of Archer, Stokes, Plunkett and Buttler against New Zealand. 'Where's Ian Austin?' he asked. 'What's going on? Why isn't Tuffers smoking at fine leg? Why are there people leaping about doing athletic stuff?' He also posits that 'Neil Diamond must be amazed at the important role he plays in English cricket.'

Miles also tells a lovely story about the time he got to play at Lord's, where he represented the Actors' XI in a match against the Authors' XI on the Nursery Ground. He ended up concussed after lining up underneath a high ball and getting the catching process badly wrong. After coming to, he initially thought he was fine but quickly realised otherwise when it became clear he was surrounded by a concerned circle of onlookers, including both batsmen and all his fellow fielders.

It being quite a high-profile match, the captain of the Actors' XI was Hollywood star Damian Lewis, and it was he who was holding Miles's head. 'Hang on a minute, I've just been watching *Wolf Hall*!' was the first thought that popped into his brain, unsure whether this was reality or hallucination. When renowned author Sebastian Faulks was then dispatched to fetch him a chair, the concussion fever dream stepped up to the next level. Eventually, he was removed back into the Pavilion, where David Soul from *Starsky and Hutch* was sitting quietly in a corner for no apparent reason. 'I remember seeing him in the corner of the room and thinking, *Is he a symptom of my head injury?*' he concludes.

'He didn't sing, did he?' asks Aggers drily, before Jupp goes off to enjoy the rest of his day, which has come about despite him telling his wife 'cricket is done' after the World Cup.

The action returns to the middle, debutant Jofra Archer is returned to the attack and he immediately starts to bowl one of the most stunning spells of fast bowling seen in an England shirt for a great many years. It begins with the removal of Paine, caught smartly at short leg by Jos Buttler, but really starts to fire up when Smith gets to the other end. First Archer bowls him a mean short delivery that the Aussie ducks into, getting painfully caught on his elbow. Swelling is immediately visible, with the joint turning a shade of red that would not have looked out of place as a charity contribution on Day 2. The

Australian physio applies tape and a tardy arm guard, but Smith has clearly been hurt. Archer runs in remorselessly, emptying bars around the ground as word gets out that something special is happening here.

'This is a great spell of bowling,' says Mitchell Johnson, a man who has produced a few in his time. 'England have sensed something. Can they capitalise on it?' Every ball from Archer is flying through at over 90mph and Smith and Pat Cummins are utterly on the ropes. The ground then falls into stunned silence as Archer digs in another short ball, a rocket of a delivery, and Smith ducks into it. The ball cracks him, hard and noisily, on the side of the head and he is felled like a tree. After lying, poleaxed, for some time, Smith groggily climbs to his feet, once more in the company of the physio, and considers his options.

'Smith looks like he feels like he's okay, but he didn't look okay when he was flat on his back,' says a clearly concerned Johnson, as Smith is eventually led from the field, having had the decision taken out of his hands by the team doctor.

'There are not many players on debut who clear the bars like Jofra Archer has,' says Vaughan, who earlier in the day was comparing his confidence and impact with the emergence of a certain Kevin Pietersen during the Ashes in 2005.

Chris Woakes replaces Archer and removes Peter Siddle, whose 40-minute innings has given Smith time to retune, recover and convince the doctor he is all right to continue. He receives a hero's welcome as he comes back out to the crease and starts to play with significantly more aggression before being trapped LBW by Woakes for 92. He reviews the decision but, bizarrely, still walks off and is nearly at the boundary's edge by the time it is confirmed. 'The previous 21 times Steve Smith reached the 90s he went on to make a hundred,' points out Andrew Samson. An incredible stat like that would normally cause general astonishment, but such is the brilliance of Smith that almost nothing surprises anybody anymore where he is concerned.

'It has been compelling. There is nothing better than fast bowling to get you on the edge of your seat,' says Tuffers, before a change of pace sees left-arm spinner Jack Leach remove Nathan Lyon to claim his first Ashes wicket. Broad then ends the innings, giving England an eight-run lead and effectively turning the match into a one-innings game, played across four sessions.

Tea arrives and with it a visit from *Strictly Come Dancing* professional Anton du Beke, who is another celebrity very much enjoying the game today. Eliminated in the first round of the 2018 edition of the show alongside his partner Susannah Constantine, he says he is 'hoping to bat on a better wicket' in the new series this autumn.

'The game is at an interesting stage,' says Johnson. 'For the limited time we have had, it has been a great Test match. Will Jason Roy come out and play a one-day innings? I think that has to be on England's mind to get the runs up.'

Whether that was his intention or not becomes moot as Roy is squared up and pops a caught and bowled chance into the air that Cummins takes nicely. Joe Root comes in and is then caught behind first ball to go for a golden duck – the first time he has ever been dismissed this way in Tests, as Samson points out. Maxwell and Johnson are jubilant, but Joe Denly sees off the hat-trick ball and forms a solid understanding with Rory Burns as England set about building a target. As Geoffrey inevitably remarks, 'They can't win it, but they certainly can lose the match tonight.'

David Warner drops Denly, Lyon misses a review that would have seen the back of Burns, and Isa Guha notes that Australia coach Justin Langer is grimly clinging onto a stress ball on the balcony. 'I wouldn't fancy being JL's stress ball,' laughs Tuffers. 'What a life that would be.'

Conditions deteriorate, but Siddle continues to steam in cartoonishly and takes a brilliant caught and bowled to remove Denly before Warner drops another one, as Ben Stokes edges to the slip position where Smith – absent from the field as he is next door in hospital, getting his elbow checked out – would normally have been fielding. Siddle then gets Burns gloving to Paine and the game is right back on, with England 71 for four. 'We said last night all four results were still possible – and they still are,' says Simon Mann, desperately hoping the umpires keep the players on the field despite the poor light and slight mizzle.

Stokes and Buttler battle hard and, when the rain gets a little heavier shortly before 7 p.m., head off with England 96 for four, a lead of 104. 'If England get a lead of 200, they win the game,' thinks Isa, while Vaughan, less specifically, adds, 'Tomorrow is going to be a special day. We're in for a nipper. Something is going to happen.'

Sunday 18 August
England v Australia – The Ashes – Second Test
Match, Day 5
Lord's Cricket Ground, St John's Wood, London

Team *TMS*: Jonathan Agnew, Simon Mann, Jim Maxwell, Isa Guha, Phil Tufnell, Michael Vaughan, Geoffrey Boycott, Mitchell Johnson, Andrew Samson

Shortly after midday, with this game's final bout of bad weather seen off, *Test Match Special*'s own Isa Guha rings the bell to indicate play at Lord's Cricket Ground is just five minutes away. Her technique – she tells the team her pre-ring plans were centred on giving it 'a good tug' – is far superior to that of Shane Warne on Day 3 but still slightly lagging behind the undisputed kings of the art, Day 2's Luca and Sam Strauss.

Ben Stokes and Jos Buttler are reunited at the crease, just a month after they dragged England back into the World Cup final on this very ground. A similar partnership here could see them allowing their side to declare in the middle of the afternoon and have a decent try at bowling Australia out. However, the tourists will also be thinking that the clatter of a few England wickets early on could see them right back into the game. 'I don't think there is enough time for England to win,' declares Geoffrey Boycott, 'because they won't declare until the lead is 220 or so.'

'The best way for England to win this is to be bowled out,' reckons Tuffers. 'Goochy used to say it only takes nine balls to win ...'

'Er, I think Goochy used to say it actually took ten balls to win ...' says his former Middlesex and England team-mate Mark Ramprakash, who again joins the programme before play and demonstrates better cricketing maths than Tuffers.

As play gets under way, a major media advisory from Cricket Australia is issued. Steve Smith, struck on the neck yesterday by Jofra Archer, has been ruled out of the Test match with delayed concussion symptoms and, under the new ICC rules, has been replaced by Marnus Labuschagne, who becomes Test cricket's first ever concussion substitute. Not only that but, given that the Headingley Test starts in four days' time, there is a very high chance of Smith being ruled out of that one, too.

On the field, Stokes and Buttler get off to a good start, scoring slow but safe runs. Stokes survives an LBW review that sees him openly giggling at Tim Paine after it was referred, such was the size of the inside edge. 'Ben Stokes is playing with a mindset and an approach that suggests that England are looking at a number,' says an intrigued Michael Vaughan, who is desperate for England to show aggression and push for the victory.

After an hour, the lead is extended to 150. Shortly afterwards, Stokes brings up his half-century and England reach lunch without having lost a wicket, leading by 165. 'No risks taken,' says Mitchell Johnson, sounding concerningly like Geoffrey. 'They've just played a very solid session. It's really going to set them up for after lunch.'

After a traditional lunchtime journalist panel is hugely enlivened by Aussie Geoff Lemon's Potteresque description of Broad as 'Malfoy on stilts', play restarts and Johnson is close to spot on. England come out with a decidedly more aggressive approach. Buttler pays the price, caught on the leg-side boundary, but Jonny Bairstow immediately looks purposeful and starts scoring quickly with Stokes.

Sixes are struck, with Stokes boffing Nathan Lyon into the Mound Stand off consecutive deliveries, which gives Andrew Samson the chance to roll out another truly wonderful stat, noting that 'Nathan Lyon has been hit for more sixes than anyone else in Test history, up to 213 now.'

Simon Mann wants a lead of 270 before declaration, but Vaughan is satisfied with 250, and when England batting coach Graham Thorpe is spotted gesturing with three fingers on the balcony, it becomes clear that a declaration is imminent. Fortunately for Stokes, he is able to reach three figures beforehand, earning one of the highest compliments in cricket, as Boycott mutters 'played, lad' before commencing an odd form of applause he has mastered over the years, banging his wrists together to give the physical look of clapping, but without making the loud noise that would be easily and irritatingly picked up over his microphone.

'It's a special hundred on this special ground,' says Jim Maxwell beautifully. 'The second time in a couple of weeks that he's been the star on Sunday at the Home of Cricket.'

Mann is the commentator who gets his way as, with England 258 for five, Joe Root rises to his feet on the Pavilion balcony and beckons Stokes and Bairstow back in. Australia will require 267 to win, in a minimum of 48 overs – without Steve Smith. It delights Samson, who immediately reports that it's the first time England have ever scored the same total in both their first and second innings.

The experienced heads of Maxwell and Boycott are both concerned for them. 'You wouldn't think Australia would collapse in 48 overs,' says Geoffrey. 'But having said that, sport throws up unusual events. If you look at the Australian batting on paper, without Steve Smith, it looks very rocky.'

'If you've got one bloke scoring 40 per cent of the runs who's not batting, all of a sudden there's a massive hole in it,' agrees Maxwell. 'I don't know what effect that will have on the rest of the team.'

Jofra Archer is again thrown the new ball and claims David Warner early, taken by Rory Burns at third slip. Any nerves felt among *TMS*'s Australian contingent are then multiplied when Usman Khawaja is caught behind to leave the tourists 19 for two. Labuschagne comes in at No 4 in place of Smith and is hit hard on the grille by Archer's second ball. The helmet has to go off and be replaced, but Labuschagne is allowed to stay after a long examination from Australia's physio, who could be forgiven for casting a rueful glance at Archer on the way off, such is the extra workload the England speedster is creating for him.

Just like yesterday afternoon, Archer is generating a superstar feeling every time he bowls, with the crowd responding to his every move. The speeds are both box office and incredibly hard for batsmen to deal with and, even if England remain unlikely to force the win, it is abundantly clear that they have unearthed a truly special cricketer. 'Jofra has grabbed these Ashes by the scruff of the neck,' says Tuffers. 'I was driving home from Edgbaston and I couldn't see how, without Jimmy, they'd take 20 wickets. Jofra has turned it on its head. I haven't seen that for a long, long time.'

Cameron Bancroft and Labuschagne make it to tea battered and bruised but unbeaten. Tufnell is preaching a very likely draw, but Maxwell is less sure. 'Don't go too far – the game is not over, folks,' warns the old pro. 'Australia are a bit wobbly.'

The tea interval brings *TMS* a man who is potentially the programme's first ever Transylvanian guest, Pavel Florin. Pavel, a full-time bodyguard, is better known as a thoroughly charming recent online sensation who plays for Romania's Cluj CC in the European Cricket League, a competition recently held in La Manga, Spain. His unique bowling action caused something of a stir on social media, with initial mockery of his floaty deliveries turning into huge respect for his love of the game.

Loving the sport the way he does in a country that is largely unaware of its charms has its difficulties, Pavel admits. 'People are not used to cricket in Romania,' he says. 'When I go on the street with my cricket bat, they think I'm going to use it in a fight!' Pavel has only just left the microphone when the game moves on again, Bancroft giving an easy LBW decision to Jack Leach. 'If England can get a couple more – look out Australia,' warns Johnson.

Travis Head starts nervously, battling some determined England efforts before nicking a straightforward catch to Jason Roy at slip, which goes straight in and out and offers him another life. It is gratefully accepted as Head remains unbeaten and, although England controversially dismiss Labuschagne – the Australian having a few words with Joe Root as he leaves the field after a low catch is claimed and verified by the TV cameras – Australia hold out for the draw.

The dying minutes will be remembered for an incredible catch by Joe Denly, bringing back memories of Stokes at The Oval in the first game of the World Cup, with a one-handed effort in the deep that a startled Aggers describes as 'absolutely magnificent'. By the very end, England are crowding the bat with close catchers, Leach and Denly bowling in the growing Lord's gloaming and, when the bails are finally removed by the umpires, it is certainly a 'winning draw' for England.

The second match in the series has delivered more classic Test cricket and introduced another star player to the stage of the Ashes. 'As big an impact as Shane Warne?' Tuffers wonders as an appropriate amount of rain falls on Lord's after play. Whichever way, Archer has made an immediate impact and, with the series still poised at 1-0 to Australia, he will be hoping to continue his headline-grabbing ways when the Ashes resume in Leeds at the end of the week.

England 258 (77.1 overs; Burns 53, Bairstow 52) and 258-5d (71 overs; Stokes 115*) drew with Australia 250 (94.3 overs; Smith 92, Broad 4-65) and 154-6 (47.3 overs; Labuschagne 59).

CHAPTER 18

Stokes Keeps the Ashes Alive

Thursday 22 August
England v Australia – The Ashes – Third Test
Match, Day 1
Headingley Cricket Ground, Leeds

Team *TMS*: Jonathan Agnew, Simon Mann, Jim Maxwell, Isa Guha,
Michael Vaughan, Geoffrey Boycott, Glenn McGrath, Sir Alastair Cook,
Andrew Samson

Michael Vaughan is wearing a baby-blue blazer, sitting atop a large green heavy roller and trying to work out if it's going to rain or not. The Headingley groundsman is looking on, ready to take evasive action should the former Yorkshire skipper's foot go anywhere near the accelerator pedal, and Jonathan Agnew, Sir Alastair Cook and Glenn McGrath are watching, terrifically amused. There is an unusual whiff coming from the back of the groundsman's shed, which turns out to be Shane Warne having a cheeky fag.

And with that, *Test Match Special* is on air for the third Ashes

Test, one England really need to win to retain any hope of a Test victory. A win for Australia would deliver the urn Down Under. The good news in this regard is that the concussion Steve Smith sustained at the hands of Jofra Archer at Lord's has ruled him out of this Test. 'I've no doubt that if things had been left to Steve Smith he would have said he was fine to bat on the final day,' reckons Glenn McGrath, 'but head injuries are taken a lot more seriously now and rightly so.'

Back on the roller, conditions are grim. Aggers thinks that Archer looks like he's heading off to the Antarctic, with his hoodie pulled up over his head, and both Vaughan and Cook are reporting that it could be a good toss to lose, such is the difference between conditions on the pitch and overhead. A social visit to the roller from Peter Siddle indicates that he has missed out on selection for this one.

The toss comes, England win and choose to bowl, but before the action gets under way the dreary mizzle of the morning gives way to full-on rain and the start is delayed for just over an hour. When play does get going, Archer receives a hero's welcome and quickly justifies his ovation, producing a succession of beauties before one of them clips the edge of Marcus Harris and gets England off the mark, just before the rain returns and the rest of the players follow Harris back into the pavilion, albeit more temporarily than the Australian opener.

Geoffrey Boycott, delighted to be commentating on home turf, is unimpressed by the new delay. 'It's a good day in Yorkshire, this,' he declares, to a general lack of surprise from those around him. 'We'd have played in some of this rain. If you didn't play in that, you'd never play in Yorkshire!'

While Headingley provides a lovely spread, members of the team bring back smaller than usual portion sizes at lunchtime because sustenance has largely been provided in the form of some well-received Fat Rascals. There is much conjecture as

TEST MATCH SPECIAL DIARY

to their identities, with more lovingly unkind comments about Mike Gatting passed around, but these particular Fat Rascals are delicious 'Yorkshire scones' that have been provided by Betty's Tea Room in Harrogate and go down wonderfully.

Vaughan is tucking into one on air while quizzing Isa Guha, who has yet to dig in, as to her favourite kind of baked goods. His eyes are agog when she replies that, actually, she prefers savoury cheese scones. Were his mouth not completely full, the response could have been even stronger.

With the remaining Rascals safely stowed away at the back of the box, the lunchtime discussion is about the iconic Headingley Test of 1981. Once everyone has got over the fact that Henry Moeran was not born at the time of Botham's heroics, memories are shared and commentary replayed before the question is asked, 'Will we ever get a Test as good as that again?' The consensus is that the greatness of Test cricket should be never underestimated and anything is possible, albeit guarded by the knowledge that the statistical improbability of a turnaround like that happening again is pretty small.

At 2 p.m., Boycott finally gets his way and play resumes like it never went away, Stuart Broad immediately bending one around David Warner's outside edge that Isa neatly calls 'unplayable'. The bowling continues to be of the highest quality, which means that Broad's dismissal of Khawaja, strangled down the leg side and caught by Jonny Bairstow, is officially 'earned' rather than 'unfortunate for the batsman'. Marnus Labuschagne joins Warner and, with England fielding five slips behind the batsmen, Vaughan is convinced that 'it's just a matter of time' before the out-of-form opener goes cheaply yet again, but the rain returns and everyone troops off once more, downcast.

As spontaneous games of cricket break out in the crowd – including one where a man in Richie Benaud fancy dress is bowling to a regularly attired small boy with a man dressed as Hulk Hogan at silly point – the players attempt to return, and after a bit more toing and froing the game restarts for a few minutes before bad light causes the next stoppage, at least out in the middle.

There is yet another resumption, and Warner and Labuschagne start to make hay, upping the scoring rate and causing Vaughan to be 'officially concerned' and Simon Mann to describe England as 'ragged' since the break, adding that 'This is not the day England had in mind when they put Australia in.'

A drinks break is taken and Archer benefits from the interruption, finally catching Warner's outside edge and breaking the partnership. Warner receives his traditional boo-filled send-off, much to Boycott's chagrin, who takes aim at his fellow countrymen, gesturing around angrily as he says, 'Stop booing, it's ridiculous! Come on, Yorkshire, you're better than that . . .' Jim Maxwell agrees, adding, 'This is very poor from the crowd to be booing a man who has just made 61.'

Business then picks up for England, with Broad castling Travis Head ('No feet,' says Boycott, likening Head's crease to quick-drying cement) and then bowling Matthew Wade when the ball deflects onto the stumps off his body, to unexpected sympathy from the Yorkshireman, who still has nightmares about potentially losing his wicket like that, despite being 78 years of age. England are then properly on top when Broad whacks Labuschagne in the most sensitive area there can be.

While Farmer Cook says there is rain on the way, Chris Woakes opens his account by getting Paine LBW on review, Archer finds James Pattinson's outside edge and then completes his five-wicket haul by nicking off Pat Cummins, who clearly doesn't think he's hit it, despite UltraEdge telling a very different story.

Labuschagne is LBW to Ben Stokes, somehow missing an 82mph full toss before, at 7.29 p.m., Nathan Lyon is LBW to Archer, who ends with six for 45. 'A stunning performance,' says Isa, while Vaughan has already taken to social media to declare that Archer will take 400 Test wickets during his career, adding on air that, 'If England get 300, they should win the game, [but] if England are bowling again tomorrow, game on.'

The evening ends with *TMS* kindly being asked to enter a team in a quiz run by Test match sponsors Specsavers for the assembled written and broadcast media at Headingley. Normally such a run-of-the-mill event would not require further description, but tonight, disaster strikes. Firstly, there is an outrageous piece of disloyalty from one of the most trusted members of the team, Simon Mann, who deserts the official *TMS* side to line up with a rival. Offence is quickly and liberally taken and Team *TMS* is named 'Mann Overboard' in his honour for the evening.

The quiz is progressing nicely until a thorny question is raised. 'Which of the 20 wickets at Old Trafford 1956 did Jim Laker not take?' asks the quizmaster. 'I know it, I know it, I know! Leave it to me!' comes the cry from statistician and international guru of cricket knowledge Andrew Samson, who then quickly writes down 'Colin McDonald' on the sheet. Sadly, the answer – as correctly identified by a number of other teams – is 'Jim Burke'. The humiliation of Samson is swift and unremitting, and even though he helps the side to a creditable finish that is rewarded with some delicious bottles of champagne, he goes into Day 2 only partially forgiven.

Friday 23 August
England v Australia – The Ashes – Third Test
Match, Day 2
Headingley Cricket Ground, Leeds

Team *TMS*: Jonathan Agnew, Simon Mann, Jim Maxwell, Isa Guha,
Michael Vaughan, Geoffrey Boycott, Glenn McGrath, Mark Wood,
Andrew Samson

Leeds on the morning of Day 2 is like an entirely different city. Gone are the mizzle, the wind, the bad light, the low cloud and the shivering crowd of Thursday and in their place are blue skies, settled forecasts, shorts, newspapers and picnics. The *TMS* pundits are buoyed by conditions too. 'England couldn't have scripted this any better with the weather,' admits Sir Alastair Cook, who has already had to bust out his knighthood to gain former team-mate Mark Wood access to the pitch before play. 'The sun is out and it's going to be a good day for batting. They've got an opportunity with the bat now to get a long way ahead in this game.'

Michael Vaughan, a veteran of Headingley for at least two decades, is also positive but slightly more guarded, preaching early hard work and caution to allow a cash-in at the end of the day. However, Glenn McGrath is also guardedly positive that while luck has not been on the side of his Australians, they can still have a good day. 'Yesterday it almost did too much; today it will just do enough,' he reckons. 'If they get enough in the right area today, they will create ten chances.'

It's Sir Alastair who sums it up as Rory Burns and Jason Roy walk to the crease, concluding the preview by simply saying, 'It's going to be a brilliant day of Test cricket because the series is on the edge.'

Aggers is convinced that today is going to be 'a Jason Roy day', but that is quickly undone when, after unfurling a lovely punch for four, he drives a ball from Josh Hazlewood that he could easily have left and is caught at slip. The dismissal comes just two balls after Cook had praised him for looking very comfortable at the crease and the former England captain is utterly mortified at collecting his first commentator's curse.

Joe Root then goes, nicking off Hazlewood in his next over, and England are 10 for two, with Warner again taking the catch. In the back of the box, the old sage Jim Maxwell laughs uproariously at the mortified Cook, who is turning a whiter shade of pale as all thoughts of England making hay while the sun shines have disappeared within half an hour. Despite this, Cook backs the decision for Root to move up the order, adding, 'He's England's best batter, and I think it's the right move for the captain to bat at three.'

When Vaughan replaces Cook in the chair, he couldn't disagree more. 'Joe Root is England's best player,' he states. 'Put him at four. Virat Kohli – where does he bat? Steve Smith – where does he bat? It's only one position but it is a huge difference.' The debate continues as the ball keeps zipping around, Burns and Denly struggling mightily and Vaughan unmoved.

Pat Cummins bowls an over that Jim Maxwell wonderfully describes as containing 'six moral victories' before Burns goes to hook him in his next set of six and is caught behind. 'That's two out of three wickets which have been a real batting error,' bemoans an increasingly irate Vaughan in the summariser's chair, before, to great trepidation, he finishes his stint and hands over to Geoffrey Boycott, who immediately backs his fellow Yorkshireman on the 'Root at four' argument.

Ben Stokes is the next to go, chasing a wide one and, as ever, Simon Mann needs minimal words to describe the situation. 'England are in tatters,' he says simply, and no one can disagree.

Boycott goes longer and harder, accusing Stokes of both poor thinking and poor batting during a general torrent of disappointed rage. 'If England lose any more wickets between now and lunch, it's dire straits,' warns McGrath, who then beams from ear to ear as Denly plays a loose drive and is snaffled by Paine. 'A hard-fought 12' is McGrath's verdict, but then again you might well expect kindness from a man in as good a mood as he is.

Disaster then becomes catastrophe as Jonny Bairstow offers Warner his fourth catch of the innings and Isa Guha is absolutely correct when, with a flabbergasted, slightly morbid tone, she describes it as 'extraordinary stuff'. England reach lunch at 54 for six. It is just two hours after the pre-play positivity of Cook, Vaughan and Agnew, and as Buttler and Woakes troop off, all Isa can say is that 'England have managed to get to lunch without being bowled out.'

Lunchtime is an attempt to reach back to happier times, as World Cup-winning fast bowler Mark Wood is the special guest. He succeeds in raising spirits by talking listeners through the extraordinary World Cup final from within the England dressing room. Myths are busted, including the implacability of Buttler, who was apparently punching the physio's bench and jumping around after the amazing 'six' caused by the ball striking the bat of a diving Stokes. He also reveals how the umpires came into both dressing rooms prior to the super over, explaining the new rules of engagement to both sides.

Finally, he talks about the morning after the night before. As a teetotaller, he woke up without a hangover and spent hours lying in his hotel bed, watching videos of people celebrating in front rooms, cricket clubs, pubs and streets across the country. 'That's when it hits you . . .' he ends wistfully. Wood's time on air was due to end as the interval finished, but after some gentle persuasion from Vaughan, he is persuaded to stick around and try his hand at some summarising. If he thinks his presence will have any positive impact, though, he is quickly set to rights as Woakes goes first ball after lunch before Buttler whacks a half-volley to cover off the first ball of the second over.

Jofra Archer smacks a baseball-style four that Wood brilliantly says was 'just missing the Batman *"Kapow!"* when he hit it', but then gets a bizarre nick as he tries to leave a short one from Cummins but leaves his bat above his head a bit like a periscope and edges it through to Tim Paine. 'It's your opening spell on *Test Match Special* and you're three for 13 from 3.1 overs. You'd take that, wouldn't you?' Vaughan asks Wood as Jack Leach walks out. 'I wish I was bowling!' replies Wood like a shot.

In double-quick time, Leach is comprehensively bowled and England are all out for 67, losing their last four wickets in less than the time it has taken for Henry Moeran to eat his lunch. Wood and Vaughan specialise in words beginning with 'R' when discussing Australians, Wood choosing 'ruthless', which he repeats for extra emphasis, and Vaughan choosing 'relentless'. Another one knocking around the box is 'remarkable'. On what seemed like the best possible morning for batting, England have been bowled out for 67 and, despite bowling Australia out for 179 on Day 1, are staring at a deficit of 112.

The doom and gloom is almost total. 'It has been a devastating morning,' says Mann, summing up the mood in camp. 'England's bowlers have got to get them back in the Test match – but it's near on impossible,' admits Vaughan. 'I fear for this. This could get ugly for England this afternoon.'

However, Sir Alastair feels like he can play a useful role in the nation's mood. 'England will believe they can get back in the match,' he says. 'If those 11 players don't believe it, there's no chance of it happening. You can still win after being 100 behind in a low-scoring game. Everyone is doom and gloom, so I have to be positive.'

He reminds Simon Mann about a game he played for Essex in the County Championship just last week. Kent got 226 before his Essex side struggled and only posted 114 in their first innings. However, they then somehow managed to bowl Kent out for 40 before knocking off the 153 runs required with seven wickets down to win by three wickets. Amazingly, the first-innings deficit is identical in both games. 'Apparently lightning doesn't strike twice, although they say that's in the same place,' replies Simon. 'Where were you?' 'Canterbury,' replies Cook as Simon nods sagely and returns to the game in hand.

Not currently on air, Aggers has taken to social media to express his thoughts on the disastrous batting performance of the morning. 'That's one batting collapse too many,' he tweets. 'Crucial day thrown away. Bowled out in 27 overs simply isn't good enough. Will take a miracle for Australia not to retain the Ashes this weekend.'

David Warner comes and goes quickly, LBW to Broad – making the Englishman the all-time leading Test match wicket-taker at Headingley, overtaking *TMS*'s own Freddie Trueman – but Australia show sticking power that was not evident with England this morning and gradually build an utterly dominant position. Aggers decides to take matters into his own hands, appointing Sir Alastair as a concussion sub. The problem he has is that, while England have not batted well this morning, none of the players is actually concussed. He has a plan to get around this though and is going to get his long handle out and hit Jason Roy around the head, enabling him to be replaced. 'We need you out there, Alastair,' he concludes. 'It's no good having you up here!'

Conversations on air flit from one desperate subject to another. Would England have preferred to win the World Cup or the Ashes? Will Joe Root still be captain once this series is over? Who else could be picked in this team? Listeners are contacting the programme in their droves, trying to sell tickets for Sunday's play – some even trying to give them away.

Spirits are lifted by a hamper of Wensleydale cheese arriving in the box, but even the hero of Lord's, Jack Leach, removing Marcus Harris with his first ball only lifts morale temporarily as the suspicion is that it turned so much that Nathan Lyon will be the happiest person in the ground to see it, knowing he gets to bowl on this pitch last. Khawaja is caught by Roy off Woakes – another poor shot on a day full of them – and when, after a period of calculation, Andrew Samson reveals that 'Joe Denly's 12 in the first innings is the lowest highest score in a Test innings for England', the Great British sense of humour starts to kick in and a few grim smiles are raised in the back of the box.

Given what's occurred today, it seems appropriate for the *TMS* batting gurus Cook, Vaughan and Boycott to gather together during the tea break and try to get to the bottom of matters. To the sound of backs stiffening and children being hushed out of range of the radio across the nation, Geoffrey Boycott goes first, and nobody is safe. 'When I was growing up as a kid, my Uncle Algie used to say to me, "Listen, youngster, you can't make runs in the pavilion, you need to stay in. And to stay in, you need to have a good defence. Then from defending, and staying in, you can move forward to playing shots and scoring,"' he begins.

'I think it's as simple as that. They don't stay in; their defence is poor. By that, it's not just the technical sense of playing defence, it's the mindset of playing defence and getting in. I had all of the shots if I needed them,' he continues. 'But I didn't use them because I knew that playing upfront against wonderful bowlers like Cummins and Hazlewood, I would've said to myself that I wasn't going to drive through the off side or punch off the back foot, because if it moved a bit, I would be gone. I'm looking to leave and play so well in the corridor that they bowl straighter and I clip it off my hip. These England batsmen are hitting it on the up like it's one-day cricket.'

'Does Jason Roy have too many shots in his head?' asks Aggers.

'Does Jason Roy have *anything* in his head?' replies Boycott harshly, having really built himself up to full speed quite quickly.

Alastair Cook admits that, when playing, he only mastered one and a half formats and had only three shots going into age-group cricket. 'Take someone around my age like Ravi Bopara,' he adds. 'He had a lot more shots but then had to make more decisions, so it was harder for him to master four-day cricket.'

'I've seen a lot of junior cricket,' continues Vaughan. 'All I hear is dot-ball percentage – you've got to score off every ball. Jason Roy has got too many clubs in the bag. He needs to play pitch and putt. Too many batsmen don't trust themselves.'

With the final session approaching, Boycott returns for a final salvo, calling on junior cricket coaches to solve the issue in the long term. 'I understand the kids have three formats to play and I know it is difficult to change between them, I accept it. But they have coaches teaching them T20 but not Test cricket,' he says. 'All the kids at Yorkshire are being taught in the nets is T20. All the administrators promote is T20 and we're getting this hundred-ball competition next year! All they want is money, they don't care. Some kids don't want to slog it, but that's all they are taught.'

Mark Wood returns after tea, having spent the break in the England dressing room. 'Batting coach Graham Thorpe was there telling the players, "Come on, lads. If it's 270 or under we can chase this",' he reveals, underscoring Cook's earlier points about positivity in the camp.

Root drops Labuschagne early in the session, but Stokes removes Travis Head with a lovely yorker, causing Wood to punch the air. 'I said Stokesy was the man to do it! England's go-to man, he never stops fighting,' he says with delight. Stokes continues charging in, dragging a well-oiled Headingley crowd with him as his 'never say die' attitude rubs off in the stands.

The atmosphere is then lifted another few notches when a beach ball that is being batted around the stands, in contravention of regulations, accidentally lands on the outfield and falls into the possession of one of the Yorkshire stewards, generating the standard chorus of loud boos. However, Archer decides to run 70 yards across the field, takes the beach ball off the steward and bats it back into the crowd. 'You know, that's the biggest cheer for an England player I've heard today,' observes Mann sardonically. 'Brilliant!' says Sir Alistair admiringly, as the Western Terrace launches into a chorus of 'Super, Super Jof – Super Jofra Archer!' that continues for some considerable time.

'We are seeing a Ben Stokes special this evening,' says Cook. 'He's not dragging England back into the game, but he's making Australia work for every run.' The Durham all-rounder continues bowling all the way up until the drinks break, when he is removed in favour of Archer. Archer gets through four balls of his spell before breaking down with debilitating cramp and Stokes immediately returns, completing the over and resuming his spell from that end.

As the day wears on and Labuschagne is caught behind off a no-ball, it becomes apparent that the fire in Boycott's belly at tea might have caused a secondary issue, because when Vaughan comes on air to replace him, the fire alarm immediately goes off in the *TMS* commentary box. 'That's it, fire alarm. Call the game off!' pleads the ever-alert Vaughan. '1-0, two to play, off we go!'

An increasingly knackered Stokes induces an edge from Labuschagne that is dropped by Bairstow, causing Wood to abandon his nascent commentary career. 'I'm going to stop coming on,' he decides. 'Every time I do, something bad happens to England.' However, he decides to stay in position for just long enough to witness Stokes bowl a fine short ball to Matthew Wade, getting his man via a glove to the keeper. Stokes sinks to his knees, roaring and exhausted as he is mobbed by admiring team-mates. 'He deserves that!' shouts Wood, torn between delight for his mate and disappointment that he is not on the field helping with the mobbing.

Tim Paine is next to go in a moment that, somehow, manages to raise smiles on England fans' faces across the ground. The Australia captain is given out LBW off Stuart Broad and immediately reviews the decision, pointing out to Root that he got an inside edge. Root then calmly replies that that doesn't matter because the ball was also caught. The replays are rolled, the nick is confirmed, the LBW decision is overruled and one of caught is given. Headingley explodes as Paine ruefully shakes his head and turns tail.

Australia close on 171 for six. The lead is already 283, higher than what Graham Thorpe was hoping for, and before the day is done there is time for one more pundit to come off their long run, this time Michael Vaughan. 'It's just not good enough,' he says. 'You have to play with discipline. You have to earn the right to score. Look at what Labuschagne has done; he's worn the opposition down. I don't see that from the England team and I haven't seen that for four years.

'They aren't willing to put the hard work in in the middle. It's a real concern that every time the batting line-up has been put under pressure, they get blown away. Were there any unplayable balls this morning? It's so predictable from England. This batting line-up, at 10 for two you know what's going to happen.

'I could see two years ago that the Aussies were working as a group, they have come here with a plan. They are better prepared for an Ashes tour of England than they have been for many years. England are not prepared for this. Last year they had two spinners, neither of whom are playing now. The opening partnership is new, Root has moved around, it's haphazard.

'Let's be honest, the Ashes have been retained. England have taken their eye off Test cricket, Joe Root is under pressure but it has all been about winning the World Cup. Winning the World Cup was great, but this is our bread and butter. How do we get the Test match team to play the Test match way on a consistent basis? England were chasing the ball. Did you see Ben Stokes chase the ball like that when he scored a hundred at Lord's? No! There's no way the planning went into this series that went into the World Cup.'

Vaughan heads home before his temperature sets the fire alarm off again, and the rest of the team shuffle away to reflect on an extraordinary day of cricket that seems like it may well have decided the destination of the Ashes.

Saturday 24 August
England v Australia – The Ashes – Third Test
Match, Day 3
Headingley Cricket Ground, Leeds

Team *TMS*: Jonathan Agnew, Simon Mann, Jim Maxwell, Isa Guha, Michael Vaughan, Geoffrey Boycott, Glenn McGrath, Andrew Samson

'It feels like the Ashes are gone for England and that is a crushing disappointment. It could have been so different. It should have been so different.' It's a sobering Aggers who greets listeners on the morning of Day 3. To be fair, Australia are a long way ahead, have every chance to stretch that lead even further this morning, and there is a fair to middling chance that, by the end of the day, they will have secured a critical 2-0 lead in the series.

However, Michael Vaughan has woken up in a better mood than he left the ground in last night and is preaching. 'West Indies chased down 330-odd here a few years ago,' he points out. 'England need to improve by 90 per cent, but it's not impossible.'

Isa Guha and Sir Alastair Cook are stood in the middle, with Isa busily brushing a stray insect off Sir Alastair's collar as he delivers his verdict: 'They have to deliver today, because if they don't there will be some changes. Turnarounds can happen. England can turn this around. It's a 100-1 chance, but they can.'

There is no early breakthrough as England start their quest to take the final four wickets, but it's a lovely day in Leeds and with observations like Vaughan's 'Marnus Labuschagne is an expansive chewer', it somehow feels a little less tragic than it did yesterday. Simon Mann adds, 'Australia still need ten wickets to win. So there's that.'

The expansive chewer is then dropped by Bairstow – and, as Mann points out, with three drops and a nick behind off a no-ball, he is now into his fifth life of the innings. The bowler, Stuart Broad, is once more doing plenty of rueful head-shaking and furious 'double teapotting'. Jofra Archer, fully recovered from yesterday's cramp, makes the key breakthrough when James Pattinson is held at slip, giving Andrew Samson the chance to make a point he's been brewing for a while. 'That is 100 Test catches for Joe Root. He's the ninth England player to that mark – Alastair Cook is number one on 175.'

'This is a sad day,' comments Geoffrey Boycott as Australia continue to take the game away.

'Cheer up, Geoffrey,' replies Aggers.

'No,' comes back the immediate reply from the stubborn Yorkshireman, just before Pat Cummins offers Rory Burns a chance at gully, the opener taking a good diving catch.

Labuschagne, finally, is next to go. Ironically, after the number of chances he received during his knock, he is relatively unlucky in the end, as Joe Denly misfields at deep point before making amends with a thunderous throw as the Australians break the cardinal rule and run on a misfield. As he walks off, to generous applause, Aggers reckons, 'He's put his side into an Ashes-retaining position.'

The innings ends ten minutes later when Archer, doing what many observers thought he'd do to tailenders the world over, fires in a fast, straight delivery that is too much for Nathan Lyon, whose castle comes crashing down around him. England need 359 to win and keep the Ashes alive. If they do so, it would be the highest successful chase in England's 141-year Test match history.

'It's the hope that kills you,' says *Tailenders* host Greg James on social media. 'No matter how pessimistic you are, there is still a very small part of you that thinks this chase could happen ... even though it absolutely won't. Still the best game in the world, though. Even when it makes us feel completely miserable.'

Rory Burns and Jason Roy survive a tricky 20-minute session and are roared from the field like heroes. 'The crowd are imploring England to go on and do something special,' says Simon Mann as he makes way for the latest *View from the Boundary* guest: the mountaineer, author and motivational speaker Joe Simpson, who was the subject of the immensely popular film *Touching the Void*, which chronicles an incredible mountaineering accident he suffered in Peru in 1985.

Now one of the most sought-after motivational speakers in the world, Simpson's first question from Jonathan Agnew is what words of motivation he would offer England were he to be in the dressing room at that exact moment. 'I'd just say give up now, you're stumped!' he replies.

'Would you?' asks a shocked Aggers. 'I don't think you would say that. You couldn't say that!'

'No,' he replies, 'but there are certain realities you have look at and, I'm sorry, but after yesterday I was so depressed by the whole thing, I thought it was going to be over before I got here today!'

Simpson continues to recount his extraordinary story before becoming the first person in the history of *Test Match Special* to use the almost unprecedented phrase 'crevasse wanker', as he tells a story of a teenage pupil who contacted him on social media after failing a GCSE exam question set about his book. Aggers' eyebrows go through the roof and an apology is quickly issued!

The afternoon gets under way with the wickets of first Burns (Warner's fifth catch of the match) and, three balls later, Roy, who is bowled by a delivery that underlines exactly why Pat Cummins is considered the best Test bowler in the world. Roy, frequently described as a genius earlier in the summer, has copped a lot of criticism since the World Cup, but on this occasion has clearly been dismissed by a moment of genius from the bowler. 'That is a jaffa!' glories Jim Maxwell. 'You couldn't blame a batsman for getting out to that. A sizzler!'

'I don't think many are hitting that. That is a serious ball,' agrees Cook, as Joe Denly joins Joe Root, with the two quickly forming a productive partnership. Such is the certainty the two are batting with, Isa decides to throw Shane Warne under the bus and reveal, similarly to Tuffers at Edgbaston, that she saw him check out of his hotel this morning, full of confidence that Australia would secure the win today.

Root and Denly continue, largely untroubled, as a grand cake is delivered to the back of the commentary box, specifically for the attention of Aggers. The baker has decided that it is poor form that Agnew was unable to make good on his World Cup final bet of eating Geoffrey Boycott's hat and decided to help out by recreating the iconic piece of millenery in cake format, adding a lovely little touch of detail by making the cake into a rhubarb sponge. It is a glorious creation and demonstrates the wonderful humour, creativity and generosity of *TMS* listeners perfectly.

England make the drinks break with no further loss and Aggers is now confident that the game will still be going tomorrow. The next landmark is passing the 67 runs the side totalled in the first innings and then, with 30 overs in the tank, Cook reveals an interesting conversation he had with Root. 'Joe Root asked me this morning, "Can we get to 30 overs without too much damage?"' he discloses. 'And you can see that the ball isn't doing quite as much now.' Tea is then taken with Root and Denly still together and England 90 for two. Once again, the players head back for a break to a rousing ovation.

The tea break sees Aggers head over to the lovely new Headingley stand to interview former Yorkshire and Australia coach Darren Lehmann, who will return to the ground next year to coach the northern team in The Hundred. The most remarkable thing about the interview is its surroundings. Not only does the new stand transform Headingley; it also oversees the Western Terrace. Beneath Aggers and Lehmann, a man dressed as a French chef can clearly be seen bowling to another man wearing a full Australia kit from the 1992 Cricket World Cup – and having him well caught by another man dressed as a can of spam at short leg.

The final session of the day is characterised by yet more careful accumulation. Root and Denly continue as if they'd never left and continue to tick off key moments. A standing ovation is received when England reach 100 and again when Root gets his fifty. 'This partnership has got to fight and fight,' says Vaughan, and that's exactly what they do.

'England are battling really well,' says Mann, adding that 'A few people in this crowd believe.' Vaughan hands over the summariser's mic to Alastair Cook, beseeching him 'not to get any wickets' and, in one of the glorious contradictions of Test match cricket, as the partnership grows, so does the tension. Root is given out but immediately reviews it and forces the decision to be overturned when it becomes clear he has practically middled the delivery, before the tension is alleviated slightly by another fascinating visitor to the box, a young man by the name of Alfie Juckes.

Alfie made a bet with his brother that if Sir Alastair Cook made a century in his final Test match, he'd have Cook's Test batting average tattooed on his ankle – and has come into the commentary box to show the man himself the evidence. After a quick moment of dreadful confusion when Cook misremembers his own average and Alfie briefly thinks he has got the tattoo wrong, the two have a lovely moment before everyone goes back to nervously rooting for Root (and Denly).

Australia burn a review, causing Boycott to amusingly cry, 'Desperation!' in a such a gleeful manner it wouldn't have been out of place on the Western Terrace, but finally, just after reaching his fifty, Denly perishes, caught behind off a very good bouncer from Josh Hazlewood, who has kept coming hard all day. 'Well played, Denly,' says Geoffrey respectfully. 'He's given England a sniff.'

The final 40 minutes of play are a remarkable exercise in patience for Ben Stokes, who bats through to the end of the day, scoring just two runs from the 50 balls he faces. Given his natural proclivity towards aggressive hitting – and the amazing stint he put in with the ball yesterday – it's a superhuman effort and is justly rewarded by a knowledgeable and appreciative crowd as he leaves the field alongside Root, who has slowly progressed to 75 not out at the end of the day.

England still need another 203 runs and are clearly huge underdogs, but they've had as good a day as could possibly be hoped for – and responded in style to the strong criticism they received yesterday for being unable to bat time and accumulate runs. 'Game on. That partnership has given England a sniff. We're in for a hell of a day tomorrow,' says Cook in the reckoning, while Vaughan – similarly to the Jonny Bairstow incident that marked a turnaround in England's World Cup form – is claiming part of the credit.

'If it needs criticism to fire them up to play the right way, I'll criticise them all the time. You've got to put the hard yards in, and England did that today. But I feel yesterday's batting will still cost them this Test,' he says. Perhaps influenced by Cook's entrenched hope, Vaughan ends Day 3 on a far more positive note than 24 hours ago. 'England have the chance to make history. Let's hope they get over the line because the atmosphere at Headingley will be incredible if they do.'

Sunday 25 August
England v Australia – The Ashes – Third Test
Match, Day 4
Headingley Cricket Ground, Leeds

Team *TMS*: Jonathan Agnew, Simon Mann, Jim Maxwell, Isa Guha, Michael Vaughan, Geoffrey Boycott, Glenn McGrath, Sir Alastair Cook, Andrew Samson

The day Shane Warne did not expect to see dawns, with a mixture of nerves, excitement and entreaties for England to, variously, 'see off the new ball' or 'make it to the afternoon with a chance of winning'. 'For England to win the game, it will take a long time. For Australia to win the game, it could happen very quickly. I'd rather be Australia,' says Glenn McGrath, taking his classic bullish stance.

While usually it can take anywhere up to an hour for a Test match ground to fill up, every seat in the house is full by 11 a.m. and, despite what has gone before over the past few days, the air is thick with expectation. 'There's something about a Sunday crowd which is just a bit different,' says Aggers, shortly before the first aggressive appeal of the day from Tim Paine erupts against Joe Root. 'There's nothing worse than getting out midway through the Barmy Army's rendition of "Jerusalem",' adds Alastair Cook ruefully, but grateful that his occasional fate has not befallen his successor as England captain.

Josh Hazlewood, unsurprisingly, is fired up and hits Ben Stokes on the helmet with 'a thumping blow' early in the action. It looks incredibly dramatic as bits of his helmet come flying off left and right, but Stokes remains unfelled and, mercifully, the debris misses his stumps.

TMS commentary stints tend to last around 20 minutes and the programme is on its second commentator of the morning, Simon Mann, before Root dabs one into the off side and scampers through for the first run of the day. It has taken 26 balls and, as Simon says, the applause that greets it 'is like the applause for a hundred'. However, in the next over, Root trots down the wicket to Lyon and attempts to hit one through the leg side. Instead, he gets an inside edge onto his pad and initially it seems like he might get away with it as the ball balloons over Paine's head and prevents a stumping or caught behind. But then David Warner, continuing his superb game at slip, dives Superman style and takes a two-handed blinder directly behind the keeper, bringing Jonny Bairstow to the crease at his home ground.

In the 80th over of the innings, Andrew Samson reveals that a Stokes clip through midwicket for four is the first boundary in over 80 balls, and it seems to spark a change in direction for England. The long-feared new ball is taken by Australia and, slowly, the momentum begins to shift.

'It really is down to these two and Jos Buttler. You can't leave the tailenders to get you 100 or so,' says Michael Vaughan, who is characteristically chipper. Even Boycott is positive, thinking, 'There's just a chance they can win. Talent is not a problem in many of these England players. What has been lacking is the concentration and patience. When England bat well, and play properly, the people are behind them.'

Stokes reaches double figures – 'the longest time it has taken an England player to do so since Ian Salisbury against India in Calcutta in 1993', says Samson brilliantly – and then underlines the new approach by hitting the first six of the match when he pulls Cummins behind square, Samson coming back to say England have hit 60 in the eight overs of the new ball. 'While England are building this partnership, and building it quickly, the pressure is back on Australia,' admits McGrath as 'Grumpy' Simon Mann shocks everyone who knows him by saying simply, 'What a great day to be alive!' Nobody disagrees; there is just a little shock at the identity of the messenger.

As Bairstow forces a single to a boundary rider, England reach lunch at 238 for four and there is a huge roar as the batsmen leave the field. 'Bairstow and Stokes are giving England a real chance,' says Mann, nerves still palpable in his voice as the two troop off to adulation from the Western Terrace, who can sniff something in the sporting air this sunny Sunday lunchtime in Yorkshire.

The second session starts with Jim Maxwell at the controls,

stating that 'The fans are so on the edge of their seats they are in danger of falling off.' It's one of those perfect statements that in some cases is literally true and the wider sense makes a figurative point superbly. Those who were literally on the edge of their seats then do topple off when Bairstow is given out caught behind, but clamber back up and retake their positions when it is overturned. It is the sixth decision Chris Gaffaney has had overturned in the match, compared to Joel Wilson's one, says Samson.

However, there is no overturning Bairstow's flash outside off stump to be caught by Marnus Labuschagne at second slip. 'That is one of the worst balls that Josh Hazlewood has bowled today,' says Alastair Cook. 'It's a fine 30-odd, but it needed to be at least a 70-odd.'

Jos Buttler comes to the crease and 'England are still in the game,' says a more buoyant Maxwell. 'But they need that Jos Buttler–Ben Stokes World Cup final partnership,' he cautions, managing his own expectations as much as those of the listenership.

There is then no overturning a disaster in the middle for England as Stokes calls Buttler through for a single, only to send him back when it's far too late and Travis Head has had time to collect the ball, aim and fire underarm at the stumps from a short midwicket. 'That is a massive moment,' says Isa Guha as Alastair Cook hisses noisily through his teeth in the background before summoning his legendary inner strength and adding, 'I haven't got any words for that. An absolute disaster for England,' as he peels himself out of the summariser's chair, making way for Glenn McGrath, who pats him heartily on the back by way of thanks for the two crucial wickets that fell during his spell. Stokes, clearly annoyed by the run-out, then takes out his frustration on a short ball from Nathan Lyon and angrily hammers it to the boundary. 'Ben Stokes still believes,' says Isa wistfully.

As the *Great Escape* theme pipes out of the Western Terrace from a lone trumpeter, Stokes and Chris Woakes reduce the arrears to 100 before Woakes drives Hazlewood uppishly to extra cover to give Matthew Wade a straightforward catch. 'Extra cover was perfectly positioned. Australia are closing in on winning the Ashes,' says Simon Mann. 'His job was to stay there with Stokes. There was no need for that shot,' adds Glenn McGrath, starting to relax and anticipate an Australia victory.

According to the win percentage on the *TMS* monitor, the three wickets in seven overs have reduced England's chances of victory from 61 per cent to 11 per cent. 'England are going nowhere at the moment. Australia are on top and closing in. But Ben Stokes is still there,' says Mann, stretching out the tension and calling for belief shortly before Aggers takes his mic and immediately describes new man Jofra Archer 'cracking' one through the covers for four.

Boycott replaces McGrath and the tone of the summaries changes somewhat. 'Australia will get fidgety if this gets down to 50 needed with three wickets still remaining,' he says, needling expertly. 'The next 30 to 40 runs are crucial.'

Stokes carts Lyon down the ground for four, earning a 'Shot, boy!' from Geoffrey, and Archer hits two cross-batted smashes off consecutive balls that a newly relaxed Jim Maxwell calls 'pretty good whacks' before – after receiving the biggest cheer of the lot for blocking the next ball – he goes again and picks out Head on the square leg boundary, who takes a neat catch.

Fortunately for Archer, Boycott has recently moved on to be replaced by Michael Vaughan, so the criticism is slightly less cataclysmic than it might have been, but Vaughan is still unimpressed. 'He's in his second Test. You can get drawn into that,' he says. 'He was hitting with the spin, so it wasn't the silliest option. But with Stokes at the other end he had to dig in.'

No 10 Stuart Broad gets a very full ball from James Pattinson, tries to jam his bat down but misses entirely. While not quite the patented Broad 'celebrappeal', the Aussie shout has more than a degree of expectation to it and the finger of Chris Gaffaney is duly raised. Broad immediately reviews, but there is no chance of success and all four boxes rapidly turn red and send him back from whence he came. England need 73 to win, with one wicket left. Jack Leach comes to the crease.

'Sri Lanka's Kusal Perera and Vishwa Fernando added 78 for the final wicket to beat South Africa in February this year,' says Andrew Sansom, raising hope the only way he knows how. 'Perera got 67 of those, Fernando got 6 and there were some extras. That's the world record in all first-class cricket. England need 73.'

With Jim Maxwell sat next to him, bristling with anticipation at the thought of calling home an Australian Ashes victory, Vaughan jokingly offers his own suggestion for a way forward: 'If Ben Stokes can push twos and then hit a six off the fifth ball and a single off the last, then England will have this done in 11 overs. Simple.'

Then, as if he's wearing a *TMS* earpiece underneath his helmet, Stokes blocks away three balls before launching Nathan Lyon for a huge six. 'What a terrific blow,' says Maxwell, slightly spoiling his unusual magnanimity by adding, with a glittery-eyed grin spread across his face, 'Just ten more of those!'

Stokes finds the single from the last ball of the over, sees off another five balls, entrusts Leach with the final ball and the game continues. Lyon returns and Stokes clonks him for six more, narrowly clearing Hazlewood on the boundary, but clearing him nonetheless. Now it's Vaughan's turn to echo Maxwell's earlier line, gleefully asking for 'ten more of those, please!' Shifting slightly uneasily in his seat for the first time in an hour or so, Maxwell offers up that 'Stokes is certainly living dangerously here. He may well hole out, but he's keeping us interested.'

Stokes then plays one of the most extraordinary shots seen on the field of play during an Ashes Test match, reverse-sweeping Lyon for a huge six. Vaughan screams as Maxwell bellows over the ecstatic crowd, 'A colossal shot! He's hit it for six! Over backward point which is really backward square! Straight out of the World Cup manual! A reverse sweep into the Western Terrace for six!'

The next ball is again worked for a single, Leach survives one ball and Stokes continues. 'Do not go to sleep in Australia. You cannot possibly do that,' beseeches Maxwell of his fellow countrymen, for whom it is between 10 p.m. and midnight, depending on their longitude. 'Australia are getting a bit edgy about how they can finish it off. They have to respect Ben Stokes's ability to find the boundary,' admits Maxwell. 'Can he be England's hero – again?!' before laughing in disbelief and adding, 'This is Stokes's summer!'

Vaughan is replaced by Alastair Cook, who immediately calls back World Cup final memories by imploring a winning partnership to be put back together. 'If I was Adam Mountford, I would be calling on the Vaughan/Agnew partnership to call it home again! The World Cup final – and now can Stokesy . . . can he do it?!'

The all-rounder pulls an extraordinary ramp out to send Pat Cummins for yet another six, causing Cook – a very different style of cricketer to Stokes – to wonder, 'How that goes for six, I do not know!' Stokes slips then during a scrambled two and almost causes a game-ending run-out, soundtracked for *TMS* listeners by a jittery Cook repeatedly saying 'no' in the background – but the throw goes to the wrong end and England continue.

TMS has a long tradition that the top commentator from the winning nation should be at the mic when the game, or indeed the series, concludes. For some instinctive reason, it is at this point that Adam Mountford decides to switch from Maxwell to Agnew. With 33 runs required to win, the Australian doyen hands the mic to his English equivalent. 'This is getting like Edgbaston in 2005,' he nervously chuckles. 'So Aggers should come in to call the England victory.' The box echoes with the edgy laughter of others as Agnew picks up the microphone, not knowing if his stint will last for one ball or – surely not again? – for 33 English runs.

This is how the final 30 minutes played out on air:

SHOES OFF IF YOU LOVE BEN STOKES

A short play for three actors presented by BBC Test Match Special

THE SCENE: A commentary box in the Broadcast Centre at Headingley Cricket Ground, 25 August 2019. Three men sit at the front, dressed in open-neck shirts and dark trousers, watching a classic Ashes Test match unfold from the best seats in the house. Between them they have been involved in over 600 Test matches as players and commentators.

All are wearing wrap-around microphone and headphone sets, like those popularised by the popstar Madonna in the 1980s. Next to them is a statistician, with an old-fashioned lip mic lying on some grey foam next to a laptop, scorebook and an assortment of colourful stationery. Behind them is a producer, sat at a raised desk, also wearing a microphone.

Elsewhere in the small box are other experienced commentators – English and Australian – and an assistant producer. At the back is a window offering a view into an engineers' studio. On a desk at the rear of the box is a half-eaten rhubarb sponge cake made to look like Geoffrey Boycott's hat, a number of Melton Mowbray pork pies and a messy pile of correspondence.

Jonathan Agnew: And now we have Hazlewood, from the Football Stand End, bowling to Ben Stokes, here he comes, he bowls [*loud noise of leather on willow*]. And he's flogged that away into the leg side!

Sir Alastair Cook: Go on!

Agnew: That should go for four, the fielder, no, they can't get it! And Ben Stokes has reached a truly remarkable hundred. Absolutely incredible hitting. That ball was just short of a length [*pause*] and he thrashed it through to midwicket to reach his eighth Test century. And out there on the terraces, every single man, woman and child are on their feet. Even our friends the Australians down there, well done, they're on their feet too. What a finish we're all having here.

Cook: He never celebrated. He didn't even raise his bat once.

Agnew: What an ovation, he's in the zone! He's 100 not out! Hazlewood comes in, bowls to him – and that's way oh! Way over deep square leg! That's six!

[*Pause for disbelieving crowd noise*]

Cook: [*whispered*] Oooaaah!

Agnew: A full toss, shovelled away with lots of bottom hand. Well, well, well! Twenty-seven needed! Twenty. Seven. Needed.

Glenn McGrath: [*on mic, unannounced*] He can't do anything wrong, can he?!

Agnew: [*surprised*] Oh, hello, Glenn! You've popped up! Well done.

McGrath: The pressure's been relaxed, hasn't it? So, he just has to go out there and play. You think that last over, threw to the wrong end, could have been all over. Really firing up out there! One ball!

Agnew: Twenty-seven more to win, to reach the highest score England have ever made to win a Test Match. 332 for nine, Ben Stokes now on 106. Hazlewood comes in, bowls to him – AND HE'S HIT WAY OVER TO DEEP MIDWICKET AGAIN. THERE ARE TWO MEN DOWN THERE – IT'S SIX! IT'S SIX.

[*Pause for increasingly raucous crowd noise*]

Agnew: Straight into the Western Terrace, where they are going utterly mad! Look at all those missiles, projectiles being thrown in the air! Plastic beer glasses, I would say. All sorts of stuff that's been chucked upwards into the air! And now Tim Paine, look at him, has come down to speak to his bowler. Twenty-one to win. Ben Stokes is playing a most outrageous innings here. You'd have to say that Hazlewood has rather lost the plot. That was a length.

McGrath: That's harsh! That's harsh, Aggers! You've got a guy who's got no fear, no pressure. He's hitting it well enough to get it over the rope.

Agnew: [*in the background*] Full toss. Length ball. Whooah.

McGrath: One mishit here?

Agnew: We're in one-day mode here. 338 for nine, 21 needed.

McGrath: I'm not even sure it's one-day mode!

Agnew: Hazlewood on the way, he just pushes that away. He'll want two if he can.

Cook: He's got it!

Agnew: Is he going to come back for two? He is coming back for two. And the fielder there is flat on his tummy. It's Lyon. He's helped to his feet.

Cook: He played the sweep like he did in the World Cup, to the yorker and hit it into the stand. A back-of-a-length ball six and then he's still calm enough to not go again. Just bat on ball, everyone's out, he gets an easy two. It's UNBELIEVABLY clear thinking. I mean, you talk about performing under pressure, pressure moments, mental toughness – whatever you want to call it. This kid's got it.

Agnew: Nineteen to win. Stokes on 114. And in comes Hazlewood again. Listen to the crowd – they're silent. Hazlewood bowls and Stokes pushes it into the same place, this time it will be one. And that leaves Leach with one delivery, with 18 more required by England to win this match. 341 for nine. Leach hasn't scored a run yet and these two have put on 55.

Cook: Watch Ben Stokes now. At the non-striker's end, Aggers. His head's down; I don't think he watches the ball. I don't think he even watches what Jack Leach does. Come on, Jack.

Agnew: Well. We've had the World Cup final – and now this. Ben Stokes central to both. And the noise out there, just as deafening as it was at Lord's. Jack Leach. Pulls on his gloves.

McGrath: What a game!

Agnew: You've got two No 11s sitting alongside you here, Cooky – and we know exactly how poor old Jack feels. He's got an incredible man at the other end, but you don't want to let him down. That's the thing. You just want to survive the ball and give it back to him.

Cook: We've got two No 11s, maybe like Jack Leach. But we haven't got the other person at the other end sitting here!

McGrath: You don't think you can do this, Cooky? Just swing!

Agnew: [laughs]

Cook: No. Only on Brian Lara's Cricket with the cheat mode on!

McGrath: Just clear that front leg, mate!

Agnew: Can Leach survive? Hazlewood's on his way, short leg

is crouching there. He bowls to Leach, it's down the leg side. Almost took that leg stump but misses it! Paine collects and Stokes is on strike with 18 more runs required by England to keep the Ashes alive!

McGrath: Ooahah.

Agnew: It looks to me like there's a very big call being made here.

McGrath: [*surprised*] Nathan Lyon.

Cook: Three hits. Three hits off Nathan Lyon.

McGrath: Well, they rope it off that much these days. This ground is too small for Ben Stokes.

Agnew: Are you surprised by this?

McGrath: It's gutsy!

Cook: It's seriously, seriously gutsy.

Elsewhere in the Broadcast Centre, through the lack of any more technical methods available, Tim Peach, a BBC 5 Live producer, shouts down a long corridor to TMS assistant producer Henry Moeran, indicating that 5 Live have now handed over their network to Test Match Special. Moeran immediately shouts into the box, alerting TMS producer Adam Mountford, who quickly passes the message on to the three broadcasters.

Agnew: Welcome to our 5 Live listeners who have just joined us! What a time to come to Headingley! Where England now need 18 more to win. The game was over half an hour ago when Stuart Broad was out LBW, but Ben Stokes is playing the innings of a lifetime but, well it may well prove to be. But we've already seen one of those this year in the World Cup final. He's 115 not out. He's with the No 11, the last man, Jack Leach, who's got nought. But these two have put on 55! Ben Stokes has been hitting sixes and fours – an amazing reverse sweep for six into the West Stand and the people in there, and in fact all around Headingley, are going ballistic. It's an amazing atmosphere. It has been since the very start of the day. And Stokes is over his bat, a gamble here by the Australian captain, he's brought the off-spinner, Lyon, on. He goes in and bowls to Stokes. He goes for the reverse sweep. [*Sound of a lone Australian appealing, quickly drowned out by sarcastic crowd cheers*] Paine's appealing; he thinks he's got him, but nothing from slip, nothing from the bowler. Well.

McGrath: [*laughs*]

Agnew: I think Tim Paine, the captain, was quite keen to . . .

McGrath: He would have reviewed it! He would have reviewed it if . . .

Agnew: And listen to the crowd!

McGrath: [*frustratedly*] Just to fire the crowd up a little bit more.

Agnew: Lyon again goes skipping in from round the wicket, he bowls to Ben Stokes. Who goes for the edge, is it?! No, it's spun out of the footholes!

Cook: [*simultaneously*] No, oooaah!

Agnew: [*to disbelieving background laughter from McGrath*] It's caught at slip, but it spun out of the footholes! As Stokes swung the bat it – oh that just adds to the tension, doesn't it?!

McGrath: A little luck here for the Aussies would be nice, wouldn't it, Aggers?

Agnew: I'm not going to comment on that. Lyon, again, bowls and Stokes tries to fiddle that away. He's not going for the big shots; he's only for the little fiddly ones here.

McGrath: It's closing in. Only 18 now! This game could have been over. [*Looks at Cook*] Three hits?!

Agnew: I love it when Glenn McGrath's chirpy. It's a sign of nerves, Cooky. It's a sign of nerves in the big man.

McGrath: You're not nervous?

Agnew: [*nervously*] No, just loving it. Here's Lyon, round the wicket, bowls and Stokes goes onto the back foot and, no, they don't take the one. There's an easy single there to be had – but they don't take it. Two balls to go. He's daring Paine to bring the field in, to go for a big one. [*Pause*] Lyon again, round the wicket, moves in, bowls to Stokes, who goes back and clubs that away into the off side. They are going to take one run. So, as we were, with Leach needing one ball to survive. Seventeen more runs needed by England to win. And Stokes is 116 not out. It's been an incredible explosion really. For Andrew, just put into context the sort of two halves – if there are two halves, maybe there are three thirds, I don't know – but the two halves of this innings.

Andrew Samson: Well, he was three off 73 balls at one stage. Took another 79 balls to get to 50. He's now faced another 56 balls to get from 50 to 116.

Cook: And this is the guy who bowled a 24-over spell, uninterrupted, up the hill in 30-degree heat yesterday.

Agnew: He is an incredible cricketer. And he's down here at the non-striker's end; he's helpless. That must feel awful as well. You've got a No 11 down there. The vultures around. There are four men catching, plus the keeper, as then Lyon goes in to bowl the last ball. And it's pushed away by Leach! [*Pause for loud cheering*] The ball trickles to mid-off. Leach survives. Stokes is on strike. There are 17 more to win! Ruth Hodd is asking about a super over? No, I'm sorry, you're not going to get one of those. But it feels like every over is a super over at the moment! And who are they going to bring on?

McGrath: When's tea, Aggers?!

Agnew: Tea is 40 minutes. [*Pause, then, forlorn*] Ohhh. Jack Leach is polishing his glasses.

Cook: Henry Moeran has called him Alan from accounts.

Agnew: Does he? He does look like him. But he's putting his helmet on. Oh well, I hope you can hear this and feel this atmosphere, it's really wonderful. So many spectators here can't sit, they're standing up. Standing up and watching. There's some booing breaking out down there because an Australian has dared to go and field in front of the West Stand.

Cook: I think it's David Warner.

Agnew: Is he out there?! Phwoar, that's brave!

McGrath: Yeah. Pat Cummins on as well.

Agnew: Cummins on. Seventeen needed. Stokes on strike. The field completely scattered. [*Pauses*] Here's Cummins, fast bowler – it's thrashed into the air! 'Catch it,' they shout! Third man's coming in; DROPS IT!

McGrath: Ohhhh no!

Agnew: DROPS IT!

Cook: Aargh!

Agnew: Not an easy chance!

McGrath: [*disconsolate*] Was that Harris?

Cook: It's a Simon Jones moment from 2005 – the same, similar catch down at third man.

Agnew: He dropped it. Harris!

McGrath: Did he drop it? Or not get to it . . .

Agnew: Let's have a look – did he get there? Ohhh, he got there.

McGrath: Ohhhh.

Agnew: It was a difficult chance, he was running at full tilt. Has he just dropped the Ashes?

McGrath: [*nervous laughter*]

[*Off-mic deep groan*]

Agnew: Oh, a groan from Jim! [*Loud, friendly cackle*] 342 for nine. I love it! Here's Cummins again, bowling to Stokes who waits – and hits that hard into the leg side! There's two men out THERE! It's four! Again that could have been a really difficult chance. He was running at full tilt.

McGrath: Is that another catch?

Cook: From here, it looked like it carried.

Agnew: Thirteen to win!

McGrath: He can't do anything wrong, can he?

Agnew: [*deep sigh*]

McGrath: Or can he? [*Nervous laugh*]

Agnew: Well. We've seen some games of cricket between us up here. I haven't seen a Test match finish like this before. Highest-ever total that England have scored to win a Test match. Ever. [*Pause*] The umpire confirms that was four but only just, there was a fielder getting round there. There's one, two, three, four, five men on the leg-side boundary. One, two, three, four on the off-side boundary. Cummins on his way again from the far end and bowls to Stokes [*sound of cricket bat making a strong connection with a cricket ball*] who hammers it past him straight down the ground! It's a very short boundary down there! And the fielder dives – it's gone for four!

Cook: Wow. Wow!

Agnew: The noise tells us it's gone for four! It's in the shadows. We can't see from here but they know down there! An incredible shot, the 350 comes up. It's nine to win. Nine!

Cook: What a shot, a back-of-a-length ball. Laced it straight, straight past the stumps.

Agnew: Well, Stokes is taking a breather. Leach is coming down. I hope he's not offering too much by way of advice apart from 'Carry on, Stokesy' is about all he can offer! All these men on the boundary. Is he going to go big again? Is he going to take that risk? Or is he going to play one of those little dinky ones now everyone is back?

Cook: How many balls to go?

Agnew: Two! We've got how many balls an over? One to go? Four? Three to go! Here's Cummins, runs in and bowls to Stokes. There it is, the little dinky one!

Cook: No, no, no, no!

Agnew: Leach is slow setting off! That's not there! They've taken one and Stokes has his arm up. Is this Australia's opportunity now? Two balls to go, to bowl to Leach. He's got his helmet off again, he's mopping his brow.

Cook: [*smiling*] He's cleaning his glasses!

McGrath: He's looked pretty solid, hasn't he, Leach?

Agnew: He has, he has! Simon Rossman says, 'It's too tense for me, I've turned off. Send me an email when you know what's happened.' Okay. Coward! We've got to watch it! You've got to listen to it. What a finish! All of you out there, sitting in your gardens, BBQs going. What an afternoon! 351 for nine, with everything on this in this series. England have to win to keep the Ashes alive. And they need eight more runs to do it and to score the highest they've ever made batting last to win a Test match.

McGrath: You'd get silly point in as well, wouldn't you? You'd get plenty around the bat.

Cook: What about that little tickle past third slip for four? Is that getting greedy, Aggers?

Agnew: I think I've got them all catching. I think this is Australia's moment.

McGrath: Now, now! Reverse psychology doesn't always work, Aggers! I know you too much!

Agnew: Stewards appearing down there! Stokes is on his knees up at the far end!

Cook: He's not watching.

Agnew: He's not watching – he's not looking! Now he looks up, Cummins on his way, bowls, a bouncer! I think that's a waste. I think that's a waste!

McGrath: A little short – a little short!

Agnew: Leach has played that short ball so well.

Cook: He's pushing him across and he's going to go leg-stump yorker. I'm convinced they're going to try to get him out the same way they got him out in the first innings. He's got a bit of a trigger going across the off stump, exposes his leg stump a little bit when the pace gets up.

Agnew: The Stokes body language is fascinating!

McGrath: This is the ball. I've got a good feeling.

Agnew: [*chuckles*] Glenn, don't do this to me: 351 for nine. Leach taps furiously at the ground, bat now raised, Cummins on his way, Stokes not looking at all! And it is that leg-side yorker, you're absolutely right, Cooky. It hit him on the boot, though!

McGrath: [*partially off mic*] Just outside.

Agnew: Pitched outside the leg stump, the Aussies are talking about it – are they going to review it? I think they might as well. It's been given not out. They are going to review it, but with absolutely no confidence whatsoever this is actually out. This says a lot about how the Aussies are feeling.

McGrath: Would you review it?

Agnew: Yes.

McGrath: [*laughs*]

Agnew: Let's have a look. Stokes is literally not looking at this delivery from the non-striker's end. He's looking straight at the ground, it's incredible! This is going to pitch outside leg stump.

Cook: Yeah.

Agnew: The crowd know it! They're a knowledgeable lot up here! And Lyon is going to bowl. I mean, if this comes off you're going to say 'hats off to Tim Paine', because this is a gamble now. He's got the off-spinner bowling to Ben Stokes. [*Huge crowd cheer*] There's confirmation of not out.

McGrath: You wouldn't go for the big shot. He's been pushing the twos nicely, hasn't he?

Cook: I think he's going big shot.

McGrath: You're probably right.

Cook: I think he's going big shot.

Agnew: What are you doing, Cooky?

Cook: If they had this field for me? [*Pause to look around*] I might be able to get a one. [*McGrath laughs*]

McGrath: You're looking to go straight down into the stand? Up on the roof?

Agnew: Do you feel, does he feel that he has got to do it this over?

Cook: I don't feel that he's got to do it this over. I just think he's thinking, the last 70 runs, he's played every attacking shot. He's played the reverse sweep for six. He's come down twice and hit Lyon from the crease for six here. He's got to carry on the same way. If he gets one boundary, then what do Australia do?

Agnew: Well, absolutely. Stokes is leaning on his bat. Lyon dries his hands. The off-spinner. To Ben Stokes. On 125. Round the wicket he goes. Bowls to Stokes, it's short, cracked off the back foot. He's saying, no, I'm not taking a run. Oh, there's a bobble out there! Ohhh, waah!

McGrath: Could have come back for two!

Agnew: The fielder there, for no apparent reason, it bobbled up and out of his hands.

Cook: Ben Stokes a little bit annoyed there because it was a short ball. I know if he'd hit it really cleanly and gets it in the gap he could have got a boundary there.

Agnew: Lyon again, off a few paces, goes round the wicket and bowls. And Stokes on the back foot again chops that away but he's not taking the run.

[*McGrath makes a partially inaudible onomatopoeic nervous noise*]

Agnew: Well, mid-on was thinking about coming up but

actually was just trotting into position. 351 for nine. England need eight. They've got one wicket left.

Cook: Interesting now. If he blocks two balls, does Paine bring the field in? Does he?

Agnew: And if he does, does Stokes go for it?

Agnew: Lyon. [*Whispering followed by short pause to demonstrate utter silence in the ground*] The crowd falls silent as he bowls and Stokes has scythed that! IT'S SIX OR OUT? ... IT'S SIX! IT'S SIX! [*Pause for ecstatic crowd noise*] I didn't think he'd hit that hard enough.

McGrath: No, he didn't. He didn't get it – but it still carries nicely.

Agnew: Two to win!

Cook: It's your boundary ropes, Glenn. They're in there, ten yards.

McGrath: In the old days – he'd have been out ten overs ago.

Agnew: It's Edgbaston 2005. Jim's trying to jinx me here. Sit down, Jim! Sit down! It's two to win – oh my!

McGrath: Got to bring them in now.

Agnew: I really thought that was going to be caught, I must be honest. It sounded horrible off the bat. I think Stokes thought it was, too.

McGrath: It should have been, but he got enough on it.

Agnew: Now, what on earth do Australia do?

McGrath: Got to bring 'em up.

Agnew: Two to win.

McGrath: Or this game's over.

Agnew: Stokes on 131, in goes Lyon, he bowls to him, he forces off the back foot. The fielder ... does very well! Very well fielded there at point under pressure!

[*McGrath makes another partially inaudible onomatopoeic nervous noise*]

Agnew: It's Khawaja. Had to roll to his right. How many balls to go? One? Two to go! Two to go! Two balls, two runs, one wicket. We can't have a tie, can we? In goes Lyon, bowls, reverse sweep, fielder fields. [*Inaudible shouting*] HE'S SET OFF!

Cook: OH NO NO NO NO NO!

Agnew: HE'S SET OFF!

Cook and McGrath: ARRRRRRGGGGGHHHHHH!

McGrath: No!!

Agnew: Lyon's dropped it! Lyon's dropped it!

McGrath: No . . .

Agnew: He was run out by yards.

McGrath: No . . .

Agnew: And Lyon has dropped the ball.

McGrath: No . . .

Agnew: Leach. Survives. He set off for that run. I don't know why; Stokes wasn't going anywhere. He should have been run out by two yards.

McGrath: Well.

Agnew: And Leach, Leach was well short and Lyon dropped the ball. He dropped the ball!

Cook: Aargh!

Agnew: They're showing it on the screen.

McGrath: Orrhh, ho ho ha. Well, that's just spoiled it, hasn't it?

Agnew: It's still two to win. It's the last ball of the over. What's Stokes going to do?

McGrath: [*mournfully*] He's going to slog it.

Agnew: In goes Lyon, bowls to him. He does slog it!

Cook: [*quietly*] Oh no!

Agnew: Appeal for leg before wicket! It's umpire Wilson! They're beseeching him!

McGrath: [*much louder*] Oh no!

Cook: No reviews!

Agnew: He's going to give it not out!

McGrath: [*quietly*] No.

Cook: No reviews!

Agnew: Not out! No reviews! Umpire Wilson has said not out.

McGrath: Oh, hoh hoh.

Agnew: From a sweep.

McGrath: If that is out, with the way Wilson's had this ...
Ooooh. Ooohaa.

Agnew: What an over again – and what drama.

McGrath: [*laughing*] Well, it's still not over yet.

Agnew: And Australia had their moment. They had their
moment. This could be tied.

Cook: What about that? Was it going down?

Agnew: [*confidently*] Pitched outside leg, I reckon.

Cook: No. I don't think it pitched outside. Just whether it might
be sliding?

McGrath: If that's hitting the stumps? Ooooh.

Agnew: Lyon wanted that.

McGrath: Why wouldn't you give that? [*Laughs*]

Agnew: Lyon wanted that.

McGrath: Because England have reviews.

Agnew: Well, that's a good point.

Cook: [*firmly*] No, because then it's umpire's call.

McGrath: Well, then it's out! [*Laughs*]

Agnew: That's a good point.

McGrath: [*laughs*]

Agnew: [*settles himself*] Oh dear, right. Okay. Jack Leach is going
to face the start of an over.

McGrath: Well. Could it get any more exciting, Athers? Aggers!
I'm calling you Athers now!

Agnew: Calm down, Glenn.

McGrath: I got all excited then.

Agnew: I've never seen you like this before. Jack Leach.

McGrath: [*watching replay that has been shown on a monitor*] OH NO!

Agnew: Pitching. Hitting. Middle and leg!

McGrath: Absolutely dead! He's given every one out except that one!

Cook: Oh, sheesh.

McGrath: Ohhh . . .

Agnew: Well, that's out. I'm looking into the Australian dressing room there.

McGrath: That is very poor. [*Brightly*] Anyway . . . [*Laughs*]

Agnew: Ohhh . . . That should have been out LBW.

McGrath: But there's still a chance!

Agnew: Well, that review that they burned off earlier. They burned off that one where you said should they do it? They did it.

McGrath: [*angrier*] Yeah, but still.

Agnew: They took a gamble. It was a bad decision.

Cook: [*quietly*] It was a bad decision.

McGrath: No. It's a horrible decision, not even bad.

Agnew: Right. Where are we? Two needed, Leach on strike.

McGrath: How many chances do the Aussies need?

Agnew: Cummins. Bowling. The crowd going mad. Fine leg's coming up. Oh, a little nick and it's all over.

Cook: That's brave. That is brave.

Agnew: No third man.

Cook: Back up, Stokesy. Surely, Stokesy, you're going to back up?

Agnew: Well, he's not looking at the moment again, he's crouching. But I think he should back up. Mind you, if it goes out, it's runs. Cummins on the way, bowls to Leach. A bouncer. [*Pause for celebratory crowd noise*] Ducks underneath it.

McGrath: Well!

Agnew: Simon Jones is in the Eurotunnel.

McGrath: [*laughs*]

Agnew: Waiting for the last bar of reception to go. 'I can't bear it,' he says! We can't bear it either, Simon. Drive carefully. Everybody in their cars, gripping the steering wheels.

McGrath: It reminds me of the semi-final in World Cup '99. Edgbaston. Missed a couple of chances and it ended on a tie. Do you reckon a tie's a fitting . . . ? [*Trails off into laughter*]

Agnew: Well, I suppose it probably is?

McGrath: No.

Agnew: Cummins, over the wicket, comes in, bowls to Leach, who steers that away, round the corner! And there's two fielders there. It beat one! That short fine leg was up.

Cook: Good decision from Tim Paine. I'd say he probably should be back for this.

McGrath: No, no.

Agnew: Two to win. A wicket now and Australia retain the Ashes. One run and out, it's a tie. Two runs, well, England win.

McGrath: It's four balls. Australia have got four balls to win this game.

Agnew: 357 for nine. Stokes has gone down for a conversation with his No 11, Jack Leach, who has taken his gloves off, he's cleaned his glasses, he's put them back on again. You have to say well done to him. He's nought not out!

McGrath: Gutsy.

Agnew: Nought not out! Very gutsy.

McGrath: Here we go.

Agnew: 357 for nine. Here's Cummins, bowls and it's short – but very well played! STOKES GOES FOR THE RUN! THROUGH THEY COME! ENGLAND CAN'T LOSE!

[*Long pause for riotously celebratory crowd noise. McGrath presses a button on the ISDN machine on the desk in front of him, muting*] *his microphone. He shakes his head and Cook and Agnew exchange a nervous glance.*]

Cook: Wow.
Agnew: The Ashes are alive!

[*Pause for further riotously celebratory crowd noise. McGrath now removes his headset entirely, sighs, shakes his head and turns to face the producer behind him, silently, angrily, mouthing, 'Joel Wilson'.*]

Cook: Wow. What do you do with the field now?

[*McGrath shakes his head one last time before putting his headset back on and pressing the button to reactivate his microphone*]

Agnew: Well played, Jack Leach, he's off the mark. [*Pause*] And he's going to give Stokes a little tap of the gloves. Stokes is on strike, England need one to win. They can't lose!
Cook: The last tie, in a Test match?
Agnew: I've never seen one.
Samson: There's only been two.
McGrath: [*resigned anger*] Well, there you go, Aggers. I've always said that DRS will cost you. If you use it badly, you'll lose a Test match. If you use it well, you'll win it. And it's cost them this match.
Agnew: They gambled that one, didn't they?
McGrath: They did. And it cost them the Test match.
Agnew: 358 for nine. Stokes on strike. England need one. To win. And in comes Pat Cummins from the far end. He bowls to Stokes [*noise of cricket ball perfectly hitting the sweet spot of a cricket bat*] WHO HAMMERS IT FOR FOUR! AND STANDS THERE WITH THE BAT RAISED. I CAN'T BELIEVE WE'VE SEEN THAT!

Cook: That is the most extraordinary innings ever, *ever* to be played by an Englishman.

Agnew: He punches the air, his helmet's off. He was hit on that helmet this morning. Bits flew off all over the place. And he's slumped to his knees. One Australian is there, it's Lyon I think, who knew, he knew he could have run him out. He's got his hands on his knees, he's feeling dreadful. One or two team-mates go and pat him on the back, that won't help him. And there's shaking of hands, there's hugs there. And that is a fantastic sight by the way. In the absolute heat of Ashes battles, there are hugs and embraces from Australians to the England batsmen. And a shake of hands to the umpire. I'm not sure if Nathan Lyon will shake Mr Wilson's!

McGrath: Well, that's an amazing, amazing innings from Stokes there. Anti-climax finish from an Australian perspective. I think their finish was poor, but Ben Stokes – absolutely incredible. Man of the Match without a doubt. Without a doubt.

Agnew: I just don't . . . understand how he's played that innings? It's absolutely amazing. And I don't think he can believe it. He's standing there. He's just taking it in. He's got his hands on his head and he's just looking around the ground.

Cook: To do that after as well? The World Cup, how he played there. To even . . . That innings happens once in a lifetime. He's done two in six weeks.

Agnew: He is an INCREDIBLE cricketer. [*Pause for crescendo in crowd noise*] And he's showing his bat all the way around the crowd who are on their feet, obviously. And the Australians, down there, are on their feet. They'll remember this. And Australia will come back to fight another day, there's still two Test matches left. And the Ashes are alive!

[*Exit Agnew, pursued by Henry Moeran, to speak to the principals on the field of play*]

As everyone comes to terms with what has just happened, it becomes clear that many people in the box have been moved to tears by the momentous events that have just unfolded in front of them. While a lot of those in the team are obviously delighted for England, there is a deeper reason. As broadcasters and promoters of cricket, the engagement seen during this game has been extraordinary and the public are clearly fully tuned into this series and learning to love cricket. For Australia to win and secure the Ashes after just three Tests would have been fully justified from a sporting perspective, but would have removed the chance of a classic finale. With the result today, the series is poised at 1-1 and the next Test at Old Trafford, just ten days away, will be yet another seismic event.

Another thing that becomes clear as the dust settles is what Simon Mann was up to when England were winning. About 16 minutes before the end, he nipped into the engineers' studio to provide a quick two-minute update for BBC World Service. Such was the drama during those two minutes, regular programming was immediately suspended, and Simon asked to continue. As the ultimate professional, he provided listeners around the world with a one-man description of the unfolding events.

Sadly for him, though, as Stokes flayed the winning runs towards the boundary, such was the excitement of Jon and Phil, the redoubtable engineers who ensure *TMS* makes it out of the commentary box and onto broadcasts around the world, that his view was completely blocked and he had to take evasive action to avoid being utterly taken out. Such is his commitment to the cause that it was unanimously decided to forgive his treachery earlier in the match.

An emotional Stokes joins Aggers for an interview shortly after close of play – and heaps praise on Leach. 'Jack,' he says, 'has got some serious bollocks!' For a programme that usually has little cause to be called up in front of the BBC's language police, it is a second use of unfortunate vernacular in a week. However, given the gravity of the situation and the size of Stokes's feats, it's hoped he'll be allowed to get away with it.

As the day continues, messages flood in. One that particularly entertains everyone is a tweet from the BBC's chief political correspondent, Vicki Young, who is covering the G7 Summit in Biarritz. There is widespread international interest in the event and, as such, the open-plan international broadcast centre is incredibly busy with journalists from many countries constantly wiring back bulletins in an array of different languages. The British area is located next to the German and French sections, and correspondents from both nations happened to be broadcasting at the precise moment Stokes hit the winning runs. While there was no effort made to explain the rules of cricket to their viewers, given the volume of the celebrations, it's fair to say that far more people around Germany and France were aware of the result than one would normally expect.

After interviewing Stokes, Leach and Root on the outfield, Aggers walks to the car park and quietly climbs into his car to drive home. Alone for the first time since the end of the match, he takes a deep breath and reflects on the incredible events before the two-hour drive. On the road his phone rings and, via hands-free, he takes a call from Ben Stokes's mum, all the way from New Zealand.

An incredible woman, at one stage she was the only bereavement counsellor on the south island of New Zealand – a place that sadly has been visited by a number of tragedies in recent years. She had stayed up all night in New Zealand to listen to the action, which finished at approximately 3 a.m. her time. She was still 'ticking' and was delighted to hear, first-hand, how proud the English cricketing world is of her son.

Back in Biarritz, early the next morning, Boris Johnson meets his Australian counterpart Scott Morrison and, as they greet each other, the pair can very clearly be heard discussing the result. After 2005, people said it could never happen again. After the World Cup final, people said it could never happen again. It's happening again. To quote Aggers, 'The Ashes are alive!'

Australia 179 (52.1 overs; Labuschagne 74, Warner 61, Archer 6-45) and 246 (75.2 overs; Labuschagne 80) lost to England 67 (27.5 overs; Hazlewood 5-30) and 362-9 (125.4 overs; Stokes 135*, Root 77, Denly 50, Hazlewood 4-85) by one wicket.

AN XI OF *TMS* LISTENERS FROM DAY 4 AT HEADINGLEY

1. In Fowey, Cornwall, Roddy Kemp told his family he had to leave them and listen in peace. The only place he could find was a nearby graveyard. After a while, it became clear he was not the only person in the graveyard doing this – by the end, everyone there was crouched over a gravestone, gasping and shouting together! Fortunately, nobody expired due to the tension – although they could easily have been interred had the worst happened.

2. Lee Colton was waist deep in the River Trent on a fishing trip, listening along nervously. Cogent of the cricketing superstition of not moving when something was going right, he stood stock still amid a rising tide that was getting ever closer to the top of his waders. He still smiles today when remembering the faces of people on a passing boat seeing a large 50-plus-year-old man in waders, jumping up and down, shouting, 'Get in, Stokesy!'

3. Simon Rogerson was working as a tour guide in York. When he switched his phone on after a tour finished at 4 p.m., he saw that England needed 19 runs with one wicket left. Coincidentally, this was the same equation as a successful partnership he had been part of the day before and he felt it was a sign. Briefly abandoning work to hunker down amid the cigarette butts around the back of the Jorvik Viking Centre, bemused tourists had to have it explained exactly why their guide was punching the air and cheering so loudly.

4. Ned Salvin was sat rigid on his combine harvester on Overtown Farm, mid-harvest. He continued with his harvesting up until Jack Leach took a single, when Ned decided to temporarily stop for the benefit of his blood pressure.

5. Alex da Costa was with his son at the Notting Hill Carnival. After seeing that Woakes was out, they stopped checking for updates. On the tube home they checked again and realised England only needed 18 to win. They managed to cling to signal between Paddington and Euston Square, where it dropped out. By the time signal was regained at Farringdon, England needed 2 to win. After an agonising journey to Barbican, they got off and followed the final few balls, before throwing their arms up in the air 'Stokes style'!

6. Robert Hodgson listened to the game in his back garden, putting in the foundations for a small retaining wall. It seemed that every time he switched on the concrete mixer while the match was in play, a wicket went down. The job took quite a lot longer when he decided he was only allowed to mix during the breaks between overs.

7. Janek Wichtowski was at a music festival called Stevofest in Surrey. As the band kept playing, the audience became increasingly distracted by the cricket. Realising what was happening, the band started to ask for updates before eventually stopping the performance to join the crowd and listen to the game. A few minutes after the finish, to much cheering, they came back on and restarted their set.

8. At 2 a.m. on Sunday, James Hallam's wife, Zoe, went into labour. This wasn't great news since the baby was in the breech position and they were booked in for a c-section in two days' time. In the ward waiting for surgery, he forgot about the cricket as they were trying to control the contractions, but briefly remembered when his phone buzzed to say that Joe Root was out. Going into surgery, dressed in scrubs, James took his phone with him so he could take the first photo of his new son, Stirling. He felt a few buzzes in his pocket but couldn't get the phone out and gave up on the game. Thirty minutes later, at 3.42 p.m., the baby was born. After the initial period passed, his wife was taken to recovery and he was sent to an empty room for an hour. As he sat down, his phone buzzed again and told him that England had won. He immediately started to stream *TMS* to listen to the aftermath. When he rang his parents to give them the good news, they answered the phone saying, 'Have you been watching the cricket?!'

9. At 1.30 p.m. on Sunday 24 August, Robert Price's dad peacefully passed away, surrounded by his loving family. After saying their last goodbyes, the family travelled back to his garden in Leicestershire to have a couple of drinks and share memories. With the radio on in the background, his mum asked for the commentary to be turned up. For the last six or seven overs, the family was enthralled and overtaken by the excitement. Being a proud Welshman, his dad probably wouldn't have been so taken in – but would have loved the sunshine, a cold beer and being with his family who loved him dearly.

10. During the morning's play, four-year-old Arthur Dennis Ball was digging a hole on the beach in Weymouth with his dad while listening to *TMS*. By lunchtime, the hole was so deep that Dad had to dig some stairs to allow them to get out. They carried on digging after lunch, with Dad vowing not to stop until they either beat Australia or found it! By the end, quite a crowd had gathered and, as England won, his dad's head could just be seen bobbing up and down at the top of the hole as everyone jumped around celebrating!

11. After listening to the three previous days' play, Ian Scrace's wife decided that the family would go on a Sunday day trip to West Midlands Safari Park. As the car crawled around a busy safari park with its windows open, the African animals taking shelter from the blazing Birmingham sun were roused by the loud cheers emanating from the car after the final shot, looking on at the celebrations in perplexity.

CHAPTER 19

Smith Returns to Seal the Ashes

Wednesday 4 September
England v Australia – The Ashes – Fourth Test
Match, Day 1
Emirates Old Trafford, Manchester

Team *TMS*: Jonathan Agnew, Jim Maxwell, Daniel Norcross,
Alison Mitchell, Michael Vaughan, Geoffrey Boycott, Glenn McGrath,
Vic Marks, Ebony Rainford-Brent, Andrew Samson

'It's like being back in Tasmania but without the fresh air and the views!'

The Australia captain Tim Paine is in an uncharitable mood as his side attempt to get their Ashes campaign back on track in Manchester. To be fair, though, he has a point. It is more than a little brisk in Manchester, and even renowned northern tough man Michael Vaughan is wearing a gilet underneath his sports jacket this morning.

As well as Steve Smith, whose return from concussion looms over the game, Mitchell Starc comes into the Australia side, and for England, Craig Overton is making his first start of the series, replacing Chris Woakes. Vaughan is unimpressed. 'I'm staggered they've gone with Craig Overton,' he says from underneath his many layers. 'It's a big call by the England team. In a few days' time, we'll know if it's a good one or not.'

Paine decides Australia will bat first and Stuart Broad strikes in the first over, David Warner once again nicking one he tries to leave and offering Jonny Bairstow a simple chance. The early wicket causes an interesting discussion about Broad to break out on air. Aggers references early-summer suspicions that Broad could have been looking at a classic Oval retirement but, given the success he has seen in this series, may now be considering extending a career that, as Andrew Samson points out, has made him England's third most successful Ashes bowler of all time (behind just Sir Ian Botham and Bob Willis).

'Stuart Broad does seem to grow a bit when James Anderson isn't playing,' thinks Vic Marks. 'He seems to relish it.' This fine piece of cricketing instinct from Victor is backed up by Samson, who reveals that 'Stuart Broad has played 114 of his 131 Tests with James Anderson and averages just over 29. In the 17 he's played without Anderson, he's taken 55 wickets at 25.5.'

Broad then follows up by having Marcus Harris LBW, an Australian review being narrowly overturned, and the moment that everyone has been waiting for arrives early, as Smith walks to the crease to a far more mixed ovation than he received earlier in the summer, his brilliance clearly converting some of the boos to respect. Jofra Archer, who has been ineffective so far this morning, remains on and the tension in the ground can be cut with a knife as he steams in to bowl to Smith for the first time since Lord's. A few well-directed bouncers are ducked under, but Marnus Labuschagne and Smith, batting together for the first time, dull the threat and progress well to lunch.

Lunchtime sees the first play of a superb interview conducted between Aggers and Ben Stokes in the build-up to this game. As well as reflecting on the magnitude of his achievements in the last Test, which he is keen to move on from as the series is still alive, he reveals the terrific amusement in the England dressing room over the video of the *TMS* commentary box during the final stages of the game that was posted on social media shortly after the match. A particular figure of fun seems to be *TMS* producer Adam Mountford, whose open-mouthed stare in the background has developed something of a cult following over the past week or so, not least within the England camp itself!

Wonderfully, Stokes talks first-hand about the increased love for the game that he has witnessed during the incredible summer of cricket that *TMS* has been lucky to be part of. 'This summer has made cricket bigger than I ever remember it to be and the Headingley Test has made cricket go even higher than it was after the World Cup,' he said. 'You see even tiny little things, like the number of people who wait at the hotel for autographs, has gone through the roof. That has something to do with what we have managed to achieve this summer so far.'

The interview is followed up by another appearance from Mark Wood, one of Stokes's best mates, who doesn't have his commentator wicket count to worry about this time, because sadly the lunch break has seen full covers pulled across the square. 'Ben is a really down-to-earth guy,' he says. 'He's a bit of a legend after the World Cup and Headingley. It's great that the kids think of him like that, that he's someone everyone looks up to, but he's still the same lad. He's got time for everyone.'

The incredibly strong wind is causing havoc with the covers, with Wood reflecting on a large marquee he once tried to erect for an engagement party in his garden. It didn't end well. 'We had to call the fire brigade because we couldn't keep it down,' he recalls. 'It was blowing into next door's garden.'

As well as a sensational on-air discussion about some of the incredible places listeners tuned into the Headingley climax from (all brilliant and an amazing follow-up to the jaw-dropping news earlier in the summer that someone was tuning in while paragliding over Mont Blanc), the other excitement of the rain break is the summer's second sighting of global pop superstar Ed Sheeran.

TMS first encountered Ed at The Oval in 2017 before seeing him again at Lord's earlier this year. Once again, emissaries are dispatched to try to secure an interview, but once again he just wants to enjoy the cricket – which is, after all, more than fair enough and why he's here in the first place! Sheeran does come over from his box to visit some friends in the Media Centre, which allows some of the team to witness the elaborate routine that must be undertaken every time he needs to go out in public. The hoodie-cap-scarf arrangement is quite something, but does allow him to traverse the ground and get back to his seat largely unbothered, which must be a triumph in itself.

A brief restart sees 16 balls bowled and is highlighted by a beach ball blowing across the field at quite a rate that is then helped to the boundary by a, naturally, well-timed flick from Smith, cueing up a million 'seeing it like a beach ball' jokes.

After another quick break, play resumes once more but the action is incredibly stop-start because of the amount of litter that is being blown across the ground by the Mancunian gale howling around. Daniel Norcross spends a good four minutes describing a pack of Wotsits heading over towards backward point, adding that he's not seen a wagon wheel yet, but there is an empty packet of chocolate currently in the eyeline of

Labuschagne. Things are then compounded by the bails repeatedly blowing off the top of the stumps, the helmet on the ground behind Jonny Bairstow blowing around, and even a pair of glasses being blown off the face of one of the umpires! 'It is chaos,' says Norcross accurately, before the umpires decide to remove the bails and briefly carry on without them.

TMS embark on one of the more niche conversations of the summer when heavier 'lignum vitae' cricket bails are discussed at some length. More practically, the Old Trafford ground staff are simply able to hammer some nails into the ends of the existing match bails to try and add enough weight so that they become windproof.

Smith reaches his half-century with one of the more amazing shots of the Ashes so far, dropping down to one knee and almost doing the splits as he drives another ball to the boundary. 'What a player he is,' gasps Vaughan admiringly, before Overton breaks the partnership by bowling Labuschagne.

'What time's play due to finish tonight?' Jim Maxwell asks Andrew Samson.

'Oh, about midnight,' comes the uncharacteristically sarcastic but perfect response. It has been an odd old day at Old Trafford, that's for sure.

The tea interval sees former England wicketkeeper Jack Russell in the box, talking about his successful retirement career as an artist and his ongoing project to paint the first ball of every Ashes Test this summer. However, sadly the interview is broken up by news of more rain, more covers and more wind. Play is called off shortly after 6 p.m. and *TMS*'s day ends many hours later with Norcross back in the bar at the hotel, explaining the intricacies of the follow-on to the German man who operates the new 'Spidercam' system that is being used by the TV networks in this series. It's all a bit surreal but fits perfectly with today.

Thursday 5 September
England v Australia – The Ashes – Fourth Test Match, Day 2
Old Trafford, Manchester

Team *TMS*: Jonathan Agnew, Jim Maxwell, Daniel Norcross, Alison Mitchell, Michael Vaughan, Geoffrey Boycott, Glenn McGrath, Vic Marks, Ebony Rainford-Brent, Andrew Samson

'Woke up, fell out of bed. Dragged a comb across my head.' The Beatles didn't say that the next thing to do was open the curtains and check the state of the wind, but that's how Day 2 of the fourth Ashes Test begins. Fortunately, a good night's sleep seems to have made everything a bit better and the sun is actually shining to the extent that Jim Maxwell has donned his sunglasses. It has also allowed Mark Wood to rock a pair of the whitest trainers ever seen, hugely impressing Ebony Rainford-Brent.

'If England don't get Steve Smith out in the first hour, he will be eyeing a double hundred,' warns Michael Vaughan concerningly, especially when Aggers adds, 'It's bright, it's fresh – it feels like a batting day. England have got a big hour ahead.'

Given everything that happened yesterday, Smith playing and missing and then causing play to be stopped after three minutes because the bright sunshine is reflecting off the windscreen of a van this morning is an unexpected beginning. The play and miss gives England hope, though, especially when it is repeated shortly afterwards. However, the big chance comes and goes when Smith offers a difficult caught and bowled shout to Jofra Archer, who gets his fingers to it but can't cling on. 'Archer will think he should have caught that,' rues Aggers, with McGrath thinking that the cold weather that was clearly bothering Archer yesterday might be partially to blame.

Travis Head is the first wicket to fall, 'celebrappealed' by Broad on an LBW he doesn't bother reviewing, but Matthew Wade comes in and continues to offer Smith support as the Aussies bat on and on. A ten-minute rain break doesn't change things, but a rash decision to come down the pitch and hit Jack Leach over the top does and Wade is well caught by Joe Root at a still breezy mid-on.

'This is a chance for England. Paine has been out of touch,' reckons Maxwell as the Australia captain walks out to bat, but the pair navigate to lunch, with the main further attraction of the morning session being the latest Smith hundred, called home by Alison Mitchell, who describes him as an 'unstoppable, eccentric run machine'.

Andrew Samson says that Smith is now the third highest century-maker in the history of the Ashes, with 11 tons against England. That he is behind just Sir Donald Bradman (19) and Sir Jack Hobbs (12) suggests that those who say we are watching true greatness are not speaking hyperbolically. Given that he's only 30 – and has now scored eight consecutive Ashes innings of over 75 – there is a good chance that The Don's record could be in danger come the next series bar one in 2023.

The presence of Stephen Fry in the back of the box is a confusing factor for those who watch the video of Alison's commentary that is posted on social media shortly after the century. The comedian, author, Hollywood star and general Renaissance man is in the box as a lunchtime guest, helping to discuss the greatness of the Headingley Test.

Writer, actor, comedian and performer Stephen Fry, a long-term friend of TMS, joined the programme at lunchtime on Day 2 to answer the question, 'What makes a Test match great?' This was his answer:

Of course, everyone will have different views about what precisely makes a game the most memorable, or the most dramatic, but I think your body tells you as much as your mind. Your bladder, your heart rate, your breathing – whether or not you can sit down. It's as simple as that.

I remember the Edgbaston match in 2005 and I couldn't sit down. I couldn't even be near the television or you on the radio; I had to go into the garden and then run in. It was extraordinary, rather like love is. Catullus, '*odi et amo*' (I love, and I hate). It's almost too much to bear. That's partly what it is.

You need big characters, but you need big characters on both sides. You need a great opposition; you don't want to steamroller. There has to be a point in the match where everybody who is knowledgeable doesn't believe England is going to win; they think it's all over. All the fans think it's over and that little voice that says *believe* is just a tiny squeak that is smothered by the obvious fact that we cannot win. *It. Isn't. Possible.* It is like Headingley in 1981, 500/1 against – and that is generous from the bookies.

And yet, despite that, something happens. Unlike a great one-day match, where it's moments of brilliance – an extraordinary catch, an incredible six – it's a session, and then it's another session – that's the glory of Test matches.

Things get worse for England early in the afternoon when Jason Roy drops an easy chance offered by Paine, and then utter disaster strikes as Smith is caught off Leach. Seemingly, this is exactly what England want, but the tragedy only unveils itself as Smith is halfway back and it becomes clear that Leach has overstepped and it's a no-ball. 'A reprieve!' yelps Maxwell. 'The last thing England want is for that to occur. That is one of the great crimes of cricket, for a slow bowler to be done for a no-ball.' Boycott, who comes on air shortly afterwards, rapidly describes it as a 'muppet moment', and after that Samson reveals that so far in his career Leach has bowled more than 15,000 deliveries and it was his eighth no-ball.

Smith and Paine continue, England are really struggling and Aggers is getting grumpy. 'Glenn McGrath's starting to get one of those smug and frankly annoying looks on his face,' he sighs to everyone and no one at the same time. The atmosphere at Old Trafford is flat and when a grimacing Ben Stokes goes off holding his side, it somehow becomes worse. 'That is a very worrying sign for England,' says Maxwell correctly.

Smith reaches 150 and when Sam Curran (on the field as a replacement for Stokes) shells the second straightforward chance Paine offers, heads really do drop. 'The wheels are coming off,' warns Vaughan, while Maxwell praises Australia's 'remorseless' attitude and people start to describe black clouds wheeling around the ground as 'encouraging'.

Tea passes, Stokes returns, and then, the first ball after tea, a loosener from Craig Overton clips the edge of Paine and he is caught behind. Pat Cummins goes next, caught slip off Leach, and if England's post-tea strategy was 'let Smith bat and focus on getting the other blokes out', it's working terrifically well. Smith reaches his double century and, for the first time this summer, the ground rises to its feet in applause. 'Old Trafford is on its feet and that is good to see,' says Aggers. 'Everyone is applauding this remarkable, eccentric and extraordinary batsman. He is the best in the world.'

'It is a huge honour to watch him,' adds Ebony Rainford-Brent. 'To come back and play like this after Lord's – what character.'

Then, amazingly, with 211 runs in his pocket, Smith gets out, reverse-sweeping Joe Root straight to Joe Denly at backward point. He is absolutely fuming with himself as he leaves the field, garnering another standing ovation in the process. 'Forget what has happened in the past, you have got to appreciate you are witnessing greatness,' says Vaughan succinctly, before adding, 'If it wasn't for that blow at Lord's then Australia would have retained the Ashes by now.'

To pile on further misery for England, Mitchell Starc and Nathan Lyon smash a few more while everyone looks on for signs that Paine is going to declare, which eventually comes at 497 for eight. Burns and Denly sprint off to pad up, something Aggers feels they will not be anticipating with great fervour. 'Joe Denly will be feeling pretty sick in his stomach,' he says. 'England's openers are going to have to go out there and bat for their lives.'

The two survive for 6.4 overs, defending a lot, scoring the odd run and playing and missing at a few, before Matthew Wade takes a superb catch at short leg after Denly turns a ball into his pad. Craig Overton is the new night-watchman and helps Burns to the end of the day without further incident. As has been the case for much of this series, Vaughan is concerned. 'England have three days of real discipline and technical nous ahead,' he says. 'It will test their mentality.'

Taking on those who criticise his punditry for too often erring on the negative side, he continues, 'Many say I am always critical, but this is a must-win match and what I have seen is an England side that looks a little dejected. It has felt like this game has been played in Australia on the back of a long tour. It hasn't felt like England are 1-1 with two matches to play. They just haven't looked right.'

'It is going to be a huge day tomorrow,' concludes Aggers. 'England have got to bat well, or they will lose.'

Friday 6 September
England v Australia – The Ashes – Fourth Test Match, Day 3
Old Trafford, Manchester

Team *TMS*: Jonathan Agnew, Jim Maxwell, Daniel Norcross, Alison Mitchell, Michael Vaughan, Geoffrey Boycott, Glenn McGrath, Vic Marks, Ebony Rainford-Brent, Andrew Samson

Last night, to celebrate Steve Smith's third Test match double century, Australia fast bowler Peter Siddle nipped across the road from the team hotel to Sainsburys and bought him a large bar of Dairy Milk chocolate. Smith then had the latest in a series of glorious night's sleeps that he has enjoyed in the UK. Why did he get such a good night? It's because he has discovered an app on his phone that plays the sound of gentle rainwater into his room every night. Did Smith have a good day yesterday? If he's giving relaxed revelations like that to Ellie Oldroyd in the morning, it's fair to say he probably did.

England are in game-saving mode, so – while it's a shame for another sold-out crowd – they are not at all displeased to see the grim conditions that blanket the Greater Manchester area all morning. On *TMS*, Glenn McGrath and Michael Vaughan are looking back at the Old Trafford Test from 2005, where they memorably did battle for a famous draw.

The next entertainment is a superb interview with England and Lancashire legend, and now *Top Gear* frontman, Andrew 'Freddie' Flintoff, who is enjoying a highly successful second career as a TV presenter but still has goals within the game. 'Coaching is definitely an ambition,' he reveals. 'There are probably two or three coaching jobs I'd like – England, Lancashire or the Lancashire Academy. I'd love to be England coach one day, just not quite yet. At the minute I've got quite a bit on but further down the line – you wouldn't believe how much cricket I watch. I'm around it a lot and I really enjoy it.'

Hilariously, he also reveals that he has already applied to the ECB once since retiring. 'A few years ago, I applied for the England coaching job, just before Peter Moores came back. We were getting beat, I was in the office, and I thought, *You know, I'm going to apply!* I wrote an email for the interview, a month passed, and I'd heard nothing. I chased it up and I got a phone call saying we thought it was somebody taking the mick! Further down the line, I'd love to have a go. I've got two of my coaching levels – me and Steve Harmison might do our level threes soon.'

The rain eventually passes, and the players get out on the field for the start of the second session, with Craig Overton falling early to Josh Hazlewood and getting Joe Root out there early in the day. 'This feels like a key phase now,' thinks Aggers. 'He's the one player capable of playing the long, really big innings England require.' Ebony Rainford-Brent agrees, adding, 'England need a couple of centurions.'

The pair start nicely, with an all-run four from Root drawing strong appreciation, and continue with little alarm, facing down some superb Australian bowling. In the box, Jim Maxwell is utterly delighted with a *Shipping Forecast* T-shirt that he has been sent by a very kind listener. It lists all the different destinations that are forecasted for and is a patriotically bright shade of canary yellow. The Australian stashes it neatly away to ensure it is packed for the return trip in a few weeks' time. Maxwell's love for the *Shipping Forecast* is becoming more and more of a theme for the summer; indeed, last week he was asked to try reading one out on the BBC World Service's *Stumped* podcast, a task he performed splendidly.

Burns and Root continue unabated on the field. 'It has been good cricket,' says Vaughan appreciatively. 'Good bowling and good batting,' before he turns his ire on the Old Trafford stewards for spoiling the fun of those in the Party Stand. 'At least let the unicorn watch the cricket,' he pleads. The fact that this line raises no eyebrows at all indicates that summer is nearly over, and it's been one of those Tests!

A second delivery comes into the box shortly afterwards: an incredible cake that is topped with a marzipan version of Michael Vaughan. The cake itself is covered in references to *Test Match Special* and the *Tailenders* podcast, including signs next to Vaughan, asking if his jacket is from River Island or Mango, and the podcast's own hashtag #tailendersoftheworld-uniteandtakeover, alongside a very kind sign that simply says, 'Thank You TMS'.

It is brought into the box by its creator, Julie, who is also wearing one of the most amazing T-shirts seen this summer. On the front it says, 'The Ashes are Alive!', and on the back are more of Aggers' lines from the culmination of Headingley. She is hugely excited to be in the box with the team and everyone is grateful for the cake, which is one of the creations of the season.

Fifty for Burns is acknowledged with what Alison Mitchell calls 'a fairly muted celebration' from the opener, 'but enthusiastic applause around Old Trafford'. As Vic Marks drily adds, 'He's the only opener who has done well this series', and, to complete a triumvirate of compliments, Andrew Samson concludes with, 'All the other openers on both teams average under 11.'

England reach their ton and carry on nicely. Root is hit in the 'bullseye' by Starc and calls a new box out to the middle because the impact has shattered his existing protector. A few nervous looks are exchanged in the commentary box, particularly among those who have had the privilege of facing internationally quick bowling. The next standing ovation comes for the hundred partnership between Burns and Root, and Ebony adds that the crowds this summer have 'been like a 12th man at times – especially at Headingley'.

Throughout the day, the Old Trafford crowd have been cheering Nathan Lyon whenever he receives the ball from one of his team-mates, echoing his missed run-out at the death at Headingley. As Lyon has been bowling for large spells of the afternoon, this has been happening a lot. The crowd's stamina for this gag is remarkable and Lyon's patience is beginning to run thin, so when he accidentally drops a ball that has been gently tossed from mid-on and the crowd explodes, his mood descends from 'impatient' to 'thunderous' quite quickly, as slyly noted by both Australian saboteur Daniel Norcross and the more mild-mannered Vic Marks. Root reaches his fifty and acknowledges it in the same taciturn manner that Burns did earlier. Victor describes him as 'stern-faced' – and it is clear that Root knows there is a lot more work to do.

Australia burn a review, much to the chagrin of Glenn McGrath, who is by no means fully over the reviewing calamities suffered at Headingley and, brilliantly, Maxwell suggests the ICC impose 'a $100 fine for every review you muck up – that goes to the umpires' retirement fund. Too many are unnecessarily reviewed.' As Root rolls around the floor for a bit, having been cracked on the knee, Samson reveals that 'England have been successful with 13 out of 30 reviews in this series. Australia have six out of 25.'

While McGrath gets mixed up between Day 3 and Day 4, Agnew is on the edge of his seat as Cummins continues to steam in for his tenth straight over either side of the tea interval. 'This is compelling viewing,' he says. 'Pat Cummins has bowled absolutely beautifully but got nothing to show for it.'

Cummins is replaced by Hazlewood, and it's the New South Wales seamer who finally does the trick. Burns plays slightly away from his body at one that bounced on him a little bit, gives the nick and Steve Smith gobbles up the catch at slip. 'A very gutsy innings,' says Aggers, as the Surrey captain drags himself off, distraught.

Root's vigil then comes to a close, LBW to Hazlewood, and when the Australian removes Jason Roy's middle stump soon afterwards, England have slipped from the relative comfort of 166 for two to the nerves of 196 for five. Roy gets a serve from Vaughan as he exits, with the former England captain imploring him to play a forward defensive shot to balls like that instead of trying to drive them.

Then, less than ten minutes after Roy's dismissal, the umpires come together and decide that the light has dropped to the extent that that's it for the day. This gives Vaughan a second bite at the cherry as he adds, 'This highlights how bad a shot Jason Roy's was. If you're going to be a Test match cricketer, you've got to have an awareness of the game and what's happening above you.'

A day that looked like it was going to belong firmly to England has skewed back in Australia's favour after the last 40 minutes, but to take it down to another Oval decider, all England need to do is get the draw. The save could still be on. Vaughan isn't convinced, though. 'They say it's grim up north,' he ends. 'It *needs* to be grim up north for England to get out of this one.'

Saturday 7 September
England v Australia – The Ashes – Fourth Test
Match, Day 4
Old Trafford, Manchester

Team *TMS*: Jonathan Agnew, Jim Maxwell, Daniel Norcross,
Alison Mitchell, Michael Vaughan, Geoffrey Boycott, Glenn McGrath,
Vic Marks, Ebony Rainford-Brent, Andrew Samson

There have been plenty of surreal moments this summer, but standing on the outfield with one of Australia's much-trumpeted pace battalion and seeing a genuine look of delight creep across his face when he is presented with a Grimsby Town mug is right up there with the best of them. This has come about because it has been discovered that James Pattinson – who partially grew up in the UK and is the brother of former England seamer Darren – is a big Grimsby Town fan. Despite living on the other side of the planet, he keeps up to date with scores and has fond memories of his dad drinking out of a similar mug (exported to Australia when the family moved out there) for large parts of his childhood.

Interviewed by BBC 5 Live's Ellie Oldroyd, Pattinson talks lucidly about how the family car was broken into the first time he visited Blundell Park, how they used to eat fish 'n' chips from a local spot next to the Cleethorpes pub where his aunt worked, and how his dad only started supporting Australia when he started playing for them. Opening an attached letter from the club, he even tries to pretend they wrote 'Go Aussie Go!' at the bottom, before admitting that was a lie.

Despite a sea of blue sky over Old Trafford, Glenn McGrath says it's a 'perfect day for bowling', with Michael Vaughan not holding out a lot of hope for England's tail on this pitch, who need to produce a further 98 runs to reach a follow-on that Aggers doesn't think Australia will enforce anyway. 'I would have thought that England need to get 150 from the last five wickets,' adds Vic Marks, 'and even then, they'll be batting again tomorrow night. So it's a huge task . . .'

Ben Stokes and Jonny Bairstow start things off for England and Aggers identifies a real sense that 'the crowd believe Stokes could do something extraordinary here'. Nathan Lyon opens up for Australia and immediately receives a loud cheer when he successfully receives the ball from a team-mate, the manner of his taunting now a Barmy Army tradition – much to his evident chagrin. The crowd are further buoyed by a Josh Hazlewood misfield that sees Aggers describe the bowler as 'going down like a collapsing giraffe', but excitement dims when Bairstow is bowled by Mitchell Starc in a dismissal that is very similar to Jason Roy's yesterday, and irritates Vaughan just as much, who laments that Bairstow is getting bowled in Test cricket too often.

Any hopes that are being pegged on Stokes on this occasion go when he edges to slip, where, inevitably, it's Steve Smith who takes the catch, and then Jofra Archer is dismissed, caught behind. Stuart Broad bats for a good amount of time, allowing Jos Buttler the chance to play some shots that drag England closer to the follow-on and a lunchtime total of 278 for eight. As Ebony says, 'The number one objective for England was to get as much time out of the game. They have a chance to just regroup and see how far they can take this.'

The penultimate *View from the Boundary* guest is the Emmy award-winning journalist Jeremy Bowen, who is currently the BBC's Middle East editor but has reported from over 80 countries, including broadcasting from the Balkan Wars of the late 1990s and interviewing figures including Muammar Gaddafi and Bashar al-Assad. He is also a cricket nut and talks happily about his playing days, both in his childhood and as a young journalist, as well as his early love for Brian Close, having watched him stand up to the West Indies at this very ground back in 1976.

As Jeremy and Aggers continue, the number of people in the commentary box grows and grows, as word gets around the Media Centre what a remarkable interview is being conducted. Bowen talks about his experiences as a BBC foreign correspondent for over 30 years, during which he has reported on 'maybe 20 wars'. He tells Aggers about a time when he and his crew were standing in a square in Grozny, the capital city of Chechnya, during the winter of 1994/95. Half of the buildings surrounding them were on fire and, were they not waiting for a colleague, they'd have left the area long before. As they waited, a fleet of Russian planes came over and bombed the square, causing Bowen to curl up in his flak jacket, trying his best to find some cover while thinking he was either going to die or be badly injured.

The feature continues with stories about being driven around Syria by an army officer who was drinking a glass of Johnnie Walker and toting a Kalashnikov, and reporting from Sri Lanka on the Boxing Day tsunami of 2004, during which time he was surreally able to pick up end-of-play summaries from *Test Match Special*, with England in South Africa at the time.

'Does the experience of war teach you something?' asks Aggers.

'Yes,' he replies immediately. 'I'm very conscious that our hold on life is quite tenuous. It doesn't take a lot to extinguish a life. Life is pretty fantastic and sometimes we don't appreciate it quite as much as we ought to.'

Given that he has only recently completed a three-month course of chemotherapy after being diagnosed with bowel cancer, they are strong words. The quality of the interview is another reminder of the incredible breadth of *TMS* – and also a relief, because it could have gone very differently. Twenty minutes before it was due to begin, Daniel Norcross and Henry Moeran were standing next to Aggers at the back of the commentary box, having an obviously loud conversation.

'What do you think *Bullseye* would be like if it was hosted by Jeremy Bowen not Jim Bowen?' asks Norcross. Moeran laughs loudly, before replying, 'I know! Isn't it amazing that they're brothers? You just would never expect that!' Aggers, his attention attracted, quickly turns around and joins in the conversation. 'Is he? Wow! I had no idea!' he says before heading off to research another couple of questions. Norcross and Moeran decide to allow this to continue for around 15 minutes before informing Aggers that he has been the victim of a wind-up and Jeremy and Jim – in very different ways icons of British TV – are no more related than Moira and Alec Stewart.

The game restarts and, powered by Buttler, England avoid any chance of being asked to follow on before quickly getting all out and conceding a lead of 196. The Australia reply gets off to an uproarious start for the Old Trafford crowd as David Warner departs at the end of Stuart Broad's first over for a duck, completing his pair and meaning that Broad has now dismissed Warner six times this series, conceding just 32 runs while doing so. Should *TMS* be on in the Aussie changing room, Warner's mood would surely worsen five minutes later when Andrew Samson pops up to reveal he has become the first Australia opener to record a pair since Mark Taylor in Karachi in 1994 – and the first to do so in the Ashes since Ross Edwards at Headingley way back in 1972.

Broad traps Harris LBW soon afterwards and, as is now

almost traditional in the 2019 Ashes, a side has lost two early wickets. However, as is definitely traditional, Steve Smith arrives and looks utterly invincible. Broad and Archer come in hard but once again are unable to trouble him too much. Labuschagne goes LBW and Archer bowls Travis Head, but so long as Smith is still there, Australia hold all the cards. At 44 for four, England have the merest sniff, but Matthew Wade partners with Smith, adding another 19 before tea, where *TMS* are joined by Olympic bronze medallist, and now the excellent BBC voice of swimming, Steve Parry.

For Ebony Rainford-Brent, the interval is a particularly delicious one, as she spends a great deal of it successfully digging around for brownies underneath Michael Vaughan's bottom. This is brought up when she replaces Vaughan on summary duties during the final session. 'It's good to replace Michael Vaughan,' she says. 'I've just stolen a brownie underneath his bottom.'

'What's that?!' asks a shocked Jim Maxwell.

'You know the cake up there that has a Michael Vaughan on top of it?' replies Ebony, pointing behind them. 'There's one brownie left on top of it and I've just spent ten minutes trying to see if I can get it out from under his bottom. I did it successfully!'

'These are the sort of things you can only say on radio and get away with it, you realise that?' says Maxwell, laughing and slowly shaking his head.

Smith and Wade spend the final session extinguishing any hope England may briefly have held of rolling the Australians cheaply and getting started on the chase. 'There was a moment when we thought Tim Paine wouldn't have to think about a declaration,' remembers Victor, adding that 'Steve Smith is yet again holding the Australia innings together.'

The two continue, with Smith in particular noticeably

upping his scoring rate. As Aggers says, 'England are getting towards damage-limitation territory,' and Vaughan adds, 'Steve Smith has completely frazzled England. They have no idea how to bowl to him.'

Smith continues to accelerate, and this aggression is what accounts for him being dismissed 18 runs short of his hundred, Ben Stokes taking a good catch on the boundary as Smith tries to hit Jack Leach's first ball for a big six. Again, despite the situation in the match, he is clearly livid that he has got out. However, as he leaves the field of play, Andrew Samson reveals that Smith 'now has scored 671 runs in the series at an average of 134.2. He has batted for 26 hours and 15 minutes and faced 998 balls.'

Wade goes next over, very well caught by Bairstow, and Australia eventually declare on 186 for six, leaving England needing 383 to win. To keep the Ashes alive, they need to survive tonight and then bat all day tomorrow. Happily, Andrew Samson is on hand to provide examples of when that last happened.

'The last time England batted out the final day to draw was in Auckland against New Zealand in 2013,' he says. 'They batted 143 overs in total and Matt Prior got a hundred. They also did it twice in South Africa in 2009-10. The last time they did it at home was against India at The Oval in 2007.'

'There is a bank of cloud right in front of the sun, but it is bright behind it,' says Aggers as Rory Burns and Joe Denly come out to start the vigil. 'It is dark. I am glad I am up here and not facing. The umpires are twitchy.'

By the end of Pat Cummins' first over, England have lost two wickets. Burns is caught at mid-off after being turned around by one that might have stuck in the pitch, and Joe Root gets one of the balls of the series that holds its line, nips back and cracks the top of his off stump. Cummins will rarely bowl a better delivery and Aggers is torn between lamenting England's horrendous start and praising the class of the Australian bowler. Jason Roy gets one of the biggest cheers of the day for blocking out the hat-trick ball, and he and Denly successfully see off the rest of the day as England end on 18 for two.

'There was a time in the afternoon when England shifted the momentum,' says Alison Mitchell almost nostalgically, before Vaughan comes in with his latest hammer blow of realism. 'It was a miracle at Headingley and it will take a miracle to survive the draw here,' he says. 'To face that attack on this pitch now for 98 overs it will take an incredible innings.'

At least the equation is simple: England will need to bat all day tomorrow to save the Ashes. The weather forecast is good.

Sunday 8 September
England v Australia – The Ashes – Fourth Test
Match, Day 5
Old Trafford, Manchester

Team *TMS*: Jonathan Agnew, Jim Maxwell, Daniel Norcross, Alison Mitchell, Michael Vaughan, Geoffrey Boycott, Glenn McGrath, Vic Marks, Ebony Rainford-Brent, Andrew Samson

On the morning of Sunday 23 July 2017, *TMS* producer Adam Mountford was getting dressed for a big day at work and decided to wear the Women's Cricket World Cup polo shirt he had been given by the ICC. England won.

On the morning of Sunday 14 July 2019, Mountford was once again making his fashion decisions ahead of a big game, this time the men's World Cup final. Deciding the shirt he wore two years earlier could potentially be 'lucky', he pulled it on. England won.

On the morning of Sunday 25 August 2019, at a hotel in Leeds, Mountford was making the same decision, but it was easier this time. The shirt had now delivered two World Cups to England, so was officially imbued with magical qualities. He pulled it on without a moment's hesitation, aware he was doing his bit. England won.

It is thus that Mountford, a definite spring in his step, walks into the *TMS* commentary box in Old Trafford early on the morning of Sunday 8 September 2019, clad in a Women's World Cup 2017 polo shirt and full of optimism for England to take this Ashes series back to The Oval. 'There's a British, back-to-the-wall spirit at Old Trafford here today. You just never know,' says Aggers, as 'Jerusalem' is pumped out to let everyone know it is time for action and Jason Roy and Joe Denly take their guards.

Up in the box, noted incrementalist Daniel Norcross has decided to count the day down, ball by ball – all 588 of them. He has also enlisted an only relatively willing Mountford in this pursuit. If nothing else, the activity gives the pair something to distract themselves from the overwhelming tension both know will settle in should the game still be going at 4 p.m. and beyond. After the first over, Norcross sidles up behind Mountford and just says, '582.' It's going to be a very long day indeed for the producer and his lucky shirt, especially after Norcross starts associating his numbers with classic innings, such as 501 (Lara, v Durham, June 1994) and 499 (Hanif Mohammad, v Bahawalpur, January 1959).

Norcross gets all the way to 480 (unattributed) before the first heartbreak of the day, as Pat Cummins produces another ball of the very highest quality to slide through Roy's defences and hit the top of his off stump. 'Exceptional' is Glenn McGrath's verdict, while Norcross compliments Roy warmly on the 82 minutes he has survived this morning. The loss of Roy brings Ben Stokes to the crease, thereby increasing the sense of anticipation even more. It's unlikely, but given what he's already done this summer, nobody can object to the heightened sense of expectation that follows the all-rounder at the moment.

However, the air is sucked out of Old Trafford after he has faced just 17 balls. Stokes tries to leave one from Cummins but gets an edge through to Tim Paine. Initially, nobody is sure if it's out or not, but to his immense credit, Stokes knows he's nicked it and immediately walks off. 'It's not often you see a batsman walk,' says Vaughan admiringly. 'Ben Stokes is that kind of player.'

Norcross murmurs '426' (unattributed) to Mountford as he sidles off to get his lunch. Desperate as the producer is for England to take this summer to the best possible denouement, he knows that if it does, it's going to be a long afternoon indeed. Denly starts the second session by bringing up his fifty but struggles to deal with a ball from Nathan Lyon that fires viciously out of the rough and gloves to Marnus Labuschagne at short leg. Norcross mutters '394' (Naved Latif, v Gujranwala, November 2000) before adding, on air, 'This is really England's last partnership of note,' as Jos Buttler walks out to bat.

Predictably, Boycott is unimpressed with England's batting, likening its quality to that of Norcross's shirt, which is a blue number covered in yellow parrots. 'That's harsh,' replies Daniel, accepting the limitations of his shirt more readily than the England line-up.

Jonny Bairstow and Buttler survive until drinks but, first ball after the break, Bairstow is hit on the pads and Australia explode towards the umpire, who gives it out. 'First ball after drinks. You could write a book about how many times that happens,' remarks Maxwell as Bairstow decides to review, to no avail.

Norcross says '311' (Amla, v England, The Oval, July 2012) as Mountford studiously looks at some correspondence and tries to block it all out. England's last partnership of two recognised batsmen has fallen and Craig Overton is heading to the crease. Hopes are not high among the English contingent, but Glenn McGrath in particular seems to be quite rapidly shedding emotional baggage that he has carried since Leeds.

Overton endures a tricky period before being given LBW to Cummins and immediately referring it. It's clear that 'he's smashed it' (McGrath) but, for some reason, to a chorus of boos from the crowd, this doesn't seem to be apparent to the third umpire. 'This could be controversial,' worries Alison Mitchell as the outraged crowd erupts upon hearing the third umpire say he can't see any bat and please proceed to ball tracking. Fortunately for everyone, it turns out to also have been pitching outside leg stump, so the correct decision is reached via incorrect means. 'There was only one person in the ground after seeing the replay who wasn't sure whether that hit the bat, and that was the third umpire,' says McGrath, astonished. Keen as he is to secure the Ashes today, the Australian is confident enough not to need decisions like that.

The two make it to the tea break with 216 (Thorpe, v Somerset, The Oval, August 1992, notes Surrey man Norcross) balls left to be faced to take it to The Oval, but with 184 (Trott, v Pakistan, Lord's, August 2010) balls remaining, Buttler disastrously leaves one from Hazlewood that cuts back and, fatally, hits his stumps.

Nine balls later, Jofra Archer gets a shooter from Lyon that raps him on the boot, and he is stone-dead LBW. There is no point in reviewing and he is sent on his way, cueing the entrance of England's second cult hero, Jack Leach, whose batting endeavours this summer seem to have moved him above Stuart Broad in the pecking order. There are 175 (Gayle, v Pune Warriors, Bangalore, April 2013) balls remaining.

Leach begins confidently, but 'England are on the brink of being on the brink', as Norcross beautifully puts it before handing over to Aggers. The light is definitely fading, but despite repeated entreaties, it seems that for whatever reason the umpires aren't listening to *TMS* and the game carries relentlessly on. As the balls tick down, the crowd gets noisier and noisier. Leach's glasses have never been cleaner and when Cummins 'chirps' Leach, to the huge amusement of Vaughan in particular, it becomes clear that England have successfully got under their opponents' skin. Suddenly, Leach and Overton have been together for an hour, there are fewer than 100 balls remaining, and everyone is believing. Norcross is still counting down individual balls but, to Mountford's relief, has abandoned the individual innings conceit due to surfeit of choice.

The tailenders have seen off all four of Australia's senior bowlers, so Tim Paine decides to try the part-time leg spin of Marnus Labuschagne. 'This is a good move – get the ball spinning back into Jack Leach,' says Vaughan, and he's right; the ploy immediately works as Leach gloves a catch to Matthew Wade at short leg. The ground is silent as Leach walks back, before bursting back into life as Stuart Broad, England's last hope, makes his way out.

In the box, conscious of retaining the tradition of having commentators from the victorious side on the air at the crucial moment, Adam Mountford makes the tough decision to replace Jonathan Agnew with Jim Maxwell. Aware of what is happening, Agnew tells listeners, 'I've just been told I have to go. Don't blame me if England lose!' as he hands the mic to Maxwell.

Then, with emotions at boiling point all across the nation, Hazlewood hits Overton hard on the knee roll. He goes up for the appeal and gets the decision. At 6.14 p.m. on Sunday 8 September 2019, Australia have won the Ashes. But wait – have they? 'Overton is going to review it,' says Jim Maxwell, almost wearily. 'Oh, it's out,' says Geoffrey Boycott, already starting to prepare himself to leave.

As the third umpire talks over the PA system, the replay rolls in front of him and, as Glenn McGrath nervously shifts from foot to foot behind him, Maxwell talks listeners through the dying embers of the match. 'Umpire's call could decide the Ashes here . . .' he begins.

'It's a bit of melodrama here at the end – if it is the end? If it's clipping the bails that'll be enough . . . We're looking at the buttons now and it's out, it's all over! Australia have won this game by 185 runs. They're all hugga mugga out there – delighted to have retained the Ashes, in what has been an extraordinary campaign!' In the height of the moment, nobody has the heart to question the great man about what 'hugga mugga' might mean.

There will be no trophy presentation until The Oval, but nonetheless, with the destination of the urn all wrapped up, there is a post-mortem to be had. 'The best team won. Simple as that,' says Boycott, emphasising the simplicity of his point by adding, 'The best team won the match, the best team won the series.'

Aggers espouses the general view when he admits that 'Australia deserve to win, I don't think anyone can deny that.' But Vaughan gets specific, adding, 'English cricket focused on winning the World Cup, and they delivered that, but it was at the expense of the Test match team. There's no denying that.'

It's been a rollercoaster week in Manchester, and with the Test going down to the final hour of the final day, nobody – commentators and players alike – has much time to put their feet up before The Oval. The urn will be going Down Under, but it's not yet been lost. England's greatest summer of cricket only has five days to go, and they will be played out back where it all began, at The Oval.

Australia 497-8d (126 overs; Smith 211, Labuschagne 67, Paine 58, Starc 54*) and 186-6d (42.5 overs; Smith 82) beat England 301 (107 overs; Burns 81, Root 71, Hazlewood 4-57) and 197 (91.3 overs; Denly 53, Cummins 4-43) by 185 runs.

CHAPTER 20

England Square the Series

Thursday 12 September
England v Australia – The Ashes – Fifth Test
Match, Day 1
The Oval, Kennington, London

Team *TMS*: Jonathan Agnew, Jim Maxwell, Simon Mann, Isa Guha,
Phil Tufnell, Michael Vaughan, Sir Geoffrey Boycott, Glenn McGrath,
Andrew Samson

Recently, there have been a lot of concerns raised about playing Test matches in mid–September. Those who are worried should note this: on Wednesday 8 May a damp *TMS* team were sitting in the commentary box at The Oval, desperately checking weather apps. On Thursday 12 September, each member of the team blinks as they emerge from the London Underground to be greeted by sunshine across south London. There is a bit of cloud around but that is due to move on. A quick check of the same app used in May indicates the situation won't be changing for quite some time.

The destination of the urn may have been decided in Manchester but, as Isa Guha says very early on, 'The Ashes themselves may have gone, but this is still an Ashes Test match.' On the field, Ben Stokes's shoulder injury at Old Trafford means he is playing purely as a batsman, so Sam Curran has been called in for his first Ashes game in place of Jason Roy. Chris Woakes is also back, replacing Craig Overton. Australia are giving Mitchell Marsh his first game of the summer and have brought Peter Siddle back for Mitchell Starc.

Tim Paine wins the toss and, to general surprise, chooses to bowl first. 'That is a big, big call from Paine,' reckons Jim Maxwell. 'I can understand it with the cloud around, but the pitch is dry underneath.' Alec Stewart, a man so associated with The Oval that *TMS* have all walked through gates bearing his name this morning, thinks Paine has misstepped, adding, 'I personally would have batted first, knowing it was going to be difficult first up.' Andrew Samson points out that it is just the fourth time in 19 Tests a team has been put in at The Oval.

Before play starts, *TMS* bears witness to the start of a new Oval tradition as a large bell is rung to mark five minutes before the start of play. It is similar to what happens at Lord's, but the bell, having formerly been hung on the deck of the Royal Navy aircraft carrier HMS *Illustrious*, is huge. The first ringer is 81-year-old Admiral Sir Jock Slater, the original commanding officer of the ship, who says that it is the first time he has seen the bell since he commanded *Illustrious* during the Falklands War.

As expected, early conditions are helpful to the Australia bowlers, but England are able to resist. Rory Burns narrowly overturns an LBW decision and Joe Denly edges to a juggling

Steve Smith at slip, but otherwise the morning session is one of calmness and authority. In the commentary box, Glenn McGrath is upbraided by Simon Mann for saying that he's 'not being biased now but I'd say that 3–1 would be a fair reflection of the series'. Mann looks him up and down and, with just a hint of a headmasterly tone, informs him he 'can't not be biased'.

Drinks arrive on the field and there is a most welcome interjection in the back of the box from two lifeboatmen representing the Royal National Lifeboat Institution. Not only are they impressed by Jim Maxwell's sterling promotional work on behalf of the *Shipping Forecast*, they also bring with them a wonderful RNLI cake. They are joined by Admiral Sir Jock, he of the earlier bell ring, who turns out to also have been the chairman of the RNLI for many years.

Siddle, who has bowled poorly when called upon so far, compounds his forgettable morning by dropping an easy chance offered by Joe Root, and the England captain gets another life when Paine drops a diving catch that also sees him almost punch David Warner in the head and hit the ball into Smith's face.

'Australia have got the dropsies,' says an aggrieved Maxwell, who, despite the on-field malpractice, is still wonderfully relaxed. This is because he and the team are joined by his wife Jen for the duration of this match. She is very comfortable watching the cricket, knitting and socialising – and is hugely looking forward to their post-Ashes holiday, where they are heading to the Faroe Islands for some open-water swimming.

JIM MAXWELL'S CHICKEN CURRY RECIPE

On a number of occasions over the summer, Australia's voice of cricket, Jim Maxwell, discussed the qualities of his homemade chicken curry – a staple of his diet back home in Sydney. Below, straight from the man himself, is the recipe and technique to follow along with at home.

Ingredients:

Portion of chicken thighs (skinned)	Onions
Cardamom	Garlic
Cumin	Olive oil
Turmeric	½ pint/285ml chicken stock
Dry chillies	Rice
Soy sauce	Lime leaves
Ginger	Lemon or lime juice
	Bay leaves

To serve:

Poppadums	Mango chutney
Naan bread	Yoghurt
Lime pickle	Saffron (optional)

Method:

Take the cardamom, cumin, turmeric and dry chillies and grind them in a bowl. When complete, tip them into a separate bowl, add a couple of squeezes of lemon or lime juice and the soy sauce. Mix together. Put the skinned chicken thighs in the bowl and marinade overnight in the fridge.

The next day, chop up the ginger, onions and garlic and put them in a heated pan with a dash of olive oil. Add the marinated chicken and run it around for a little while.

Add the chicken stock to half a litre of boiled water. When ready, throw the chicken into the mix, also adding the lime leaves and bay leaves. Bring it to the boil and then leave for an hour while it simmers.

Wash the rice and bring a pan of water to the boil. Add the rice to the water, stir with a teaspoon and boil for 12 mins. The teaspoon is key as it stops the rice sticking. You could add saffron to the mix, but Jim has it straight.

Remove the chicken from the other pot and serve. Get the lime pickle, mango chutney and yoghurt out separately with a few poppadums and naan breads and, if available, serve it up alongside a couple of Crown lagers.

Lunchtime comes with England 86 for one and the newly knighted Sir Geoffrey Boycott is delighted. 'England couldn't wish for anything better than being 86 for one at lunch after being put in,' he says. 'Those dropped chances don't matter.'

This is England's final Test in the Trevor Bayliss era, and lunchtime sees the final *TMS* interview with the inscrutable Australian. Oftentimes when a coach knows they're leaving, their last interview with an old interrogator is the time for some light-hearted revelations or old stories. For Bayliss it's nothing of the sort. While always friendly, polite and honest, he remains taciturn to the last, keen to give his successor the best chance to impose their ideas without him looking over their shoulder.

'That would have been an interesting lunch break,' says Tuffers as he opens up the afternoon session in the summariser's chair. 'The fast bowlers looking at the captain and going, "Skip, did you mean to win the toss and bowl?"' Root is then dropped for a third time, again by Smith, and England continue on. After all his lives, Root brings up a significant career landmark with a four off Josh Hazlewood, taking him to exactly 7,000 Test runs. 'He's the 12th Englishman to get there and third youngest overall – only Alastair Cook and Sachin Tendulkar were younger,' remarks Samson, providing interesting context to a fine achievement.

Following an emotional treatise from Tuffers on how the Oval Test always makes him sad because it forces him to realise that summer is coming to an end – possibly fuelled by childhood memories of coming to the ground with his dad, who always slightly worried that the game in question might be the last he'd ever see – the conversation between him and Simon turns to the unusual sense of relaxation that is being engendered by the quality of this partnership and the security with which the two are batting.

There has been much discussion of the 'commentator's curse' this season and this instance is a real doozy. As the conversation about the pair's qualities continues, Josh Hazlewood comes in with his characteristic vigour and bowls to Burns, who attempts a pull shot, gets it all wrong, and splices the easiest of catches to Marsh at mid-on. Tuffers and Simon are mortified, exchanging wide-eyed looks like a pair of naughty schoolboys. 'Are we that powerful?!' wonders Tufnell. 'Sorry, Rory …'

Then, after a couple of glorious shots have the sold-out crowd *ooh*ing and *aah*ing, new man Stokes falls in not dissimilar fashion, miscuing a pull to point where Nathan Lyon gratefully accepts the chance. 'England have got to be careful here that they don't let Tim Paine off the hook,' warns Vaughan. 'They should be making 350-plus.'

Root's fifty ('He's 50 for three!' cackles Tuffers) comes up and Jonny Bairstow becomes the second landmark hitter of the day when he tucks one through midwicket to score his 4,000th Test run – the 34th England player to do so, according to Samson. As the two Yorkshiremen continue to advance England's cause, the time comes for Isa Guha to hand the microphone over to Simon Mann. Normally such a transfer is done with no fervour whatsoever. However, on this occasion, shortly before the mic is passed, Isa observes that she thinks Simon looks a little bit Hollywood star Harrison Ford! It's fair to say that the observation is not shared by Isa's colleagues, or indeed the *TMS* inbox, and when Simon later discovers that Harrison Ford is now 77, he is further aggrieved by her suggestion.

Teatime sees a guest appearance by former BBC *Breakfast* host Bill Turnbull and then the final session begins with Aggers convinced that 'These two look like they're wanting to dig in and bat a long time.' That may well be their desire, but it's not the reality as Root has his timbers rearranged by a jubilant Pat Cummins and Bairstow is quickly LBW to Marsh.

'The Duke's ball has been the player of the series. It's just never out of the game,' says Maxwell. Curran hooks Cummins for six but is LBW later in the over, before becoming the latest batsman to benefit from a late recall due to an overstep. Such is the look on Cummins' face that, even sitting four flights up behind a pane of thick glass, Tuffers is still nervous about facing the next delivery.

The all-rounder doesn't last much longer, as Marsh has him caught at slip and then follows up by trapping Woakes LBW soon afterwards and, again, England have officially collapsed – this time from 170 for three to 205 for seven. Woakes does not refer the decision and McGrath thinks 'that was missing off and leg stump', before seeing the replay rolled. 'Ah. Okay. Leg stump in the end. But still very, very out,' he concludes.

Hazlewood removes Jofra Archer after some brief resistance, causing Jos Buttler to enter what Maxwell calls 'full one-day mode'. He slaps Hazlewood for back-to-back sixes and then reaches his first Ashes half-century of the summer by clobbering the same bowler over the leg side. 'He could really hurt Australia if he keeps going here,' notes Tuffers, who is enjoying the flashback to Buttler's early-summer brilliance.

As ever, Jack Leach is superb at the other end, delighting the crowd and enraging the Australians in equal measure with the production of his patented glasses cloth and playing the perfect foil as the two add 45 in the London gloaming before gratefully walking off, shortly after the new ball is produced by Australia, with England on 271 for eight.

At the close, Simon Mann shows once again how he is the favourite commentator for time-poor listeners by nailing the entire day in 25 words. 'England did well for half a day. Collapsed. But then have recovered again thanks to Jos Buttler, with Jack Leach playing a determined supporting role.'

Vaughan goes over his familiar concerns about the lack of 'Test-style players' in this England team, but it's actually McGrath who lands the biggest punch at the end of play, accusing the Australians of inconsistency and adding that 'If they bowled like they did at Old Trafford, England would be all out and Australia would be batting by now.' As it is, the Test is beautifully poised, with England very much still in with a chance of drawing the Ashes.

Friday 13 September
England v Australia – The Ashes – Fifth Test
Match, Day 2
The Oval, Kennington, London

Team *TMS*: Jonathan Agnew, Jim Maxwell, Simon Mann, Isa Guha, Phil Tufnell, Michael Vaughan, Sir Geoffrey Boycott, Glenn McGrath, Andrew Samson

While *TMS* have enjoyed a quiet night back at the London billet, it seems like it hasn't been that straightforward for everyone else, as the team arrive at The Oval to be greeted by the news that Joe Denly has rushed off home overnight to attend the birth of his second child. The batsman is planning on returning to the fold this afternoon, but it is nonetheless a dramatic and happy development. Surprisingly, he actually has form in this, after retiring from an innings he was playing for Kent in 2016 in order to try to be at the birth of his first child, which he missed by five minutes.

Back at The Oval, *TMS* are joined by Surrey CCC Chairman Richard Thompson before play to discuss the development of the club's splendid ground and preparations for next year's Hundred competition. Simon Mann even manages to secure the exclusive announcement that Australian coach Tom Moody will lead the Oval-based team next summer.

Jos Buttler and Jack Leach start nicely, with Andrew Samson statistically proving Leach's value to the England batting cause as he reveals that 'Jack Leach's average is 21 but England now average 58 runs per dismissal while he is at the crease'. Pat Cummins bowls Buttler and, when Mitchell Marsh finally prises Leach from the crease, England are all out for 294, a good 106 less than the minimum everyone was calling for yesterday.

Nonetheless, David Warner obligingly edges one from Jofra Archer behind in the second over and, when Archer then follows up with the wicket of Marcus Harris, caught by Ben Stokes at slip, Australia are 14 for two and once again it's England v Steve Smith and Marnus Labuschagne. Aggers, whipping out his crystal ball, is convinced that Sam Curran – playing his first Ashes Test of the summer – is the man for the occasion. 'Smith lbw b Curran. It'll be before lunch,' he predicts, with 37 minutes for his tea leaves to be proved correct.

It initially looks unpromising, but then Curran loops one back into Smith's pads and goes up for a big appeal. It is turned down and, after some hard conversations out in the middle, England decide against reviewing it. Tuffers correctly diagnoses that it's going just over before Smith shoulders arms to another and is whacked in front. Again, a short conversation decides not to appeal, correctly, but there is suddenly a buzz around The Oval. Could England have found the man to somehow trouble Smith?

After a lovely lunchtime interview with former BBC royal correspondent Jennie Bond, the battle resumes. Readers of the BBC Sport live text commentary service have nicknamed the Australian pair Death and Taxes, such is their seemingly constant presence. On balance, it is agreed that Smith should be Death, because he is always there at the end. 'Surely Smith's not going to get another ton, is he?' asks Simon Mann unconvincingly. 'If he's still there at tea, he'll get a century,' replies Michael Vaughan, taking a slightly more realistic look at the situation that is currently facing England at the Vauxhall End, and fidgeting annoyingly.

Denly returns to the field, receiving warm greetings from his team-mates, and his presence inspires the breakthrough as Archer has Labuschagne LBW for 48, allowing England – under the assumption that Smith is going nowhere – a new batsman to target at the other end.

While Smith may not be conventionally dismissible, it's still good to have fun with him, as two incidents this afternoon demonstrate. Firstly, Alec Stewart, working for BBC 5 Live next door, brings two unusual guests into the back of the commentary box. Although Stewart – as previously stated – is King of The Oval, eyebrows are raised when he is seen being accompanied around the place by two uniformed police officers. Fortunately, it turns out they are Oval regulars, and had bumped into Stewie outside, who had kindly offered them a tour of the Media Centre.

It's fair to say that Isa Guha and Glenn McGrath, on air at the time, were a little surprised to feel the long arm of the law on their shoulder as they commentated on England trying to get among Matthew Wade early on – but the true winner in the whole situation is producer and pun master Adam Mountford, who suggested that seeing as England have been unable to all summer, perhaps the officers could 'nick' Steve Smith. Sadly, the policemen were more interested in having their photo taken with Phil Tufnell, which is understandable.

The other incident takes place out on the field, with Jonny Bairstow providing one of the great moments of the series. Wade hits the ball down the ground to Leach, who returns the ball with interest to the bowler's end. Smith is running towards the batsman's end, his back to the throw, and Bairstow – through a combination of an artful shout and good command of the art of mime – is able to convince him that he's in trouble, forcing Smith into a desperate full-length dive. The crowd erupts in cheers, the commentary box finds the whole thing hilarious and, after a few seconds, Smith also starts to see the funny side.

'Bairstow has absolutely done Smith there. I like that. Smith is covered in dust,' says a giggling Aggers, before Smith, inevitably, has the last laugh as he dashes another one off his pads for a four 'like he was swatting a fly', according to (Sir) Geoffrey. Curran then accounts for his first Australian of the summer, getting Wade LBW on review. 'It was only clipping,' remarks McGrath, before being upbraided by Simon Mann, who reminds him that 'That's the same as hitting.'

Smith then 'clonks Leach over Cow Corner' (Jim Maxwell) for six to bring up his tenth consecutive Ashes half-century, causing Tuffers to reach for pen and paper. A little-known fact about The Cat is that, in one of his many guises, he is an artist who has sold paintings for not insubstantial amounts. On this occasion, though, he decides to go more diagrammatical, penning something that resembles Leonardo da Vinci, demonstrating his theories on how to get Smith out. It's a beautiful thing but isn't easily understood by the rest of the team. 'We could have an ice age and, after it thawed, Steve Smith would still be at the crease,' says a diagram-toting Tufnell as the teams emerge for the final session of the day – one he describes as 'a game breaker'.

England have first joy, Marsh gifting a soft dismissal to Archer, before what seems like the entirety of south London explodes as Smith nicks a tricky chance to Joe Root at slip. Root gets a hand to it but cannot cling on. Curran – and 24,000 people inside The Oval – are already celebrating, as is Tuffers, who almost falls off his chair and is clinging onto the desk in front of him for stability as he shouts 'NO!' repeatedly.

Curran keeps coming, though, and gets his reward and then some when Tim Paine nicks a full delivery to Bairstow and then Cummins is LBW first ball to the perfect left-armer's delivery that swings back into the pads and hits the Australian plumb in front. Cummins reviews it, but when Maxwell has to use the word 'very' three times to describe how hopeful it is, the picture is clear. A well-directed fast yorker comes in as the hat-trick ball, which Peter Siddle is just able to jam his bat down on and edge past the slips for four, as Geoffrey muses that 'England have to find a way to get Sam Curran in their Test side more.'

Drinks are taken, Chris Woakes is brought into the attack and the seamer drifts onto what, to Smith, is a slightly straight line. However, to gasps around the ground, the Aussie misses a seemingly regulation flick into the leg side and is hit in front. The umpire's finger is slowly raised and Smith has to go, knowing there is no point in a review. 'I cannot believe what we have just witnessed. Steve Smith has missed one on his pads,' says a visibly shell-shocked Isa. 'It was an innocuous delivery!'

Sitting next to her, McGrath is equally shocked. 'Well then, he is human!' he declares, before exhibiting the sympathetic side to his character and adding, 'I feel for Simon Mann – he really wanted that wicket.' Smith was out for his lowest score of the series (80) and Andrew Samson doesn't waste time in coming to the party with the full stats. 'Steve Smith has now scored 751 runs at an average of 125.16,' he says. 'He has batted for 1,854 minutes, just short of 31 hours.' When contextualising this, it's important to remember that Smith missed the entire Headingley Test and the second innings at Lord's.

After some brief wagging, Archer records his second Test five-wicket haul by bowling Nathan Lyon, and the innings ends soon afterwards with Rory Burns taking one of the catches of the series, diving low to his right and grabbing the ball inches off the turf to get rid of Siddle and leave Australia 225 all out. Tuffers explodes with excitement on air, likening it to Ben Stokes's memorable effort at Trent Bridge in 2015, and Archer walks off with six wickets in the innings, holding the ball aloft to an adoring Oval crowd.

As Burns and Denly walk out, there's some talk about what total England require to make the game safe, but their primary motivation is simply surviving the 20 minutes until close. This they do successfully, despite Denly being dropped by Harris at gully and Burns being hit early on and then receiving a barrage from Cummins.

A roar of anticipation greets the final ball, which sees Burns given LBW. However, the opener immediately refers it and it's quickly clear that the delivery pitched outside leg stump. The decision is overturned, generating a different kind of roar and England end the day on 9 for no wicket. They will come back tomorrow looking to create a winning position that could see them secure a drawn Ashes and a successful end to the summer.

Saturday 14 September
England v Australia – The Ashes – Fifth Test
Match, Day 3
The Oval, Kennington, London

Team *TMS*: Jonathan Agnew, Jim Maxwell, Simon Mann, Isa Guha, Phil Tufnell, Michael Vaughan, Sir Geoffrey Boycott, Glenn McGrath, Andrew Samson

The sun continues to shine on south London, and confidence and positivity are the themes of the morning as everyone prepares for play beneath the famous old Kennington gasholders. 'If England bat all of today, I think they will win the Test match quite convincingly,' says Michael Vaughan, changing his tune from recent times where he has been one of England's chief critics. He's not entirely convinced, though, adding, 'But, as we have seen, don't rule out 50 for five!' Alec Stewart is even more certain, saying, 'If England are batting at 6.30 p.m., I am convinced they will win this game.'

Rory Burns and Joe Denly continue the good vibes into the morning session, putting away the bad balls with some panache and offering very little in the way of chances from the good ones, with Denly bringing back memories of Jason Roy in the World Cup semi-final by lofting Nathan Lyon for six in the spinner's first over of the morning.

'Merely a checked drive,' says an excited Isa Guha, who is spending the day between the *TMS* box and a hospitality box just down the corridor where the England women's team of 2009, who won both the World T20 and the Ashes, are having a ten-year reunion celebration. *TMS*'s Ebony Rainford-Brent is very much part of the festivities, to the extent that she has decided to stay well away from the airwaves today.

While Andrew Samson tends to specialise in statistics that astonish the listener by dint of wondering how on earth he could access such complex information so quickly, this morning he makes jaws drop in a very different way, purely by pointing out that when Burns and Denly's partnership reaches 33, it is the highest opening stand of the English Test summer, surpassing William Porterfield and James McCollum's 32 for Ireland at Lord's.

Burns brings up the fifty partnership, Samson returning to form with the revelation that it snaps a run of '15 innings without a fifty opening stand – the longest run in England's history' – but when Lyon bowls one of the ranker balls of what has been a poor morning for Australia, he tries to cart it for four and gets an under edge through to Tim Paine. 'What a way to get out on a sunny Saturday on your home ground,' says Simon Mann mournfully as Burns troops off, head bowed. Sad as Burns will be by his dismissal, his record for the series will hopefully raise his spirits eventually. The 390 runs he has scored, at an average of 39, is the most runs by an England opener (other than Sir Alastair Cook) since Andrew Strauss got 474 in the 2009 Ashes, ten years ago.

Joe Root comes to the crease and – after a slightly unsavoury incident with Matthew Wade, which causes the umpires to step in and have a word with the Australian – picks up where Burns left off. Vaughan says he looks like he wants to play a 'busy' innings and he appears to be enjoying himself in the middle, no less than when a smile dances across his face after Denly goes down following a 'bullseye' strike not dissimilar to the one Root himself suffered at Old Trafford and requires a fresh box.

A buoyant Tuffers comes on air, convinced England will win, and adding, 'Retain the Ashes, jolly good, whatever. But 2-2 is a draw. You ain't won the Ashes then!' Simon Mann is not convinced, pointing out that Australia will still retain the urn and will do so until England win a series, but the ensuing debate shows that neither Simon nor Tuffers is down on energy at the end of a long season. The debate is then neatly entered by Samson, who says that 'If the series does finish 2-2, Australia are way ahead on the boundary count.'

Root's eventful knock comes to an end just before lunch, edging Lyon to slip, and England hit lunch at 88 for two. The interval is notable firstly for the arrival of Daniel Norcross on air for the first time this Test, and secondly for the last *View from the Boundary* guest of the summer, the actor Toby

Jones. Toby is known for his variety of roles, which included BAFTA-nominated turns in *Detectorists* and *Marvellous*, as well as more high-profile parts in films like *Jurassic World: Fallen Kingdom*, *The Hunger Games* and a number of films in the Marvel Cinematic Universe.

While interviews more commonly reveal fascinating intricacies in their subject, this one actually begins with the interviewer (Daniel Norcross) gloriously admitting that the reason he is a cricket commentator is because he gave up his previous career, 'because I got sick of inventing meetings that didn't exist just so that I could go and watch a Test.' Dan talks to Toby at length about his deep love for the game of cricket, born both from an experience of watching the West Indies play England at The Oval in 1976 and a career playing halcyon village matches in a beautiful part of Oxfordshire.

He also discusses the brilliant breadth of career he has been able to achieve, describing how taking roles in huge Hollywood films, rather than being the goal of his career, is something that actually allows him complete freedom to take parts in a wide range of mediums, including radio plays, stage work and television. The actor also talks about how, recently, for the first time, his work has brought him into contact with his cricketing passion, as he provided the narration for *The Edge*, a documentary about the England cricket team of eight to ten years ago that has already featured once on *TMS* this summer and has a soundtrack composed and performed by 'Tailender' Felix White.

Speaking of Felix, he is a welcome sight in the box today as *Test Match Special* are visited by his fellow Tailender 'Mattchin Tendulkar' for the first time. It's an exciting meeting for both parties, as commentators who have loved the podcast all summer enjoy the chance to meet Mattchin and he gets to see the programme in action for the first time. A particular friendship is struck up between Jen Maxwell and Mattchin, who is very impressed at the knitted codpiece she appears to be creating.

On the field, for a long period after lunch, Denly and Ben Stokes produce what Jim Maxwell wonderfully terms 'pretty tranquil cricket'. The two bat together in a cohesive manner that has rarely been seen this summer, only pausing to see Smith drop a regulation chance from Stokes off Lyon and then Denly clipping one off his legs to the boundary to bring up his fifty. 'He averages 15 in the first innings and 41.28 in the second,' says Samson, once again bringing a thought-provoking fact to the table.

As the two progress, there is an unexpected and welcome reunion in the commentary box when listener Jason Stocks arrives with Eoin Morgan and Kane Williamson. Sadly, though, Morgan's head has fallen off and is lying on the ground next to his right boot. Before rumours start, there has been no *Game of Thrones*-style medieval retribution for England's World Cup triumph; these versions of the England and New Zealand World Cup captains are only inches tall and were last seen atop the wonderful cake that was presented to *TMS* by HRH the Duchess of Cornwall at the World Cup final.

Celebrating after England's dramatic victory, Jason had attended numerous after-parties and found himself, in the early hours of the morning, with a pizza in one hand and a beer in the other. Seeing these two fabulous figures unattended and seemingly without an owner, he slid them into his pocket and walked around with them, showing them off for the rest of the evening. The following morning, Jason went straight to his office, allegedly fresh as a daisy. He installed the figures as features on his desk until, a few days later, he received an email from a colleague pointing out from whom he had, unknowingly, purloined them. While on holiday later in the summer, he tuned into the Lord's Test match and heard a desperate plea for their return from Aggers. Knowing he had secured Oval tickets, a plan was formed and here he is today.

Denly and Stokes continue on, with Tuffers accusing Denly in particular of batting for an extended period purely to avoid changing nappies, and England reach tea at 193 for two. 'You feel this is potentially a winning position,' suggests Simon. *TMS* mark the interval with a chat to Cricket Australia chief executive Kevin Roberts, who tells Aggers that, 'if you boo David Warner, you don't understand the mind of a champion'.

Stokes is bowled soon after tea, with Lyon getting one to turn an appreciable amount. 'It's seen the back of Stokes, but England won't mind seeing that,' reckons Agnew, knowing that Australia have to bat last. Heartbreakingly, Denly then does have to go and change nappies, being caught by Smith at slip for 94, and England, while still firmly in control, are now 222 for four.

Sam Curran comes and goes relatively quickly, but England continue to go aggressively, with Buttler playing another impressive knock that suggests he has found his red-ball form just in time for the end of the series. 'Everything about Jos Buttler's play this week has looked more balanced,' says Vaughan. 'He just looks to have much more time. He needs to write down everything he has done in this Test and try to replicate it.'

There is still time for another piece of brilliance from Smith, though, as Chris Woakes gets a thick edge off Mitchell Marsh and the Australian propels himself violently to his left and takes a one-handed catch at full length, his arms and legs fully extended to the point where he looks like an extremely athletic, white starfish. A further demonstration of its quality is the five 'wows' that Tuffers needs to get through before he is able to start describing the moment. 'There are not many better catches than that,' underlines Aggers later on.

The theory that Marnus Labuschagne is an attempt by the Australians to engineer a Smith clone then gets another outing as he takes a blinder at the start of the next over to get rid of Buttler, throwing himself full length in the deep to take the catch low to the ground in front of him. Jack Leach comes to the crease to a massive ovation and prevents the team hat trick by gently blocking his first ball back down the pitch, and there is a real end-of-term atmosphere at The Oval, as the crowd rises to its feet to sing repeated choruses of 'Stand Up If You Love Jack Leach'.

The final highlight of the evening is Leach wheeling out a wonderful on-drive to hit a decidedly displeased Pat Cummins for three, and when Jofra Archer blocks out the final ball of the day, England have achieved the challenge set for them by Vaughan and Stewart and successfully batted through an entire day, generating a lead of 382 as the stumps are pulled from the ground.

While Vaughan points to the outrageous events that have dotted this extraordinary summer, and McGrath reflects on a poor decision at the toss and the puzzling inclusion of Peter Siddle over Mitchell Starc, the day's final word goes to Stewart, the hometown hero, who says, conclusively, 'I'll give Australia a one per cent chance of winning this match.'

Sunday 14 September
England v Australia – The Ashes – Fifth Test
Match, Day 4
The Oval, Kennington, London

Team *TMS*: Jonathan Agnew, Jim Maxwell, Simon Mann, Isa Guha,
Phil Tufnell, Michael Vaughan, Sir Geoffrey Boycott, Glenn McGrath,
Andrew Samson

'Til we have built Jerusalem – in England's green and pleasant lands . . .

'I love Sunday crowds. They're just a bit different,' says Jonathan Agnew as the final strains of the William Blake anthem ring out across The Oval and two of England's biggest successes of the summer, Jofra Archer and Jack Leach, take to the field with the adulation of a nation ringing in their ears. After Jofra's heroics in the World Cup and Leach's unlikely success with the bat, the pair have both been vaulted from relative obscurity to become cult heroes across the nation, and it feels somehow appropriate that what could be the final day of the summer begins with the pair together at the crease.

It's not for long, though, as Archer is quickly caught down the leg side off Pat Cummins. Stuart Broad then provides a sold-out crowd with a very entertaining ten-minute spell as he rolls back the clock to blast two big sixes – one of which 'was like someone hacking a tree down', according to Aggers – and causes Tim Paine to install Steve Smith at backstop, which is not a position that many of the team have seen used at Test level for some time. However, Leach then top-edges Nathan Lyon and the fun is over. England have set Australia 399 to win the match and take home the Ashes 3–1. Anything less will see an England win and a final series result of 2–2. Given the time left in the game and the near-perfect weather forecast, a draw can now basically be ruled out.

The atmosphere can be cut with a knife as Broad takes the ball in his hand and stares down David Warner at the other end. 'Is this the day Dave Warner scores all of his runs for the series?'

asks Glenn McGrath hopefully. 'Today might be the day he gets a massive hundred.'

Warner and Marcus Harris stay together for five overs, which incredibly is long enough for them to form their highest opening partnership of the series, 18 runs, before Harris is bowled by Broad, his off stump charismatically cartwheeling back in a way that is seen far less frequently than it once was. 'Comprehensively castled,' says Simon Mann satisfyingly, before McGrath adds that 'There is no better feeling as a bowler than when you rip out that off stump.'

An already charged crowd then explode when Warner goes for the final time this summer, inevitably falling victim to Broad, who has utterly tormented him throughout the Ashes. A loose drive is taken by Rory Burns at third slip, giving Broad his seventh dismissal of Warner in ten innings. The polarising Australian ends the series with an average of 9.5 – and Broad with figures of seven for 35 against the opener.

As before, 'Death and Taxes' (Steve Smith and Marnus Labuschagne) are at the crease, and with the two trying assert a bit of grip to the Australia innings, conversation in the box turns to any impending Hollywood adaptation of *TMS* that might be made, and what the casting process would be. Tuffers wasn't happy with being assigned Martin Clunes, but has accepted Nicholas Lyndhurst; Aggers is settled with comedy veteran Tim McInnerny; and Alec Stewart has been told that under no circumstances is he allowed Daniel Craig. Ellie Oldroyd is immensely offended when it is suggested that she could be played by Dame Judi Dench, but slightly mollified when the thought is clarified to a 'young' Judi Dench; and an ebullient Henry Moeran happily takes either Hugh Grant or Matt Smith, both of which are suggested as options for him.

However, far earlier than expected, Taxes' (Labuschagne) series is ended by a combination of Leach and Jonny Bairstow, as he comes too far forward, misses the ball and is stumped. He has scored just 14 and his removal immediately triggers a thousand conversations about whether England might just be able to win this today. The dismissal is particularly pleasing for Andrew Samson, who quickly points out that Labuschagne has just become the 100th Australian to be stumped in an Ashes Test match.

Matthew Wade is the new man and, alongside Smith, sees Australia safely to lunch. 'England know if they get Steve Smith out in the afternoon then this will finish quite quickly today,' says Michael Vaughan as the final journalist panel of the summer gets into position. 'Smith is the one player who could take this into tomorrow.'

Proceedings resume after lunch before, shortly after 2 p.m. on Sunday 14 September, England finally dismiss Steven Peter Devereux Smith for less than 50. A plan is put in place, with England's premier catcher Ben Stokes sent to field at quite a square leg slip. Broad bowls a slightly straighter line, tucking Smith up slightly and, with a little extra bounce for good measure, he shovels it towards Stokes, who takes a good diving catch away to his right.

As Smith leaves the field for the final time, the contrast with his first arrival at Edgbaston could not be starker. Every man, woman and child in The Oval rises to their feet to applaud the final act of a summer of such extraordinary dominance that it may never be seen again, creating quite an emotional moment. Any boos that might be expressed are quickly shut down as Smith's disappointed last walk is soundtracked by pure, hard-earned respect. 'Well played, Steve Smith,' says Tuffers warmly. 'It's been something to behold this summer, a joy!'

The new man, Mitch Marsh, doesn't seem long for this world, as he's caught by Rory Burns at slip, but he becomes the latest resurrection by posthumous no-ball as it turns out

Chris Woakes has overstepped. Samson later reveals that the no-ball is Woakes's first ever in Test cricket, after more than 5,000 deliveries.

Yesterday, when Wade was fielding close in at short leg, there was clearly a degree of unhappiness at some of the 'sledging' that was taking place, so, when Archer is brought on to bowl at him and immediately produces an aggressive bouncer that hits Wade hard on the back, a different kind of buzz enters the commentary box. 'Jofra Archer clearly relishes bowling at Matthew Wade,' says Simon Mann, as the pace moves up into the 90mph category later in the spell and the aggression levels stay high.

While the Archer spell may be tantalising the crowd, it's the part-time spin of Joe Root that gets the breakthrough, as Marsh knocks one straight to Jos Buttler at short leg. 'Marsh will be cranky with himself for getting out in that manner,' suggests Jim Maxwell, who actually sounds slightly cranky himself. Tea is reached with Australia 167 for five and there are more conversations – described by Vaughan as 'a lot of chirp' – between the England players, particularly Stokes, and Wade as he walks off.

TMS: THE OPERA

More normally known as a spoken-word programme, the undisputed highlight of the tea interval on Day 4 at The Oval is the world premiere of the opening chorus of *TMS: The Opera*. This wonderful tribute to the programme was written on a canal boat earlier in this summer before being recorded by a choir at Asheville College in Harrogate. The Wilby sisters, who composed it, also very kindly sent in the music, which is being published for the first time in this book.

Full Tosca (TMS: The Opera)
Opening Chorus

Anna and Sarah Wilby

After the break, Archer continues in his previous vein to Wade, firing up two more terrific bouncers that are well ducked, before following on down the wicket and engaging in a very long stare-down with the Australian. The tension is highlighted by the crowd's engagement in the conflict and the umpires get Archer and Tim Paine (now batting alongside Wade) together, with Vaughan describing it as 'like they were in the naughty corner'.

Paine is then dismissed by Leach, appropriately ending his series with a failed review, before Archer v Wade resumes, with more bouncers and intense stare-downs. 'Don't forget these two are team-mates in the Big Bash,' adds Vaughan, who is loving every minute of it. 'There were a few whispers at Old Trafford that Jofra Archer is moving to the Adelaide Strikers. I don't think Matthew Wade is impressed.'

Archer continues for an eighth straight over, throwing everything he's got at Wade, with a 91.2mph yorker almost doing the job and Burns nearly taking a spectacular catch at gully. With the Australian on 96, though, Archer is withdrawn, and Glenn McGrath, taking the role of judge, says, 'It was a good contest. Give the points to Wade. He is still there.'

Similarly to Burns earlier in the series, Wade goes through a number of serious scares in the late 90s but eventually reaches a well-earned century, vaulting the stumps – 'almost like Michelangelo the streaker at Lord's', according to Aggers – during a passionate celebration before surviving both a missed stumping and dropped catch. The partnership between Wade and Cummins is ended by Broad, Cummins caught behind going for the big drive, and the conversations about a potential finish tonight move into the next gear, with Tuffers calling for the application of Leach to remove the final three wickets – and immediately getting his way.

It's the other spinner who gets his man, though, as Root

tempts Wade down the pitch before beating him with some Day 4 turn and bounce. This time, Bairstow does complete the stumping and, with Wade gone, the chances of England securing a win before close increase again. 'Now the game is going towards the end,' admits Jim Maxwell, 'you would think Australia are just about resigned to their position.' Not even Maxwell can predict how quickly the end eventually comes, though, Leach taking two in two balls to finish the match, tie the Ashes and draw the summer to a close. Both are caught by Root – the first at square leg, where he is perfectly picked out by Lyon, and the second, brilliantly, at mid-wicket, where he dives low to take Josh Hazlewood with his left hand.

'It's somehow fitting that this summer should end with a moment of brilliance like that!' shouts Aggers as The Oval erupts around him, hands are shaken, deep breaths exhaled, and friendly smiles exchanged. The Ashes is over, England have won the Test and secured the drawn series they were desperately hoping for. In a summer that has rewritten the record books many times over, it is the first drawn Ashes series in 47 years. 'It is probably a fitting result,' thinks McGrath. 'Some will say Australia played better, but England just found a way to hang on.'

Jonathan Agnew leaves the commentary box for one final time this summer, heading down to the outfield to report on the trophy ceremony – assured that there will be no members of the royal family he doesn't recognise on this occasion. As well as Henry Moeran, he is accompanied by a great man called Brian Mack. *TMS* listeners will not be familiar with his name, but they should be with his work. For the last 29 years, Brian has been *Test Match Special*'s chief engineer, as well as working across numerous other BBC live productions. At times almost single-handedly, he has kept *TMS* on the air in a wide variety of locations and conditions and has been a beacon of sense, reliability and good counsel for all. He is presented with a signed England T-shirt by Joe Root to mark his final match – and is rather embarrassed by the glowing tribute paid to him on air by Aggers.

Root and Paine come together on stage to officially share the series trophy, before the England captain has to slink off and see the Australian squad gleefully lift the Ashes urn. As ever the tiny, 137-year-old urn will not actually travel back to Australia (it will stay in its climate-controlled environment at Lord's), but symbolically it is considered to reside Down Under, and England will not get another chance to wrest it from the Australians until the winter of 2021-22.

Once the celebratory formalities are over, the players disperse, and the unofficial celebrations begin. After completing the interviews, Aggers moves away from the crowds and stands on the outfield, wistfully looking up at the old gasholders, and takes *Test Match Special* off the air for the final time in the historic summer of 2019.

From Friday 3 May in a misty Malahide to Sunday 15 September in the heart of London, the cricketing summer of 2019 has been an extraordinary run. Over the course of the summer, BBC Sport have broadcast 4,289 hours (178 days) of live cricket, including their county commentaries. Throughout this time, *Test Match Special*, responsible for approximately 1,143 of those, has been lucky to be at some of the greatest moments in the history of the game.

From Tom Curran and Ben Foakes dragging England to victory over Ireland, through some staggering scores in the one-day international series against Pakistan, across England's Lazarus-like comeback to reach the World Cup final, and then for every ball of the most incredible limited-overs match in the history of the game, *TMS* were there, fuelled by cake, for every beat.

After England once again overcame the odds to defeat Ireland, from an uproarious Birmingham to a classic St John's Wood, from the wonders of Leeds to the disappointment of Manchester and, finally, to the uplifting denouement in Kennington, one of the most memorable Ashes series of the modern age has played out spellbindingly on the BBC's historic airwaves.

Throughout the years, the likes of John Arlott, Brian Johnston, Henry Blofeld, Peter Baxter and Christopher Martin-Jenkins took generations of *Test Match Special* listeners through what are considered to be some of the finest moments in sporting history. When the museum of *TMS* is opened (with an excellent café for afterwards), the summer of 2019 will surely require its very own wing.

England 294 (87.1 overs; Buttler 70, Root 57, Marsh 5-46) and 329 (95.3 overs; Denly 94, Stokes 67, Lyon 4-69) beat Australia 225 (68.5 overs; Smith 80, Archer 6-62) and 263 (77 overs; Wade 117, Leach 4-49, Broad 4-62) by 135 runs.

ACKNOWLEDGEMENTS

Every *TMS* listener, all over the world

Adam Mountford and Henry Moeran

The entire *TMS* team, on and off air, past and present

Andy Zaltzman, Andrew Samson and Phil Long

Emily Dubois

Amy Lofthouse, Matt Henry, Jack Skelton and Mark Mitchener

Stephan Shemilt and Tom Fordyce

The *Tailenders*, Greg James, Felix White, Jimmy Anderson, 'Mattchin' Tendulkar and Mark Sharman

Anna and Sarah Wilby, composers of *TMS: The Opera*

Ian Marshall and Melissa Bond at Simon & Schuster

Ellie Caddell and Shavina Goreeba

Rachel Surtees